THE ONCE AND FUTURE
Budapest

THE ONCE AND FUTURE

Budapest

Robert Nemes

Northern Illinois

University Press

DeKalb

© 2005 by Northern Illinois University Press

Published by the Northern Illinois University Press, DeKalb, Illinois   60115

Manufactured in the United States using acid-free paper

All Rights Reserved

Design by Julia Fauci

Library of Congress Cataloging-in-Publication Data

Nemes, Robert.

The once and future Budapest / Robert Nemes.

p.   cm.

Includes bibliographical references (p.   ) and index.

ISBN 0-87580-337-7 (hardcover : alk. paper)

1. Budapest (Hungary)—History—19th century. I. Title.

DB991.N46 2005

943.9'12—dc22

2004023579

Title page art is of the Pest Town Hall, a front line of the language campaign in 1848. See page 145 of the text for more information.

Contents

Illustrations

Preface

When I embarked on this project in the mid-1990s, I had an apartment in Pest, not far from the Nyugati (Western) train station. There was much to like about this neighborhood: its careening red trolleybuses, village-like local market, and proximity to the Danube River. As an aspiring historian, I was fascinated by the district's street names: I lived on Balzac Street, near a park named after an early Hungarian king and around the corner from two streets honoring heroes of the Second World War. But the most intriguing local street bore two names, not one. Next to the new "Ernő Hollán Street" sign was one that read "Sándor Fürst Street"; the only difference was that the latter had a bright red diagonal stripe running through it. I later learned that Hollán had served as a colonel in the Hungarian Revolution of 1848–49, whereas Fürst had been an early martyr of the underground Communist Party. My eighty-year-old neighbor recalled that the street had borne Hollán's name before the communist takeover in the late 1940s, and in the 1990s, Budapest's postcommunist government had decided to restore it. Like Marx, Lenin, and the hammer and sickle, Sándor Fürst was destined for the dustbin of history; the crossed-out sign itself would be removed several years later.

The street with two names captured my attention because it exemplified the way different political movements leave their mark on cities. In this work, I have looked at how nationalism and urbanism intersected in nineteenth-century Budapest. Few cities grew as fast, and in almost none was nationalism woven so tightly into the urban fabric. My research thus tries to uncover what came before nationalism, why this political movement mobilized so many men and women, and how it shaped the development of Budapest. The account has been colored by my sources—a mix of archival materials, newspapers, memoirs, and travelers' accounts—which have allowed me to study nationalism's influence on painting, architecture, dress, horse racing, and street names. This book concerns the nineteenth century, but it is a testament to the enduring influence of the national idea in Budapest that many of the individuals, places, and buildings described here will be recognizable to twenty-first-century visitors to the city.

Names can pose a challenge for historians of Central Europe, particularly when nineteenth-century nationalism is the topic at hand. In this book, difficulty starts with the title, because the autonomous towns of

Buda, Pest, and Óbuda united to form "Budapest" only in 1872–73. Before then, writers used a number of names to describe the towns collectively. I have chosen the most common, "Buda-Pest," which was used by British, Hungarian, and German authors from the 1830s onward. It seems preferable to "Pest-Buda," which is favored by modern Hungarian historians, but has significantly fewer nineteenth-century precedents and less tradition in English-language scholarship. For other cities and regions, I have used a mixture of familiar English names (Vienna and Prague) and nineteenth-century usages (thus, Pressburg instead of Bratislava); when needed, I have given the modern equivalent in parentheses. For individuals' names, I have used English forms for the Habsburg rulers, and thus Francis Joseph makes an appearance here rather than the Germanic Franz Josef or the Hungarian Ferenc József. Since the Habsburg rulers were, with few exceptions, emperors as well as kings of Hungary, I refer to them as emperor-kings and their authority in Hungary as "imperial-royal" *(kaiserlich-königlich)*. Otherwise, individuals' names mostly appear as they do in the sources. Finally, I often use the term "Magyars" (as Hungarians call themselves) as shorthand for the Hungarian-speaking cultural community and the term "Magyarization" to describe the process, both coercive and voluntary, by which more people became linguistically and culturally "Hungarian."

This venture into Hungarian history surely would have failed had it not been for the many institutions, colleagues, and friends who helped me along the way. I am grateful for the assistance of countless archivists and librarians, and especially those at the Hungarian National Archives, Budapest City Archives, Széchényi National Library, and Ervin Szabó Library, all in Budapest, as well as the staff at the Haus-, Hof- und Staatsarchiv in Vienna. In the United States, Butler Library at Columbia University, the Library of Congress, and Case Library at Colgate University greatly aided my research and writing. So too did generous grants from Columbia University, the Fulbright-IIE Fellowship program, the International Research and Exchanges Board, and the Mrs. Giles Whiting Foundation. The American Council of Learned Societies has been very supportive of my work, as has Colgate University. I am especially indebted to Mary Lincoln and the wonderful staff at Northern Illinois University Press, as well as to the press's readers, who provided thoughtful advice and insightful criticism on this project.

Sections of different chapters have appeared previously in other works, and I would like to acknowledge gratefully the permission of the editors and publishers to use this material. Parts of chapter 3 appeared as "Associations and Civil Society in Reform-Era Hungary," *Austrian History Yearbook* 32 (2001), pp. 25–45; chapter 4 as "The Politics of the Dance Floor: Civil Society and Culture in Nineteenth-Century Hungary," *Slavic Review* 60, no. 4 (winter 2001), pp. 802–23; and chapter 6 as "The Revolution in Symbols: Hungary in 1848–1849," in *Constructing Nationalities in East Central*

Europe, ed. Pieter Judson and Marsha Rozenblit (Berghahn Books, 2004). I would also like to thank the Hungarian National Gallery in Budapest for permission to reproduce *Woman in a Striped Dress* and *Recapture of Buda Castle in 1686*.

My graduate advisor, István Deák, has provided unfailing encouragement and patient answers to my many questions on nineteenth-century Hungary. Gábor Vermes has likewise been a careful reader and constant supporter. Thanks are also due to to the many other people who helped me at various stages of this project, including Karen Barkey, Greg Brown, Alice Freifeld, Pieter Judson, Howard Lupovitch, Elizabeth Marlowe, Marsha Rozenblit, John Swanson, Dan Unowsky, Isser Woloch, and Richard Wortman, as well as the members of the history department at Colgate University. In Hungary, Professor Gábor Pajkossy of Eötvös Loránd University generously shared his time and expertise; I would not have been able to navigate the Hungarian archives without his assistance. I have also benefited from conversations with a number of Hungarian historians, especially Attila Pók, Árpád Tóth, Miklós Zeidler, and the late Péter Hanák. Friends in Budapest have been no less important, and I would like express my gratitude the Varró family, Tibor Milcsevics, and Judít Dávid. Special thanks are due to Matt Caples, who has long shared his enthusiasm for East European languages and distant Hungarian towns.

Finally, I would like to thank my parents, sister, and brother for their cheerful acceptance and long endurance of my fascination with Hungarian history; they have helped me in more ways than they know. My greatest debt is to my wife, Elizabeth Marlowe, who shared her remarkable skills as art historian, editor, and critical thinker; this project would be much poorer without her love and support. I dedicate this book to her.

THE ONCE AND FUTURE
Budapest

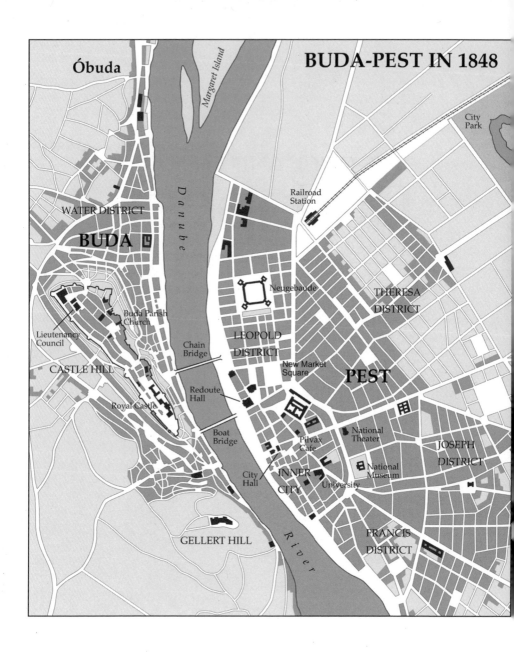

BUDA-PEST IN 1848

Óbuda

Margaret Island

City Park

Railroad Station

WATER DISTRICT

BUDA

D a n u b e

Neugebäude

THERESA DISTRICT

Buda Parish Church

Lieutenancy Council

LEOPOLD DISTRICT

Chain Bridge

New Market Square

PEST

CASTLE HILL

Redoute Hall

Royal Castle

Boat Bridge

Pilvax Cafe

National Theater

JOSEPH DISTRICT

City Hall

INNER CITY

National Museum

University

FRANCIS DISTRICT

GELLERT HILL

R i v e r

Introduction

This book is about a city and the political visions that shaped its character. "Every nation," the nineteenth-century novelist Mór Jókai wrote, "has a holy city which it thinks about with piety and pride."[1] For generations of Hungarian nationalists, this "holy city" was Buda-Pest, and they sought to remake it in their own image—to recapture its lost glory and guarantee its future greatness. Wanting to make Buda-Pest entirely "Hungarian," they took their campaign into all corners of the city: into ballrooms, music halls, and restaurants. But there was much more at stake than the carnival dresses, concert programs, and menus they fought over. The nationalists' struggle in Buda-Pest had a profound impact upon modern Hungary's political culture, which held the potential for liberalism, progress, and inclusion, as well as for xenophobia, intolerance, and exclusion.[2] To understand why the stakes were so high, we need to look first at the city itself and then at the political dimensions of its development.

From Huns to Habsburgs

In the mid-nineteenth century, the Englishman John Paget recorded his first glimpse of the city as his steamer came down the Danube: "I shall never forget my astonishment at the picture I then saw. The mountains, which had receded from the river, seemed again to approach its very edge; for some distance they were covered with vineyards almost to the top, but, as we approached Buda, these yielded to buildings which appeared to us a succession of magnificent palaces."[3] He and his fellow passengers "declared that we had never seen a more magnificent sight than that presented by our first view of Buda-Pest." The Danish writer Hans Christian Andersen arrived a few years later and was no less enthusiastic: "There is Buda, the capital of Hungary—the castle with its white walls, the Hungarian acropolis, rising above the verdant gardens."[4] If Buda was Hungary's acropolis, then Pest was its agora—dynamic and bustling, its residents, in the words of one observer, "lacking all refinements but expert in the *lucri bonus odor* [pleasant scent of profit]."[5] The staid dignity of Buda and the commercial tumult of Pest seen in the early nineteenth century were roles the towns had long been playing.

The twin towns' good fortune owes much to geography. They lie near the center of the Carpathian Basin, a fertile lowland surrounded on three sides by a thousand-mile arc of mountains. Buda-Pest also sits astride the

Danube, one of Europe's great rivers. The Danube has at times served as a barrier and a border, but, more commonly, it has helped link the twin towns with the Austrian lands to the west and Serbian and Romanian territories to the south. The hills on the Buda side of the Danube have made them an ideal site both for fortifications and viticulture, a combination that produced the castle, palaces, and vineyards so admired by nineteenth-century visitors. Pest, by contrast, lies on flat ground, which until recently was swampy in some places and dusty in most others. Pest was far less defensible than Buda, but in times of peace, its accessibility made it a focal point of communications and transportation—in Hungary, all roads (and later railroads and airplanes) lead to Pest. Unchecked by the hills that girded Buda, Pest could expand much more easily in the modern era, with the result that today more than 70 percent of Budapest's 1.7 million inhabitants live in Pest.

For more than two millennia, the towns have witnessed repeated cycles of prosperity and decline. The first flowering came with the Romans, under whom Aquincum (today Óbuda) developed into a sizeable settlement, complete with baths, a palace, and a large amphitheater.[6] Roman rule did not last, and in the ensuing centuries, waves of invaders swept through the towns with dismaying regularity: Huns, Lombards, Avars, and, in the late ninth century, Magyars. The Huns and Magyars were unrelated, even if both were nomadic horsemen who came from Asia in search of plunder and pastureland. (The name "Hungarian"—in French *hongrois*, in German *Ungar*—derives from the Turkic words *on ogur*, which means "ten arrows" and perhaps described some aspect of the early Magyar tribes.) Yet the idea that the Magyars were somehow connected to the Huns lingered through the nineteenth century, and this explains the long-held view that Buda took its name from the brother of Attila the Hun, who appeared in sources as *Budli* or *Bleda*. Other writers said that the town's name came from an early Hungarian or Slavic word for "water," possibly in reference to the area's hot springs. Scholars today suggest, less colorfully perhaps, that "Buda" derives from a male name, likely of German origin, from the period after the Magyars' arrival.[7] "Pest" comes from a Bulgarian or Slavic word for "oven," likely a reference to the area's lime kilns.

Hungary became a Christian monarchy in AD 1000, and the early Hungarian kings spent at least some of their time in Buda and Óbuda. Scattered evidence from toll and tax records suggests that trade and crafts gradually developed on both sides of the Danube. By the thirteenth century, documents described Buda and Óbuda as *medium regni*—the middle of the kingdom—a phrase with administrative, as well as geographic, connotations. There were setbacks as well: Mongols sacked the towns in the mid-thirteenth century, and the neglect of later kings slowed their recovery. This changed decisively under King Sigismund of Luxembourg (reigned 1387–1437), who made Buda his permanent royal seat. Under his patronage, construction boomed, local craftsmen flourished, and merchants prospered on shipments of local wines and cattle from the Hungarian plains to Austria, northern Italy, and Bavaria. The *Ofner Stadtrecht,* or Buda Charter, compiled between 1405 and 1421, eloquently testifies to the town's extensive rights of self-government and to the flourishing local economy.[8] The burghers' success was confirmed when Sigismund made the kingdom's chartered free towns, which included Buda and Pest, the fourth estate in the realm, the first three estates being the prelates, magnates, and nobles of the counties. The estates were represented in the National Diet, which often met in Buda. On those occasions when the king died without a legitimate heir, the estates would assemble to choose a new ruler either in Buda or on the Pest side of the river, in a meadow by the Rákos stream. The elective monarchy came to an end in the late seventeenth century, but Rákos Field in Pest remained an important symbol, as the Englishman William Hunter later recorded: "The Hungarian nobles still venerate the spot, as it recalls to memory those proud days of tumultuous freedom, in which they had the privilege of aspiring to, or bestowing a crown."[9]

Prosperity continued under King Matthias Corvinus (r. 1458–90), who dominated the second half of the fifteenth century. The son of the general János Hunyadi, who had twice defeated the Ottomans, Matthias was a skilled warrior in his own right. As king, he conducted successful campaigns in Bohemia and in 1485 besieged and occupied Vienna, thereby earning the sobriquet "the second Attila." Matthias's marriage to Beatrix of Aragon, the daughter of the King of Naples, brought a host of writers, artists, architects, and scholars from the Italian states to the court in Buda, and with them came the ideas and styles of the early Italian Renaissance. A refined patron and avid collector, Matthias "took pleasure in all rare things," noted Giorgio Vasari in his *Lives of the Artists.*[10] Matthias amassed a great royal library, the *Bibliotheca Corviniana,* a collection of more than 3,000 manuscripts and incunabula. In 1473 a Buda printer named Andreas Hess produced the first book ever printed in Hungary, a history of Hungary in Latin. The population continued to grow under Matthias, and by the late fifteenth century Buda, Pest, and Óbuda combined had as many as 20,000 residents, putting them on par with Vienna, Prague, and Cracow.[11]

Matthias died without an heir in 1490, and neither the glory of his court nor his military conquests long survived his death. His successors failed to stop the advancing Ottoman armies, and at the battle of Mohács, in 1526, Süleyman "the Magnificent" decimated the Hungarian forces and the Hungarian king died in flight from the battle. Ottoman armies briefly occupied Buda and seized it for good in 1541 after defeating the armies of the Habsburg Ferdinand I, who claimed the Hungarian crown based on an earlier dynastic marriage. Ferdinand had to be content with a strip of land in the north, which was called "Royal Hungary." A pasha, the governor of Ottoman Hungary, was meanwhile installed in Buda, but not in the royal palace, which was reserved for visits by the sultan. Buda gradually became the economic center of Ottoman Hungary, although trade was now oriented toward the Balkans rather than westward, as it had been previously; the population included Muslims, Jews, and both Orthodox and Catholic Christians. The Ottomans altered the townscape by turning churches into mosques (the Church of Our Lady became the Süleyman Khan Mosque), strengthening the walls and defenses of Buda, planting gardens, and opening baths. "You are as beautiful, fortress Buda, as Istanbul itself," wrote a seventeenth-century Turkish poet.[12] Edmund Brown, who traveled in Hungary in the 1670s, observed that "the natural Baths of *Buda* are esteemed the noblest of *Europe*, not only in respect of the large and hot springs, but the Magnificence of their Buildings."[13] Yet the frequent warfare and sieges—enemy armies advanced on Buda six times between 1541 and 1686—also took their toll.

Habsburg-led forces expelled the Ottomans in 1686 after a long, destructive siege. With bells ringing in Vienna, Rome, and Barcelona, the capture of the city was celebrated as a triumph for the House of Habsburg and all Christendom. The victors found a ruined town, which an eighteenth-century historian sadly described as little more than "toppled, broken walls; collapsed arches, palaces and chambers; badly smashed banquet rooms; fallen towers; shattered walkways; yawning cellars, which emit every kind of pestilential vapor."[14] The Muslim and Jewish population, which had once numbered 6,000, swiftly disappeared. Mosques became Catholic churches, and the tomb of the Dervish holy man Gül Baba, a Muslim pilgrimage site in Buda, was turned into a Jesuit chapel. Later observers would find few traces of the Ottomans, as the traveler Robert Townson noted in the 1790s: "The Turks having been in possession of Buda from 1541 to 1686, I expected to have found here some remnants of Turkish arts; either in buildings, manufactures, or handworks; but there are no remains of Turkish buildings, except the baths, worth mentioning, nor any arts that I could hear of."[15]

The victorious Habsburgs swiftly put their stamp on the twin towns. In 1703, Leopold I bestowed new charters upon Buda and Pest, raising both to the status of royal free town. Pride of place was given to Buda, which had maintained the aura of a royal seat or capital even through the Ottoman occupation. Thus, its charter referred to it (and not to Pest) as *Metropolis Hungarae*, roughly the "capital of Hungary."[16] The charters gave both towns wide privileges, including the right to send deputies to the Diet as part of the fourth estate, to own land on the same footing as nobles, and, most important, to govern themselves.[17] With these charters, the towns won a large measure of juridical, political, and economic autonomy from the imperial-royal government as well as from the surrounding noble county. This freedom, however, had limits, as the Royal Treasury kept a close watch over the towns' finances and the Vice-Regal Council sometimes intervened in local politics. But Townson captured the essence of the charters: "The burghers being under the particular care of the sovereign, and having their own magistrates, are pretty independent of the nobility, and have only to bear the burdens of government."[18]

The twin towns benefited from Habsburg favor in other ways as well. Before 1686, the town of Pressburg, which was close to the court in Vienna, had been the administrative center of Habsburg-controlled Hungary. After the expulsion of the Ottomans, however, Buda-Pest offered a much more central location in the Hungarian lands. Over the course of the eighteenth century, Habsburg rulers relocated a number of key institutions to Buda and Pest, including the Royal Treasury, which managed revenues from mines, customs duties, and the salt monopoly, as well as Hungary's highest law courts, their names—the *Curia Regis* (Royal Curia), *Tabula Regis* (King's Bench), and *Tabula Septemviralis* (Septemviral Court)—a reminder that Latin was the language of administration in Hungary. Maria Theresa (r. 1740–80) ordered that Hungary's lone university be relocated to Buda from Nagyszombat (today Trnava, in Slovakia), a small town not far from Pressburg. Her successor, Joseph II (r. 1780–90), championed administrative centralization and thus transferred from Pressburg to Buda the Royal Treasury, the military command, and, most significantly, the Vice-Regal (or Lieutenancy) Council, which oversaw most political, economic, and military matters and acted as a conduit between administrative institutions in Hungary and those in Vienna. As a finishing touch, Joseph also relocated the university, Hungarian archives, and the Royal Curia from Buda to Pest. The clear loser in all this was Pressburg, whose newspaper bemoaned the loss of its former splendor and the "support of the worthy state."[19] The Buda Town Council, by contrast, asked Joseph for permission to erect a statue in his honor; with a characteristic mix of modesty and ambition, Joseph replied that he would accept a statue only "when I have put a stop to all spiritual and secular abuses, when I have awakened activity and industry, made trade flourish, [and] provided the country from end to end with streets and navigable canals."[20]

Trade was already flourishing across the river in Pest, as its large, crowded quarterly markets plainly showed. Other towns had the right to hold markets and fairs, but none could compete with those of Pest, which lasted for up to two weeks and often attracted more than 20,000 people. Pest's market revenues more than quadrupled between 1730 and 1790 as thousands of wagons clogged its roads and hundreds of barges and boats filled the Danube.[21] Grain and livestock were the most important commodities, but one could also purchase soap, saddles, wagons, wool, and wine. To capture the most buyers, publishers released new books just before the fairs. Count Hofmannsegg, a visitor from Saxony, was impressed: "There is just as much noise and crowding as at the Leipzig fairs, only the marketplace here is much more attractive."[22] The population grew as well, and by the late eighteenth century Pest had nearly 25,000 inhabitants, roughly the same as Buda.

Both towns welcomed immigrants from near and far, especially if they were Roman Catholics. A few hundred Protestants (Lutherans and Calvinists) lived in the twin towns, and the Jewish population was not much larger. The Buda Town Council had attempted to expel thirty-two Jewish families in 1746, and only the intervention of the imperial-royal authorities had prevented the expulsion from taking place. Pest was no more hospitable, and its town council grudgingly granted residency permits to several Jewish innkeepers only in the 1780s. In this hostile environment, many Jews settled in Óbuda ("Old Buda"), a small market town on the Buda side of the Danube. Once a substantial settlement and a center of medieval trade, Óbuda had been decimated in the Ottoman wars. It then passed into the hands of the Count Zichy family and later to the Royal Treasury. Eighteenth-century Óbuda was a small settlement of workshops, low houses, and surrounding fields. Its residents, for the most part German-speaking Catholics, lived from agriculture, viticulture, and small crafts. But the Zichys had also welcomed Jews into Óbuda and other market towns on their estates. The Royal Treasury continued this policy, and by the mid-1780s 1,650 Jews lived in Óbuda.[23] The Jewish community appointed its first rabbi in 1746 and eventually had a synagogue, yeshiva, cemetery, and ritual baths. Óbuda's Jews could go into Buda and Pest on market days, but they were forbidden to spend the night in either town.

By the late eighteenth century, then, Buda and Pest had regained their status as Hungary's acropolis and agora. Yet for all their antiquity, the towns must have appeared remarkably new to observers, because both had been almost entirely repopulated and rebuilt after the expulsion of the Ottomans in 1686. Few residents had lived in the towns for more than a generation or two, and few buildings had stood for much longer. The towns nonetheless retained a wealth of historical resources and associations. Potentially, there was something for everyone: the Habsburgs could boast of their liberation of Buda in 1686, the burghers could look back to their medieval charters, and noblemen could imagine the days when they elected kings on Rákos Field. Whether this multifaceted past would weigh lightly or heavily on the twin towns as they continued to develop remained an open question at the turn of the nineteenth century.

The Nationalization of Buda-Pest

Buda and Pest changed dramatically in the nineteenth century. Few cities grew as rapidly: in the early 1800s, the towns of Buda, Pest, and Óbuda (which would unite to form Budapest in 1872–73) were muddy and small, with a total population of little over 50,000, most of them German-speakers. The reformer Count István Széchenyi warned visitors that they would find bad hotels, worse restaurants, and a barren cultural life; he later wrote a book called *Buda-Pest's Mud and Dust*. This began to change in the 1830s, and by the end of the century, Budapest had become a capital city and a burgeoning metropolis with nearly 800,000 inhabitants. It had also become, in almost every respect, a distinctly Hungarian city, as could be seen in its theaters, schools, street signs, and public monuments.

The activists who wanted to paint Buda-Pest in the Hungarian national colors had much in common with their contemporaries in Rome, Berlin, Athens, and Prague.[24] This nationalizing trend was most pronounced in the capital cities of newly unified or independent states, which proudly displayed their cultural achievements in freshly built national museums, libraries, academies, and theaters.[25] Even London built its Houses of Parliament between 1837 and 1868 in a neo-Gothic architectural style to express the uniqueness and antiquity of British political traditions. Nineteenth-century regimes also used monuments, holidays, and street names to display their national achievements and ambitions. In Rome, for example, the national-liberal government commemorated Italian unification by completing *via Nazionale,* whose cross streets bore the names of Italy's cities—*via Torino, via Firenze,* and *via Napoli.* Few of these interventions were politically neutral, and nearly all emerged from intense competition between liberals, monarchs, conservatives, republicans, and, at the end of the century, socialists and political Catholics.

In Hungary, nationalists pursued their aims within an imperial framework. Nineteenth-century Hungary was part of the Habsburg Monarchy, a European great power that encompassed what are today a dozen twenty-first-century Central European states, including all of Austria, Croatia, the Czech Republic, Hungary, Slovakia, and Slovenia.[26] The Habsburgs had ruled the Austrian lands since the twelfth century; they later became Holy Roman emperors and from 1526 kings of Hungary as well. The Habsburg rulers kept their court in Vienna, the "imperial capital and residential city" of their realm.[27] Vienna in 1800 was a celebrated city with roughly 230,000 residents, making it more than four times the size of Buda-Pest. The Habsburgs would in fact do much to foster the economic and administrative development of Buda-Pest, but they had no interest in creating a rival capital to Vienna. When needed, they were ready to use their police and censors against their opponents, including Hungarian nationalists. This would change only in 1867, when Hungary was made an equal partner with Austria in the Dual Monarchy.

In Buda-Pest itself, Hungarian national activists had to confront the heterogeneity of the local population.[28] A geographer once described Hungary as "Europe in miniature," and the same could be said of the twin towns of Buda and Pest, with their mixture of languages, classes, customs, and religions.[29] An 1845 guidebook observed that the population included Magyars, Germans, Slovaks, Jews, Serbs, Greeks, Romanians, Czechs, Poles, Italians, and French; an 1851 census reported that the twin towns were roughly one-half German and one-third Magyar, with the balance a mix of Jews, Slovaks, and Serbs.[30] Disparaging this diversity, some Hungarian activists declared that many natives of Buda-Pest were in fact "foreign," and they set out to nationalize the population and the surrounding city. But their tireless promotion of Hungarian language and culture was at odds with the towns' polyglot and cosmopolitan traditions, just as their insistence that the nation should be the primary locus of political loyalty was a direct challenge to the population's layered allegiances to ruler, church, kingdom, and hometown.

With a suspicious regime and an inhospitable population, how did Buda-Pest become a manifestly Hungarian city in the nineteenth-century? Historians have paid close attention to both the emergence of Hungarian nationalism and the development of Buda-Pest, and the present study is partly based on their findings.[31] Most accounts, however, typically view Hungarian nationalism "from above," that is, from the perspective of political and cultural elites.[32] Particularly in studies of the period before 1848, the stress is on Count Széchenyi, Lajos Kossuth, Baron József Eötvös, and other political leaders, and the context is often the Hungarian National Diet (the feudal parliament), which became the scene of long, running battles between the liberal opposition and Vienna. It was in the National Diet, for example, that reformers secured the place of Hungarian (instead of Latin) as the official language of the kingdom in 1844. Studies of Buda-Pest's cultural life typically adopt a similar perspective, often focusing somewhat myopically on Hungarian-language institutions: the theater, press, and literature.[33] For all the richness of this scholarship, we still know surprisingly little about how the wider urban population understood, embraced, and redefined the sustained political and cultural agitation connected with nineteenth-century nationalism.

When they have looked at the mass of the population, scholars have stressed the role of immigration, schools, and voluntary assimilation in changing the national character of Buda-Pest. The emphasis here shifts to the second half of the century, and the twin towns are frequently held up as examples of what have been called "sinking islands," ethnic enclaves that gradually submerged into the surrounding sea of peasants.[34] (Another oft-cited example is Prague, where waves of Czech-speaking peasants ostensibly overwhelmed the German burghers.) In the case of Buda-Pest, scholars point out that German-speakers accounted for more than 50 percent of the population in 1850 but less than 10 percent in 1890.[35] The arrival of tens of thousands of Hungarian-speaking peasants and artisans from the 1830s onward surely strengthened the hand of Hungarian nationalists in Buda-Pest. Yet many accounts tend to treat national allegiances uncritically, assuming, for example, that the Magyar peasants who came to Pest already possessed a strong sense of national loyalty. Similarly, nearly all scholars describe the linguistic assimilation of the towns' Germans, Slovaks, and Jews as a painless, if not inevitable, process.

The present study borrows from the "top-down" and "sinking islands" models described above, but it also seeks to provide new perspectives on the nationalization of Buda-Pest. A growing literature on the urban dimensions of nationalism greatly helps in this effort.[36] In nineteenth-century Buda-Pest, displays of national allegiance encompassed dances, costumes, language, paintings, and architecture. Why did Hungarian nationalism take so many different forms, and why did many residents of Buda-Pest embrace them so enthusiastically? Did these men and women in turn influence the direction taken by the Hungarian national movement? In thinking about these national-minded town dwellers, one must consider the full range of political and national loyalties in nineteenth-century Buda-Pest: what did it mean, for example, to be "Hungarian" or "German" in the nineteenth century? Could a person be both? Neither? And what was the position of the city's growing Jewish population? Finally, the role played by Vienna and its supporters in Buda-Pest should be taken into account as well. How did they respond to the challenges posed by the Hungarian national movement? What vision of Buda-Pest guided their actions?

To answer these questions, this study treats nationalism primarily as a political strategy. Its advocates across Europe wanted to create new political communities, whose members would be joined by their common language, religion, customs, or residence.[37] Nationalism can usefully be distinguished from patriotism, a loyalty to state or homeland, and to the ruler of this territory. Historically, nationalism is best understood as part of a much larger reordering of the European political landscape in the wake of the French Revolution, which in turn shaped the language, symbols, and aims of all national movements in Europe and beyond. If the French model encouraged revolutionaries in Spanish America, Greece, Belgium, and Italy to take up arms to fight for their "national" independence, it also heartened historians, poets, and philologists, who fought with their pens. No matter what their weapons, the proponents of nationalism used language, history, myths, and aspects of cultural life to legitimate a wide range of political and cultural claims. Nineteenth-century nationalists may have spoken in terms of freedom, progress, and emancipation, but they often had their sights on more tangible rewards: state employment, social status, economic power, cultural autonomy, and, in some cases, independent statehood.

The political struggle in Buda-Pest initially pitted a thin stratum of Habsburg loyalists against an equally small number of Hungarian national activists (chapters 1–2). On the Habsburg side stood imperial-royal officials, the town governments, and the Catholic Church; theirs was a political system rooted in tradition, confident in its authority, and responsive to the needs of the population. Habsburg loyalists held a strong position in Buda-Pest in the early nineteenth century. Hungarian activists, however, increasingly challenged the loyalists' nonnational outlook and the corporate social and political order upon which it rested. The Hungarian cause would draw support from feudal institutions—the Hungarian National Diet and Pest County—but activists claimed to have the entire nation behind them as well (no matter that "nation" was, and is, a rather slippery term). In reality, the Hungarian national movement at first comprised a narrow circle of noble landowners, writers, and students. From the start, then, the nationalists' campaign to remake Buda-Pest depended on their ability to win over the towns' burghers, professionals, clergymen, merchants, artisans, and even peasants freshly arrived from the countryside.

As in other parts of Europe, Hungarian nationalists had their greatest success outside existing political structures. In an era of stunted political life—of limited suffrage, strict censorship, and monarchical power—national activists everywhere had to be imaginative, energetic recruiters and to use a wide range of strategies to broaden their base of support. They formed clubs, launched newspapers, took up collections, and hosted banquets; they championed national symbols, including flags, anthems, plays, and dances; and they took their campaigns to the streets, which they filled with parades, mass meetings, and monuments. Not all these efforts succeeded, and the national activists' dreams often outran their limited resources and the enthusiasm of the wider population. Yet their many initiatives helped create a domain of informal political activity that extended far beyond the narrow confines of electoral and legislative processes. This, in turn, allowed men and women usually excluded from public life to discuss, debate, and make known their political and national commitments.[38]

In Hungary, the political class was always small, and even in the late nineteenth century, no more than 6 percent of the population had the right to vote. Before 1867, the Habsburg authorities not only stifled established political forums, but also attempted to close off entire areas to Hungarian nationalists, including schools, administrative bodies, and economic institutions. More often than not, this canalized the nationalists' dissent into the realm of civil society, into a world of newspapers, voluntary associations, and public meetings.[39] As studies of club life, the dance floor, and public space show (chapters 3–5), the Hungarian nationalists used institutions of civil society to gain a more prominent role in Buda-Pest in the 1830s and 1840s. Potentially, this opened the door for new social groups to enter public life, including women, workers, and Jews. But Catholics, political conservatives, and Serb and Slovak activists also learned from the Hungarian national movement and formed their own societies and newspapers. When viewed in this light, nationalism can be seen as a catalyst for the creation of a wider, more pluralistic political life.

Nineteenth-century nationalism had a darker side as well. The forging of national political communities can involve chauvinism, coercion, and segregation.[40] This frequently took the form of exclusionary practices: in nineteenth-century Central Europe, institutions of civil society generally remained the preserve of propertied and educated men, and even the more public national rituals (concerts, balls, and parades) had little room for members of the lower classes. Similarly, the rhetoric of nationalism that animated this new public life routinely involved attacks on perceived domestic or foreign "enemies." The violent language of the *Marseillaise,* the French anthem that inspired so many others, is typical: it warns citizens against "cut-throat soldiers" who come "to slaughter our children, our wives." Xenophobia could take on even higher significance when nineteenth-century nationalists gained control of the state and translated their fears into official policies. In such cases, regimes at times denied the full rights of citizenship—local autonomy, control of schools, and use of certain languages in public life—to identifiable religious, political, or linguistic minorities (and even majorities).

Exclusion, intolerance, and intimidation all had their place in nineteenth-century Buda-Pest.[41] As the boundaries of nationhood became more distinct in the nineteenth century, to refuse to embrace all things Hungarian, especially in moments of political crisis, was to invite suspicion. In the 1830s, Magyar students threw rocks through the windows of shops with German-language signs; a decade later, they would burn German-language newspapers in public. Belligerent rhetoric was even more common: Mihály Táncsics, a democrat and defender of the working classes, suggested in the 1860s that all non-Magyar workers in Buda-Pest should be forcibly shipped to the countryside and replaced with Hungarian-speakers from the provinces; this compulsory exchange, he promised, would create a more industrious, sober, and homogenous working class.[42] Táncsics's ideas were extreme (and never implemented), but he was not alone in searching for ways to make the twin towns exclusively Hungarian. Indeed, as the book's final section (chapters 6–7) suggests, the Hungarian state ultimately played an important role in the nationalization of Buda-Pest. Events took a decisive turn with the Compromise of 1867, which created the Dual Monarchy and gave Hungary a free hand in its internal affairs. In 1872, parliament passed a law that would create the unified city of Budapest in the following year. That Hungarian was declared to be the official language of city administration was unsurprising, yet it was a clear signal to the towns' sizeable German-speaking population that the new government had absorbed the nationalist agenda. Budapest, it was clear, was to be a Hungarian city in the future. What it once was, and why this matters, are the subject of this book.

CHAPTER ONE

Buda-Pest, Ofen-Pest

"When we speak of the metropolis, we generally consider the three towns which compose it, as one: so here we may consider the cities of Pest and Buda as one; for they are only separated by the Danube, over which there is a bridge of boats, and then this city is very respectable in its extent and population; Pest contains fifteen, Buda or Ofen twenty-two thousand people."

—Robert Townson, *Travels in Hungary* (1797)[1]

The British natural scientist Robert Townson visited Hungary in the early 1790s, something few of his compatriots did in this era. Hungary was far off the beaten path, and its bad roads and sparse accommodations did little to encourage visitors. But Townson was no Grand Tourist, and while in Hungary he captured animals and birds, collected fossils and rare plants, and explored remote mountains and valleys. He also proved to be an astute observer of urban life and especially of Buda-Pest, which he recognized as Hungary's leading city. The tireless Townson investigated the towns' markets, gardens, hospitals, theaters, and antiquities. The baths of Buda fascinated him, and the animal fights in Pest horrified him.[2] He lingered in the coffeehouses, which he admired for their elegance and their mixed clientele: "all ranks and both sexes may come; and hair-dressers in their powdered coats, and old market-women, come here and take their coffee or drink their *rosolio* as well as Counts and Barons." An assortment of peoples only added to the diversity. In Buda-Pest, Townson saw Jewish, Armenian, and Greek merchants in the marketplace, as well as Germans and Magyars in the streets. His description of them is revealing:

> The common arts, here, as well as in the rest of Hungary, are chiefly in the hands of the Germans. On Corpus Christi day there was a great procession, principally of the different trades. The Germans wore the common dress, and the Hungarians their national dress: the latter made by far the best appearance, partly through their more elegant dress, and partly by being finer men; but the former greatly exceeded the latter in numbers.[3]

Townson's partiality toward the Magyars is a recurring theme in his book—"the Hungarians," he writes elsewhere, "are a brave, generous, and hardy race of men."[4] Yet his account also makes it plain that German was widely spoken in the twin towns.

Was it surprising that German resounded so loudly in Buda-Pest? Many towns in eighteenth-century Habsburg Central Europe in fact had a German character. What we today call Zagreb, Ljubljana, Bratislava, and Prague were better known by their residents as Agram, Laibach, Pressburg, and Prag. Dennison Rusinow has observed that "until the rapid growth of cities, usually only after 1850 and only sometimes associated with industrialization, the towns of the [Habsburg Monarchy] were almost all German in language, culture, and (where such existed) national consciousness."[5] To be urban, he writes, was by definition to be "German," a capacious category defined by education, social status, and language rather than by ethnicity or origins. Germanness was thus something that could be acquired, and because German was the primary language of administration, commerce, and culture, newcomers who hoped to better themselves or their children had a strong incentive to make it their own. In this way, steady immigration at first did not alter the German character of the towns of Central Europe.

By all accounts, German was by far the most common language of the twin towns in this era. Buda had a German name, Ofen ("oven"), and later writers and officials sometimes referred to Ofen-Pesth, the German equivalent of "Buda-Pest."[6] The magistrates of the Pest and Buda town halls may have known several languages, but when they discussed the day's business, issued orders, and took down the minutes, they used German more frequently than any other language. Admittedly, residents could petition the town council in Hungarian or Serbian and expect an answer in the same language; and each year on September 2, the anniversary of Buda's liberation from the Ottomans, speeches were given in German, Hungarian, and Serbian. Yet the towns' Catholic priests typically said their weekly sermons in German, and the most common language in workshops and warehouses was also German. Hotels in Pest had names like Zu den 7 Churfürsten (The House of the Seven Electoral Princes) and Zum goldenen Adler (The House of the Golden Eagle). The towns' first newspapers, including *Ofnerischer Mercurius (Buda Mercury)* and *Pester Intelligenzblatt (Pest Intelligencer)*, appeared in German. German-language theatrical companies were established in 1774 in Pest and a decade later in Buda. While these companies flourished, their Hungarian-language counterparts struggled to gain a foothold in the twin towns: there would be Hungarian theater in the first part of the 1790s, but none through the first decades of the nineteenth century. Latin meanwhile remained the language of secondary and university education, although some instructors at Pest's Piarist school began to teach in Hungarian from the late 1770s onward. The towns' elementary schools used Hungarian, Serbian, and, again most commonly, German.

Patterns of immigration help explain the prevalence of German in Buda-Pest. Over the course of the eighteenth century, sustained migration from Austria and the Holy Roman Empire brought numerous German-speakers to the twin towns. One analysis of parish registers suggests that nearly 70 percent of newcomers in Pest came from outside the Hungarian lands.[7] Local migration also strengthened the towns' German character, because many surrounding villages were populated by German-speaking peasants. The same forces, of course, also brought speakers of Serbian, Slovak, and Hungarian to the twin towns. As a rule, though, German-speakers appear to have occupied a higher social position in eighteenth-century Buda-Pest than other groups. This gave them greater prominence, especially to the era's travelers and guidebook writers, whose ears were attuned to the language of the leading citizens.

To many contemporaries, immigration and social groupings told only part of the story. In their eyes, supposed national characteristics also explained the towns' German character. Typical was Professor Martin Schwartner's landmark *Statistics of the Kingdom of Hungary* (1809–12), a sweeping survey of Hungary's political institutions, economy, and society.[8] German-speakers, he explained, had been in the Hungarian lands for centuries: some arrived in the time of Charlemagne, others were invited by medieval kings, and still others came as colonists in the eighteenth century. To Schwartner, Germans were identifiable not only by their language and origins, but also by their frugality, industry, patriotism, and piety. Schwartner reminded his readers that Germans had settled Hungary's towns, introduced Lutheranism (Schwartner's religion), and helped develop mining, urban crafts, and commerce. His depiction of the Magyars was markedly different: "It seems that the Magyars loathe town life as much as Tacitus's Germans hated it. Only the free, open fields match their inclinations and are suitable for their freedom; and even today the Hungarian burghers, when they are encountered in towns, prefer to live in the outer suburbs, away from the inner city."[9] To be Magyar, then, was to live in the countryside, apart from the diligent, town-dwelling Germans.

Such stereotypes proved remarkably durable. They appear again and again in memoirs, travelers' accounts, guide books, and statistical literature, the details varying only with the perspective of the writer. A Dutch traveler thus described the population of Pest in 1843:

> The Magyars are bold, warlike, generous, amorous. They hunt and are not very disposed to work; they look down on the Slavs with scorn and consider them to be their conquered enemy. . . . The Slavs are merrier and less passionate than other nationalities, but are often sly and dissembling, having been oppressed for centuries. . . . The Germans are here what they are in Germany. Commerce and industry are mainly in their hands, [because] the Slavs are too little civilized, the Magyars out of prejudice are too proud.[10]

How the proud, indolent Magyars could hunt game in a growing city is not explained, but the general picture of the different groups is clear enough: the cities belong to the Germans, the countryside to the combative Magyars and the servile Slavs. If nothing else, this "prism of petrified prejudices," in Péter Hanák's apt phrase, shows how ideas of nationhood were bound up with language, social status, and culture.[11]

More insightful observers recognized the diversity and dynamism of Buda-Pest's population. The eighteenth-century polymath Matthias Bél, who once described himself as a Slav by birth, a Hungarian by nationality, and a German by education, noted in 1737 that it was impossible to describe the customs and manners of the towns' inhabitants because of their varied origins. "The residents of the town of Pest," observed geographer András Vályi sixty years later, "are for the most part Germans, with fewer Magyars, Slovaks, Greeks, Dalmatians, Serbs, Cincars, and Jews."[12] In light of this heterogeneity, some knowledge of multiple languages was common, at least among the educated classes. The roster of the Pest magistracy, which included the wealthiest and most influential burghers, bears this out. Of the ten magistrates in 1789, nine members spoke or wrote German, nine Latin, eight Hungarian, six Slovak, two French, and one Illyrian.[13] The head magistrate, Móric Bálint Hülff, spoke German, Latin, Hungarian, and French; three others knew German, Latin, Hungarian, and Slovak. Contemporary writers also noted how the different languages affected one another. Townson claimed that German had colored the Latin spoken in Hungary: "*Schmutzidum tempus,* for instance, is a common term used to express bad rainy weather; *Schmutzig* is a German word, and signifying 'dirty' it is therefore as if an Englishman speaking Latin should say, *dirtydum tempus.*"[14] It is not difficult to imagine that in Buda-Pest, German had a similar influence on Hungarian, and vice-versa.

This brief survey of polyglot Buda-Pest suggests two conclusions. First, this evidence, however impressionistic, should caution us against viewing the urban population as comprised of fixed communities, neatly divided by ethnic, linguistic, or national differences. We can speak of "Germans," "Magyars," and other groupings in Buda-Pest, but we also need to remember that the populations' mobility, varied origins, and linguistic adaptability constantly blurred such divisions. But if there was a general tendency in eighteenth-century Buda-Pest, it was for the towns' residents to become linguistically German. The guidebook writer Franz Schams described how this might work: "Magyars, Slovaks, Székelys, Austrians, Czechs, Moravians, Styrians, Tyroleans, Italians, French, Bavarians, Swabians, Saxons, Rhinelanders, Swiss, Lotharingians, etc. ceaselessly migrate to Pest; they try their luck and to some extent they find it and naturalize."[15] Because German was the leading language of the twin towns, to "naturalize" most often meant to learn how to function in a primarily German-speaking world. Precise figures are impossible to come by, but it appears that German-speakers far outnumbered Hungarian-speakers in the late eighteenth century. In this sense, Buda-Pest was no different from many other towns in the Habsburg Monarchy.

Second, this patina of Germanness covered a diverse population. Potentially, this meant that any number of national movements could be formed out of the residents of Buda-Pest. Across the Habsburg lands, national activists would eventually emerge among many of the groups mentioned by Schams—Magyars, Slovaks, Czechs, and Italians. But not every group produced an eponymous national movement, as was the case with Schams's Székelys, Bohemians, Saxons, and Lotharingians. Language, culture, and common origins could serve as the basis for a wide range of national loyalties, but only political intervention would turn townsmen into nationally conscious Germans, Hungarians, and Slovaks.[16] To map the emergence of nationalism in Buda-Pest, we need to look closely at the centers of political power in the twin towns: the royal castle, Pest and Buda town halls, and Pest County hall.

The Emperor and the Towns

In Habsburg Central Europe the town "represented the site where the imperial met the local."[17] The most visible reminder of this in Buda-Pest was the royal castle. Perched high above Buda, it gazed down "with princely dignity at the Danube flowing at its feet, at rapidly growing Pest, and at the entire surrounding countryside."[18] Ruined in the siege of 1686 and largely rebuilt over the course of the eighteenth century, the castle contained an astronomical observatory, chapel, armor collection, garden, and numerous offices. To Townson, it was "a vast and stately pile of building."[19] It was also a royal residence, but one that was seldom used: Maria Theresa, for example, visited Buda only once during her forty-year reign. The castle was nonetheless an indelible symbol of the eighteenth-century political order. The Habsburg dynasty stood atop this system, and it had powerful allies on the local level: aristocrats, burghers, and the Catholic Church.

The Habsburgs took a direct interest in the twin towns. Over the course of the eighteenth century, they granted the towns important economic and political privileges, sponsored buildings and Baroque festivities, and shaped religious practices and institutions. Imperial-royal activity peaked under the energetic Joseph II.[20] To facilitate transportation and development in Pest, officials ordered the demolition of the town gates and walls encircling the Inner District. They then surveyed and began to sell land parcels in the adjacent New District (Leopold District after 1790), the first neighborhood in Buda-Pest to grow according to a regular plan. Officials also planted trees on the outskirts of Pest, which would lead to the establishment of Buda-Pest's first park in the nineteenth century. Joseph's ban on Catholic contemplative orders (1782) had much more immediate consequences for the towns, because it opened up prime urban real estate for a variety of purposes. As a result, Buda's handsome Carmelite church, which had been built in the 1720s on the site of a ruined mosque, became a theater. A German-language theater company had its first performance there in 1787, and three years later László Kelemen's troupe presented the first Hungarian-language play in Buda-Pest. Joseph also envisioned building a theater in Pest and permanent bridge across the Danube.

To accomplish his many plans, Joseph had to rely on the towns' imperial-royal officials, an important prop of Habsburg power. Their numbers were remarkably low by modern standards, and as late as the 1840s, the Vice-Regal Council, which was responsible for everything from censorship and commerce to religious affairs and education, had a staff of just over 100. These bureaucrats formed a separate caste: "[I]n the castle itself," observed Johann Csaplovics, "as the site of the various governing bodies and their officials, a certain self-esteem and superiority, mixed with a legal tactfulness, sets the tone."[21] Some officials spent only a few years in Buda and then moved on to other posts; many were aristocrats who had come to Buda with the Vice-Regal Council in the 1780s. A good example is Baron József Podmaniczky, an ardent but not uncritical supporter of Joseph II.[22] A skilled conversationalist who spoke five languages fluently, Podmaniczky was also a talented pianist and hosted lively musical evenings in his Buda palace. For those fortunate enough to be admitted to them, these aristocratic households offered lively and cultured society: "Social calls, supper, theater, games, and dinner, these have been my main occupations," wrote Count Hofmannsegg fondly of his time in Buda.[23]

As a Protestant, Podmaniczky had entered public service in the wake of Joseph II's celebrated Edict of Toleration (1781). In Buda-Pest, the edict allowed local Calvinists and Lutherans to establish congregations. Joseph also ordered that Jews be allowed to settle in most royal towns in Hungary, including Buda and Pest. In the short term, these measures were more symbolic than substantive, and Buda-Pest effectively remained a Catholic city.[24] At a time when Catholics comprised roughly 60 percent of Hungary's population, they made up well over 90 percent of Buda-Pest's. A sizeable clergy met the towns' spiritual and educational needs: the 1787 census turned up 587 Catholic priests, many of them members of the towns' forty-seven monastic orders. Well-to-do laymen demonstrated their devotion by joining pious associations with names like the "Society of the Annunciation" and the "Society of Christ's Five Holy Wounds." Each craft guild had its own patron saint and proudly marched in the numerous religious processions that filled the calendar. So great was the guilds' zeal that Joseph II eventually forbade religious banners that could not be carried easily by three men (one guild apparently had a banner that required ten men to raise it and as many as twenty-five men to carry it). The townscape itself reflected the Catholics' preeminence: Buda-Pest (with Óbuda) had two dozen Catholic churches and chapels, but only three Orthodox churches, two small synagogues, and no Protestant churches. It is a small but telling detail that watchmen atop Pest Town Hall marked the hour by shouting *"Gelobet sey Jesus Christus!"* (Praised be Jesus Christ!).[25]

The town halls of Buda and Pest were the final pillar of Habsburg rule. On paper, both towns' charters upheld the doctrine that *Stadtluft macht frei* (town air makes one free), but in practice, town government was resolutely oligarchic and became even more so over the course of the eighteenth century, as local administration slowly ossified and fell into the hands of a small coterie of wealthy merchants, master artisans, and property owners. Here, too, Joseph II attempted to shake things up. Declaring that he would rather work with "a seasoned man" than "some bootmaker or other master artisan," Joseph effectively purged the Pest Town Council and installed Móric Hülff, a retired army officer, as mayor.[26] Hülff had been born into a burgher family in Pest—his father had come from Bavaria in the early eighteenth century—and had married a wealthy Pest widow. But Hülff had little respect for the town council, which he repeatedly accused of incompetence, greed, and corruption. As mayor (1785–87) and then head magistrate (1787–90), Hülff attempted to push through reforms favored by Joseph and presided over a newly formed building committee. Its greatest accomplishment was to break ground on a large military structure in Pest. Known simply known as the *Neugebäude* (New Building), it was an early example of the neoclassical style that would dominate early nineteenth-century architecture. Yet, to some observers, the massive, unfinished edifice symbolized the incomplete and overreaching nature of Joseph's reign.[27] Hülff himself had few admirers, and he was turned out of office soon after Joseph's death in 1790.

Joseph's successors proceeded more cautiously, but they would not shy away from exercising their authority over the towns. The balance of power between crown and town was tipping decisively in favor of the former. But town leaders were neither resourceful nor representative, which partly explains why Vienna's strong-arm tactics met with so little resistance. Fewer and fewer town dwellers were in fact being admitted to the rights of full citizenship, and by the turn of the nineteenth century, no more than 2–3 percent of residents of Buda and Pest were fully privileged citizens (*Bürger,* in a legal sense) of the towns.

The corporate social order had never been premised on equality. A relatively thin stratum of urban elites—imperial-royal officials, aristocrats, untitled nobles, the Catholic hierarchy, and successful burghers—enjoyed the array of privileges that held it together. Collectively, these groups dominated political, economic, and religious life in the twin towns. This was, to be sure, a heterogeneous leadership, and a world of difference existed between Buda's urbane aristocrats and Pest's industrious artisans. But a commitment to the corporate order, fidelity to the Habsburgs, and, with few exceptions, the Catholic faith linked these elites. These allegiances could be seen in the large celebrations held in Pest in 1803 to mark the centenary of the town's royal charter. Underlining the Catholic, corporate nature of urban institutions, the festivities included a procession of the burgher militias, guilds, and town magistracy, as well as the singing of a *Te*

Deum (a thanksgiving service) and mass in the Inner City parish church. "It is necessary and proper," said the Pest magistrate János Boráros, "that today's commemoration awaken in us the gratitude to which we owe God, our Monarch, and our forebears and forefathers in this town; this day, on which we celebrate the centenary of our recently renewed freedom, should be sacred to us."[28] As Boráros's words make clear, loyalty for the town leaders encompassed their faith, ruler, and hometown.

It would be a mistake, however, to assume that these burghers, officials, aristocrats, and Catholic priests did not also have a strong attachment to the Hungarian Kingdom in which they lived. A handful may have shared Joseph II's unitary conception of the monarchy, but in Buda-Pest declarations of loyalty almost always had a Hungarian inflection. Loyalty to the crown, church, and town, in other words, did not preclude a strong attachment to the traditions of the Hungarian Kingdom and to the welfare of all its residents. This patriotism was neutral with regard to language: the key element was simply loyalty to the Hungarian homeland, no matter whether this was expressed in Hungarian, German, Slovak, or Latin. Scholars sometime refer to this state patriotism as *Hungarus* loyalty, after the eighteenth-century writers who proudly identified themselves abroad as *Hungari*.[29] There is a whiff of antiquarianism about the *Hungarus* concept, and Hungarian scholars have often treated it as little more than a relic, but it was a tradition with deep roots in eighteenth-century Buda-Pest.

The leaders' multiple loyalties closely reflected the towns' corporate social order, with its interlocking guilds, parishes, town councils, and imperial-royal offices. Since authority in this system flowed downward from the ruler, it may make sense ultimately to describe the towns' various elites as "Habsburg loyalists" and "Hungarian patriots." This does not mean that all officials, aristocrats, or magistrates supported every decree emanating from Vienna, but rather that they felt an attachment to the ruling dynasty and the social and political order upon which it rested. C. A. Macartney once described the widespread attachment to the dynasty as a "special nationalism," but in eighteenth-century Hungary, Habsburg loyalty predated modern nationalism and would later compete with it.[30] Buda-Pest would be a focal point of this struggle.

The Trojan Horse

There was another center of political power in the twin towns: Pest County Hall. The unadorned, two-story building was not much to look at, but it is difficult to overstate the importance of the political system it stood for: "The county, and nothing else, was the unit and motive force of this old Hungary," wrote one historian.[31] Because the noble counties dominated the National Diet, collected taxes, and allotted recruits, they possessed significant leverage against the imperial-royal government. Pest County (in full, Pest-Pilis-Solt County) was one of the largest and most populous of Hungary's fifty-two noble counties. Much of it was covered by wide, treeless plains—the *puszta* in Hungarian, a word that means both "desolate" and "prairie." Nobles owned nearly all the land and typically used serfs to cultivate it; there were also free peasants, village craftsmen, and clergymen. The county's population, estimated at 272,000 in 1787, was five to six times larger than Buda-Pest's.[32] As the county seat, the town of Pest housed its administrative offices and hosted meetings of its assembly, which took place around the quarterly markets and were well-attended and lively.

In theory, nobles lived in the countryside and burghers in the towns. But with the County Hall as a kind of Trojan horse, the nobility had long ago breached the juridical barriers that separated the royal free towns from the surrounding county. As a result, more than 1,400 nobles appeared in the 1787 census of Buda and Pest.[33] These nobles accounted for 6 percent of the adult male population, which was similar to their proportion in the kingdom as a whole. This sizeable nobility set Hungary apart from its neighbors: in the Austrian lands, less than 1 percent of the population could claim noble rank; only in Poland and perhaps in Spain were nobles so thick on the ground.[34] Although the Hungarian nobility was deeply divided along economic, confessional, and regional lines, legal tradition enshrined the concept of *una eademque nobilitas,* a nobility equal in rights and duties: exemption from taxes, the right of habeas corpus, and freedom from all services except fighting for the king. Nobles could wear swords, sit in the front pews in church, and race their coaches through the streets of Pest. Their political privileges were no less impressive. All nobles could claim membership in the *natio Hungarica,* the Hungarian political nation. Townson is again instructive:

> But what is the nation? Who constitutes the people? To whom do these valuable rights belong? In this country, as in others where society is in childhood, the nation, alas! is only the great aristocratic body of nobles and clergy; and the productive part of the community, the citizens and peasants, have few or no rights, and no interference in public affairs; yet must submissively bear *all* the burdens of the state.[35]

As this definition makes clear, membership in the feudal political nation depended on birth and rank. Command of the Hungarian language was secondary, and, although most nobles would have known some Hungarian, an equal number knew Latin and other languages as well, if for no other reason than to communicate with their peasants (nobles had no compunction about exploiting and abusing their Hungarian-speaking serfs). The Hungarian national character of the feudal nation was largely fictional: the "nation of nobles" embraced only a fraction of people who could claim to be Hungarian through language, origin, residence, or loyalty.[36] Like many fictions, it had its uses; whether it could be rewritten to accommodate the claims of modern nationalism was a question that arose in the late eighteenth century.

The reign of Joseph II was again the crucial period. Joseph's reforms and seeming endorsement of Enlightenment ideas won him many admirers in Hungary, particularly among Protestant nobles. One barometer of Joseph's standing among the nobility was the attitude of Hungary's Masonic lodges. Masonry, which spread like wildfire across eighteenth-century Europe, first entered Hungary from Austria, where it had gained a relatively small but influential membership. A similar pattern held in Hungary, which by the early 1780s had around thirty lodges with anywhere from 600 to 2,000 members.[37] If these figures appear low in comparison with Western Europe—France had an estimated 50,000 masons—they are proportional to the size of Hungary's political public. One of the most famous lodges, the Magnanimity lodge in Pest, had only seventy-eight members, but they included aristocrats, officials, military officers, and landowners. In the words of one member, "the best brains of each county were drawn together and united here."[38] Pest's burghers had their own lodge, The Three Silver Anchors, and the First Innocence in Buda brought together reform-minded officials, many of them recently transferred to Buda with the Vice-Regal Council. Freemasonry was ostensibly above politics, but it was only a small step from the masons' lofty language of improvement, freedom, and virtue to the more prosaic reality of public affairs. As a rule, Hungary's freemasons had started out as loud defenders of Joseph II's program: it is characteristic of the Enlightenment in Central Europe that reformers placed their hopes in the state and especially in "enlightened absolutists" such as Joseph. By the second half of the 1780s, however, most masons had fallen silent or even turned against Vienna.

Why had Joseph lost so much support so quickly? From the outset, Joseph's wider campaign against the Catholic Church and his attempts to reshape lord-peasant relations had earned him the enmity of large parts of the Hungarian nobility. Nor did it help that Joseph was deaf to the tenor and pitch of Hungary's political life and willfully disregarded the kingdom's traditions and symbols. He had refused to be crowned King of Hungary and in 1784 ordered that the Hungarian Crown, which was believed to have been worn by St. Stephen in the year 1000, be transferred from Pressburg to Vienna, where it would be kept as a museum piece. (The Bohemian Crown of St. Wenceslas, formerly in Prague, suffered the same fate.) Joseph's cavalier handling of the crown was widely unpopular, and the thunderstorms that broke soon after the crown left Pressburg were taken as a sign of divine displeasure.[39]

Undaunted, Joseph rapidly issued a number of decrees that were of great consequence to the Hungarian nobility. He first ordered that a population census be carried out, in the apparent hope that military conscription could be extended into Hungary. When the nobles discovered that their households were to suffer the indignity of being counted, they responded "by evincing an impudent and irrational opposition," as Joseph put it.[40] The emperor's plan to replace or supersede the fifty-two noble counties with ten larger, more uniform administrative districts aroused an equal measure of hostility and resistance. Finally, Joseph also issued a decree replacing Latin with German as the language of administration, justice, and education in Hungary. To Joseph, the German language was foremost an administrative tool and was not meant to be imposed upon the mass of the population. Yet the preamble to his decree spelled out German's great promise: "What great benefit it would be to the common good, if only one language prevailed in the entire Monarchy, in which all governmental matters would flow, and through which every part of the Monarchy would be drawn tightly together, and its inhabitants united in a closer kinship."[41] German, the decree suggested, could function in the Habsburg Monarchy as French did in France or Russian in the Russian Empire. It thus ordered that German be used by all imperial-royal, county, and town officials, as well as in courts, schools, and the National Diet; those who did not know German were given up to three years to learn it.

Joseph's decrees raised a storm of protest in the noble counties. In particular, county officials—who tended to know Latin and Hungarian, but not always German—resented the language decree. Similarly, Joseph's attempt to weaken the county system threatened the economic and political existence of the provincial nobility, for whom the counties were an important source of income, prestige, and power. At first, the majority of noble counties opposed ending the use of Latin and recommended Hungarian as the alternative only if Latin had to be abandoned. The assembly of Pest County, for example, favored retaining Latin but was willing to allow lawsuits to be conducted in the vernacular languages.[42] But Pest County also complained to Joseph about the many "worthy patriots" who had been excluded from public service because of his actions. Joseph's decree was never fully implemented, but he had unintentionally turned the language of administration into a political football.

During his reign, Joseph had done much for the twin towns. His death, ironically, was no less significant. On his deathbed in February 1790, Joseph withdrew many of his reforms, including his decrees on the census, counties, and the German language; only the Edict of Toleration, the church decrees, and several edicts related to the peasantry remained in effect. The dying Joseph also ordered that the Hungarian regalia be returned to Hungary. The Crown of St. Stephen was thus delivered to Buda with great ceremony in April 1790. "Patriotism awakes in all its force," recorded Townson, "everybody wears Hungarian dress, such a scene of joy was never known before."[43] On the next day, the Archbishop of Esztergom celebrated a *Te Deum* amid thunderous cannon salutes. Feasts and parades filled the following days. To Townson, the celebrations had unmistakable revolutionary overtones, as "whole crowds of people paraded with music, and cried

'Huzza! The freedom of the Hungarian nation forever!' I can now form a pretty good idea of the revolutions in France and the Netherlands."

Joseph's successor Leopold II apparently agreed. Determined not to make the same mistakes as his older brother, Leopold had himself crowned in Pressburg, promised to fill the vacant office of palatine (or viceroy), and summoned the Hungarian National Diet to Buda. The Diet had not met in thirty-five years, and Leopold's announcement unleashed a torrent of ink, as hundreds of writers churned out pamphlets in German, Latin, and Hungarian. Many pamphlets advocated religious toleration and social reforms, and others called for everything from the abolition of capital punishment to the admission of women as spectators to sessions of the Diet. Politically, the pamphlets were all over the map. A handful of radicals entered the lists, as did conservatives: *All Change is Dangerous* was the title of one pamphlet. Casting about for allies, Vienna commissioned several works by the Pest professor Leopold Alois Hoffmann, who railed against the Hungarian nobility's monopoly on political power and its "enslavement" of the burghers.[44] In an equally provocative pamphlet, the Lutheran minister Johannes Molnár sharply attacked both the Hungarian aristocracy and Catholic prelates for their lack of patriotism and at the same time urged Leopold II to promote the German language and to complete the work left unfinished by Joseph II.[45] A greater number of pamphleteers, however, argued the opposite and called for the wider use of Hungarian. Samuel Decsy, a medical doctor and later newspaper editor, compared the Hungarian language to a phoenix rising from the ashes.[46] To Decsy, the development of commerce, the foundation of a scholarly society, the improvement of women's education, and other reforms would allow Hungary to shake its "present misery" and regain the splendor that it had enjoyed under Matthias Corvinus.

The National Diet opened in Buda in June 1790. Mixing hardnosed political calculation with genuine enthusiasm, the National Diet loudly championed the cause of the Hungarian language and at the outset declared that its deliberations and minutes would be in Hungarian. The Diet remained in session in Buda through October, and then reconvened in Pressburg, where it met until May 1791. This marked the high point both of the nobility's resistance to Vienna and of its influence in Buda-Pest, where demonstrably Hungarian costumes, dances, and plays were suddenly all the rage. But it remained to be seen how this "nation of nobles" would respond to the French Revolution, and how deep its commitment to the Hungarian language actually was.[47]

The Descendants of Attila

"I have written this book in Hungarian, because in it I wanted simply and solely to satisfy Hungarian hearts."[48] So begins András Dugonics's preface to *Etelka,* his 1788 novel of love, war, and nationhood among the ninth-century Magyars. The son of a provincial merchant, Dugonics became a Piarist monk and professor of mathematics at the university in Pest. Dugonics had fiercely opposed Joseph's 1784 language decree and much else about the emperor's reign, which he saw as a threat to Hungary's traditions and independence. Against this background, he not only wrote *Etelka* in the Hungarian language, but also filled it with descriptions of the costumes, customs, and language of the ancient Magyars, whom Dugonics linked to the Huns, Scythians, Turks, and other warrior tribes. Dugonics wanted to offer his compatriots a source of hope and pride, an antidote to their supposed suffering under Joseph II. The landscape of Buda-Pest itself offers solace:

> With such thoughts in mind I was on the Rabbit Island near Buda and, standing amid the sad ruins of the splendid buildings of our ancient Kings, saw before my very eyes the grievous remains of Attila's castle on the Danube's opposite bank. It seemed to me as if, looking across the water, the very pieces of stone offered consolation to each other, as those famous ruins of Carthage might have comforted the great Marius when, exiled from Rome, that great spirit placed his head to rest among them.[49]

Dugonics's Huns and early Hungarians proved to be very popular, and *Etelka* soon became a bestseller. It was said that many young women changed their names to Etelka (the heroine of the novel) soon after its appearance.[50]

Dugonics was part of a growing movement of writers, poets, journalists, linguists, and scholars who shared a commitment to all things Hungarian, including history, costumes, dances, theater, and, above all, language. Socially diverse and geographically diffuse, these national activists first made their presence felt in Buda-Pest in the 1780s and 1790s. In describing this movement, scholars often speak first of an older generation of writers, most of them nobles who had spent time in Vienna, often serving in Maria Theresa's Noble Hungarian Bodyguard (to which each noble county could send two young men) or attending the Theresarium, a school for the sons of the Hungarian nobility.[51] Led by György Bessenyei, these writers emerged in the 1770s, but then gave way to a younger and more radical generation of educated commoners. Although there is some truth to this picture, Hungarian activists were always a heterogeneous lot whose ranks included Catholic priests, titled aristocrats, and poor tutors, as well as political radicals who embraced the Enlightenment and conservatives who denounced it.[52] These activists were united in the belief that the Hungarian language had been neglected and should be used more widely, especially in Buda-Pest.

Boosters of the Hungarian language faced a long road. Millions of people spoke Hungarian; it had few dialects and a long literary tradition. But scholars were uncertain even of its origins: prevailing opinion held that

Hungarian had Turkish, Hunnish, or Scythian roots (offering a much less glamorous pedigree, nineteenth-century linguists would establish its place within the wider Finno-Ugrian language family, which includes, among others, Finnish and Estonian). Hungarian also had a limited social reach, particularly in the towns and among the aristocracy. Before the 1780s, there were few Hungarian-language novels, newspapers, plays, or publishers. Undaunted, the literati set out to standardize the language, translate foreign works, write original pieces in Hungarian, and compile grammars and dictionaries.

These linguistic labors helped cement the bond between language and nationhood. "One language, one nation," announced the late eighteenth-century preacher József Péczeli.[53] This simple equation had great consequences, at least potentially. By suggesting that the Hungarian national community was coequal with the kingdom's Hungarian-speakers, the literati were at once stretching its boundaries beyond the feudal confines of the *natio Hungarica* and at the same time defining it more narrowly than the Habsburg loyalists and Hungarian patriots, for whom language was a secondary consideration. Many historians have emphasized the democratic aspects of this transformation, seeing in it the influence of the Enlightenment and the emergence of modern, bourgeois Hungarian nationalism.[54] From this perspective, the expansion of the national community beyond the nobility placed Hungary in the mainstream of currents unleashed in Europe by the French Revolution. For a handful of scholars, however, the connection between language and nationhood forged in the late eighteenth century had terrible consequences. To George Barany, this link accelerated "the transformation of Hungarian, essentially pluralistic patriotism into modern or exclusive Magyar nationalism."[55] No matter what their perspective, such accounts often obscure the fact that the emerging Hungarian national movement was far from monolithic and that other forms of loyalty were far from extinguished.

The emerging national movement in Hungary also had many parallels both at home and abroad.[56] Within Hungary, the creation of a suitable literary language was a central concern to Slovak, Croat, Romanian, and other national activists, just as it animated the Czech, German, Greek, Italian, and other national movements. Neither spontaneous nor predetermined, the creation of national languages was, in the words of Geoff Eley and Ronald Suny, "a complex process of cultural innovation, involving hard ideological labor, careful propaganda, and a creative imagination."[57] Although activists worked under very different conditions, they often had common goals: to define and standardize the national language; to prove its antiquity; to promote its literature and increase the size of its reading public; and to encourage the cosmopolitan upper classes to use it. These efforts took on political dimensions when activists invariably declared that their languages should be used in schools and the administration.

For Habsburg Central Europe, the standardization of the German language in the late seventeenth and eighteenth centuries was of signal importance. It at once made possible Joseph II's language decree and at the same time provided a model for his opponents. In Hungary, the active support of several noble counties and the National Diet aided the cause of the Hungarian language, and in 1790–91 activists hailed the National Diet's early moves on behalf of Hungarian. But the Magyars' fixation with their language had deeper sources as well, including the Enlightenment in both its French and German forms. The key figure here was the landowner and onetime member of the Noble Hungarian Bodyguard, György Bessenyei, who argued that the vernacular offered a unique means of spreading Enlightenment ideas through all classes of society. His assertion in 1778 that "all nations gained their education in their own language, never in a foreign one" became a mantra repeated by generations of Hungarian national activists.[58] Not all of them shared Bessenyei's belief in progress and the diffusion of knowledge, but they agreed that the Hungarian language alone—and not Latin, German, or French—was the only suitable instrument for scholarship and learning in the Hungarian lands. It followed that Hungarian should be used in schools: "Do not let us force young people to learn unnecessary things," reads an anonymous pamphlet from 1790, "until now the dangerous practices introduced among us by Latin and other foreign languages have impoverished many."[59] Learning in Hungarian ("our own dear language"), it concludes, "will also enhance the happiness of the whole country." In this way, Enlightenment notions of progress and education could be harnessed to the activists' demands on behalf of the Hungarian language.

So too could the broad intellectual and artistic movement later known as Romanticism. Switching almost in the same breath from optimism to pessimism, activists claimed that they were fighting a desperate battle for linguistic (and hence national) survival. They urgently warned that the Magyars would end up like the Irish or Welsh, who had lost their "national" languages. The influential German philosopher Johann Gottfried Herder lent substance to these fears in 1791, when he wrote that the Magyars would soon disappear into an encircling sea of Slavs and Germans and that, by the end of the nineteenth century, the Hungarian language would no longer be heard.[60] Even before Herder, however, writers often warned of an impending national death. "If the Magyar nation loses its own language," wrote the Pest professor Miklós Révai, "it will also be entirely lost, and the Magyars will no longer be Magyar [a' Magyar nem leszen már Magyar]."[61] The fate of the nation seemed to hang in the balance: until Hungarian is used more widely, declared Ferenc Kazinczy, "our homeland will always be foreign, and the nation not a separate nation, but simply a colony."[62] To prevent this from happening, activists saw it as their duty to propagate the language more widely.

From the beginning, the Hungarian side focused its attention on Buda-Pest. In light of the growing economic, administrative, and cultural importance of the twin towns, this was unsurprising. With few exceptions, national movements in Europe almost always took root in cities and towns before spreading to the countryside.[63] But Buda-Pest held a symbolic importance for Hungarian national activists, even those who lived in the provinces. This can be seen in one of the most popular literary works of the late eighteenth century: Count Joseph Gvadányi's long poem *The Village Notary's Journey to Buda* (1790). An unlikely poet, Gvadányi was a retired cavalry officer whose work first appeared while he was in his sixties. As its title indicates, *The Village Notary* tells the story of a provincial lawyer who travels to Buda, which he imagines to be "a paradise," "the seat of kings," and "the ornament of our nation."[64] Upon his arrival, the notary marvels at Buda's many attractions—its castle, baths, and pontoon bridge—but his wonder soon gives way to disillusionment. Expecting to meet the descendants of Hungarian heroes of old, he sees only foppish aristocrats affecting foreign fashions. To make matters worse, the notary scarcely hears a word of Hungarian during his stay in Buda. In frustration, he finally bursts out at a young count dressed in English clothes:

> So it's the fashion, it? Is that the only reason you can state
> That you and every noble youth these foolish things must prate?
> No Magyar blood flows in your veins! You're all degenerate!
> I never saw such madness, no! in all my life to date![65]

The message is clear: leading town dwellers should wear the national costume (described elsewhere in the poem as "the most beautiful in the world") and speak the national language; only then will Buda shed its foreign character and reclaim its former glory.

But how could Hungarian activists accomplish this? How could they win over the Habsburg loyalists? How could they challenge the dominance of the German language in the twin towns? While activists had high hopes for the National Diet, they also used two key institutions—newspapers and clubs—to broadcast their views, rally their followers, and, it was hoped, shape the course of events. Print was the cornerstone of this emerging civil society. Ironically, its foundation had been laid by Maria Theresa's educational reforms, which had made primary schooling mandatory and provided funds to pay for new schools, and Joseph II's moves to reduce censorship and untie the hands of publishers. Buda-Pest in the late eighteenth century thus had a number of printing presses, booksellers, and libraries, which catered to a small but growing reading public.[66] Although almanacs, prayer books, and cheaply printed tales of crime and adventure remained the bestsellers, German and French classics, as well as Hungarian-language translations, novels, and poetry, were also available. From the 1780s onward, the number and circulation of newspapers expanded rapidly. Led by *Magyar Hirmondó (Hungarian Messenger)*, which was launched in Pressburg in 1780, the Hungarian-language press made impressive gains, and there were new German and even Latin newspapers as well.

Residents of the twin towns also had more places where they could meet to discuss and debate the latest ideas.[67] In 1779, Bessenyei had launched a short-lived society in Pest with the aim of contributing to the development of Hungarian language and literature. A number of reading rooms *(Lesekabinette)*, which both sold and lent books, later opened, and in 1791 a group of literati formed a reading club in Buda. Devoted to self-improvement and sociability, the club had 126 members and subscribed to 45 newspapers and journals, including several French papers.[68] Its reading room rapidly became a gathering place for leading reformers in Buda, and the house of Baron Orczy played a similar role in Pest. In the early 1790s, Baroness Anna Beleznay also established Pest's first literary salon.[69] Her gatherings were particularly notable for bringing together men and women of different social ranks and religious confessions.

This network of newspapers and reading clubs gave Hungarian activists a beachhead in Buda-Pest. These gains in civil society, however, were not matched in the Hungarian National Diet. After opening to great promise in 1790, the Diet achieved much less than the activists had hoped. The Diet did score a number of notable successes, including a law stating that Hungary was an independent kingdom that was to be governed in accordance with its own laws and customs and not according to the norms applied to other Habsburg lands. Another law (Act 1791:38) upheld the right of Jews already residing in royal free towns to remain; at the very least, this prevented their expulsion. Leopold II also promised to convene the Diet every three years and obtain its consent for taxes and recruits. But the French Revolution had rattled the Hungarian nobility, and in the end conservatives won the upper hand. The gains for the Hungarian language were accordingly slight, and the Diet closed in 1792 with Latin still firmly in place as the official language.[70] Yet Joseph's plan to introduce German was long dead, and Vienna had consented to the Diet's proposal to install and fund instructors of Hungarian literature and language in all secondary schools. The formation of nine Dietal committees, which met from 1791 to 1793 to consider economic, social, and legal questions, also kept alive the possibility of further reforms in the near future.

But the atmosphere in Hungary was rapidly changing. From July 1791 onward, censors would not allow newspapers to mention events in France. The authorities began to watch closely for any signs of dissent. In 1792, Palatine Alexander Leopold anxiously wrote to the emperor-king: "I learned several days ago that Pest maintains a club whose aim is supposedly an uprising of the burghers and the villagers; secondly, I have heard complaints from different people that the French events are spoken about in the coffeehouses, and what is more, that in one of them they toast the

French."[71] Vienna soon launched a full-scale crackdown. Its main target was the so-called Jacobin movement, led by Ignác Martinovics. In turn a member of the Franciscan order, professor of physics, and police informer, Martinovics organized two secret societies in Hungary in May 1794. The first, the Society of Reformers, was exclusively for the nobility, who were kept in the dark about the existence of the second club, the Society of Liberty and Equality, whose members included young nobles, teachers, and writers with much more radical aims. The total membership of the two groups, however, never exceeded a few hundred, and the secret police likely knew more about them than the public did. Vienna moved against them in the summer of 1794 and in the following year conducted trials that led to eighteen death sentences, seven of which (including that of Martinovics) were carried out in Buda (the rest were commuted). Long prison sentences awaited many other Jacobins. The authorities removed several university professors from their posts and placed others under police supervision. They also introduced strict new censorship laws and closed down most newspapers and reading rooms.

The Hungarian cause in Buda-Pest suffered setbacks in other areas. For years, activists had denounced "foreign" fashions and extolled the antiquity of the national dress. In 1790, Magyar costumes and dances had suddenly come into vogue, but this fad soon passed. When he attended masked balls in Buda and Pest in 1793, Hofmannsegg humorously noted the noblemen who insisted on wearing spurred boots on the dance floor, but otherwise recorded that "nothing seemed more familiar than such entertainments, and I did not notice anything extraordinary that would not be allowed at home [in Dresden]."[72] A similar story played itself out on the stage. National activists, who saw the theater as an indispensable tool for polishing and popularizing the Hungarian language, despaired that performances in Buda-Pest's theaters were almost exclusively in German. When parts of an opera in Buda were sung in Hungarian in July 1790, a Hungarian-language newspaper rashly boasted that this was "manifest proof that the German stage is already [voluntarily] Magyarizing."[73] A Hungarian-language theater company held its first performance in October, and actors presented dramas, tragedies, and musicals in Hungarian on the towns' stages for the next five years. When financial difficulties arose, the theater companies turned to Pest County for support, proudly writing in 1795 that, "because the establishment of this company took place in the name of the nation, its survival is connected to the maintenance of the national honor in the eyes of foreigners."[74] But national honor could not fill seats, and Hungarian-language performances had difficulty drawing audiences after the close of the National Diet. This was to be expected, because Hungarian-language theater had shallow roots and too few potential customers in Buda-Pest. In April 1796, Pest County officially announced that the Hungarian theater company had disbanded.

By the end of the decade, visitors to Buda-Pest would be hard-pressed to find places where they could read foreign newspapers, discuss the most recent events, or meet writers and journalists. Nor would they be able to see manifestly Hungarian dances, costumes, or plays. The nascent civil society in Buda-Pest seemed to have collapsed, and with it the Hungarian national movement. The poet Mihály Vitéz Csokonai grimly took stock of the situation in 1798: "Our theater has died in its cradle, our best authors have either died or fallen into misfortune, and the rest are silent, with none to rouse them."[75] But the nationalist project would not die so easily. With their noisy protests in newspapers, pamphlets, coffeehouses, and clubs, national activists had quickened the efforts of language reformers and spurred the development of Hungarian-language literature and theater. In the National Diet and county assemblies, the Hungarian nobility had voiced its support for the vernacular. This combination of heated agitation from below and repeated remonstrances from above was a powerful legacy for the Hungarian national movement in the nineteenth century.

With the benefit of hindsight, squinting perhaps, we can find hints of Buda-Pest's remarkable future: portents of its role as the center of the Hungarian national movement, as the capital of the 1848–49 Revolution, and as a twentieth-century metropolis. But we should not let these signs, however compelling, obscure our view of the twin towns in the late eighteenth century. Both the prestige and population of Buda-Pest had grown impressively over the course of the century, yet the towns remained relatively small and unimposing. A circle of imperial-royal, Catholic, and corporate elites dominated local affairs; only a minority of the wider population spoke Hungarian as their first language.

On the surface, then, Buda-Pest did not appear to be promising terrain for the Hungarian national movement. Yet as the events of the early 1790s had shown, the towns possessed unequal political, material, and cultural resources for national activists. Nowhere else did so many influential aristocrats, noblemen, officials, and writers come together, and nowhere else had such a vibrant and diverse social and cultural life. Buda-Pest, moreover, occupied a central place in the national imagination: it was the city of Attila, St. Stephen (or at least his crown), and King Matthias; it was the "the light of the Magyars' eyes, the capital of the whole country."[76] For national activists, the past provided a clear direction for the future. But public life had changed dramatically in the mid-1790s, and whether these Hungarian nationalists would have their way in Buda-Pest was far from certain at the turn of the nineteenth century.

CHAPTER TWO

Mud, Dust, and Horses

"Public life stormed and raged in the theater and concert hall because there was nowhere else it was allowed to storm and rage."

—Wilhelm Heinrich Riehl, an early nineteenth-century Bavarian reformer[1]

On May 3, 1819, Károly Kisfaludy's *The Tatars in Hungary* opened on the Pest stage.[2] Kisfaludy had written the play seven years earlier while an art student in Vienna, and its simple, unadorned language told the story of the Hungarians' heroic but doomed resistance to Mongol horsemen in the thirteenth century. Because Buda-Pest did not have a Hungarian-language theater company, provincial actors performed the play. From all reports, the opening night audience was large and rowdy, and when an actor intoned the line "Long live freedom," the crowd roared back "Long live Hungarian freedom!" Kisfaludy's themes of foreign oppression and Hungarian opposition may have stirred the audience; according to a police informant, the seditious outburst also had social causes: Hungarian-speaking tailors, cobblers, hatters, and bookmakers had left their workshops for the theater, where they had noisily cheered the actors' every utterance. Upon learning of the disturbance, Count Sedlnitzky, the head of the police and censors in Vienna, demanded a full report from Pest. Such occurrences, he fulminated, can "heighten the ruling stupor and encourage passions under the enchanting name of nationalism and patriotism."

The authorities ultimately refrained from action, and *The Tatars in Hungary* was repeated many times over the next two years. Emperor-King Francis (r. 1792–1835) himself watched the play during a visit to Pest in 1820. Why, then, did the authorities react so strongly, at least at first? For that matter, why was a police spy in the theater? Perhaps we should not be surprised, since paranoid policing is consonant with the usual picture of Francis's regime, at once stifling, suspicious, cumbersome, and entirely unable to tell the important from the trivial. In this era, balls with an orchestra of three or more instruments required the permission of the authorities, who also opened letters, searched rooms, and set spies even on imperial-royal officials. But Vienna's fears about the Pest stage may not have been entirely unfounded. "Indescribable joy roused my patriotism," wrote one Pest resident who attended the premiere of *The Tatars in Hungary*.[3] A contemporary newspaper greeted the play as evidence that Pest should have a Hungarian National Theater. Censorship and policing, in short, may have put a damper on public life in Buda-Pest, but it did not extinguish it altogether, as would-be club members and journalists found new outlets for their energies. With this in mind, we need to look closely at the political dynamics of the first decades of the nineteenth century and examine how Hungarian national activists in Buda-Pest adapted to this repressive environment. Far from being a period of *Ruhe und Ordnung*—stultifying quiet and order—the era witnessed a wide range of cultural, literary, and linguistic initiatives.

The twin towns themselves changed dramatically during these years. The Pest Theater was a visible symbol of this: built at great cost between 1808 and 1812, it was the first building in Buda-Pest constructed expressly to be a theater. With its handsome neoclassical exterior and spacious interior—it could seat 3,000—it reflected the towns' growing population, prosperity, and cultural aspirations. These changes posed a challenge both to the leaders of the twin towns and to the Hungarian national movement. For the former, the boom of the early 1800s was a mixed blessing, at once filling the towns' coffers and boosting real estate values, but at the same time loosening the hold of guildsmen and privileged merchants over the local economy. In this situation, political initiative continued to shift from the Buda and Pest town halls to the imperial-royal authorities, who rarely saw eye to eye with the burghers. For their part, national activists were slow to grasp the wider significance of economic expansion and urbanization. Many dismissed commerce and industry as the concern of "foreigners," meaning German-speakers, burghers, and Jews. This blinkered view would give way only in the mid-1820s, when an aristocrat and erstwhile German-speaker, Count István Széchenyi, would use horse races, a social club, and a learned society to push public life in Buda-Pest in a new direction.

From Marsh to Marketplace

The French Revolution and Napoleonic wars were trying times for the Habsburg Monarchy.[4] The nadir came in 1809, when Napoleon trounced its armies (not for the first time), occupied Vienna and carted off its art treasures, and then imposed a steep indemnity on the monarchy and redrew its borders. As a final humiliation, Napoleon unceremoniously exchanged his first wife for the favorite daughter of Emperor-King Francis. The Austrians emerged victorious from the wars, and much was salvaged at the Congress of Vienna (1814–15). Although Francis's regime is often associated with political immobility, in reality it implemented a number of administrative, legal, and military reforms. This was meager compensation to his subjects, who had to bear the burden of warfare, casualties, occupation, inflation, and shortages, as well as continued policing and censorship when the fighting was over. But, even as it grumbled and tired of the endless war, the population responded with remarkable endurance and a high degree of loyalty.

This was above all loyalty to the dynasty. While the fighting lasted, the authorities in Vienna cultivated this allegiance through propaganda. They installed Anton Zauner's equestrian statue of the popular Joseph II in front of the imperial palace, commissioned Joseph Haydn to compose the imperial anthem *Gott erhalte (God Preserve [the Emperor])*, and allowed Josef Hormayr to produce the *Patriotic Journal for the Austrian Empire*.[5] Once the danger had passed, however, the regime had little use for the widespread energies awakened by the Napoleonic wars. Hence the oft-repeated anecdote about Emperor Francis: when one of his subjects was recommended to him as a clever and ardent patriot, Francis supposedly retorted: "I hear he is a patriot for Austria. But the question is whether he is a *patriot for me*."[6] For this reason, it has often been alleged—most forcefully by Oscar Jászi—that from the late eighteenth century onward, the Habsburg dynasty did little to encourage the continuing loyalty of its subjects and, where such allegiance existed, did less to use it to advance reforms or to bind together the monarchy's disparate territories and populations.[7] When Francis added a new imperial title in 1804, it was as Emperor of Austria and not as Emperor of the Austrians: French ideas of popular sovereignty clearly had no place in the Habsburg realm. Nor would there be a Habsburg equivalent to the "myth of national liberation" that took root in Prussia or Russia; the wars did not create "Austrians" as they did "Britons" out of the peoples of England, Scotland, and Wales.[8]

But the Habsburgs kept armies in the field for nearly a quarter century. In Hungary, there were few signs of open dissent. No doubt aware of what the French principles of "liberty, equality, and fraternity" might mean for their feudal privileges, the noble estates dutifully approved Vienna's repeated requests for money and men. Tensions still remained, and the National Diet repeatedly called for wider use of the Hungarian language and denounced Vienna's economic policies. The customs barrier between Austria and Hungary was a frequent target of criticism, and only its modification or elimination, the Diet suggested, would bring an end to Hungary's "colonial status."[9] But such complaints had a formulaic quality, and the nobles were unwilling to renounce their exemption from taxes or seriously discuss the condition of the serfs. In 1809, with Napoleon's forces already in Vienna, the Hungarian nobility gave battle to a well-equipped French army, which rapidly swept the noblemen off the field. This must have been a moving display of both bravery and military obsolescence, even if later tributes to the nobles' "valiant" and "manly" courage and to the Hungarian national spirit—which had stood like a "stone wall" against the French—could not disguise the totality of the defeat.[10] The monarchy's chronic financial woes ultimately undermined relations between Vienna and Hungary, and in 1812, after the Hungarian estates refused to accept new fiscal burdens, Francis simply dissolved the Diet and did not summon it again until 1825.

The suspension of the National Diet reflected Vienna's wider approach to all competing sources of political power, including the towns of Buda and Pest. Superficially, the revolution and war increased the dignity of the twin towns: the Hungarian National Diet met three times in Buda (1790–91, 1792, and 1807) and Emperor-King Francis visited the towns on several occasions.[11] Indeed, with the end of the Holy Roman Empire in 1806, Friedrich von Gentz, a confidant of Prince Metternich, even suggested that the center of the monarchy should be moved from Vienna to Hungary. This happened quite unexpectedly three years later, when the court fled to Buda ahead of Napoleon's advancing armies. But appearances can be deceiving. Francis and his court soon returned to Vienna, the three National Diets were in session for only fourteen months, and after 1807 the Diet would not return to the twin towns for more than forty years. At the same time, Vienna systematically stripped away privileges enshrined in the towns' 1703 royal charters. By the early nineteenth century, neither town could construct buildings, raise their employees' salaries, or spend more than fifty florins (a paltry sum) without the permission of the Royal Treasury in Buda. Imperial-royal officials also nominated all candidates for the highest town offices (mayor, head magistrate, and town captain); the town council could then choose from among the approved candidates. As a result, the *Bürgertum* (wider citizenry), already a fraction of the population, had almost no say in local affairs and its outer council became little more than a rubber stamp. For many successful town dwellers, including merchants and manufacturers, local citizenship promised few rewards and may not have been worth pursuing.

Sustained economic growth put a different set of pressures on the towns. Untouched by fighting and buoyed by high agricultural prices, the twin towns enjoyed an upsurge in commerce, population, and construction in the first decades of the nineteenth century. War was the engine of growth: it created huge armies that needed to be clothed and fed, disrupted the international grain trade, and brought Napoleon's Continental System, which helped local manufacturers. Buda-Pest rapidly became a commercial entrepôt for a wide range of products, and enterprising merchants and large landowners made great fortunes shipping grain, cattle, and wool to Austria. That servants were said to dress as well as their masters and that coachmen now carried pocket watches suggests that some wealth was trickling down to the lower strata of society. The boom came to an end after 1815, as the collapse in world agricultural prices, together with the resumption of industrial imports from Britain, checked Hungary's economic growth for more than a decade. The career of the Jewish merchant Joachim Zappert is instructive: he started the century selling jewelry and precious stones in Pest, switched to wool—a much more profitable commodity—and flourished for a time, before struggling through the 1820s and dying penniless in Vienna in 1832.[12] But if growth slowed

1—New Market Square, the center of commerce in Pest. Its tall buildings stood out in a town where one-story houses were the rule.

after 1815, it did not cease entirely. The guidebook writer Franz Schams rapturously described New Market Square (fig. 1), an emblem of Pest's continued economic expansion:

> There, where marshes, reeds, and devastating quicksand once covered the land, where only 40 years ago the townsmen's bodies were laid to rest in the churchyard of the Tailors' Chapel, where the murderous spectacle of bull-baiting once entertained the public, is now the central point of the annual markets' enormous traffic and the parade ground of the local garrison; a most beautiful arrangement of houses has formed the new square, which surpasses all its cousins in the Austrian Empire (excepting St. Mark's in Venice) and deserves to be compared with the greatest and most beautiful squares in Europe.[13]

As many as 30,000 people attended Pest's fairs in the nineteenth century, prompting the German traveler J. G. Kohl to remark that the mixture of peoples in the marketplace would reward a six-month ethnographic study.[14]

Demographic and physical growth provided further evidence of Pest's dynamism, particularly in comparison with Buda and Óbuda. After growing rapidly in the 1780s, Buda now developed more slowly, and its population held steady at roughly 24,000. The number of houses in Buda reached nearly 3,000 in 1809, but a devastating fire the following year destroyed 600 houses and left soot and burn marks that were still visible more than two decades later.[15] The story in Óbuda was similar, and although the population expanded from 6,000 in the 1780s to more than 7,000 in the 1810s, it grew at a slower rate than in the early eighteenth century. Immigrants instead headed to Pest, whose population swelled from 22,417 in 1787 to 35,349 in 1809, an increase of 58 percent in just over two decades. There were much larger cities in Europe and in the Habsburg lands—Vienna at this time had around 230,000 residents—but Pest's growth rate outstripped that of every other town in Hungary, a trend that would continue into the twentieth century. The number of houses in Pest increased from 1,981 to 2,850 during the same period, prompting one visitor to remark that "more than half the present town looks as if built but yesterday."[16] There was a marked expansion upward in the older parts of town, as builders put up two- and three-story structures and rent-hungry land- lords tacked new floors onto existing buildings.

Pest also expanded outward. Most newcomers settled in districts that ringed the Inner City and bore the names of eighteenth-century Habsburg rulers: Theresa, Joseph, Leopold, and Francis. Theresa District, for instance, had only a few hundred residents in the early eighteenth century, but an estimated 10,600 inhabitants in 1806, nearly 15,000 a decade later, and more than 21,000 in the early 1830s.[17] With the exception of the prosperous, orderly Leopold District (discussed below), the outer districts were almost always described by travelers and guidebook writers as village-like and disorderly, which meant that the streets were wide and unpaved, the houses were low and poorly built, and the residents had gardens and kept animals (a wealthy person, contemporaries said, lived in a house without cows). The residents of the outer districts spoke a number of languages—Joseph District was called a "Slavic fortress"—and came from different regions of Hungary.[18] They were united, however, in their abysmal living conditions, which included high infant mortality rates (one in three infants died), widespread hunger, and frequent epidemics.

Most immigrants earned their living as day laborers, peddlers, artisans, and servants. They worked as vinedressers in Buda and sold firewood, water, chickens, and homebrewed brandy in Pest's markets and squares. Better jobs were hard to come by, because there was only a handful of factories (and such work paid poorly in any event), and the guild system, itself in deep flux, proved unable to increase output in key trades or to find places for the many newcomers from the countryside. Almost as old as the towns themselves, the guilds were tightly woven into the fabric of social, religious, and political life. Although this tapestry was fraying in places and showing signs of wear, guild privileges remained important, and at the end of the eighteenth century there were scores of guilds in the twin towns, including masons, tailors, millers, butchers, carpenters, and glaziers, not to mention chimney sweeps, goldsmiths, glovers, soap boilers, card painters, bookbinders, and surgeons.[19] The number of master artisans in Buda-Pest rose from 1,039 in 1774 to 4,158 in 1828, a significant increase, but one that disguised increasing diversity. Some enterprising guildsmen oversaw large workshops and subcontracted jobs to other masters, whereas most artisans scrabbled to make ends meet, often relying upon small gardens and, particularly in Buda, vineyards in the surrounding hills.[20] Guildsmen complained that the towns were filled with *Störer* (literally, troublemakers) or *Pseudo-Magister* (pseudo-masters), artisans who produced goods outside the guild system. Many of these nonguild artisans worked as masons, carpenters, and tailors in the underserved outer districts, and, although most were Catholic, the guilds directed much of their anger against the handful of Jewish artisans who had established themselves in the twin towns.[21]

The guild masters' hostility to Jews was shared by the Pest Merchants Corporation, which included only Roman Catholic, Greek Orthodox, and, later, Protestant merchants.[22] The merchants' ill will had two sources. On the one hand, the corporation worried about the mass of peasants, tinkers, and peddlers in the towns—it claimed that there were fifty peddlers for every legitimate merchant—and singled out Jews for selling bogus goods, using loaded scales, and practicing usury.[23] This fear was surely exaggerated: although there were a growing number of Jewish peddlers in Pest, most were desperately poor "rag-and-bone merchants" who eked out a living in the outer districts. But the Pest Merchants Corporation was also alarmed by successful Jewish wholesalers. Orthodox merchants (called "Greeks" or "Serbs," but in reality from across the Balkan peninsula) had traditionally played a leading role in long-distance trade through Pest. As they prospered, these Orthodox merchants reinvested their capital in urban real estate and sometimes obtained noble titles, with the result that many of them had abandoned commerce by the end of the eighteenth century. Jewish merchants often stepped in to take their place. At times possessing significant capital, professional expertise, and connections in Vienna, Jewish wholesalers soon accounted for a large share of the trade in grain and textiles, two commodities high in demand during the Napoleonic wars. Risk-taking members of the Pest Merchants Corporation also entered long-distance trade during this time, and some, like the Lutheran Johann Samuel Liedemann, made fast and fabulous fortunes. Vera Bácskai has nevertheless estimated that more than 70 percent of Pest's largest merchants in the early nineteenth century were of Jewish origin, although she rightly observes out that this represented only a small fraction of the Jewish population.[24]

By the early nineteenth century, there was a growing sense among many burghers that Jews, either as well-connected merchants or price-cutting *Störer,* were the source of their economic worries. Contemporary travelers did nothing to dispel this image and uncritically blamed Jews for

urban misery. "The entrance into Buda," wrote Townson, "is the most unfavorable that can be conceived. There are no fortifications nor even gates
to this city, and you enter the metropolis of Hungary as you do one of its
villages; and as the Jews have occupied the first part of the town, it is not
necessary to say that the first thing that strikes you is poverty and filthi-
ness."[25] That Jews were barred from the Merchants Corporation, craft
guilds, and most professions (including teaching, the law, and civil service) was not part of the discussion; rather, the burghers simply attempted
to exclude them from Buda-Pest, even after Joseph II had ordered in 1783
that Jews could settle in royal free towns. In the 1790s, the Pest Town
Council set fines for landlords who rented rooms to recently arrived Jews
and tried to expel the married children of Jews who had been granted residency permits. The town later announced that legal residency and the
right to trade in Pest could be passed on to only one son per family.[26]
These and other measures were as ineffectual as they were harsh, but residential restrictions would remain in effect until 1840.

In this situation, Óbuda continued to function as a suburb of Pest.
(Some of Buda-Pest's first omnibus lines would run between Óbuda and
Pest.) By 1810, Jews comprised roughly two-fifths of Óbuda's population.[27]
The Jewish community's most visible symbol was its new synagogue (built
1820–21). Schams visited Óbuda soon after its completion and declared,
"This recently-built synagogue takes honors over all religious houses
found in the Austrian Monarchy."[28] The synagogue won accolades partly
because of its exterior's pronounced neoclassicism, which was also the
style used for most churches and public buildings in early nineteenth-
century Buda-Pest. But a neoclassical façade could not erase deep religious
and economic prejudices, and in the same breath that he praised the
Óbuda synagogue, Schams criticized strong Jewish adherence to tradition
and what he called "speculative spirit."

The prevalence of such views makes the rapid growth of the Jewish
community in Pest all the more remarkable.[29] Despite the town's opposition, approximately 1,000 Jews lived in Pest in 1800 and nearly 4,000
three decades later, making it one of the largest Jewish settlements in the
Hungarian lands. Pest's Jewish population surpassed Óbuda's in the late
1820s. How this happened is not yet fully understood, but at least three
factors were involved. First, Pest attracted large numbers of young, unmarried men, drawn by necessity, opportunity, and a willingness to take risks.
Second, Jews already living in Pest used a range of family strategies to
maintain their position in town. A well-to-do father with several sons, for
example, would pass on his residency permit to a younger son, while giving the older ones sufficient capital to allow them to apply for residency
on their own. Finally, Jews in Pest often enjoyed the support of the
imperial-royal authorities and of aristocratic landlords. If the former were
broadly interested in the town's economic development, the latter often
saw Jews as potential tenants. Thus, many Jews settled in Theresa District,

which was near New Market Square and also home to several apartment buildings whose aristocratic owners were willing to rent to Jews. The largest and most famous was the Orczy House, which had forty-eight apartments, warehouses, three restaurants, and a coffeehouse, and acted as a "harbor" in Theresa District for newly arrived Jews. In time, everything required by the Jewish community was available in the Orczy House: baths, a savings bank, a bookstore, an abattoir, and a synagogue. Baron Orczy was richly rewarded in return, and the building was reportedly the most profitable piece of real estate in Pest.

The Orczy House and the sprawling suburbs were just as much signs of Pest's growth as the Pest Theater or the New Market Square. Coming by the thousands, these newcomers slowly, imperceptibly, weakened the bonds of the corporate order. Divisions on the Habsburg side only hastened this process, as town officials, master artisans, and merchants could not always count on the support of the imperial-royal authorities or aristocratic landlords. Even the Catholic Church lost some of its influence, since there were too few churches in the outer districts. Political power in Buda-Pest increasingly lay with the imperial-royal authorities; how they used it the early nineteenth century would have great consequences for the twin towns.

A Patriotic Archduke

Even in the better parts of Buda-Pest, rapid growth and newfound prosperity did not create a safer, healthier, or more attractive city. Streets lacked sewers, trees, and sidewalks, and the center of Pest contained ponds, cemeteries, slaughterhouses, and the burghers' shooting gallery. The geographer J. C. von Thiele wrote of an "intolerable stench" caused by the putrefaction of human and animal waste in streets, squares, and riverfront areas.[30] Deforestation, an alluvial soil, and a steady wind made sandstorms a frequent occurrence: "This sand is one of the miseries of Pest," wrote Paget. "It is so fine, that it enters into everything, destroys furniture, and blinds and chokes the inhabitants worse than a London fog."[31] In *Buda-Pest's Dust and Mud* (1834), Széchenyi examined, among other topics, why houses in Buda-Pest were so often wet, smelly, and noisy. The Danube, a source of the towns' prosperity, was part of the problem: floods were a constant threat in the spring, and low water often made it impossible to unload goods on the Pest side in the summer.

Clearly, some form of urban planning was desperately needed, especially in Pest. Its town council, however, was rent by personal rivalries and unwilling to encroach upon the rights of property owners (most magistrates owned land in Pest). This made the active intervention of the imperial-royal authorities all the more necessary. The crucial figure here was Archduke Joseph Anton, Emperor-King Francis's younger brother and, from 1796 onward, Palatine of Hungary, effectively the intermediary between the ruler and the Hungarian estates. The office of palatine *(nádor)* was an old one, dating back to the fifteenth century, but it had been vacant for much of Maria Theresa's and all of Joseph II's reigns. Archduke Alexander had served as palatine from 1790 until his untimely death in a fireworks accident in 1795. Before his death, Alexander had secretly urged Vienna to take a tough line on Hungary and, if necessary, to use troops, censorship, the clergy, and propaganda to maintain order.[32]

Palatine Joseph took an entirely different approach. He worked hard to show that the imperial-royal government was interested in the development of the Hungarian lands. In a memorandum to the emperor-king, Joseph suggested that Pest, which he called *"die Hauptstadt Hungarns"* ("Hungary's capital"), had the potential to be a flourishing commercial center as well as the most attractive town in Hungary. The local magistrates, he added, would accomplish nothing on their own.[33] Undeterred by the monarchy's endless wars and troubled finances, Joseph sponsored the establishment of an Embellishment Commission *(Verschönerungs-Commission),* which began work in 1808 with the twin aims of fostering economic growth and developing Pest's infrastructure.[34] Its funds came primarily from the sale of properties held by the town; the commission's members included the town engineer, an architect, a mason, and a carpenter, as well as six magistrates, but the commission was under the leadership of the Royal Treasury and entirely independent of the town council. The Embellishment Commission planned to create new squares, dig sewers, pave streets, and plant trees against the ubiquitous dust. It also wanted to erect a new theater, dance hall, work house, and barracks for the local garrison. Most ambitiously, it commissioned the architect Josef Hild to draw up plans for Leopold District, a rapidly developing neighborhood to the north of the Inner City. In contrast to the old city center, with its narrow streets, small building lots, and mix of residential and commercial real estate, Leopold District would have a grid pattern broken only by squares, parks, and long, radial avenues; residential blocks with plots large enough to accommodate sizeable houses; and a riverbank both protected against floods and suitable for promenades. There was little room in this scheme for the working poor, who would presumably have to fend for themselves in Pest's swelling outer districts.

The Embellishment Commission achieved a great deal, if not all that had been anticipated. Property sales had raised a sizeable sum, but the Embellishment Commission spent the money quickly and often unwisely, so by the early 1810s its capital and momentum were nearly exhausted. In 1818, the imperial-royal authorities quietly suggested that the commission be placed under the purview of the Pest Town Council. Although the commission retained its autonomy and continued to meet until 1858, it never regained the dynamism of its first few years. A review of the commission's activities in the mid-1820s nevertheless revealed that it had accomplished two-thirds of its stated objectives. It put up several needed buildings, tore

2—The Pest Town Theater (built 1808–12). Károly Kisfaludy's *Tatars in Hungary* was performed here in 1819.

down the remaining town walls and gates, and helped introduce street lighting (that these lights were not used five days before and after a full moon suggests that the towns had not fully shed their provincial character). The commission actively promoted and directed the growth of Leopold District. Its streets were wide and straight, its squares orderly and spacious, and most of its building three stories high, their elegant, neoclassical facades testifying to the growing wealth of the area. Foreign visitors lavished praise on Leopold District, in no small part because its geometric order and symmetry conformed to European trends in architecture and urban planning. "At the first, fleeting glance," G. L. Feldmann wrote, "one sees that this is the newest district and that because of its position directly on the Danube, it is destined to be the center of Pest's future greatness and European importance."[35]

The crown jewel of Leopold District, and the most visible accomplishment of Palatine Joseph's Embellishment Commission, was the "royal town theater" in Pest (fig. 2). The theater opened on February 9, 1812, with original works by the popular playwright August Kotzebue and music by Ludwig van Beethoven.[36] The building's grand exterior made a strong first impression, and one German traveler even suggested that the main theaters in Vienna and Berlin were but playhouses in comparison, adding that both would fit comfortably inside the Pest Theater. The interior was gracefully decorated and, in a continuation of the classical theme, loosely modeled on an amphitheater. Unfortunately, it was also a cavernous space: the Pest Theater, judged Baron Podmaniczky, "is almost as large as the great theaters of Paris or London; but is a gloomy-looking place and badly adapted for the transmission of sound."[37] Actors' voices could not be heard in the balconies, which were often empty after the public's initial enthusiasm had worn off. In light of its vast proportions, the poor acoustics, and the small size of the theater-going public in Pest, it is re- markable that the theater did not immediately go bankrupt. Its directors relied mostly on opera and ballet to fill seats, but also bravely staged dra- mas by Shakespeare, Schiller, Goethe, Hugo, and Dumas. Although a con- temporary critic dismissed the theater troupe as twelfth-rate, it had a handful of talented, popular actors, as well as a steady stream of perform- ers from the Viennese stage.

The Pest Theater's directors soon learned that patriotism sold tickets. One of the theater's first big successes was Theodor Körner's *Zrínyi*, a Hun- garian historical drama, and Kisfaludy's *The Tatars in Hungary* was also a hit. But the development of a distinctly Hungarian (or German, for that matter) repertoire never took priority. Kisfaludy's first play accepted by the Pest Theater, for example, had also been a tragedy set in historic Hungary. By the time it hit the stage, however, it had been given a happy ending and transplanted to Spain, apparently because the director thought the unusual setting and colorful costumes might be popular with audiences. At the same time, although nearly all the productions were in German, the theater's size militated against the intimate dramas and nuanced comedies popular at that time in Vienna, and even Schiller's *Robbers* sold out only when horses, wagons, and scores of extras filled the stage. The theater directors, in short, were motivated more by financial concerns than by national goals (Hungarian or German), and they guiltlessly mixed Shakespeare's tragedies, Mozart's operas, a recreation of the Battle of Leipzig, patriotic tableaux, and colorful spectacles aimed at the widest pos- sible audience. By all accounts, they had some success, particularly in the late 1820s and the early 1830s. Baron Podmaniczky, who otherwise de- scribed the theater as cold and ill suited for drama, recalled that perfor- mances were always well attended by the towns' burghers, nobles, and aristocrats.[38]

The theater's broad cosmopolitanism and undisguised commercialism did not sit well with the more outspoken Hungarian national activists. In their eyes, the Pest Theater was "German" and a painful reminder that Buda-Pest lacked a standing Hungarian-language theater. When the Pest Theater was being built, a number of noble counties, with Pest County at their head, had suggested that the German and Magyar companies share its stage. There was little evidence that Hungarian-language productions would be popular or profitable, but national activists were still deeply disappointed when nothing came of this proposal: "I sigh, I ache, I weep, that there is no mention of Hungarian drama in connection with the large, new Pest Theater," wrote Gábor Döbrentei.[39] The Hungarian company moved to the Rondella Theater in 1812, but its demolition in 1815 forced the company to disband. One actress bitterly recalled: "Poor Magyars! There is no place for the Magyars to establish themselves in the capital of Hungary."[40] Visiting a decade later, Kazinczy complained that Hungarian-language plays had been "banished" from Pest and suggested that "a splendid building exists in the Hungarian capital for foreign theater, where a visitor from afar will find everything except that which will remind him of Hungary."[41]

In this manner, the "royal town theater" irrevocably became the "German theater" (and was thereby written out of most histories of the Hungarian stage). And if the Pest Theater was "foreign," it followed that those who attended its productions were disloyal to the Hungarian cause. Such is the Manichean logic of nationalism, which creates—at least on the level of rhetoric—friends and foes, "us" and "them."[42] Perhaps unwittingly, Schams illustrated this view when he called for a national monument to adorn New Market Square. Schams suggested that it could be dedicated to the memorable deeds of the early Hungarians (die alten Ungern) or the succession of the Hungarian crown to the Habsburgs.[43] Nothing came of his proposal, but it hints at the choices that national activists wanted the residents of Buda-Pest to make: was their primary allegiance to Hungary or the Habsburgs; were they "Magyars" or "Germans"?

But loyalty to Hungary and the Habsburgs was rarely exclusive. Certainly this was the belief of Palatine Joseph, who once made the remarkable assertion that "the blood of Árpád flows in my veins."[44] (This may not have been technically true, but the Habsburgs had always been imaginative genealogists and not above claiming descent from Aeneas and the Trojans.[45]) Joseph's words can be seen as part of a larger effort to win supporters under the rubric of a dual devotion to crown and homeland—that is, to strengthen and demonstrate the compatibility of Habsburg loyalty and Hungarian patriotism. Historians often speak of the abiding loyalty of the Habsburg subjects to their rulers; in Buda-Pest, this allegiance was neither innate nor accidental, but arguably the result of Palatine Joseph's efforts. Under his leadership, the imperial-royal government played a diverse, active, and productive role in Buda-Pest. Joseph, to be sure, was a member of the ruling family, who, when required, dutifully carried out Vienna's orders. But he was also an archduke comfortable in committee meetings, interested in sewage systems, and clearly partial to his adopted city. In many ways, Joseph embodied what historian Heinz Dollinger has called "Bürgerkönigtum" ("burgher-kingship"), a model of rule built less on splendor and sacrality than on values held near and dear by the middle classes: progress, paternalism, and diligence.[46] He was, in short, a leader well suited to needs of early nineteenth-century Buda-Pest.

The Language of Angels

Palatine Joseph's efforts were only one side of the coin. In the wake of the French Revolution, most Central European states had imposed strict limitations on public life, closing down newspapers, censoring books, and banning clubs and assemblies. No thaw came with the end of the fighting in 1815; instead, the Karlsbad Decrees (1819), which sought to snuff out liberalism in the German universities, carried repression into the post-Napoleonic era. In the Habsburg lands, the authorities wove a web of police spies, banned 2,500 books that had been approved under Joseph II, and tightened the screws of censorship: authors had to submit all material to the censors *before* publication, printers had to be licensed, and newspaper publishers had to put down sizeable security deposits and also submit to precensorship. "Despotism has destroyed my literary life," groaned the Austrian poet Franz Grillparzer.[47] By one count, the number of newspapers published in Hungary dropped from eighteen in 1792 to just four in 1805, and the few that remained stayed far from politics. With this in mind, historian C. A. Macartney has described "the near-complete fossilization of social, economic, and intellectual life" in the Habsburg lands in the first decades of the nineteenth century.[48]

The impact of repression should not be exaggerated. For Buda-Pest, historians chiefly interested in Hungarian-language offerings long overlooked the vibrant German-language literary and cultural life of this period.[49] The *Vereinigte Pesther und Ofner Zeitung (United Pest and Buda Newspaper)* was the towns' most popular newspaper, and in 1819 Buda-Pest's German-language periodicals had a combined circulation of 3,300, compared with 1,650 for the Hungarian-language press. Romanticism coursed strongly through these publications: this was the era of the great Hungarian-born poet Nikolaus Lenau (1802–50), and his many imitators filled the pages of German literary journals with paeans to friendship, youth, nature, and the home. But not all German writers shied away from public affairs. A good example is Ludwig Schedius, a brilliant scholar and university professor of aesthetics at twenty-five, unanimously respected by his students and colleagues. Around 1800 he launched a series of journals, the most successful of which was *Zeitschrift von und für Ungern (Journal from and for Hungary)*. It kept readers abreast of the latest scholarly and cultural developments and once included copies of the most recent maps of Hungary. By publishing in German, Schedius hoped to make Hungarian literature and scholarship better known abroad. But Schedius was catholic in his view of what constituted "Hungarian" culture, and he published reviews of works that appeared in German, Hungarian, and Slavic languages.

Publishing in the German language allowed Schedius to reach a larger reading audience at home and abroad than doing so in Latin or Hungarian would have. German was also better equipped with technical, scholarly, and literary terms. For Schedius, language had little to do with political allegiance. Like many other men of letters, Schedius combined a strong attachment to his homeland with a deep loyalty to the Habsburgs. Many of these writers were educated commoners, but they also counted merchants and noblemen in their ranks. As heirs to the Enlightenment, they wanted to direct people's energies to badly needed political, social, and economic reforms: this encompassed everything from Gregor von Berzeviczy's plans to improve the monarchy's commerce to Martin Schwartner's recommendations for the university in Pest.[50] They had little patience for the Hungarian national activists' obsessive and divisive views toward language. Thus, the geographer Samuel Bredeczky distinguished between patriotism, a "holy fire" that leads good citizens to noble actions, and nationalism, a "poisonous passion" that undermines the foundation of society.[51] These writers, in short, were Hungarian patriots and Habsburg loyalists, reformers in the mold of Palatine Joseph. Unfortunately, such patriotic reformers received no encouragement from the authorities in Vienna, who showed little interest in promoting public debate or cultivating local sources of support.

Patriotic writers thus had more limited resources than did Hungarian national activists, who could count on the sustained backing of the National Diet and noble counties. Neither the Napoleonic wars nor the crackdown on public life had blunted the nobility's enthusiasm for the Hungarian language: "I love my language, and wish that the angels also spoke it," said one nobleman.[52] The National Diet pressed for wider use of Hungarian in administration and education, repeatedly demanding linguistic concessions from the crown in exchange for soldiers and money. In 1805, Vienna made a small but symbolic concession when it granted that the Diet's addresses to the crown could henceforth be written with Hungarian and Latin in parallel columns, and that the noble counties could communicate with the imperial-royal authorities in the same manner. This was a green light for Pest County, which just two weeks later resolved not only to correspond with the emperor-king and his councils in the two languages, but also to conduct all business, including lawsuits and financial matters, solely in Hungarian.[53] It also resolved that only schoolmasters capable of teaching in Hungarian would be hired in Pest County and that Hungarian lessons should be part of every school's curriculum, measures clearly aimed at villages in which German or Slovak was the language of instruction. Reviewing these actions, the Hungarian Chancellery in Vienna characterized the paragraph on schools as "inadmissible" and the section on lawsuits as "in no way compatible with the legal freedom of individual citizens."[54] For boosters of the Hungarian language, it was small comfort that Francis's new education ordinance for Hungary (1806) made the Hungarian language a required subject in all secondary schools, because Latin remained the primary language of instruction. A pattern was emerging that would hold for the next four decades: the Hungarian estates made persistent demands on behalf of the Hungarian language, and the crown made grudging concessions but offered few alternatives to the status quo.

The support of the Diets and counties was a shot in the arm for a small but vocal movement of writers, linguists, scholars, and students. Their unofficial leader was Ferenc Kazinczy, a former freemason and supporter of Joseph II who had sat in jail for nearly seven years for his participation in the Jacobin movement. After his release in 1801, Kazinczy retreated to his provincial estate, where he received a steady stream of visitors. Letters, however, were his main contact with the wider world, and in the decades that followed Kazinczy wrote thousands of them—his side of the correspondence alone fills twenty-two volumes—peppering each with encouragement, gossip, news, and discussion of recent publications. This uncensored "salon of letters," in Anna Fábri's apt description, reached all corners of the kingdom and gave shape and succor to the Hungarian national movement.[55] Led by Kazinczy, language reformers strove to make Hungarian suitable for literature and all branches of scholarship, including medicine, law, philosophy, zoology, and military science. This necessitated the invention of thousands of new words, a Herculean labor of creative philology that proved both contentious and dramatic. Different factions fought long, running battles over orthography and word creation.[56] In crafting new words, writers rummaged through dialects, mined archaic words from Hungarian literature, and pasted together words to form compounds (technically, "agglutinated morphemes") such as "standpoint" (álláspont, modeled on the German Standpunkt) and "prejudice" (előítélet, from the Latin praejudicium). From our remove, the so-called Y War, which hinged on whether "he sees" in Hungarian should be spelled láttya or látja, may seem arcane, but at the time it was heady stuff that sparked debates across Hungary (the Y War even inspired a play by the same name).

Even with the backing of the National Diet, Pest County, and Kazinczy's epistolary network, national activists still faced an uphill battle in Buda-Pest. The crackdown of the 1790s had neutralized their leaders and frightened many supporters. Moreover, the reading public was small, and most people were indifferent to the stirrings in the Diets and noble counties. As a result, Hungarian-language cultural offerings in the early nineteenth century were meager. A handful of national-minded professors taught at the university, but their influence was far from complete, particularly since lectures were typically held in Latin rather than in the vernacular. It may not have helped that the instructor of Hungarian was Miklós Révai, whose outspoken nationalism, linguistic virtuosity, and lyrical writing were paired with a lonely, suspicious, and even paranoid disposition. He failed to win supporters among the students or his colleagues, whom he once characterized as "haters" of the Hungarian language and "enemies of the homeland."[57] This made the appearance in Pest in 1806 of István Kultsár's Hungarian-language Hazai Tudósítások (Reports from the Homeland) all the more important. Dubbed the Hungarian Times by one admirer, Kultsár's paper publicized debates among language reformers and promoted the cause of Hungarian music and theater.[58] Kultsár, a former seminarian and one-time tutor, also hosted small informal dinners, which were notable for their lively literary discussions and for bringing together Catholics and Protestants.

What activists lacked in numbers, they often made up for in intensity. One of the most devoted adherents to the national cause was István Horvát, the scholarly son of an impoverished nobleman. A follower of Kazinczy, Horvát worked as a secretary, tutor, and later an instructor and professor at the university. Horvát's passion was history, in which he combined an encyclopedic knowledge of medieval manuscripts with a fervent desire to illuminate the Magyars' antiquity and past glories. In a widely read work, he argued, improbably, that King Matthias had been a "friend, admirer, and propagator" of the Hungarian language and that the fourteenth-century court of King Louis had likewise been "Magyar in body and soul."[59] Scholars were unconvinced, but Horvát's works found many readers. By popularizing St. Stephen, King Matthias, and other national heroes, Horvát helped bolster the view that the Magyars were a "historic" nation worthy of their place in Europe. Horvát's diary also reveals how he carried the national cause into everyday life. At home—he long lived with the Ürményi family, where he worked as a tutor—he avoided taking meals when German-speakers were present. The diary also relates how Horvát and his friend Markovits went to visit a musician friend who was sick in bed. The ailing musician, Horvát wrote, "was restored to health, wholly cured" when Horvát and Markovits sang the "Rákóczi March" and other national-spirited songs.[60]

Horvát's is an extreme case, yet, on some level, the imperial-royal authorities also agreed that small acts could take on a larger significance. Their worried response to the 1819 premiere of *The Tatars in Hungary* showed this, as did their dogged pursuit of the shadowy *Csárda* (Tavern) club in Pest, which may not have existed, but whose members were said to wear the Hungarian national costume in public.[61] By the late 1810s, however, the most important changes were afoot in the world of print, not in the streets.[62] When the wealthy landowner István Marczibányi died in 1810, he left 50,000 florins to the future Hungarian academy; until its foundation, the money was to be used to reward outstanding Hungarian-language works in law, medicine, history, and moral philosophy, as well as the best translations of the classics. The first awards ceremony took place in 1817 in Pest and drew imperial-royal, military, church, university, and local officials; lending their prestige to the event, Palatine Joseph and Emperor-King Francis attended the prize ceremony that followed in 1820. The publisher János Tamás Trattner also aided Hungarian-language scholarship during this era. Another supporter of Kazinczy, Trattner eagerly promoted Hungarian-language literature, and between 1817 and 1825 he published 310 works in Hungarian, compared with 259 in Latin, 127 in German, and 11 in the Slavic languages. Trattner's most significant publication was the journal *Tudományos Gyüjtemény (Scientific and Scholarly Review)*, which began in 1817 and appeared monthly for the next twenty-six years. Its articles covered linguistics, philosophy, geography, and literature, and they included book reviews as well as obituaries of authors and scholars. Carefully edited, well-written, and widely read, the journal had 800 subscribers by the mid-1820s, making it the first Hungarian-language periodical to pay for itself through subscriptions.

Tudományos Gyüjtemény added a formidable new weapon to the national activists' arsenal. On the most basic level, the journal ceaselessly promoted the Hungarian language, cheering its every advance and celebrating its uniqueness.[63] This boasting had few limits: one author bragged that the Hungarian language had more letters than any other language— today it has forty letters (forty-four if *q, w, x,* and *y* are counted)—and that the Magyars themselves "knew more languages than any other nation." Another claimed that Hungarian was unrivaled in its suitability for prosody; he judged Greek and Latin verses to be "labored" and after quoting two lines of Schiller's poetry, sarcastically asked, "Is this a beautiful and pleasant sound?" The twenty-one-year-old Endre Kunoss listed 199 common Hungarian words of Latin, German, or French origin that he wanted to replace with what he considered to be more authentic forms: the word "knight," for example, would be *dalia* or *hős* and not the Germanic *Ritter*. To Kunoss, linguistic purification would remind people of their origins: the Hungarian language, he wrote, "is not some jumble, it is not a Western language! And our nation is Magyar! Or have our good Magyars forgotten that our ancestors came out of the East to win *Hunnia?*" Like Horvát before him, Kunoss pushed the bounds of nationalism beyond what most supporters of the Hungarian cause would have accepted. Yet Kunoss's Romantic view of history and language echoed broader developments in literary life. Classical literary models were slowly giving way to Romantic ones, as could be seen most visibly in the groundbreaking literary journal *Aurora*, which a circle of young Hungarian writers founded in Pest in 1821. Károly Kisfaludy became its first editor.

Questions of language and culture often took on political dimensions. In particular, national activists demanded that the Hungarian language replace Latin as the kingdom's official language. To support this claim, they pointed to the growth of Hungarian literature, the success of the language reform program, and the antiquity of the Magyars. But they also warned that the Hungarian language would flourish—and in fact survive—only if introduced into government offices, churches, courts, and especially schools. Writing in *Tudományos Gyüjtemény* in 1822, Baron Alajos Mednyánszky suggested not only that Hungarian should take the place of Latin, but also that elementary school students should use it to study most subjects—geography, history, and arithmetic.[64] If Hungarian became the official language, he reasoned, all the kingdom's residents would want and need to have some familiarity with it. Over the course of generations, schools would help speakers of German, Romanian, Croatian, Slovak, and other languages slowly learn Hungarian. Mednyánszky stated his opposition to coercion of any kind and modestly estimated that "even with ceaseless supervision, encouragement, and application, this may require 50 and perhaps 100 years before it reaches the county's edges." As models for this optimistic scenario, Mednyánszky pointed to Great Britain, where English dominated but Gaelic and Welsh survived, and to France, where French coexisted with Breton, Alsatian, and other tongues.

Such was the stuff of nationalist dreams. But the link between language and nationhood was very real to these activists, for whom membership in the national community required that one know and promote the Hungarian language. Those who used other languages—including even worthy patriots such as Schedius—did not belong. Mednyánszky, for example found it "deeply painful" that "every resident [of Hungary], be they Slovak, German, Greek, or Romanian, could proudly call themselves Hungarians [*Magyarnak mondja magát*], without feeling sufficient love for the homeland's language."[65] Isidór Guzmics, a Benedictine priest and supporter of Kazinczy, offered an even clearer classification of the population. Showing the influence of Herder, Guzmics argued that language, rather than "mountains, rivers, or any other natural or artificial symbols," determined the borders between nations. But he also took for granted the inviolability of the Hungarian kingdom and its political borders, as well as the primacy of the Magyars within it. It followed, then, that the kingdom's Slovaks, Germans, and Croats, no matter how long they had lived in Hungary, would be members of the national community only if they adopted the Hungarian language: "they will be state Hungarians [*Magyar országi*] but not national Hungarians [*nem magyar nemzetbeli*]."[66] With Guzmics, we have arrived at a very precise, very modern definition of the nation-state. It presupposes the existence of a coherent, closed national community, one in which language trumps loyalty, residence, social status, or origins. Speakers of multiple languages are encouraged to give priority to Hungarian; "outsiders" are to be won over through schools and other means. That Magyars were less than half the population of the Hungarian kingdom was taken as a spur to decisive action, rather than as evidence of the unsuitability of the nation-state idea in Hungary.

When national activists gazed at Buda-Pest through this prism, they discovered that many natives of twin towns were in fact "foreign." This view could be expressed lightly, as in Schams's 1821 description of Pest: "Every stranger will be astonished to find that the German language is so widespread in the largest town in the Hungarian lands—in trade and commerce, in coffeehouses and taverns, in the theater and in all public places of amusement, as well as in the largest part of the citizens' homes—that he may sooner believe that he is in a town in Germany than on Hungarian soil."[67] Like Schedius, Schams was a Hungarian patriot who published in German, and there is nothing in his writing to suggest that the residents of Buda-Pest were not loyal to Hungary. An increasing number of writers, however, showed much less tolerance. Later events undoubtedly colored the memoirs of Teréz Karács, one of Hungary's first female journalists, but they succinctly capture the Hungarian national perspective: "Everything in Pest was so foreign in the first decades of our century that the Magyar felt homeless in it."[68] Pest had no aristocrats or wealthy noblemen, she explained, only "foreigners" (presumably German-speaking Christians and Jews) with no understanding of the Hungarian language or character. Karács allowed that these outsiders were clever at commerce and even well intentioned, but she alleged that "they wanted to build a splendid, but German capital for Hungary." From this perspective, Pest's rapid development after 1800 was not a cause for celebration or pride, because it only strengthened the "German" character of Buda and Pest.

To many national-minded writers, the political and cultural machinations of the imperial-royal administration lay behind the dominance of the German language in Buda-Pest. Such thinking shaped an essay by the ethnographer Johann Csaplovics that appeared in 1822. To Csaplovics, German flourished primarily because all imperial-royal officials in Hungary insisted on using it, which meant that German was the language of commerce, mining, military affairs, and the postal service. The city of Vienna itself had an alchemical effect on Hungarian noblemen: "Whoever lives for a bit of time in Vienna," Csaplovics alleged, "comes home entirely metamorphosed, and, with certain arrogance plays the German in dress and language." German universities apparently had a similar effect on Protestants, rapidly turning Hungarian students into "perfect Germans." Csaplovics complained that in Buda-Pest German was the language of taverns, shops, the theater, and the press, in which the large number of domestic and foreign German-language papers "kept the national language in fetters." In closing, Csaplovics let his frustration show: "The besieging Germans do not consider it worthwhile to accommodate themselves to the country's language, and for the Magyars, this is perfectly acceptable."[69] The message here was unambiguous: if Magyars would only shake off their passivity and challenge Vienna, the national character of Buda-Pest could be altered in their favor.

The number of people in Buda-Pest who would answer this call to arms was still small. The first decades of the nineteenth century were nevertheless important for the Hungarian national movement. In letters, newspapers, journals, county assemblies, and the National Diet, a small circle of activists strengthened the link between nationhood and language and laid plans for how they could propagate Hungarian more widely. This was a powerful program, and one that put Magyar activists in step with national movements across Central Europe.[70] Yet the nationalists' insistence on the primacy of language posed a serious challenge to the towns' linguistic diversity, which now appeared to be a "problem" and a marker of disloyalty.

In the early nineteenth century, this view had not yet made deep inroads into Buda-Pest's schools, churches, shops, and town halls. The Hungarian national activists, moreover, were slow to explore the democratic potential of their model. Although the occasional writer brought up the needs of Hungarian-speaking serfs or workers—ostensibly members of the national community—the same activists who so eloquently extolled the virtues of the Hungarian language were frequently tongue-tied when it came to the difficult social and economic questions that Hungary faced. This made the appearance of Count István Széchenyi all the more important.

Horses and Scholars

The first horse race in Pest was held on June 6, 1827. The organizers had built an improvised track on the edge of town, amid ramshackle cottages and disreputable taverns reportedly frequented by bandits from the surrounding countryside.[71] On race day, however, the neighborhood acquired a carnivalesque atmosphere, as crowds, vendors, and coaches filled the streets. A temporary triumphal arch led to the racetrack, with admission largely limited to the highborn and well heeled: spectators included Habsburg archdukes, Hungarian aristocrats, and English racing enthusiasts. Count Széchenyi had been the moving force behind the races, and the crowd cheered loudly when his horse won the first race; that only two of the eight horses were thoroughbreds did nothing to diminish Széchenyi's triumph. Indeed, the fourth and final competition of the day, the peasant race, was open only to nonpedigreed horses. The day had a strong national coloring, from the poles along the racecourse topped with the Hungarian coat of arms to the countess who bragged about the fashionable scarves she had ordered in Pest for the event, adding that it was a sin for Hungarian women to buy clothes from Vienna. By all accounts, the races were a great success and were repeated every year thereafter in late May.

For Széchenyi, the 1827 races capped years of planning. Széchenyi in fact was an unlikely booster of the national cause in Buda-Pest. As a onetime courtier and cosmopolitan aristocrat, Széchenyi could have made a fine career in the imperial-royal administration, shuttling between Vienna and his family's sizeable estates in Hungary. Yet his first visit to England in 1815 had been a revelation: "There are three things to be learned in England, all the rest is nothing: *the constitution, the machines* and *horse-breeding*."[72] Back in Hungary, Széchenyi joined forces with a number of like-minded aristocrats, but their efforts to form a society dedicated to horse racing and breeding foundered on the opposition of the imperial-royal authorities.[73] Széchenyi persevered and by the late 1820s not only had organized the first races in Pest, but also had written a book on horses and successfully had launched a horse-breeding society, this time with Vienna's grudging consent. As a former cavalry officer, large landowner, and committed Anglophile, Széchenyi possessed a genuine enthusiasm for horses, yet he viewed his equine endeavors as a means to a greater end. Horse racing and breeding, he believed, would improve the domestic stock of horses, encourage better methods of animal husbandry, make Hungarian horses known abroad, and benefit the military. Horse racing could also draw civic-minded men to Pest, as Széchenyi wrote in an 1830 letter to a fellow aristocrat: "The fourth spring is approaching, when, to assemble the most important patriots, we set up and hold horse races in the center of the homeland. Many patriots will gather, become acquainted with one another, and deliberate on the concerns of the homeland with one heart and soul."[74]

Critics tartly pointed out that horse racing was an aristocratic amusement that encouraged gambling and that undertakings dedicated to the improvement of farm horses, sheep, and cows would be much more useful in Hungary. But such criticisms missed the point, for Széchenyi's leap from a sandy, suburban racecourse to public-minded deliberations put him squarely in the ranks of a growing number of liberal reformers across Europe. Many of these reformers pursued their goals through voluntary associations, the quintessential form of organized group life in the nineteenth century. Particularly after 1815, middle-class joiners formed charitable societies, singing clubs, cultural organizations, and a host of other public-spirited undertakings. The timing and trajectory of associational life varied across the continent, but almost everywhere it took root first in cities and among educated and propertied men. Government suspicion was another constant, and no matter how respectable a society's members or laudable its goals, it was likely to be monitored by the authorities. But the reach of even the most repressive regimes was limited, and recent scholarship has suggested that urbanization, material prosperity, and institutional innovation were just as important as state sanction in the development of associational life.[75]

Associations are a good measure of the development of civil society in Central Europe.[76] There were thousands of associations in the German lands, where they all but assumed the status of the "universal elixir." In the Habsburg Monarchy, the close of the Napoleonic wars and the Congress of Vienna brought military and diplomatic triumphs, but at home the government faced social and economic problems with an empty treasury. Under these circumstances, Vienna gradually allowed the formation of societies with lawful and useful goals. Metternich was personally hostile to voluntary associations—he reportedly called them a "German plague"—and the authorities repeatedly banned secret societies, monitored university students and writers, and spied on societies that had already been approved. In spite of these measures, Vienna itself was home to an estimated 200 associations by mid-century.[77] Potentially, there was a great difference between this emerging civil society and the existing corporate order, because associations could bring together a range of social groups under the banner of cultural benefaction, civic activism, and liberal reform.

Associational life developed slowly in Buda-Pest. Only a handful of societies remained from the 1700s, and most founded after 1800 had modest aims. Newly formed pension societies provided important services for their members, as did self-help and burial associations, whose members contributed small sums each month in anticipation of a decent burial and assistance for their families. At the other end of the social spectrum, well-to-do women in Buda and Pest formed charitable associations, which provided food, firewood, and medical aid to the poor and helped support a workhouse, an institute for the blind, and schools for orphans, foundlings, and indigent children.[78] These new societies were beneficial and innovative—the women's associations brought together nobles and burghers, Catholics and Protestants—but they hardly marked a new direction in public life. Thus, when Széchenyi pledged a year's income in 1825 to establish a Hungarian Scholarly Society (later the Hungarian Academy of Sciences), it electrified public opinion. Széchenyi made this announcement in Pressburg at the National Diet, which Emperor-King Francis had reluctantly summoned after a hiatus of twelve years. Although the Diet, which met 271 times between 1825 and 1827, achieved little in the way of social and economic reforms, it was a watershed in Hungarian political life.

Over the next quarter century, the National Diet would be the scene of running battles between Vienna and the growing Hungarian opposition. But Széchenyi's genius lay in his understanding that progress could also come outside existing structures, and here he turned to voluntary associations, which he had learned about on his trips abroad. In Pressburg, Széchenyi and Count György Károlyi converted their quarters into a gathering place for like-minded young magnates, and from this grew the National Casino. (Széchenyi deliberately chose the Italian "casino" over "club," fearing that the latter might recall the political clubs of the French Revolution.) The casino opened in Pest in 1827, not long after the first horse races. It seemed that Széchenyi's ventures might fail—the secret police noted that the new club had only five to six visitors per day and stood empty in the evening—but by the early 1830s an "associational fever" had taken hold of Hungary.[79] By 1833, there were 29 casinos and reading circles across Hungary, and by 1848, some 210 societies had more than 10,000 members.

There were many other Hungarian reformers, but Széchenyi was by far the most visible and influential in the late 1820s, so it is useful to examine the principles behind his initiatives in public life. Most broadly, Széchenyi was committed to reforming Hungary along liberal lines. His trips abroad had convinced him that Hungary, simply stated, was "backwards in everything." "The century is on the march," he wrote, "but, unfortunately, I live in a country that is dragging one leg behind."[80] In a series of landmark works brimming with ideas, Széchenyi presented a sweeping program of economic, moral, and national reform. Széchenyi foresaw the transformation of the Hungarian countryside, in which freer movement of land and labor would lead to foreign investment and greater productivity;

he also hoped that improved education and legal equality would encourage both social mobility and civic-minded behavior. Although Széchenyi believed that meaningful changes would come only with the cooperation of Vienna and through established feudal institutions, he also felt that voluntary associations were ideally suited for the first steps on the road to reform. It followed that no limits should be placed on societies pursuing legitimate goals, and Széchenyi strongly defended the freedom of association.

A commitment to openness, Széchenyi was sure, would win the goodwill of the authorities. "Everything I undertake," he wrote to Metternich, "I undertake in public and I do nothing clandestinely."[81] This applied doubly to associational life: not only was Széchenyi opposed to secret societies, but he also felt that openness was itself a prerequisite to building trust among members of an association.[82] The bylaws of the National Casino, a model for many other societies, mandated that the entire membership be allowed to attend all meetings, that general assemblies be advertised in the local papers, and that the minutes and account books always be available for inspection. Individual members paid dues, attended meetings, voted by secret ballot, and took part in biannual general assemblies, which held ultimate authority over all decisions. The associations' officers and executive committees handled day-to-day affairs, including finances, correspondence, and the admission of new members. The ubiquity of such constitutional forms of self-government has led some scholars to describe associations as "schools of public life" or as enclaves of "enlightened sociability" where a microscopic civic politics emerged.[83] In Hungary, many of the societies' members would already have had some experience in county or national politics, yet the regular meetings, printed bylaws, and attention to procedure suggest that members took the practices of openness, legality, and order—key norms of civil society—quite seriously.

Széchenyi had few illusions about the difficulties he faced. In one gloomy letter, he remarked that the bulk of Hungary's aristocrats and nobles had little idea how "ruined" and "degenerate" they were.[84] Yet, like many of his contemporaries, Széchenyi firmly believed in self-improvement and from the 1810s onward used books and travel to overcome what he saw as his own poor, impractical education. To inspire others to do the same, the National Casino was equipped with a reading room and a library, which soon had more than 3,000 works in French, German, and English, as well as a growing number in Hungarian.[85] Other associations followed suit, and, in an era with few lending libraries and a government that actively discouraged the circulation of foreign works, these libraries created a vital institutional base for reading and discussion. It is impossible to know how many members took advantage of the libraries (in the National Casino, a fine restaurant and free tobacco must have been a distraction), yet the casinos undoubtedly promoted intellectual exchange. One contemporary later recalled, "Casinos were to the exchange of ideas—to the friction of thoughts—what railroads were to communication."[86]

These exchanges often revealed a strong Hungarian national orientation. Széchenyi again was a bellwether. In his eyes, nationhood was something innate, an inalienable property of every individual. But he also understood that national loyalties had to be cultivated, and, in answer to charges that aristocrats had lost touch with their homeland, Széchenyi replied that it had little to offer them—or, as he humorously put it, too much cabbage and pipe smoke had been mixed into the national character.[87] To Széchenyi, national questions were inseparable from larger economic and social reforms, which, he emphasized, could take place only within a Habsburg framework. In more optimistic moments, Széchenyi expressed the hope that the Magyars' cultural and spiritual achievements would gradually attract the other peoples in the Hungarian lands. To this end, Széchenyi publicly supported the Hungarian language and, although his command of it was still imperfect, used it both in the 1825 Diet and in his first book, *On Horses* (1828). But language was never of primary importance to Széchenyi, who disliked empty nationalist bluster and worried about alienating supporters of reform. In the National Casino, for example, no distinction was made between German and Hungarian. Members instead displayed their commitment to the homeland in ways befitting the aristocracy: they contributed to national causes (such as a Hungarian-language theater), bought Hungarian-language books, and added Hungarian vintages to the French and German bottles in the casino's wine cellar. Whether it was with wine or horseracing, however, Széchenyi had helped set powerful forces in motion, and he would have little control over the direction later taken by the Hungarian national movement in Buda-Pest.

The French and Industrial revolutions transformed Europe in the first half of the nineteenth century. The dual revolutions may not have touched Buda-Pest directly—neither French soldiers nor many factories reached Hungary's largest city—but their influence was felt in the first decades of the century. The dynamics of political repression and economic growth forced both Habsburg loyalists and Hungarian activists to respond. On the Habsburg side, Palatine Joseph used his authority to shape Pest's physical expansion, improve its appearance, and promote its cultural life. In so doing, he fortified both dynastic loyalty and Hungarian patriotism. Hungarian national activists undoubtedly saw themselves as loyal to both their ruler and homeland, but they also wanted to rewrite the political rules of the Hungarian lands, especially with regards to language. If Vienna's heavy-handed rule put a damper on the Hungarian national movement, it did not quash it altogether. National leaders proved to be rich in expedients and found new places to gather, new ways to communicate, and new ways to propagate their ideas. Not all their initiatives succeeded—Buda-Pest still had no Hungarian-language theater—yet they had laid the groundwork for the breakthrough of the 1830s and 1840s. With Széchenyi, moreover, Hungarian nationalism had taken on a distinctly liberal coloring.

Buda-Pest had meanwhile become the undisputed center of the Hungarian national movement. Few activists could compete with Széchenyi, who moved his house from Vienna to Pest and became a citizen of the town in 1831. In what was perhaps his most widely read work, *Light*, Széchenyi suggested that Buda and Pest should be formally united and renamed "Budapest" (he also wrote "Buda-Pest").[88] Legal unification, however, was only the first step, and like Palatine Joseph, Széchenyi wanted to embellish the towns, spur their economic development, and awaken their residents' public spirit.

Unlike the Palatine, however, Széchenyi subscribed to the view that the twin towns should be more "Hungarian." He once complained that, in Pest "there is much that is German and little that is Magyar."[89] This was a surprising assertion coming from someone who had grown up speaking German and fought for the Habsburgs. As historian Robert J. W. Evans has observed, Széchenyi, like many politicians and writers of his time, long remained uncertain just where his ultimate allegiances lay—were they to the ruler, to the Hungarian homeland, or to a community of Hungarian-speakers?[90] A growing number of national-minded writers had no such doubts. They continued to insist that the twin towns of Buda and Pest were largely "foreign," an epithet that described their new theater, their German-language journals, and, it seems, many of their residents. Széchenyi's vision of a unified, modernized "Budapest" would spread widely in the following decades, but so too would the idea that the residents and the spaces they inhabited also had to become exclusively "Hungarian."

CHAPTER THREE

Club Life

> "Fifteen hundred or more had gone to the grave! Trembling, we stared
> into the dark future and from every lip hung the question: Lord! how
> long will Your punishing hand rest so heavily upon us? . . . [T]he dan-
> ger now seems to be over; we can breathe more easily, joyfully hoping
> that it will never again be as it was: horrible, dreadful, and deadly!"
>
> —A thanksgiving sermon following the 1831 cholera epidemic[1]

In July 1830, revolution again broke out in France. The July Revolution
was short, bloody, and largely limited to Paris, but its effects were immediately felt across the continent. Reports of students and workers fighting on
the barricades, respectable citizens singing the forbidden *Marseillaise,* and
the new king granting a constitution stirred radicals and reformers everywhere. Revolution followed in Belgium (1830), which won independence
from Holland, civil war broke out in Spain and Portugal, and the Reform
Act (1832) passed in Britain. In the German lands, revolution in France
sparked two years of political unrest, with petition campaigns, public debates, mass meetings, and sometimes violent demonstrations. As a result
of this pressure, rulers in several small German states granted constitutions. From the perspective of Vienna, perhaps the most worrisome development was the 1830–31 uprising in Russian Poland, which aroused great
sympathy throughout the Habsburg lands. In Prague, crowds demonstrated in support of the Poles; in Buda-Pest, a handful of young men
hatched plans to go fight alongside them. A police informant warned Vienna about the mood in Hungary: "Everyone wants reforms. They want
an annual Diet to approve taxes every year, freedom of the press, responsible ministers, and a thousand other things."[2]

This revolutionary fever coincided with a more deadly disease: cholera.
As revolution moved eastward across the continent, cholera moved in the
opposite direction. The French prime minister and the philosopher G. W.
F. Hegel were among the hundreds of thousands of victims. In Hungary,
authorities established a cordon sanitaire on the kingdom's borders on
May 29, 1831, but eastern counties reported the first outbreaks of cholera
just weeks later.[3] On July 2, Palatine Joseph ordered armed guards to close
the borders of Buda-Pest. As a further precaution, he appointed doctors for
each district and established a committee to bring the poor to hospitals;

yet it is also instructive that the authorities hired out-of-work locals to help expel unemployed nonresidents (many of them Polish Jews) from the towns. In spite of these measures, cholera broke out in Buda-Pest on July 14. Three days later, nearly 4,000 university students—angry that they could not return to their homes in the countryside—apprentices, and residents of the outer districts clashed with soldiers in the streets of Pest. The fighting left 16 dead and led to 176 arrests. The cholera meanwhile claimed its first victims. The epidemic lasted through late September and killed 2,277 people in Buda-Pest; those who survived, such as Leopold Hevánsky, the priest cited above, could only pray that the cholera would not return. The violence and deaths in the twin towns, however, paled in comparison with the devastation visited on northeastern Hungary, where cholera infected 500,000 people, half of whom died. Tens of thousands of poor peasants, convinced that landlords, doctors, Jews, and Catholic priests were responsible for the disease, took up arms. Troops ultimately crushed the insurrection, and the courts handed out 119 death sentences (later commuted to five- to six-year prison terms), as well as 4,000 lesser punishments, often whippings and floggings.

The riots in Pest and the peasant uprising exposed deep divisions in the Hungarian political leadership. For Széchenyi and his allies, the epidemic laid bare Hungary's weaknesses and showed the desperate need for substantial reforms, whereas his opponents feared that any changes to the status quo would imperil the entire system.[4] The simultaneous paroxysm of political agitation across the continent only heightened these divisions. This set the stage for the tumultuous National Diets that met in Pressburg in 1832–36, 1839–40, 1843–44, and 1847–48. Julia Pardoe exaggerated when she called the Diets "an oasis of liberty amid a desert of despotism," but this feudal institution proved to be a lively political arena.[5] From the start, the initiative lay with a small but growing number of liberal reformers and their skillful leaders: Count Széchenyi, Baron Wesselényi, Ferenc Deák, and Lajos Kossuth. Under their guidance, the Diets addressed a host of fundamental issues, including lord-peasant relations, taxation, judicial reform, railroads, tariffs, Jewish emancipation, and public education. In response, Vienna wavered uncertainly between a policy of coercion, which it followed in the late 1830s, when it arrested, tried, and imprisoned Wesselényi and Kossuth, and grudging concessions, which was the strategy favored by Palatine Joseph. The Diet's pitched battles spilled over into the noble counties, and Vienna and the liberals fought tooth and nail in many of them; the liberal Austrian *Die Grenzboten* aptly called the county assemblies a "permanent Diet."[6] By the 1840s, Pest County had become a focal point of oppositional activity and a meeting place for leading liberals.

Following in the footsteps of Széchenyi, the same reformers turned their attention to institutions of civil society. A good example is Kossuth, who was at once a leader of the liberal opposition in the National Diet and Pest County, and at the same time a journalist, a booster of Hungarian language and culture, and an officer in numerous national societies. To Kossuth and other political leaders, newspapers and clubs were a soapbox from which they could promote their ideas and broaden their basis of support. In Buda-Pest, however, these leaders had to contend with wide social divisions, a lack of resources, cautious local elites, and a mistrustful regime in Vienna. From this perspective, the remarkable expansion of civil society in the 1830s and 1840s is a measure of the reformers' success in inserting themselves into local public life and strengthening the national cause in the twin towns.

The Mania for Associations

The pace of public life quickened throughout Central Europe after 1830. Although press censorship and policing remained firmly in place, the number and circulation of books, newspapers, journals, and petitions grew everywhere. In Bohemia and Lower Austria, moribund provincial estates began to stir and demand a say in local affairs; in Vienna, writers boldly petitioned the government to ask that censorship be lightened. Reformers of all stripes also rushed to join voluntary associations. Vienna's nobles, artists, singers, and medical doctors had their own societies by 1848, as did proponents of industry, agriculture, horticulture, and homeopathy. The shared commitment to discussion, debate, improvement, and self-governance of these associations signaled a new kind of civic activism. It was not long before a number of societies took on a distinct political coloring: "By 1848," Pieter Judson has observed, "voluntary associations constituted semipublic settings where people otherwise deprived of a voice in policy formulation joined to articulate shared concerns about the community and the state."[7] At the same time, national activists in Prague, Zagreb, and other cities began to use associations to publicize their demands and rally supporters. The character of urban public life was changing rapidly.

Hungary had an estimated 500 associations in 1848, most of them founded in the 1830s and 1840s.[8] Buda-Pest alone was home to eighty associations, a development humorously described by a contemporary newspaper: "Pest has not lagged behind in fashions or even the mania for associations, which in recent times has become so rampant in Europe. We already have several dozen societies of all sorts, shapes, and colors, and soon there will also be a need for an association against the increase of associations."[9] The majority of societies dedicated themselves to sociability, self-help, philanthropy, and educational activities, but there were also agricultural, scientific, economic, and cultural associations, not to mention those devoted to such goals as the prevention of cruelty to animals and the erection of a statue to King Matthias Corvinus. (Sadly, neither cause fared well.) Conversely, there were no secret societies, trade unions, or openly political organizations. Only in the late 1840s would political "parties" emerge in Hungary, but they hardly resembled modern parties with their broad memberships, dues, and conventions.

The Hungarian national movement instead took root in a handful of social clubs, cultural societies, and economic associations. In each of these areas, Széchenyi's pioneering initiatives—the casino, scholarly society, and horse races—found both imitators and competitors. The aristocratic National Casino, for example, was joined by the Merchants Casino (founded in 1828), the equally refined Buda Casino (1841), the literati's National Circle (1841), and the artists' Concordia (1845). Not all new associations succeeded—a lack of resources undermined some, too few committed members doomed others—yet by 1848, an interconnected network of "national societies" had emerged in Buda-Pest. Perhaps one-third of the towns' associations could be given this designation: the closest they came to concerted action was in 1843, when representatives of two dozen societies gathered to discuss plans for a newspaper that would report on associational activities in the twin towns.[10] Nothing emerged from this meeting, however, and the national societies were instead loosely linked by their broad commitment to reform, a steadfast support for the Hungarian language and culture, and an often unspoken opposition to Vienna and its policies.

An interlocking leadership provided a further bond. Count Lajos Batthyány, who joined no fewer than nine associations, was more enthusiastic than most, but political leaders such as Batthyány and Kossuth commonly belonged to multiple societies.[11] Even a cursory glance at lists of officers and executive committees shows that aristocrats and untitled nobles held the reins of most societies. They dominated both economic and cultural societies, and their hold over casinos and reading societies was even tighter: commoners never comprised more than 10 to 15 percent of the National Casino's membership, and the 254 members of the National Circle included only eight merchants and seven burghers.[12] As Károly Kecskeméti has shown, county politics, intermarriages, and school ties provided close links among these noblemen.[13] If these factors gave civil society in Hungary a blue-blooded, tightly knit leadership, it also strengthened the connection between the sphere of formal politics and the realm of civil society.

But had the nobility simply reproduced the dominance it enjoyed in the National Diet and the counties in a new arena? Did this civil society merely provide a new source of legitimacy for established elites?[14] To answer these questions, two aspects of associational life in Buda-Pest need to be considered. First, many national societies encouraged meaningful social mixing. The Industrial Association, which Kossuth helped found in 1841, shows how this could work. Dedicated to the spread of useful knowledge and the promotion of domestic industry, the Industrial Association was a whirlwind of activity: its leaders met 158 times in the early 1840s and passed no fewer than 1,614 resolutions.[15] Arguably, it was through the Industrial Association that Kossuth (the vice-president of the society) came to know Batthyány (its president); they would serve together in 1848 as minister of finance and prime minister in Hungary's new government. Yet it was no less remarkable for Kossuth and Batthyány to rub shoulders with the master button makers, master tailors, and Jewish merchants who were also active in the society and regularly attended its meetings. In similar fashion, the Industrial Association allowed Buda-Pest's growing professional classes to demonstrate their commitment to the national cause. Lawyers, doctors, engineers, and teachers comprised nearly one-third of its executive committee, and, although some of them were of noble origin, most were commoners whose social position reflected their education and the services they offered. Finally, the Industrial Association also mobilized women, who not only put their names on subscription sheets, but also actively collected subscribers themselves: Countess Julia Nádossy-Forray, for example, gathered fifty-nine new members, including more than thirty women, and Countess Antonia Batthyány (one of the Zichy sisters) collected more than 800 florins in subscriptions.[16]

Second, corporate social categories may have lost some of their luster in this period, at least in Buda-Pest. What it meant to be a "noble" was slowly changing, as an increasing number of nobles took up full-time residence in the city for the purpose of earning a living. Such was the case with the statistician Elek Fényes, a tireless participant in the Hungarian national movement.[17] The son of an old but penurious noble family, Fényes married the equally poor (and nonnoble) daughter of his Pressburg landlady, published a six-volume statistical survey of Hungary, and later supported himself in Pest as a secretary, director, and editor for several voluntary associations in the 1840s. By marrying a commoner and settling in Pest, Fényes distanced himself from the vast majority of the Hungarian nobility (including his family, which frowned on his marriage). He had entered an urban world that valued wealth and education as much as feudal privileges and landed property. After analyzing housing inventories of the 1840s, Péter Hanák concluded that a common material culture was emerging in Pest, one that transcended corporate social divisions.[18] Leopold District's better apartment buildings, he pointed out, attracted noble and nonnoble officials, lawyers, doctors, and other professionals, as well as wealthier artisans and merchants who no longer wanted to live above their shops and workplaces. Uniform Biedermeier interiors hid behind the buildings' neoclassical facades, and larger apartments had separate bedrooms, parlors, and children's rooms, all filled with the era's handcrafted furniture.

The national societies that emerged in Buda-Pest in the 1830s and 1840s, then, were more than simply watering holes for the Hungarian nobility, although they served this function as well. Instead, they cast the Hungarian political leadership in new roles and brought them into contact with a relatively wide range of social groups. An Austrian journalist who visited Pest's clubs favorably noted that "one can be admitted without regard to rank, religion, and national origin." He humorously added, "At the various meetings of the clubs one has the opportunity to admire the Magyars' great skill in making toasts."[19] The titles and privileges of those who raised their glasses were important, but so too were their education, their sophistication, and, almost always, their commitment to the national cause. Buda-Pest's expanding network of national societies thus had great importance for the Hungarian national movement. Activists who had recently struggled to find places to meet and means of publicizing their ideas could now turn to a wide range of societies and newspapers.

Steam Engines and Sedition

An 1845 event organized by the National Protection Association shows how politics could infuse the national societies' activities. In November 1845, the Protection Association held three days of festivities in Pest to show the success of the "Buy Hungarian" campaign it had launched a year earlier. The festivities began with a massive torchlight parade, in which thousands of people marched to the home of the association's president, Count Kázmér Batthyány.[20] The count greeted the people with a rousing speech, saying that "public opinion of this kind must speak out, because the press is not allowed to." The Protection Association, he told the crowd, "has bound its fate so tightly to the nation that they will live or die together." At a general assembly held the next day, flags representing the association's 138 local chapters covered the stage, and behind the president's chair stood a tall obelisk wrapped in the national colors and topped by a papier-mâché steam engine. Against this inspiring backdrop, leaders of the boycott movement delivered fiery speeches, with Kossuth, the director of the Protection Association, likening the boycott's enemies to the British who had "used weapons to force opium on the Chinese." That evening the association held a large banquet and a ball, to which most guests wore the national dress and danced only when the band switched from Viennese to Hungarian tunes. A ball held the following day attracted more than 1,000 people. Over the course of the three days, an improvised industrial exhibition was held to showcase the products of factories helped by the campaign, physical proof of the Protection Association's achievements during the past year.

These festivities contain many clues about the Hungarian national movement in the 1840s. First, they made clear that national societies could mobilize hundreds, even thousands, of people behind a wide variety of causes, and they did so through mass meetings, banquets, balls, exhibitions, and concerts. Wide coverage in the press helped turn these gatherings into media events followed by a growing reading public. Second, they show the influence of Hungarian liberalism, both in the Protection Association's grand vision of industrial development (neatly symbolized by the model steam engine) and in the speakers' defiant references to Viennese absolutism. This raises an obvious question: in light of Vienna's proven wariness of public demonstrations, nationalism, and liberalism, why did the authorities permit these seditious celebrations?

Events in Pest reflected wider developments across Central Europe. Even the most watchful regimes could not quarantine associations from public affairs. This trend was most pronounced in the German lands, where gymnastic societies and sharp-shooting clubs took on a national-liberal coloring. Activists had less room for maneuver in the Habsburg lands, in part because the authorities clipped the wings of the local press, with the result that Viennese papers transcribed debates of the British Parliament but could not mention those of the Hungarian Diet, which met barely fifty miles away.[21] The authorities had less success in silencing voluntary associations, and the Lower Austrian Industrial Association and the Legal-Political Reading Society decisively shaped public opinion in Vienna in the 1840s. Although the government had the police search the Reading Society's library and sent spies to meetings of the Industrial Association, its measures were largely ineffective and ultimately counterproductive. Members of the Industrial Association, for example, were far from unanimous regarding specific economic policies; they spoke with one mind, however, when they complained about the regime's inactivity and hostility to reform.[22] By the end of the decade, these ostensibly apolitical associations had become, in the authorities' eyes, hotbeds of subversion.

In Buda-Pest, the rapid growth of the press gave voluntary associations an even greater visibility. During the 1830s and 1840s, many new journals and newspapers appeared, including specialized publications aimed at different segments of a variegated reading public. Publications in Hungarian grew most rapidly, and, by the mid-1830s, Hungarian-language papers in Buda-Pest had a combined circulation of 10,000 copies, compared with 5,000 for German-language publications (many people likely read both the Hungarian and German press).[23] Moreover, with the slight relaxation of censorship in Hungary, newspapers could wear their political colors more openly. This does not mean that Hungary enjoyed freedom of press, because the imperial-royal authorities still limited the content of domestic papers and the circulation of foreign ones. A breakthrough came with Kossuth's *Pesti Hirlap (Pest Gazette)*, which was founded in 1841 and soon had more than 5,000 subscribers and many more readers, giving it a large audience across the Hungarian lands.[24] Like many other papers, *Pesti Hirlap* frequently reported on the activities of Buda-Pest's associations.

At key moments, however, Vienna attempted to shut down this flow of information. This could be seen vividly in the case of the Protection Association. Its "Buy Hungarian" campaign had created a great stir in Vienna, and when Theresa Pulszky first inquired about it, she received this indignant reply: "A ridiculous demonstration against Austria! The Hungarians want to wear their own manufactures, and as they fabricate as yet nothing but blue cotton stuffs, the ladies attire themselves in such material for parties, although they always before appeared in Viennese velvets and silks."[25] The Protection Association also raised great alarm among high officials.[26] To Metternich, the goal of the association was simply absurd, and its concealed purpose amounted to nothing less than high treason. Sedl-nitzky likewise argued that the purpose of the Protection Association had never been the advancement of Hungarian industry, but only the promotion of separatism and the "spread of terrorism." In Buda-Pest, Palatine Joseph also opposed the boycott, but he worried that Vienna lacked clear grounds to ban the Protection Association and that attempts to suppress it would unnecessarily turn public opinion against the government.[27] He counseled Vienna instead to hinder the Protection Association at every turn without acting openly against it. Palatine Joseph's position won in the end, and, although the authorities took determined steps against the Protection Association, they refrained from the coup de grâce favored by Metternich.

Vienna thus used its police, censors, and bureaucrats to conduct a "quiet war" against the Protection Association in particular and national societies in general. The authorities first reasserted their privilege to limit the right of association. In January 1845, the Vice-Regal Council warned, "Those societies, whose bylaws have not been previously and mercifully sanctioned by His Majesty, will not be tolerated at all."[28] As part of this decree, Palatine Joseph ordered county authorities to submit lists of all local associations and to describe their origins, goals, and rules. In an unprecedented move, the palatine also prohibited imperial-royal officials from joining the Protection Association. The censors meanwhile refused the Protection Association permission to publish any materials whatsoever. This forced the leadership to communicate with its many chapters via handwritten notices and letters (a nobleman's letters were in principle not subject to censorship).[29] This method was slow, expensive, and did not reach as many readers as the press. The censors also gave the conservative press full rein in its attacks on the boycott movement, while opposition papers at first could not even mention the Protection Association by name. The *Augsburger Allgemeine Zeitung (Augsburg General Newspaper),* which circulated widely in Hungary as well as in the German lands, France, and England, published several articles hostile to the Protection Association, most likely at Metternich's instigation.

The authorities' success was far from complete. Despite the government's active discouragement, at its peak the Protection Association had 146 local chapters. With their noble-dominated leadership, many chapters enjoyed the protection of the county authorities as a buffer against Vienna. For example, in response to Vienna's demand that all associations submit their rules for approval, the Pest County assembly agreed that the origins and goals of all societies should be made public but denounced any attempt to limit the right of association. "We cannot recognize," it resolved, "that the government's right to supervise [associations] should be extended, or that free activity not forbidden by law is or could be made conditional upon the government's authorization."[30] With similar indignation, the Protection Association trumpeted the openness of its meetings, minutes, and activities, implicitly contrasting its publicity with Vienna's secret police and shadowy decision making.

Such words conveniently overlooked the Protection Association's clandestine actions and rowdy behavior. In a case that created great consternation in Vienna, the Protection Association had its statutes printed at night in the provinces and then smuggled them into Pest.[31] Similarly, until the authorities revoked his license, a Pest lithographer printed announcements for the association. Finally, the leaders of the Protection Association secretly published several pamphlets, including the *Hungarian Protection Association* (1845), whose title page bore the provocative epigraph, "The light in today's Europe no longer comes from above"—a clear message to the authorities in Vienna.[32] Although these pamphlets bore foreign imprints (Leipzig and Hamburg), they may have been printed in Hungary. Either way, they were intended not only to influence opinion at home, but also to counter Metternich's campaign in the international press. The Protection Association also showed its defiance to the government through public demonstrations (the assembly, dances, and exhibition described above), which sometimes spilled into the streets and beyond the association's control. The "Pest Youth," its young, zealous supporters, made up a large part of the crowd that serenaded Count Kázmér Batthyány. They later noisily protested outside the home of an imperial-royal official who had not allowed his county to organize a chapter of the association. Although police informants were convinced that Kossuth was behind this "cat music," as these rowdy, nighttime demonstrations were called, the leaders of the Protection Association apparently had not endorsed the action.[33]

The directors of national societies in fact rarely encouraged explicitly political actions. In the National Casino, Széchenyi repeatedly stressed that the society should remain free from politics, and to this end, the Casino amended its rules in 1845: "As an association, the Casino will not make a decision or take a step that has any shade of political coloring or that may conflict with the decrees of its executive committee."[34] The leaders of other societies likewise claimed that their actions were entirely devoid of political motivations. The picture that emerges is one in which associations encouraged debate of public issues but shied away from openly political discussions or actions. Yet, at moments during the 1840s, and during elections in particular, members of certain societies found it difficult to ignore politics altogether.[35] This was most obvious in the National Circle, which in 1845 hosted a meeting in support of Pál Nyáry, an opposition candidate running for deputy lord-lieutenant *(alispán)* of Pest County. This gathering increased divisions within the circle, and later in the year the club splintered into three separate societies, each marked by specific political tendencies.

The breakup of the National Circle helped crystallize the growing division of public life in Hungary into two clearly defined camps, the "conservatives" and the "opposition." By the late 1840s, political conservatives had their own newspapers and social club in Buda-Pest. In 1846, conservative leaders went a step further and organized themselves into a political party, issuing a program based on "constitutionalism, nationalism, and union with the Austrian Monarchy."[36] For conservatives, "nationalism" meant the defense of Hungarian rights and legal traditions within the monarchy; it had little place for public opinion or popular mobilization. The new Conservative Party did not have a broad membership or even a permanent leadership. It merely hoped to rally potential supporters with an eye to Dietal elections in 1847. Conservatives realized that they were perhaps setting a dangerous precedent, but by formally organizing themselves, they had stolen a march on the liberal opposition.

The formation of the Conservative Party helped the divided opposition overcome its differences. Former members of the National Circle reunited in early 1847 to establish the Opposition Circle in Pest.[37] Its leaders included the liberal-minded aristocrat Count László Teleki, the statistician Elek Fényes, and the poet Mihály Vörösmarty. Although the conservative press warned that the Opposition Circle was dangerously radical—even Széchenyi called it a "Jacobin Club"—it had more than 800 members and gained dozens more every week. In March 1847, the circle hosted three days of meetings and banquets, which drew 1,200 people and led to the official formation of the Opposition Party on March 15. Count Lajos Batthyány was elected head of the party and set about raising money for the coming elections. Kossuth next drafted the "Opposition Program," which Ferenc Deák put it into final form. This declaration spelled out the liberals' demands: the unification of Hungary and Transylvania, general taxation, the extension of suffrage, equality before the law, and the abolition of peasant servitude. It would serve as the basis for the sweeping reforms passed in April 1848.

Buda-Pest's national societies had helped shift the rules of the game governing the relationship between Vienna and Hungary. Their ceaseless activity (or at least plans for ceaseless activity) often put the imperial-royal authorities on the defensive. Similarly, their determination and assertiveness forced Metternich's regime and its conservative supporters, the "party of order," to adopt many of the opposition's tactics and to engage in debates on the future of the country. Even though conservatives opposed most of the liberals' proposed reforms, by establishing newspapers, joining voluntary associations, and contesting elections, the conservatives tacitly sanctioned the principle of free discourse and debate, an important characteristic of civil society. At the same time, the liberal opposition emerged as a "party of movement" broadly committed to limiting the excesses of absolutism, sweeping away the remnants of the feudal order, and building a national life in Hungary. This relentless political agitation captured the attention of more and more residents of Buda-Pest, a process one newspaper grandiloquently described in 1846: "In every corner one hears debates and different views about the day's political events, and every day the number of people grows, whom the homeland's troubles make grave, whom the homeland's moments of joy make happy, and whose breasts swell at mere mention of the names of the homeland's greatest and most honorable men."[38]

The Carriage Makers' Conversion

By the 1840s, the national press and societies had fundamentally altered the contours of public life in Buda-Pest. How did local elites respond to the dynamism of the Hungarian national movement? A brief sketch of the Kölber firm, which made high-quality carriages in Pest for more than a century, suggests how one burgher family gradually shifted its allegiance to the Hungarian side.[39] The firm's origins went back to 1784, when the German-born saddler Casimir Kölber became a citizen of Pest and opened a carriage shop. To learn the craft of carriage making, his son Jakab spent six years abroad, mostly in Vienna, where Hungarian noblemen typically purchased their carriages. Jakab returned to Pest and took over the firm in 1813. Business flourished, and Jakab was able to marry the daughter of a wealthy burgher family. Jakab Kölber actively participated in public life: he was a guild master, a citizen of Pest, and later a member of the town's outer council. In the early 1840s, his sons Philip and Karl took over direction of the business, and in their hands it continued to prosper. The Industrial Association awarded the Kölbers a bronze medal at the 1842 industrial exhibition, a silver medal in 1843, and finally a gold medal in 1846.

The Kölber firm by now employed more than thirty artisans, a mix of blacksmiths, locksmiths, wheelwrights, painters, carpenters, tinsmiths, and harness makers. This arrangement brought the Kölber brothers into conflict with the guild system, which was built upon the clear separation of the trades, and in the 1840s the Kölbers successfully petitioned to leave the saddlers' guild and have their firm recognized as a factory. Following in the footsteps of their father and grandfather, both brothers became citizens of Pest, but they also participated in a number of national societies, with Philip serving on the executive committees of the Protection Association and the Industrial Association. During the 1848–49 Revolution, the brothers joined the local national-guard cavalry and, because there was little business, urged their workers to enlist in the newly formed Hungarian army. When Kossuth triumphantly returned to Pest in June 1849, he rode in a magnificent carriage built by the Kölber brothers. In 1869, another set of sons, now the fourth generation, took over the firm. Under their leadership, the Kölber firm began to use Hungarian in the place of German in its transactions and records. The brothers even created new technical terms in Hungarian, several of which remain in the language today.

The history of the Kölber family confirms several common arguments made by historians about the Buda-Pest's "Germans"—or, more accurately, the towns' non-Jewish, German-speaking economic, political, and cultural elites. (Jews are discussed in the following section.) As a rule, Hungarian scholars describe the two decades leading up to 1848 as a crucial period that laid the groundwork for the German-speakers' support for Hungarian nationalism and rapid linguistic assimilation later in the century.[40] Unfortunately, the towns' once-proud burghers and master artisans often appear resigned and passive in this literature. But even if overdrawn, this picture suggests that German-speakers in Buda-Pest responded differently to the appearance of modern nationalism than their counterparts did in other parts of the Habsburg lands. In Bohemia, for example, some German-speakers began to adopt a self-conscious German identity in response to demands for power and status by the insurgent Czech national movement.[41] Forced to abandon their former local, Bohemian, and Habsburg loyalties, they built their own community life, relying heavily on voluntary associations and following the model already established by the Czechs. For Buda-Pest, patterns of associational life may also help explain how social groups with a large number of German-speakers—merchants and master artisans, town leaders, and writers—responded to the Hungarian national movement.

Rapid economic development and social differentiation in the early nineteenth century likely strengthened the national cause in Buda-Pest. The guilds in particular entered into slow but irreversible decline, which would end with their abolition in 1872. The formation of new guilds partly disguised this trend, and by the 1840s Pest and Buda each had nearly seventy chartered guilds.[42] The town councils also continued to support guild masters, especially in their sometimes violent disputes with journeymen over wages and working conditions. But the guilds had no defense against their old foes, merchants and independent artisans, and, as the Kölber firm demonstrated, the gap between masters with capital and those without was widening. A similar process was under way in the Pest Merchants Corporation, as competition from wholesalers, peddlers, and shopkeepers chipped away at its privileged position. In 1846, some of the corporation's most successful merchants joined with their Jewish counterparts to form the Pest Wholesalers Corporation. Wealth—not religion or local citizenship—was the barrier to entry in this society; its members had to have at least 30,000 florins in capital. These well-to-do merchants and bankers had very different interests and horizons from the majority of the towns' small traders and master artisans.[43]

These changes may have eased the entry of some successful merchants and masters—men like the Kölber brothers—into the Hungarian societies. By one count, merchants and masters comprised 15 percent of the Protection Association's membership and 28 percent of the Industrial Association's.[44] In this capacity, leading merchants and masters could provide an important link between the reform nobility and town dwellers. The printer Lajos Landerer, for example, recruited fifty-three members for the Industrial Association, and the master button maker Miklós Kajdán signed up fifteen, six of them on the Hungarian-language subscription sheet and nine on the German one.[45] A number of factors led master artisans and merchants to participate in national societies: for some, the social status that accompanied frequent contact with aristocrats and nobles may have been a reward, others may have viewed associations as a source of potential customers, and still others may have been drawn by the societies' broadly liberal political agenda. The majority of guild masters and merchants, however, kept their distance from the Hungarian national movement. There was good reason for this, because the leading Hungarian activists, most of them nobles, often showed little understanding of town dwellers' institutions, traditions, or concerns. The Hungarian-language press routinely described the guilds as an impediment to progress and cast doubts on the merchants' commitment to the national cause. Ferenc Csanády, an officer in several economic associations, bitterly charged that, "with the exception of a few praiseworthy men, the merchant class is not only unfriendly to the Protection Association and to Hungarian industry, but because of its miserable pennypinching selfishness and inaccurate understanding of its own interests, it is the most dangerous and stubborn of our enemies."[46]

Town officials had less room to maneuver than did merchants and masters. The Vice-Regal Council and the Royal Treasury had long circumscribed their activities, and from the 1830s onward, the Hungarian National Diet also began to exert an influence over local administration. The most visible sign of this was a series of language laws passed in the 1830s and 1840s.[47] Traditionally, the towns had used German for most internal matters and Latin to communicate with the imperial-royal authorities. If a petitioner or a noble county wrote to them in Hungarian, the councilors would respond in kind, but this happened infrequently. In 1830, however, the National Diet passed Act 1830:8, which ordered that all public officials know Hungarian. The Pest Town Council immediately resolved to keep its minutes in Hungarian and, as a symbolic gesture, instructed its night watchmen to mark the hours in the same language.[48] With no less enthusiasm, the Buda Town Council pledged to introduce Hungarian-language lessons into parish schools and to encourage local guilds to use Hungarian. In practice, the towns' national-spirited resolutions produced few real changes, and the trilingual administration—German, Latin, and Hungarian—continued as before. Only the Diet's language laws of 1840 and 1844, which required the towns to communicate with both the Vice-Regal Council and the Royal Treasury in Hungarian, brought this trilingual tradition to an end. Latin was the first to go and had largely disappeared by the late 1840s. German was more resilient, and although both the Buda and Pest Town Councils pledged to use Hungarian in all matters and to encourage its use in local schools, in reality German continued to be used widely in local affairs. But the trend toward Hungarian was clear, and it is revealing that the mayor of Pest in the early 1840s, János Tölgyessy, had changed his surname from the more German-sounding Eichholz (*Eichenholz = tölgy* = oak).

But Eichholz/Tölgyessy was atypical in a number of ways. At the very least, most town officials proved immune to the fashion for Hungarian surnames. Historian Lajos Schmall estimated that, in the 160 years before 1848, only thirteen of more than 2,800 officials changed their names.[49] Eichholz/Tölgyessy, moreover, had changed his name when he was ennobled, an uncommon honor for town leaders. Finally, his outspoken support for the Hungarian national cause—he promoted the use of Hungarian in the town's elementary schools—likely set him apart from other local officials. It is difficult to make general statements about the political and national loyalties of these officials.[50] An increasing number had university degrees, and all would have known several languages, but they had varied social backgrounds and included the sons of nobles, professionals, artisans, and local property owners. No matter what their origins, none could expect rapid promotion, because it typically took fifteen to twenty years for an ambitious official to rise into the ranks of the town council—it took Eichholz/Tölgyessy sixteen. These factors combined to produce few town leaders who openly supported the Hungarian national movement. The most prominent was Leopold Rottenbiller, whose father had been a member of the outer council and a master fisherman.[51] Rottenbiller entered town government in 1826 but came to prominence only in the late 1830s, and then as a financial wizard who helped improve the town's accounting practices. Elected vice-mayor of Pest in 1843, he soon became a leading spokesman for reform in town government and joined a number of national societies. The Pest councilor Boldizsár Holovits likewise served in the National Circle (as its vice-president), the Industrial Association, and the Protection Association. But even this was no guarantee that Hungarian national interests would trump those of the town, because Holovits would be the lone councilor to argue against the adoption of the revolutionaries' Twelve Points on March 15, 1848.

The Hungarian national movement had its strongest influence on the twin town's aspiring writers, journalists, musicians, and artists, including many who had grown up in German-speaking families. The Hungarians' sweeping reform program undoubtedly attracted some; others may have been drawn by the animated Hungarian cultural life, with its newspapers, novels, poetry, and operas, all of which made local German-language theatrical and literary offerings look rather limited and staid. Indeed, by the 1840s most German newspapers actively supported the national cause. Their editors and journalists, many of them Jews, took it upon themselves to inform the German reading public about the latest development in Hungarian politics and culture. They provided translations of recent Hungarian-language poetry and literature, proud accounts of Hungary's history, and endless praise for the Hungarian stage. In this environment, a number of young literati from German families threw themselves wholeheartedly into the Hungarian national movement.

An instructive case is the poet and literary critic Ferenc Schedel, who published an important German anthology of Hungarian-language poetry in 1828 and served as secretary of the Hungarian Scholarly Society in the 1840s and 1850s.[52] Schedel grew up in a German-speaking household in Buda, the son of a postmaster, but his decision to pursue Hungarian litera-ture was not the product of a youthful rebellion against parental author-ity. His father had sent him to the countryside to learn Hungarian at an early age (Rottenbiller's father had done the same) and then enrolled him in Pest's Piarist gymnasium, which Vörösmarty and Széchenyi attended at different times. The elder Schedel also subscribed to Hungarian-language journals and later supported the liberal reform movement. It would be in-teresting to know whether the father also approved of his son's decision to use the pen name "Toldy" for two decades before formally changing his name in 1847. This new surname was a clear expression of Hungarian na-tional loyalty, but also seems to have been the price of admission into the Hungarian-language world of letters.

More cautious German writers criticized what they considered to be the excesses of the Hungarian national movement—"Magyar-mania" *(Magyaromanie)* they called it. One drew a pointed contrast between what he called "true" patriotism, "the deeply and clearly understood recogni-tion of civic, national, and purely human conditions," and "false" patrio-tism, the "product of blind, benighted passion."[53] Such criticism was not limited to the Hungarian national movement, and when reports came of the premiere of a Croatian national opera in Zagreb, a German paper re-sponded with skepticism: "National opera? We find this expression almost improper! Art knows no nationality; it is at home everywhere that it is planted and cultivated. We will tolerate national songs, national melodies, but opera . . . cannot be properly given this predicate. . . . Alas, that poli-tics have become mixed with art! Nothing could contribute to its decline as much as this!"[54]

Buda-Pest's German-language press was fighting a losing battle, how-ever, in demanding that cultural life remain free from national and politi-cal sentiments. In this context, a number of writers, with Carl Maria Benkert at their head, worked to find some way of synthesizing their Ger-man and Hungarian allegiances. A somewhat shady character (he would offer his services to the secret police in the 1850s), Benkert came from a family of Pest hoteliers and Viennese artists, worked in the book trade, served as a soldier, and wrote plays and poetry ("Beer is Poison" was the name of his first publication). In 1846, he edited the *Yearbook of the Ger-man Element in Hungary,* one of the few publications of the era that claimed to speak for the German population. In the introduction, Benkert conceded that Hungary's one million German-speakers were rapidly Magyarizing. Benkert regretted their passivity and suggested that there "are many people in the land, who are perfectly Hungarian-spirited . . . but still speak German." This echoed the nonnational patriotism of Schedius earlier in the century and suggested an alternative to linguistic nationalism. But Benkert's conclusion was hardly a call to arms: he accepted in principle that Germans would eventually learn to speak Hungarian and merely asked for patience from Hungarian nationalists, arguing that the process would take generations.[55]

Only a few writers openly suggested that Hungary's German-speakers should develop national institutions in order to compete with—or at least stave off—the Hungarian side. The strongest advocate of this position was Eduard Glatz, who reportedly once expressed his regret that Germans had not colonized all of Hungary.[56] Glatz's family was from the Zips region in Upper Hungary (today's Slovakia), which had a large concentration of German-speakers, a number of whom (Ferenc Pulszky, for example) became avid supporters of the Hungarian national movement. Glatz in contrast had studied at the Lutheran university in Leipzig and taught for several years in Austrian Silesia, where he witnessed the Czech and Polish national movements and joined the local German society *(Deutscher Verein)*. Unlike many of his fellow writers, Glatz thus had firsthand experience of German nationalism. In 1842, he published in *Pesther Tageblatt (Pest Daily News)* a series of short, biting verses, which mocked both the Hungarian national movement and the German-speakers who supported it. In Glatz's eyes, Hungarian nationalists championed empty symbols (the theater, flag, and costumes) instead of building schools or helping the peasantry; most damningly, the Hungarian side's agitation upset a long tradition of peaceful coexistence:

> German, Slav, and Magyar *(Magyaren)*,
> Vlach, Serb, and Cincar
> Lived for hundreds of years
> Happily in a mixed marriage.
> And now you suddenly cry out in sorrow,
> as if you have been wronged,
> and with threatening gestures
> your nationality loudly demands
> from us another reversal:
> "That we all become Hungarian *(ungrisch)*."[57]

In the same breath, Glatz also criticized German-speakers who paraded in Magyar dress, changed their names, and studied the Hungarian language. Glatz continued to propound these views as editor of *Pester Zeitung (Pest Newspaper)*, a German newspaper that appeared in Buda-Pest from 1845 onward. Under Glatz's direction, *Pester Zeitung* hewed to a conservative course and often spoke out against liberalism and Hungarian nationalism.

Glatz's invocations of German nationhood found little response in Buda-Pest, at least in associational life. Although there were a large number of societies with many German-speakers, including burial societies, economic associations, and sharpshooters' clubs, none had an identifiably German national character. The Waiters Association, a self-help society founded in 1835, was typical: it used German in all its transactions but also had a small membership, limited aims, and a minimal impact on public life. Larger societies upheld a tradition of bilingualism. The First Pest Burial Society (founded 1842), for example, likely had a preponderance of German-speaking members, yet its statutes appeared in both German and Hungarian and mandated that the society's officials know both languages.[58] The same was true of the Pest Sharpshooting Society, one of the oldest associations in the twin towns. Membership was mandatory for new citizens *(Bürger)*, who were required to take weekly target practice for one year.[59] Yet the society's bilingual bylaws also stated that it was open to nobles and professionals, groups more likely to support the Hungarian cause. Most men who came to the shooting range in any event seem to have been more interested in sociability than politics (or target practice, because income from beer and billiards far exceeded the fees paid by recently enlisted burghers). In this way, the sharpshooters' club functioned as a modest version of the National Casino and other noble-led social clubs, but without their linguistic and cultural aims. This may also have been the case with the Burghers Circle, which was founded in 1847. It apparently had 300 middle-class members, but little evidence remains about its leaders, goals, or activities.[60]

The authorities in Vienna did little to direct the German-speakers' loyalties or to support their institutions. Perhaps Vienna took their allegiance for granted. "The German burghers feel great sympathy for the ruling house," wrote a police informant in the mid-1840s.[61] Metternich and other imperial-royal officials at times toyed with the idea of playing Hungary's burghers off against the nobility, and by the 1840s Vienna had tacitly recognized the need to counter the Hungarian national movement in the realm of public opinion. This explains why Vienna provided generous financial support and active direction to Glatz's *Pester Zeitung*. But if the authorities welcomed Glatz's conservative political orientation, they discouraged his German national activism. Vienna had no intention of fighting fire with fire, because German nationalism was no less palatable to imperial-royal officials than its Hungarian equivalent. Ultimately, Vienna rarely differentiated between language groups in Buda-Pest. Editors of German-language papers often complained that the censors treated them more strictly than they did the Hungarian press, and managers of the German theaters waited in vain for support from the imperial-royal authorities. The Pest Town Council, which wanted only to rent the Pest Theater to the highest bidder, had neither the deep pockets nor the national motivations of Pest County and the National Diet, which generously subsidized the Hungarian theater and other national institutions.

The creation of a distinctly Hungarian social and cultural life in the 1840s thus did not lead directly to the creation of comparable German institutions. There were few signs of Germanization and only faint stirrings of an incipient German national movement. If anything, currents ran in the opposite direction, as a number of young men raised in German households adopted a conscious Hungarian loyalty. It would be a mistake, however, to overstate the progress of Hungarian cause among the towns' economic and political leaders. Many town dwellers appear to have been ambivalent, torn between their loyalty to dynasty, town, and homeland and the obvious dynamism of the Hungarian national movement.

Árpád and Abraham

How Buda-Pest's Jews would respond to Hungarian nationalism was uncertain. For their part, Hungarian national leaders found them difficult to classify: "With the exception of a few families," statistician Elek Fényes wrote, "Jews use the German language; but nonetheless we cannot count them as Germans, nor as a distinct people, because presently only their persecuted religion sets them apart."[62] With its implicit criticism of the status quo, Fényes's description illustrates how many contemporary writers linked Jews' acquisition of nationhood with a range of religious, legal, and cultural reforms. In this era, many Jews would take the first, decisive steps toward the Hungarian side, laying the groundwork for what historians have called the "Magyar-Jewish symbiosis" of the late nineteenth century.[63] Although scholars have recently begun to look more critically at the meanings of Hungarianness and Jewishness, particularly for the period after Jewish emancipation in 1867, there is no question that a number of Jewish leaders actively supported the Hungarian national cause from the 1830s onward.[64] The situation in Buda-Pest again appears to be opposite to that in Prague (and other cities in the Austrian lands), where national-minded Jews first chose the German over the Czech community in the nineteenth century. What were the origins of this close relationship between Árpád and Abraham (to borrow a metaphor from a young Jewish writer of the era)?

The status of Buda-Pest's Jews in this era was greatly changed from that of just a few decades earlier. This could be seen most clearly in Pest, where Jews had carved out a precarious existence in the last decades of the eighteenth century. By the 1810s, Jews had elected a rabbi, written statutes for their community, established several schools, and organized a merchants association. The Jewish population meanwhile surged, with the result that in the late 1840s there were between 8,000 and 10,000 Jews in Pest and 4,000 to 5,000 more in Buda and Óbuda.[65] As in earlier decades, most newcomers came from within the Hungarian lands and settled in on the streets surrounding New Market Square in Pest's Theresa and Leopold districts. There they found a vibrant Jewish community, complete with schools, a kindergarten, charitable and women's associations, ritual baths, and two synagogues. Like the urban population in general, nearly all Jews

were poor, but there were also Jewish doctors, surgeons, musicians, journalists, students, and midwives.[66] Jewish artisans pursued a number of
trades—tailors, pipemakers, and painters were the most common—and
Jewish merchants played an important role in commerce and banking. By
one count, there were 142 Jewish wholesalers, in addition to 881 smaller
traders and peddlers.

The authorities were slow to react to these changes. In 1833, the Vice-
Regal Council ended the legal fiction that there was no organized Jewish
presence in Pest—only tolerated individuals and their families—and
granted legal recognition to Pest's Jewish community, now officially the
Juden-Gemeinde. The economic and civil status of Jews improved markedly
in 1840 with the National Diet's passage of Act 1840:29, which permitted
Jews to establish factories, enter all trades, take on journeymen, and settle
and own property in nearly all royal free towns, Pest and Buda included.[67]
But Jewish residents still faced restrictions and everyday obstacles that
Christians did not: they were effectively barred from most liberal professions, paid a collective "toleration tax" (through 1846, when they negoti-
ated its end), and could not become citizens of the towns. The burghers
had long been hostile to Jews, and in the 1840s, the Pest Town Council
fought a rearguard action against Jewish settlement, particularly in the
center city.[68] In 1847, it issued decrees that ordered Jews without residency
permits to leave Pest immediately and threatened to punish landlords
who housed them.[69] To this official hostility was added everyday discrimination, such as that of a journalist who warned his readers about dishon-
est Jewish peddlers in Pest: he claimed to have witnessed a Jewish merchant cheat a "good-hearted gentleman" by selling him a gold ring that
turned out to be worthless copper.[70] Hungarian liberals were themselves
deeply divided, and for every reformer who openly advocated full Jewish
emancipation, there were many more who favored a much more cautious
approach. Nearly all political leaders believed that Jews should first "reform" their religion and adopt the Hungarian language. Few liberals were
as brave as József Eötvös, who called for the immediate emancipation of
Jews, arguing that this was a necessary prerequisite to incorporating them
into the national community and to extending equal civil rights to all
parts of the population.

In this rapidly changing context, some Jews in Buda-Pest began to address publicly questions of legal emancipation, religious reform, and language use. Because most Jews had no interest in abandoning traditional
religious and communal practices, their numbers were limited. Nevertheless, urban life introduced a dynamic element into the Jewish community.
As historian Jacob Katz has observed, it was much harder for Jewish merchants to observe religious commitments in the city than in the countryside.[71] In Buda-Pest, there were pressures to conform to the wider community's languages, dress, diet, and holidays, and it was only with difficulty,
for example, that Jews persuaded the town of Pest not to hold markets on

the Sabbath. Currents of religious reform from Vienna and Berlin also began to reach Buda-Pest. In 1827 Joseph Bach gave the first sermon in Pest
in literary German, rather than in the customary Yiddish. A decade later,
several Pest Jews began to play a more active role in public life and to
reach out to the Hungarian national movement. A key figure was Loeb
Schwab, rabbi of Pest from 1836 until his death in 1857. Deeply religious
and highly cultured, Schwab had the respect of both conservatives and reformers within the Pest community. In 1840, he attracted wide attention
when he called on Jews to acquire the Hungarian language. A number of
writers and translators aided this effort, including Moritz Bloch, who
penned an influential pamphlet calling for Jewish emancipation and published the first Hungarian translation of the Torah.

Schwab's call found an enthusiastic response among students.[72] A
group of them soon formed the Society for the Dissemination of the Hungarian Language among the Israelites, the so-called Magyarization Society,
one of a number of Jewish associations in the Hungarian lands devoted to
the spread of the Hungarian language.[73] The Magyarization Society in Pest
sought to promote Hungarian language and literature through its reading
room, conversation hours, public lectures, and language classes. By 1847,
the society's library had 1,000 volumes and its language classes more than
300 students. The society also opened a kindergarten, which was directed
by a twelve-woman committee, and held well-attended monthly readings
in Hungarian. In the eyes of its founders, the existence of the Magyarization Society refuted allegations that Jews were not committed to the Hungarian national cause. As its young secretary Márton Diósy wrote, in an
era "swept away by one great idea—the idea of nationality," Jews were
unique in not clamoring for "the awakening of their long-dead nationality."[74] In response to those who might cynically say that Jews were learning Hungarian "only so that they can read bankruptcy notices," Diósy argued that Jews were in fact responding to recent advances in cultural life
(Diósy himself was an aspiring journalist and playwright). According to
Diósy, the adoption of Hungarian had three important consequences.
First, Hungarian (and not German, Yiddish, or Hebrew) would be the key
to further religious reforms: "It is certainly enough of a problem that the
prayers take place in a language that the worshipers hardly understand;
but under these circumstances, we hope that if the Hungarian language
becomes more widespread, then enlightened views will win wider acceptance, and Hungarian Jewry will not be adverse to reforms that have already been introduced in many foreign temples." Second, Hungarian
would be used in everyday life: "Let friend speak to friend in this language, lover to beloved, children to parents; let us complain to our God of
our earthly woes in this language; and let us be confident that we will
soon sing out our thanks in this tongue for the relief we have won and for
our complete emancipation." Third, the use of Hungarian would promote
the cause of emancipation. Diósy stressed that emancipation had two

sides, political and social. The former could come only from above, but the latter depended on the Jews themselves. Hungary's Jews thus had to accept that political emancipation was contingent upon a combination of religious reform and adoption of the Hungarian language.

Similar impulses lay behind a voluntary association founded to help young Jewish craftsmen.[75] The Society for the Promotion of Artisans and Farmers among the Israelites (1842) aimed to place young men into artisanal and agricultural trades from which they had long been excluded, to promote the Hungarian language among Jewish workers, and to disseminate useful knowledge and instill good morals. In practice, the society tried to place Jewish apprentices with Christian master artisans in the hope that they would learn the craft and ultimately become guild masters themselves. The society wanted to "refute a frequent and baseless protest raised against the Jews—that they dread heavy labor."[76] As the ever enthusiastic Diósy observed, both Árpád and Abraham had been farmers.[77] The society provided young Jewish workers with financial assistance and religious instruction, as well as with lessons in writing, arithmetic, and drawing. To underline its connection with the Hungarian national movement, the society also became a chapter of the Industrial Association. In spite of its good intentions, however, the society met with limited success: the executive committee regretfully discovered that most guild masters had no interest in taking on Jewish apprentices. Indeed, only the intervention of the Vice-Regal Council led some Buda masters to accept Jewish apprentices, and, in 1846, a locksmith became the first Jewish master of a craft guild.

Craft guilds were not alone in their reluctance to open their doors. Despite their professed commitment to openness, many national societies were unwilling to accept Jews as members. This tendency was most pronounced in the National Casino. Soon after its founding, Széchenyi had proposed that the Casino admit Jewish merchants, reasoning that one of its goals was to promote commerce in Hungary.[78] Although he personally mistrusted Jews and opposed their continued immigration into Hungary, the count was willing to set aside his prejudices in favor of what he considered to be the national interest. His motion found little support, however, and after a stormy debate was voted down fifty to six. According to police informants, Széchenyi's opponents argued that "it would be impossible for us to merge with the merchants, since experience has shown that magnates do not wish to associate with the gentry or the burghers."[79] That snobbish aristocrats did not want to mix with merchants is unremarkable, but there were certainly other factors at work. Historian Michael Silber has argued that, although the Hungarian nobility recognized the important contribution of Jews to the economy, they also saw this as a regrettable sign of economic backwardness and even a source of moral corruption.[80] To most members of the National Casino, then, Jewish merchants were socially inferior and represented unwelcome economic changes. In the 1830s, the Casino rejected the application of two wealthy Jewish entrepreneurs, Moritz Ullmann and Samuel Wodianer, despite the fact that both had frequent business contacts with the aristocracy. Only in the 1850s would the National Casino admit several members of these two families, years after they had converted to Christianity and gained noble titles.

Other social clubs were only slightly more hospitable. The National Circle is a good example. Although the local authorities reported to Vienna that the National Circle "had attracted numerous Jewish merchants and bankers with the offer of emancipation," the National Circle never had more than a handful of Jewish members.[81] According to a contemporary Jewish writer, the circle "did not want to accept Jews at all," a charge repeated by the editor Imre Vahot, himself a member of the circle. Although discrimination may partly explain the low figure, it is true that few of the club's members were doctors or merchants, two occupations open to Jews in the early nineteenth century. Similarly, the National Circle's emphasis on the Hungarian language excluded Jewish journalists and writers fluent in German but less certain in Hungarian. Many Jewish literati instead supported the national cause as contributors or editors to the towns' German-language literary journals, which were largely sympathetic to Hungarian nationalism.[82]

Successful Jews had more opportunities in Pest's economic societies and institutions. That the membership of the Pest Wholesalers Corporation included both Christian and Jews suggests that confessional differences could be set aside, at least in commercial matters. National societies such as the Industrial Association and Protection Association also welcomed the support of Jewish merchants. The Pest wholesaler Emanuel Kanitz, for example, belonged to a number of national societies and was three times elected to the Industrial Association's executive committee. But the case of Kanitz's brother-in-law, Jónás Kunewalder, is also instructive. The Kunewalder brothers dealt in agricultural products, second-hand goods, transportation, and credit, and Kunewalder was among the first Jews to register a house in Pest under his own name following the Diet's reforms in 1840. He was also a prominent leader of the Pest Jewish community. The Kunewalder brothers supported the Industrial Association from its inception—Jónás attended more than twenty-five of its meetings—and they organized a well-attended ball to benefit the Association's school for apprentices. It was natural that the Protection Association would also seek their support. The Pest chapter thus elected the merchants Ullmann and Kunewalder to its executive committee. Ullmann accepted the position, but Kunewalder declined it.[83] He explained that he would not accept the position "because of his unfavorable civic position arising from the 'question of the Israelites,' which the Diet has still not solved."[84] In short, he was protesting the still unfavorable legal position of Hungarian Jewry in the 1840s. In response, the Pest chapter admitted that the question of emancipation remained unsolved yet expressed its hope that the solution would soon come, adding that, "if the task of social associations is to pre-pare the road of legislation," Kunewalder's participation in the executive committee would help advance the cause of emancipation. They asked Kunewalder to reconsider his decision, but he again refused.

This exchange is telling because it demonstrates at least one Jewish leader's impatience with the unfulfilled promise of gradual emancipation. Nevertheless, it again shows the liberals' faith that activity in the realm of civil society could pave the way for formal political change. Kunewalder was not convinced, though a small but influential circle of Jews in Buda-Pest was, and they showed their support for the Hungarian na-tional movement by joining (or trying to join) national associations, forming their own societies, and supporting Hungarian-language cul-ture in the German-language press. These activists were likely to be young, educated, and in favor of religious reforms, all of which made them a minority within the Jewish community. Although many of them may have known German, becoming "German" was not an op-tion, as it would be elsewhere in Central Europe, because there was no defined German national community in Buda-Pest in the 1840s. On the Hungarian side, the low number of Jews in Buda-Pest's national so-cieties suggests not only the wide social and cultural gap that divided Hungarian noblemen from Jews, but also the nobles' ambivalence about the desirability or necessity of recruiting Jews for the Hungarian national movement.

The expansion of civil society in the 1830s and 1840s greatly strength-ened the Hungarian national cause in the twin towns of Buda and Pest. It was through national societies and newspapers that the county nobility came together with wealthy aristocrats, local writers, established profes-sionals, and influential burghers. These activists often justified their ac-tions on the grounds that they acted in the interest of the entire national community, carefully overlooking the fact that their words would reach only a few dozen listeners or several hundred readers. Yet more and more people were listening, reading, and responding, as a final example from the National Protection Association makes clear. In 1846, the local chapter in Köveskál, a small town in western Hungary, sent a letter to the execu-tive committee in Pest.[85] In ringing tones, the letter called on the Protec-tion Association's leaders to work for the establishment of a national ware-house for the purchase and sale of domestic goods, the founding of a Hungarian National Bank, and the development of railroads in Hungary. It advocated greater honors for factory owners and workers, associations for women, and legislation allowing patriotic Jews to become full citizens. If these demands suggest the broad base of support for liberal reform in the 1840s, they are also a reminder of people's readiness to view economic and social questions in national terms.

Not everyone embraced the national societies and their goals. This can be seen in another letter, this one sent to the Industrial Association by the privileged merchants corporation of the town of Neusohl (today Banská Bystrica, in Slovakia). The corporation was writing in response to the Industrial Association's proposal to organize Hungarian-language classes for merchants across the country, which had the long-term aim of replacing German with Hungarian as the language of commerce. The merchants' letter reads in part, "Whoever has the occasion and takes the trouble to observe this matter more closely and clearly in practical life without preconceived opinions or partisanship, may reach the conviction that in Hungary one can perfectly conform with regards to nationality and patriotism, without being talented in the Hungarian language."[86] This was an eloquent argument for an inclusive definition of what it meant to be "Hungarian," in which state patriotism and not language would be the measure of nationhood. Its reference to "preconceived opinions or partisanship" was also a pointed rebuke of the Hungarian national movement.

Yet the letter itself demonstrates again how the national societies and press could force people across the country to respond to their agenda. At the same time, the rapid growth of these national institutions subtly altered the twin town's relationship with Vienna. By making the case for reform and nationhood in meetings halls, reading rooms, and newspapers—in civil society—the national societies embodied the liberal faith in publicity and openness. This allowed them to criticize the regime in Vienna, which they characterized as trapped in the past and inimical to freedom. With all the fervor of a convert, the French-born publicist Auguste de Gerando drew a stark contrast between Vienna and Pest: "An absolutist nature rules in Vienna, a love of the status quo, which has hardened into stone. In Pest, however, there is a movement, a flurry of thoughts, an atmosphere of freedom, which places us on the gates of the Orient with surprise. One feels that here we are moving forward, and there they are stuck in place."[87] This was a polemic, and one that would be proved wrong in March 1848, when Vienna rose in revolution before Pest. But the identification of Pest with liberty and progress held a strong appeal for the Hungarian side, because it legitimized and ennobled their tireless activism in the twin towns. If Palatine Joseph and István Széchenyi had suggested that Buda-Pest's future lay with Vienna, the national activists turned Buda-Pest into the center of a movement increasingly oriented against Vienna.

CHAPTER FOUR

Women and Cultural Politics

"We must have images of our great men in statues and drawings, so
that they serve as symbols, to which fathers lead their sons every day
to awaken love of the homeland."

—Lajos Kossuth, 1841[1]

Kossuth himself would be painted and sketched many times in the
1840s, and once by Miklós Barabás, the leading portraitist of the era.
Born in Transylvania to a noble family, Barabás had studied in Vienna,
prospered in Bucharest, and traveled widely in Italy before settling in
Pest in 1840.[2] As a painter, Barabás helped popularize watercolors of urban life—the influence of contemporary Viennese artists was significant
here—as well as idealized, Romantic paintings of peasants. But it was as
a portraitist that he was best known, and his subjects included, in addition to Kossuth, Palatine Joseph, István Széchenyi, Ferenc Deák, Lajos
Batthyány, and Franz Liszt. Lithographic reproductions further increased the circulation and profitability of this pantheon of political
and cultural luminaries.

More commonly, however, Barabás made his living through portraits of
well-to-do burghers, nobles, and aristocrats, and in the 1830s and 1840s
he executed dozens of them in oil paintings, watercolors, and miniatures.
Portraiture, patriotism, and patronage thus come together in Barabás's
Woman in a Striped Dress (fig. 3). The subject of *Woman in a Striped Dress*
(1845) has not been identified, but she was evidently a woman of means:
the commission of Barabás suggests this, as do the jewelry and embroidered blouse in the painting itself. The composition adheres to neoclassical conventions of European portraiture, and the subject's three-quarters
pose, almond eyes, soft flesh, and rich fabric recall the aristocratic women
painted by Ingres. At the same time, the clothing, hairstyle, and furniture
also evoke the Biedermeier world of the early nineteenth century, with its
ethos of simplicity and domesticity. The book in the woman's hands
might therefore be merely a painterly convention or perhaps a mark of
leisure and cultivation; yet it also conveys a certain seriousness and, one is
tempted to add, a commitment to the literature of the day. This interpretation is possible only because of the woman's unusual hat, the key to the
painting. Although its stripes harmonize with those of the dress, the colors of the hat and tassel are immediately recognizable as the Hungarian

national colors: red, white, and green. This detail gives this otherwise very cosmopolitan painting a distinctly national flavor.

Women in a Striped Dress is one of many clues that women in Buda-Pest actively supported the Hungarian national cause. Although older literature on nationalism typically paid scant attention to women, scholars have recently begun to explore the ways in which national struggles gave new meanings to the many roles played by women: wives, mothers, readers, writers, consumers, protestors, and subscribers to a variety of causes.[3] At the same time, they have cautioned that women were often visible but voiceless contributors to national movements—present in the public realm but not able to speak for it. In Hungary, women lacked property and political rights and were denied access to the professions and university. Yet in a period of great political and cultural agitation, a small number of women gained a precarious foothold in public life. Mothers and daughters, they showed, could be just as enthusiastic about the national cause as the fathers and sons that Kossuth wanted to mobilize. Their many activities shed light on the expansion—and the boundaries—of the national public in Buda-Pest.

Hungarian as the Official Language

The National Diet in Pressburg did much to foster the development of Hungarian national culture in Buda-Pest. During the 1830s and 1840s, it provided financial support for the Hungarian Scholarly Society, National Museum, and National Theater. Some of its members would have done even more. One noble county wanted to require that a Hungarian dance always follow the opening promenade (polonaise) at all balls, and another, likely inspired by the French Revolutionary calendar of the 1790s, proposed that the names of the months be made more authentically Hungarian.[4] Yet these activities paled in comparison with the Diet's unrelenting advocacy of the Hungarian language for more than a half century.[5] Vienna gave ground only slowly, but ultimately consented to a series of language laws, including Act 1830:8, which required all public officials to know Hungarian and allowed counties to use it in their correspondence with the Hungarian Chancellery in Vienna; Act 1836:3, which widened the use of Hungarian in legislation and courts; and Act 1840:6, which made Hungarian mandatory in the internal administration of the kingdom. These culminated in Act 1844:2, the crowning achievement of the 1843–44 Diet. This law made Hungarian the primary language of administration, education, and the judiciary in the Hungarian lands. Henceforth, the National Diet would conduct its deliberations and communicate with the emperor-king in Hungarian; the law further required the Vice-Regal Council and all high judicial courts to use the Hungarian language alone, rather than the customary mix of Latin, German, and Hungarian. Act 1844:2 also made Hungarian the principal language of higher education and left open the

3—Portraiture, patriotism, and patronage: Miklós Barabás,
Woman in a Striped Dress (1845).

possibility that it would soon be introduced into all elementary schools. By the mid-1840s, then, the Hungarian language had triumphed—on paper, if not yet in practice—in the places that mattered: the imperial-royal administration, city halls, counties, courts, and schools.

Yet, rather than producing a new equilibrium, these changes contributed to an already dynamic situation. They certainly did little to improve relations between the Diet and the crown. Vienna's position on the language question had always been more tactical than ideological. At the 1843–44 Diet, Vienna and its allies (chiefly aristocrats and prelates in the upper house) had rejected the overwhelming majority of reforms proposed by the liberal opposition, and, as a result, long deliberations on noble taxation, tariff reform, revision of the criminal code, and electoral procedures in the towns had come to naught. But, because this was one of the few issues on which conservatives and liberals agreed, Vienna could not so easily turn aside the Diet's linguistic demands. For Vienna, the language question ultimately appears to have been of secondary importance, and linguistic concessions were a relatively painless way of securing recruits and taxes. In agreeing to make Hungarian the official language, Vienna nonetheless secured exemptions for the Hungarian Chancellery, Royal Treasury, and the military command, all of which would continue to use German in everyday transactions and communications with Vienna. (The language used by the military would be a bone of contention between Hungary and the crown through the end of the monarchy in 1918.) Vienna also helped forge a compromise that allowed the three Croatian counties, which were part of the Hungarian Kingdom, to continue to use Latin alongside Hungarian. Compared with what had been gained for Hungarian, the retention of German and Latin in these areas was minor, but it meant that the crown's wide concessions won little goodwill among the Hungarian political leadership.

For these leaders, the Dietal victories were only the first step. As part of their campaign for the language laws, the Hungarian side had marshaled a wide array of arguments. Some were historical and political (the Hungarian nobility, they said, had conquered Hungary in the ninth century and ruled it since); others cultural (the Magyars were as civilized as the Germans and far above the Slavs); and still others geographic (Hungarian-speakers lived in the center of the kingdom, not on the periphery).[6] Liberals also argued that the introduction of Hungarian into public affairs would not impinge upon the civil rights of those who did not know Hungarian, because they would still enjoy free use of their own languages in the private sphere of the home, workplace, tavern, and church. Indeed, because liberal leaders such as Kossuth saw the language laws as part of a much larger package of reforms, they promised that knowledge of Hungarian would be a means to education, emancipation, upward social mobility, and, eventually, political participation for much of the population. Progress and not coercion, it was hoped, would gradually draw Slavic peasants and German town dwellers into the national community.

As in earlier periods, this liberal model uneasily coexisted with less-tolerant views. Obsessed with nationhood and haunted by the Romantic specter of national death, some writers worried aloud that the Magyars, far from being dominant, were in fact alone in a world of enemies.[7] Demographic anxieties compounded these fears, as did political stirrings in the Balkans and the spread in Zagreb of the Illyrian movement—the first phase of the Croatian and south Slav national ideas. In an influential book, the opposition leader Miklós Wesselényi warned of a Pan-Slavic crusade emanating from Moscow. Journalists and poets popularized these fears: in his well-known "Fóti dal" ("Song of Fót"), Mihály Vörösmarty wrote of the "dread phantoms of the north," a clear reference to Russia. Some national leaders accordingly downplayed the model of progress and instead urged that kindergartens, elementary schools, and churches be used to spread the Hungarian language in the countryside, even if this caused conflict with local teachers, priests, and writers. There were dissenting voices, and in an 1842 speech to the Hungarian Scholarly Society, Széchenyi famously warned that forcible and fast Magyarization (which he identified with Kossuth) would produce hostile national movements among the Serbs, Slovaks, and other groups within the kingdom.

In this tense environment, societies dedicated to the cultivation and promotion of the Hungarian language took on a new importance. The most prestigious was the Hungarian Scholarly Society in Pest, which held its first general assembly in 1831, the same year in which Franz Palacký organized, with similar aims, the Czech Foundation in Prague.[8] By the end of the decade, the Hungarian Scholarly Society had six academic sections, a growing library, and a sizeable endowment; it published new grammars and dictionaries, awarded annual prizes for Hungarian-language scholarship, and held well-publicized assemblies. It also spawned many other literary societies, including the Kisfaludy Society, which friends of the late dramatist and writer Károly Kisfaludy founded in 1836. It published Kisfaludy's works and foreign literature in translation, sponsored essay contests with national themes ("What influence does dramatic literature have on the moral life of the nation?" was one), and sponsored János Erdélyi's pioneering collection of Hungarian-language folk songs, which, Erdélyi hoped, would soon free poetry from Italian and German influences.[9] Several short-lived student groups likewise aimed to promote the Hungarian language through discussion, criticism, and journals.

To outsiders, this obsession with language could be hard to understand. John Paget praised the Hungarian Scholarly Society's efforts, but tartly expressed his hope that "they will soon be able to dedicate some of their time to matters that may unite them to the learned of the rest of Europe, as much as their present studies tend to *separate* them."[10] Vienna had its own concerns about the Scholarly Society: one of its spies reported in 1839 that a "democratic tendency" dominated the leadership and that it had printed materials without first obtaining the permission of the censors.[11] Even Széchenyi, the society's first president, complained that it had become a "revolutionary club."[12] Such fears were overstated, but they signaled the extent to which contemporaries in all parts of Europe connected language, literature, and politics. As Eric Hobsbawm has observed, "There has rarely been a period when even the least 'ideological' artists were more universally partisan, often regarding service to politics as their primary duty."[13]

Other groups soon followed the Magyars' example. In 1826, Serb activists in Buda-Pest founded the Serb Foundation, a literary and educational association.[14] Orthodox Serbs lived in towns up and down the Danube and in southern Hungary, and their leaders had closely watched the Serb uprisings against Ottoman rule in the first decades of the nineteenth. Buda-Pest was far from the Serbian border, but it had wealthy

Orthodox merchants, a lively literary life, numerous presses, and the invigorating presence of the Hungarian national movement. The Foundation's quarterly journal, *Serbske Letopisi (Serb Yearbook)*, soon became the most important Serbian-language publication in Hungary. Members of the society hailed the appearance of Vuk Karadžić's landmark collection of Serb folk songs, although they were more guarded about his proposal to use the dialect of Herzegovina as the basis for the Serb literary language (existing forms relied heavily upon Church Slavonic). Under the leadership of the wealthy landowner Sava Tekelija (Száva Tököly, to the Magyars), the Serb Foundation followed a conservative course regarding language. Following Tekelija's death in 1842, however, a pitched battle broke out over the question of language reform. Those who favored Karadžić's innovations eventually prevailed, making it easier for activists in Buda-Pest to join forces with Serb leaders elsewhere. The foundation meanwhile published a number of books and held competitions for a Serb grammar, for a history of Serbs living in the Monarchy, and for biographies of Serbs living in Hungary.

Buda-Pest performed a similar function for the Slovak national movement. On the surface, Slovak nationalism faced many obstacles: although Slovak-speakers comprised more than one-fifth the population of Hungary (excluding Croatia and Transylvania), most were poor peasants in the mountainous northern regions.[15] Unlike the Serbs, Slovak activists could not look abroad to a foreign state with a Slovak population, although the Czech lands partly fulfilled this role in the nineteenth century. From the outset, the Slovak national movement was fractured along linguistic and religious lines, with Catholic reformers often at odds with Lutherans. These tensions played themselves out in Buda-Pest, which had several thousand Slovak-speakers. In 1834, a number of writers, officials, and clergymen formed the Society for the Friends of Slovak Literature, modeled on the Hungarian Scholarly Society and the Serb Foundation.[16] The society had limited resources, yet it managed to publish four issues of the literary almanac *Zora (Dawn)*. It was less successful in bridging the gap between Catholics and Lutherans, and, under the influence of the local pastor Ján Kollár, Lutherans gradually abandoned the society. One of the most dynamic figures of the era, Kollár served the Lutheran community in Pest from 1819 to 1849. Kollár had come under the spell of German Romanticism during his studies at Jena, and in Pest he forged close links with Serb and Illyrian leaders. Kollár published Slovak folk songs and wrote epic poetry, including, most famously, *The Daughter of Sláva* (1824). Filled with barbs against Magyars and Germans, *The Daughter of Sláva* was a paean to Slavic heroes, kings, and saints, and prophesied the triumphant union of all Slavs. This message of Slavic brotherhood reflected Kollár's view that the Slavs—or at least Czechs and Slovaks—should have a common literary language (only in the mid-nineteenth century would advocates of a separate Slovak language carry the day).

The Serb Foundation and the Society for the Friends of Slovak Literature did not challenge the primacy of the Hungarian national movement in Buda-Pest. But they were important nonetheless. National movements play off and strengthen one another: "The collective result," historian Jeremy King has written, "no matter which movement carries the day in individual battles, is to bolster nationhood as a whole."[17] Other forms of allegiance—Habsburg loyalty and Hungarian state patriotism, in our case—lost ground in the face of concerted national agitation. In Buda-Pest, Serb, Slovak, and Hungarian national activists shared beliefs (that nationhood should be the primary locus of loyalty), strategies (agitation through journals and societies), and aims (to promote national languages and cultures). This fostered frequent borrowings and mutual influences: Slovaks modeled their literary journal *Dawn* on the Hungarian-language *Aurora* (they shared a title); writers in the Serb Foundation's journal held up the advance of the Hungarian language as a model to be emulated; and the Kisfaludy Society attempted to produce the Magyar equivalent of Karadžić's collections of Serb folk songs. To be sure, the different national movements were far from identical, and their leaders had different social backgrounds, political programs, and intended audiences.

They also had different symbolic centers. Over time, the Serb movement's center of gravity would drift southward, just as the Slovak movement would shift northward. The Hungarian national movement meanwhile kept its eyes squarely focused on Buda-Pest. "The Magyarization of these two towns," wrote the critic and theater director József Bajza, "would be of greater consequence and significance, than if we made a millions souls Magyar in other provinces. If we truly and seriously aspire to this goal, let the Magyarization of Pest-Buda be our motto."[18] Bajza and other activists in the twin towns surely welcomed the gains made in the National Diet, which gave the Hungarian national movement legal sanction and the promise of long-term success. But many of them wanted to accelerate this process in the twin towns, and so they carried their campaign into schools, ballrooms, and private homes. This opened the door, if just a crack, for women in Buda-Pest to participate in the national movement.

Educating the Daughters of the Homeland

Nineteenth-century national leaders understood fully the importance of schools. As usual, the French had shown the way. In *The Government of Poland*, Jean-Jacques Rousseau had given this advice to the Poles: "It is education that you must count on to shape the souls of the citizens in a national pattern and so to direct their opinions, their likes, and dislikes that they shall be patriotic by inclination, passionately, of necessity."[19] During the French Revolution, the Jacobins had taken this lesson to heart and launched a great enterprise of universal public education, which they saw as "the hallmark of a progressive nation and as a key to the future prospects of the French people."[20] In the more conservative environment of the nineteenth century, regimes concentrated instead on the promotion of basic literacy, religious piety, and respect for the ruling house. The same governments closely monitored secondary and university students, who were most open to new political and national ideas. As a rule, early nineteenth-century regimes showed little inclination to "shape the souls of the citizens in a national pattern."

In Hungary, the most striking feature of the school system was its steady expansion. Credit for this is due to the imperial royal administration, which had taken the lead in education with the reforms of Maria Theresa and Joseph II, as well as to the town authorities and churches that ran the schools. In Pest alone, the number of primary schools increased from seven in 1790 to thirty-two in 1848.[21] Students seeking further education could attend the town's three gymnasiums (secondary schools with a strongly classical curriculum), two of which were Catholic and the other Lutheran (although it accepted Orthodox and Jewish students as well). All three attracted many students from outside Pest, as did the university and, after its founding in 1846, the new technical school, the imperial-royal government's most impressive educational initiative of the era.

The language of instruction varied from school to school. In elementary schools, teachers used German, Hungarian, and Slovak; in secondary schools and the university, professors held lectures in Latin, German, and Hungarian. National activists, however, had long demanded that Hungarian should not only be a required subject in all schools, but also that it should be the language of instruction. There were some steps in this direction in the late 1830s, and in Pest Mayor Eichholz/Tölgyessy urged schools in the outer districts to employ Hungarian-speaking instructors. The real breakthrough came with the National Diet's Act 1844:2, which declared simply that Hungarian would henceforth be the "language of public education."[22] This had an immediate impact on the gymnasiums and the university, where many (though not all) professors switched to Hungarian overnight. Matters were more complicated on the elementary level, and the Diet and imperial-royal authorities did not settle the question at either the 1843–44 or the 1847–48 National Diet. In 1848, Baron József Eötvös, the minister of education and religion, proposed that Hungarian be taught in all elementary schools but that instruction be in the language of the majority of a community's inhabitants. This relatively moderate proposal met with fierce opposition from many nationalists, who hoped to use schools to Magyarize the wider population. Even diehard supporters of Hungarian as the universal language of instruction, however, had to recognize the shortage of teachers and textbooks, to say nothing of schools themselves.

This again put the spotlight on national societies in Buda-Pest. Their educational initiatives were more symbolic than substantial, yet they revealed the extent to which national activists hoped to give force to the

Diet's legislation on the ground. Such initiatives greatly worried the imperial-royal officials, who jealously guarded their authority in educational matters.[23] But the Hungarian nationalists were tireless: they formed societies to establish kindergartens (1836), distribute popular Hungarian-language books to peasants and workers (1841), and publish a pedagogical newspaper (1842). The Industrial Association alone published a number of books for young workers, the first of which was a Hungarian-language adaptation of Benjamin Franklin's *Way to Wealth*. It also organized classes in mechanical drawing, opened a school for apprentices, and held public lectures on physics, chemistry, and mechanics.[24] The lectures and schools never drew more than a few hundred students, but they fired the imagination of national activists. A journalist who visited the Industrial Association's lecture hall came away convinced that, if this model were followed, "prosperity would come to our poor homeland, which, after the storms of vanished centuries amid miserable conditions, lags so far behind peaceful, cultivated peoples!"[25] The Industrial Association also offered Hungarian-language lessons for journeymen and apprentices, which were notable for attracting both Jews and Christians, as well as a handful of maids and seamstresses.

The question of female education was an important one. "The more cultured a nation, the better educated its women," explained one newspaper. "Conversely, the more influence [women] bear, the more respect and esteem they are given, the more cultured a nation."[26] Such lofty phrases frequently appeared in the contemporary press. At the same time, all observers agreed that women in Hungary were poorly educated.[27] Girls from the middle and upper social strata had long studied at home or in convents. In the first decades of the nineteenth century they began to attend an increasing number of exclusive private schools. In spite of their growing popularity with parents, these finishing schools came under sharp criticism in the press. In 1822, István Kultsár attacked them for imparting superficial knowledge and empty skills, for filling the students' heads with foreign languages, dance instruction, and novels. These fashionable schools, he indignantly added, do not even teach their students Hungarian, the "language of the homeland."[28] Kultsár's solution that girls should study at home was unimaginative and unlikely to improve female education. A much more insightful analysis came from Éva Takáts, the daughter of the writer Teréz Karács.[29] Takáts agreed that female education was superficial, but pointed out that husbands prized women who could sing, dance, and speak foreign languages. In contrast to Kultsár, she called for more and better schools for girls, and especially for institutions that would promote social interaction between nobles and nonnobles. If properly educated, she asserted, women would energetically serve the national cause.

This exchange set the terms of a debate that continued into the 1840s and beyond. The central issue remained how female education could be improved and given a more national direction. One of the most active participants was the novelist András Fáy, who firmly believed that women should "love and honor national customs," that they should "speak the national language, read and patronize its literature—in short, be Magyar women from head to toe, and raise their children as Magyars as well."[30] In the language of the era, the ideal woman was the *honleány* (daughter of the homeland). Education would prepare women to be national-minded wives and mothers, but not participants in public affairs. Fáy spelled this out explicitly: "I do not desire that women argue about the systems and theories of national government and display their knowledge and opinions; this frequently embarrasses the most learned and humble men, who do not know whether they should apply arguments of greater learning that [women] will not understand, humor the women out of politeness, or dismiss them from the debate with a joke."[31] Fáy was not alone in admonishing women not to meddle in public life. One of the more memorable characters in Eötvös's great reform novel, *The Village Notary* (1845), is Mrs. Réty, whose schemes to manipulate local politics reap a harvest of injustice and tragedy. At the end of the novel, with her plots revealed and unraveled, she commits suicide. Less dramatically, newspapers in the 1830s and 1840s frequently pointed out unseemly behavior by women in public and private—cigar-smoking women were a favorite object of ridicule—and repeatedly warned against the danger that emancipation posed to society.[32] If such admonitions suggest that women at times challenged the rules of social behavior, they also underline the heavy sanctions imposed upon those who did.

This set the stage for the first halting steps to reform women's education in the 1840s. Fáy had urged the 1843–44 Diet to establish a teacher-training institute for women, and when this did not come to pass (it was not even brought to debate), he called for a similar institute to be funded by private subscriptions. When Fáy's plan failed to find the needed support, attention shifted to Countess Blanka Teleki, who wanted to establish a school for the daughters of well-to-do families. In an anonymous newspaper article published in December 1845, she vividly described the need for her school: "The aristocratic girl has hardly left childhood—has hardly learned about life . . . when she is already a woman, a mother."[33] Teleki claimed that existing schools made the students "foreign," in that they knew several foreign languages, could recite the history of any number of foreign lands, and dreamed of living in Paris or London. The time has come, she wrote, to educate aristocratic girls in a national spirit; only this would allow liberal reforms to take root and Hungarian-language literature to flourish.

Teleki was part of a long tradition of aristocratic women engaged in educational and charitable initiatives. Yet her activism, nationalism, and independence—she was unmarried and spurned social life—are nevertheless striking. Teleki's project proceeded with difficulty: the absence of money was a serious problem, and she also had trouble attracting potential students. Police spies reported that the aristocracy was suspicious of a school run by a woman, and the untitled nobility balked at the sizable annual tuition.[34] It did not help that the imperial-royal authorities would not allow Teleki to advertise the school in the newspapers, and an announcement appeared in one only after an oversight by the censor. She instead had to promote the school by word of mouth, and, although political leaders such as Deák and Kossuth promised to help, students appeared slowly.

Teleki's school opened in Pest in 1846 and had fourteen students in the following year. In spite of its small size, it had some very good teachers and a progressive curriculum. It also attracted the attention of Vienna, as Teleki humorously noted in a letter: "The miserable [authorities] are afraid that in a few years there will be a dozen more patriotic women in Hungary!"[35] The authorities' hostility stemmed from their open mistrust of Teleki's motives. A police informant reported that she had instilled her school with a "particular political direction" and turned it into a "nursery of newly-minted female patriots [*Patriotinnen*]."[36] Teleki's political orientation, it continued, was "a patriotic, Hungarian one, but purely oppositional in spirit and exceptionally exaggerated." Reviewing the evidence, the Hungarian Chancellery wrote to Emperor-King Ferdinand (r. 1835–48) that the school was extremely dangerous and that "the personality of Countess Teleki in no way offers the guarantee that is required in educational matters with regard to the common good." Vienna thus resolved to monitor the school closely and to intercede if necessary.

That the highest levels of the imperial-royal administration devoted so much attention to Teleki's small school gives an indication of Vienna's priorities in the years leading up to 1848. But their fears were not entirely misplaced. As an aristocrat and a woman, Teleki stood out in the national movement, and her school did win some converts to the Hungarian side. One former student enthusiastically wrote to Teleki, "In the future I will be such a excellent woman that you will be able to write me into the history of notable women, and I will Magyarize my village and then other villages."[37] Another student, a young baroness, wrote, "I realize that I was a Germanized girl but now I regret my errors." Teleki herself would continue to write and serve the Hungarian national cause, particularly during the 1848–49 Revolution. These activities would figure prominently in the government's trial of Teleki in 1852, which led to her imprisonment from 1853 to 1856.

Dance Floor Nationalism

Social and cultural life in urban Hungary, as elsewhere, revolved around the theater, concerts, dinner parties, and balls.[38] As in other Catholic countries, dancing in Buda-Pest reached its peak during Carnival and its endless succession of masked, charity, opera, and public balls. By all accounts, Hungary's upper classes were cosmopolitan, which meant that they aspired to dance the same dances, wear the same clothes, watch the same plays, and speak the same languages as their counterparts across Europe. This social life had as many critics as it had observers. Dr. Anton Jankovich, for instance, confirmed that fashions in the twin towns resembled those of Vienna, Paris, and other large cities.[39] As a medical doctor, Jankovich disapproved of the women's narrow shoes, garters, and corsets: the last he called a "prolific source of many ailments, and especially consumption [tuberculosis of the lungs]." More generally, he disapproved of the rampant luxury and wide social divisions that he observed at balls, parties, and concerts in the twin towns. From the 1830s onward, however, the most pointed criticisms came from the pens of Hungarian national activists, who railed against cosmopolitanism and championed national culture in all its forms.

The idea that social life in Buda-Pest should be more national spirited dated back to the eighteenth century and had peaked during the Diet of 1790–91. After growing more muted in the first decades of the nineteenth century, such appeals again found their voice with the hothouse development in the 1830s and 1840s of the local press and of "fashion magazines" (Modeblätter, divatlapok) in particular. The first Pest fashion magazine, Der Spiegel (The Mirror), appeared in 1828 and quickly won a large, devoted readership. Hungarian-language competitors soon followed. These papers were edited and, with few exceptions, written by men, yet they helped bring before the public questions deemed meaningful to women, including mixed marriages, education, and divorce. Their fashion plates, colored sketches, and advertisements popularized the latest fashions, and their society columns brought the latest news to a large reading public, thereby making closed balls and private dinners topics of public discussion. These reports were so popular that by the mid-1840s, political newspapers carried society columns as well.

National-minded journalists attached great importance to the Buda-Pest dance floor, which they repeatedly described as "foreign." The editor of the fashion magazine Pesti Divatlap (Pest Fashion Pages), Imre Vahot, recalled that, when he settled in Pest in 1838, the Hungarian language, dances, and dress were entirely forgotten. Vahot thus became a journalist in an effort "to destroy this dangerous cancer" in social life and, as much as his talents permitted, "to help achieve a fundamental improvement and transformation of society with respect to nationality."[40] In this spirit, journalists denounced tails, waltzes, and the use of German in society and lauded national costumes, dances, and the Hungarian language. The fashion papers directed many of their appeals at women, for they understood that women exercised considerable influence in social life, even if they were barred both from formal arenas of political power and from newer forms of male sociability, including numerous associations. Newspapers and national societies thus called on women to purchase domestic goods (especially textiles), to embrace national symbols (language, dances, and dress), and to display them in public, especially on the dance floor.

4—Pest tailor Ádám Kostyál's advertisement for his "National Ball Dress" (*Tudományos Gyüjtemény*, 1832).

The campaign to nationalize the dance floor yielded its first fruit in the 1830s. Color advertisements of distinctly Hungarian fashions appeared in a number of journals at this time. Typical was an 1832 engraving in *Tudományos Gyüjtemény,* which featured a local tailor's "National Ball Dress" for both men and women (fig. 4). According to another paper, fifty-three young men had signed a petition to make Hungarian the language of social life in Pest and to persuade women to support their cause.[41] Other articles proudly described the development of national dances and music. Many journalists expressed the hope that the younger, wealthier members of local society would take the lead in making social life more national spirited. The initial response to these pleas, however, was decidedly muted. At the National Casino Ball in 1833, a number of women apparently spoke Hungarian, but the dance floor was nearly empty when the ball opened with two Magyar dances. One paper imaginatively explained that the large crowds did not permit the "appropriate Asian, serious dignity" apparently required for such dances.[42] Other national activists were less forgiving, and many soon directed angry words at the aristocracy. Complaints ranged from the local tailor who grumbled that aristocrats ordered their clothes from London and Paris to the actress who accused them of attending the Pest German Theater with their wives while sending a few retainers or maids to sit in their boxes at the Hungarian National Theater.[43] They also took the aristocracy to task for spending too much of its time and money in Vienna. Such protests seem to have had little effect, and when the Buda and Pest women's charitable societies listed the annual donations of their roughly 1,500 members, four-fifths of women used the German form of their names, compared with only one-fifth who used the Hungarian form (the surname appears first in Hungarian).[44]

This made the breakthrough of the 1840s all the more remarkable. The 1843 carnival season may have been the turning point: the secret police certainly thought so.[45] The celebrated Zichy sisters, Antonia Batthyány (the wife of Lajos Batthyány, the future prime minister) and Karolina Károlyi, lent considerable support to this campaign, and they were joined by other members of the aristocracy. Young, attractive, and wealthy, the countesses strongly supported the national cause and were instrumental in popularizing Hungarian national fashions. Police informants excitedly reported that, at a ball in the Redoute Hall, "all eyes were directed on the two countesses, and if fashion exercises a greater influence than the law, then with their good example of fortifying the national spirit, they contribute more than a [National] Diet."[46] This was an exaggeration, yet it suggests the authority of aristocratic women in social life. Over the next few years, the sisters earned repeated mention in the press by wearing dresses made of Hungarian fabrics to the theater, at balls, and in the streets. Sándor Petőfi wrote a poem in honor of these "celestial apparitions."[47] But the Zichy sisters also had a very worldly sense of the dramatic word and gesture. For example, when they returned to Pest in

1847, large crowds gathered in the streets to cheer them. Seizing the moment, Karolina Károlyi led her three children to the balcony and loudly promised to raise them in a national spirit, which earned her even louder hurrahs.[48]

The nationalist campaign embodied by the Zichy sisters reached its apotheosis during the Protection Association Ball held on January 15, 1845. The ball was open only to members of the Association and their guests, who were invited to appear in national costumes or clothes cut of domestic cloth, with the understanding that "simplicity will be the main splendor of this national entertainment."[49] With the Protection Association's popularity reaching its peak, the announcement created great excitement, and people besieged the merchants of Pest, demanding silk, velvet, or simple cotton, which they took to tailors to be cut into dresses and suits. The ball itself was a smashing success. Hungarian flags and banners blanketed the ballroom, and almost 4,000 people from different social classes attended; only imperial-royal officials were noticeably absent. According to all reports, most guests appeared in Magyar dress. Police informants noted that aristocratic women "drew attention to themselves through their admirable *toilettes* and showed that the Protection Association in no way hinders luxury."[50] Moreover, forty to fifty women wore simple cotton dresses, making a virtue of the domestic manufacturers' and tailors' inability to keep up with demand. The nationalist press crowed that this was an entirely national-spirited ball, something one fashion magazine explained clearly: "If foreigners had seen this beautiful public flooding the rooms, they would easily have believed that we are all Magyars."[51]

The Protection Association Ball revealed the degree to which national activists had turned the upper classes' traditional cosmopolitanism on its head. Language was at the center of this transformation, and, at the Protection Association Ball, almost all the guests tried to speak Hungarian instead of French or German, as was common. In a short story revolving around the ball, an aristocratic young woman who speaks German is chided by her patriotic brother: "Here only a handful of immigrant Swabians speak German, and you'll be included among them if you speak it."[52] When she continues in German, he interrupts her: "Here gentlewomen only speak Hungarian, which is perfectly natural for women born in Hungary." Abashed, the young woman switches to Hungarian, "so that she would not be considered a burgher." As this story suggests, activists continued to hope that the largely cosmopolitan aristocracy would embrace the Hungarian language and lend its considerable social status to the national cause. This aristocratic imprimatur, it was believed, would send a powerful message to the status-conscious middle classes, many of whom spoke German as their first language. According the nationalist press, this campaign was making some headway, as many burghers and merchants were reportedly beginning to use Hungarian in social life.[53]

Language, however, was only one component of social life that nationalists wanted to change. Kossuth stated this clearly: "Language alone does not represent a nationality; rather, nationality lies in a people's language, customs, tastes, and judgments, in short, in every aspect of social life."[54] These customs, tastes and judgments, however, were often difficult to define precisely, and, in practice, it seems that "Hungarian" included most everything that was not German, French, or Austrian. Hungarian dress, for example, included both the national costumes and clothes cut in Western styles but made of domestic materials. Men wore either tails made by local tailors of homegrown silk or the dashing, martial national costume, which possessed a certain antiquity, but was largely reinvented by tailors in the 1830s and 1840s.[55] Women wore the national costume less frequently than men did, in part because women's clothing had always been much more strongly influenced by Parisian, Viennese, and Italian fashions. Many women attended the Protection Association Ball in this costume, yet the women who wore simple cotton dresses attracted just as much attention. Making a virtue of necessity, Vahot emphasized the simplicity of the national dress: "The most dazzling foreign clothing obscures the beauty of Hungarian women, while the national dress doubles their charms—nay, increases them a hundredfold! Seeing on your breasts cotton, silk and velvet of domestic make, it is impossible for us not see it as a protective armor—a protective breastplate defending your hearts against the desire for foreign things."[56] Even as it underscores the importance of women as national-minded consumers, the article, with its humorous, mock-chivalrous tone, gives a sense of how the press often formulated appeals to women.

Along with dress, national dances and music also came to dominate the ballrooms of Pest and other cities, especially when the ball was organized by a national society.[57] Previously, at least three-quarters of dances were waltzes, polkas, and French quadrilles. In contrast, the Protection Association's guests danced the Circle Dance, the Diet Csárdás, the Wreath Dance, the Protection Association Circle Dance, and even the Pannonia Waltz.[58] This dizzying array of dances represented the fruits of the nationalists' campaign to remake the dance floor. The csárdás was the most celebrated of these newly popular national dances. Széchenyi had helped make it acceptable in high society in the late 1830s, and it gradually took root in the following decade.[59] The dance itself probably grew out of village recruiting dances; its name derived from the peasant word for inn, and it summoned images of popular songs and the sorrowful tunes of the Hungarian plains. But, not all national dances had such rustic roots. One writer tartly attributed the popularity of the Circle Dance to its close resemblance to a fashionable French quadrille. It is also ironic that Hungarian national activists spurned the waltz, which had itself replaced the stilted, courtly minuet and was regarded suspiciously by the authorities in Vienna for the wild enthusiasm and close physical contact it inspired.

Musicians followed the lead of dancers. To show his support for the Protection Association, the leading composer of dance music, Márk Rózsavölgyi, dedicated a tune called "Protector of Industry" to the Zichy sisters.[60] Change on the dance floor came slowly, however, as the works of Johann Strauss, Josef Lanner, and other Viennese composers continued to be favorites at balls. The greatest gains instead came in the Hungarian National Theater. In 1844, the composer Ferenc Erkel presented his opera *László Hunyadi.* Erkel had written operas before, but this was the first to incorporate successfully Magyar folk elements into the music; the historical theme also gave it a decidedly national character. Contemporaries hailed the opera as a milestone for Hungarian music and proof that homegrown operas could compete with those by French or Italian composers. In the same year, Erkel also won a competition to orchestrate Ferenc Kölcsey's *Hymn,* which was destined to become Hungary's national anthem. The composition was first performed in the National Theater in July 1844. One critic praised its "Magyar character" and "grandeur," adding that the Hungarians should be proud of it, even if it was not the best anthem in the world.[61]

This wide array of songs, dances, and costumes raises obvious questions about the definition of what constituted national culture.[62] The standardization of the Hungarian language in the late eighteenth and early nineteenth centuries had required a great amount of innovation, yet language reformers could draw upon centuries of Hungarian-language literature. Fewer domestic traditions existed on the dance floor, however, and organizers thus disguised French dances as Hungarian ones and filled ballrooms with Moorish kiosks and tropical flowers to add an "Asiatic" atmosphere.[63] Moreover, it was often hard to define the national when it came to dress, especially because fashion magazines commonly showcased national fashions that had simply been lifted from the Viennese or Parisian fashion papers and partly redrawn. Similarly, national activists were divided on whether simplicity (the unadorned cotton dress) or luxury (the richly embroidered national costume) should be rewarded.

These uncertainties reflected a larger tension among Hungarian activists between their desire to develop a distinct national culture refashioned out of provincial, popular elements—the *csárdás,* folksongs, and national costumes—and their concurrent need to prove that Hungary was in the mainstream of European cultural developments. This ambivalence revealed itself in many areas of culture, including literature and music. In the Pest-Buda Music Society, a younger generation, which favored music by Hungarian composers (admittedly few in number), squared off against an older one, which wanted to perform the works of the great German composers and thereby develop a musically sophisticated public in Pest. With characteristic vehemence, the newspaper editor Adolf Frankenburg complained that the Music Society's concerts "were of such a perfect German physiognomy that it practically hurts the Magyar's heart."[64] As a result of these attacks, the Music Society resolved in 1844 to conduct its business in Hungarian alone, thus ending an eight-year tradition of German-Hungarian bilingualism. Yet this intolerant gesture could not change the fact that most of the society's performers were trained in German music and song and that it lacked the funds to sponsor new orchestral and choral works by domestic composers.

Gender also played a conspicuous role in these debates on national culture. The overwhelming popularity of national symbols and goods testifies to the rapid transformation of social and cultural life in the 1840s. As consumers, women were central to this process, but one should be careful about linking consumption and politics too closely. Women were becoming national-minded consumers at a time of increased trade and rising expectations as well as of growing income inequality and social uncertainty.[65] Contemporary writers thus displayed a marked ambivalence toward consumption, although they uniformly resolved this seeming dilemma by ascribing different roles in the national movement to men and women. For men, the goal was denial and self-discipline; the models were ancient Sparta, Benjamin Franklin, and the zealous politician Daniel Zeyk, who said "he would rather wear a shirt of iron than see one single thread of foreign linen on his back."[66] The models for women, on the other hand, were the Zichy sisters, who ostentatiously purchased Hungarian goods for display on and off the dance floor. Yet this dichotomy between (masculine) austerity and (feminine) consumption, like all such polarities, was neither stable nor universal. There is no question that by dancing the csárdás, speaking Hungarian, and wearing the national costume, women gained an embattled presence and an unprecedented visibility in public life in Buda-Pest.

Debates in the press and in the national societies did not change cultural practices overnight, but they did create new standards by which to judge later events. Activists may have differed on the specific qualities of national culture, but they spoke with one voice in their rejection of competing cultural traditions. Typical was the description of a ball held by the Sharpshooters' Club, which had many German-speaking burghers. In the words of a Hungarian-language fashion magazine, the ball appeared "as if it had remained 20 years in the past . . . the dance order was written in another language, all conversation flowed in a foreign language, and national dances were replaced by Styrian quadrilles."[67] Similarly, journalists who celebrated every Hungarian national ball reacted with outrage when other national groups in Buda-Pest organized similar events. Describing a Serb ball held in Pest, nationalist newspapers decried the "laughable fanaticism" of the participants, who spoken Serbian and danced Serb dances. These were "the dances of a foreign, disagreeable nation," explained one paper.[68] Not all Magyar leaders were so intolerant, but as these comments make plain, the dispiriting habit of calling natives "foreigners" had taken deep root in segments of the press.

The dance floor in Buda-Pest had many parallels in nineteenth-century Europe. Closely resembling their Hungarian counterparts, Czech nationalists in the 1840s also organized a series of national-spirited balls, which drew attention to the Czech language, dances, and costumes and were widely understood as political demonstrations.[69] Not everyone was willing to invest such balls with political meanings, but the dress, dances, and language undoubtedly allowed a large number of men and women usually excluded from public life to display their political allegiances. As Lynn Hunt has written about the French Revolution, "You could tell a good republican by how he dressed. The right dress was a sign of virtue, and dress in general made manifest the political character of the person."[70] For one night at least, the participants in national balls could feel more "Hungarian." In this way, the diffuse set of ideas, feelings, and allegiances connected with nineteenth-century liberalism and nationalism spread more widely in Buda-Pest. But the same symbols also functioned as border guards, and those caught on the wrong side of the boundary—German-speaking aristocrats, women in French fashions, Serbs on the dance floor—were subject to exclusion from the national and political communities.[71] By mid-century, nationalists had drawn a clear line between "us" and "them" on the dance floor.

Everyday Nationalism

How far into everyday life did these divisions run? In Gary Cohen's history of nineteenth-century Prague, he challenged the view that Czech- and German-speakers lived in separate worlds, voluntarily segregated from one another.[72] The Czech and later the German national movements, he showed, played an important role in the segregation of public life but had much less influence in neighborhoods, shops, offices, schools, and cafés, where encounters between different groups remained common. More generally, Rogers Brubaker and Frederick Cooper have warned that national categories can mask the ambiguity and fluidity of everyday life, with its bilingualism, social mobility, mixed marriages, and schools.[73] In many spheres of life, they stress, people simply remained indifferent to the claims of nationhood.

This was undoubtedly true of nineteenth-century Buda-Pest. Hungarian activists saw language as the foremost marker of nationhood, and by the 1840s, they could point with pride to the Scholarly Society, the National Theater, and the burgeoning Hungarian-language press. But they could not ignore the limited social reach of the Hungarian language. According to Baron Podmaniczky, only university students, county officials, writers, and some lawyers used Hungarian; aristocrats, he noted, were much more likely to speak German, as were Buda-Pest's shopkeepers, waiters, coachmen, drivers, and police. "If a Magyar came to Pest and did not know German," Podmaniczky concluded, "he was lost."[74] At most, bilingualism was on the rise, at least among the middle and upper classes, as more urban elites learned Hungarian. "Most people here [in Buda-Pest]," wrote Jankovich, "speak at least two languages; the higher estates even more, which the cohabitation of so many nations in the twin towns naturally brings with itself."[75] The guidebook writer G. L. Feldmann took this a step further: "To move around the different sections of the town, one must normally be able to speak and understand the four main languages—Hungarian, Slavic, German, and Latin—and everyone who wants to lay claim to an education speaks and understands them."[76] Even if few town dwellers were in fact such accomplished linguists, such observations suggest that patterns of everyday life in Buda-Pest could weather the storms of Hungarian nationalism. The literary historian Béla Pukánszky has written movingly about the towns' publishers and booksellers, who at once played an important role in the growth of Hungarian-language literature and journalism and at the same time nurtured their own traditions and the German language in their homes and private gatherings.[77]

The diary of Etelka Schlachta Szekrényessy allows us to look more closely at the question of everyday nationalism.[78] Schlachta grew up in Sopron, a small town in western Hungary with a largely German-speaking population. Her marriage to the nobleman József Szekrényessy brought her to Pest, where he worked as a lawyer and associational official (he was the secretary of the National Casino). Schlachta therefore came into contact with a wide range of writers and politicians, including Széchenyi, who was a friend of her husband. Schlachta's diary shows that she wholeheartedly (but not blindly) supported the Hungarian national movement. Incidental details in the diary also make it clear that Schlachta moved in a bilingual world. Although she kept her diary and published a newspaper article in Hungarian, she attended both the German and Hungarian theaters and subscribed to fashion magazines in both languages; conversations with friends, family, and servants moved easily between German and Hungarian. She disapproved of the *Pesther Tageblatt,* not because it was a German paper, but because of its conservative politics. One entry in particular hints at the complex interplay of language, opposition politics, and social status:

> On our return we went into Emich's [bookshop], and my gallant Jósi subscribed to *Honderű* [a Hungarian-language fashion magazine] for me; speaking Hungarian with each other, we had no difficulties in securing *Austria and Its Future,* which is forbidden. As I flipped through the booklet, the assistant, who was German but studying Hungarian with great industry, said [in German]: "Oh, this will hardly interest the lady—it is all calculations." But of course! I was speaking Hungarian! Here [in town] the usual Hungarian speakers are all birdbrains and the like, how could a serious, above all scholarly political work interest them?[79]

To the traveler J. G. Kohl, it was simply the case that, in Hungary, German was the mark of an educated person (the way French was in his native Saxony), so that even Hungarian nationalists felt ashamed if they did not know it.[80]

Schlachta's account again reveals the uneven impact of the Hungarian national movement on everyday life. But there is also the curious detail of Schlachta's first name, Etelka. Etelka was the heroine of András Dugonics's eponymous novel of 1788, the daughter of the ninth-century chieftain Árpád and "a pure Hungarian maiden." That Dugonics had in fact invented Etelka did nothing to dampen the enthusiasm for the book or the name, which many parents gave their daughters in the following decades. And this was only one of many distinctly "Hungarian" names drawn from the distant (and often imaginary) past: for girls, there was Jolán, Tünde, and Csilla (all of them created by writers around 1800); for boys, Béla, Gyula, and Zoltán. The historian István Horvát was among the first to call his son Árpád, which apparently started a craze for this name as well.

It is difficult to generalize about parents' motives in these cases. The same is true of people who changed their surnames. Name changes had traditionally been reserved for burghers who obtained a patent of nobility; in the nineteenth century; however, a growing number of writers and professionals with German- or Slavic-sounding surnames adopted more Hungarian-sounding ones.[81] The imperial-royal authorities disapproved of the practice and attempted to regulate it, but this had little effect. Nor did the censure of writers such as Eduard Glatz, who bitterly wrote, "Magyarize your names, you German renegades!"[82] The average number of official name changes thus rose from six per year in the 1830s to fifty-five in the 1840s.[83] These included the linguist Pál Hunfalvy, the son of a farmer named Hunsdorfer, as well as the composer Márk Rózsavölgyi, who had been born Marcus Rosenthal in a merchant family. Rosenthal/Rózsavölgyi was of Jewish origin, as were roughly one-fifth of all those who adopted Magyar names. To varying degrees, careerism, youthful enthusiasm, and a desire for social status likely motivated the artists, writers, and scholars who took new surnames. One did not need to have an *echt* Magyar name to be a national activist—Adolf Frankenburg is a good example here—but the trend, no matter how limited, toward Hungarian-sounding names for children and adults points to the ways in which national loyalty could enter the domestic sphere.

A number of national activists found other ways to demonstrate their convictions in everyday life. The woman with the red, white, and green hat described earlier is but one example. Others showed their colors by disparaging the German language: a British visitor to Pest recorded that "Magyars will sometimes affect a foreign accent when speaking German, or pretend not to understand some German words."[84] Kohl likewise related a humorous anecdote about one die-hard nationalist who took exception to a catalogue of the Pest Arts Society, which had descriptions of its paintings in

German and Hungarian on facing pages.[85] Shouting, "Why is German still published in Hungary?" the young man angrily began to tear the German pages out of the book, only slowly realizing that he was also removing the Hungarian text on the opposite side. For more sensible nationalists, the Pest merchant Bernát Weisz sold handkerchiefs adorned with pictures of Hungarian political leaders (such as Kossuth and Deák), along with many other domestic products.[86]

Other supporters of the national cause followed the example of the National Casino and displayed their loyalties at the table. András Fáy, for example, refused to serve foreign wines at his house in Pest's Inner City.[87] Indeed, from the 1830s onward, there was even an association in Pest dedicated to making Hungarian wines better known both at home and abroad. Buda-Pest's hoteliers and restaurateurs likewise recognized that a touch of Hungarianness could be good for business. Kohl remarked favorably on the Hungarian music he heard in Pest's hotels, as well as on the prevalence of paprika-flavored dishes: "Only bread is not yet baked with paprika," he added.[88] (A distinctive Hungarian cuisine would emerge only in the latter part of the nineteenth century.) Kohl also observed window shades decorated with the Hungarian coat of arms; red, white, and green sofas and chairs; and servants dressed in the same national colors. He also might have mentioned the popularity of the word "national," which preceded everything from the "First National Swimming School" to the "National Tie Shop."

Superficially at least, the Hungarian national movement was rapidly moving from the margins to the mainstream. A contemporary traveler stated that "a feeling of nationality" had "taken deep, firm and widely-spreading root" in Pest. "Every detail of daily life among the Hungarians, however insignificant it may be, seems, somehow or other, stamped with the impress of this national feeling; and nothing can be done, no word spoken, that is not to some degree marked with it."[89] The secret police apparently concurred. "The nationality of the town of Pest is changing at a stormy tempo," wrote an informant in 1844.[90] According to the report, the Hungarian language was gaining daily, especially among younger people and among women who had previously never uttered a word of Hungarian. With every advance of Hungarian, it seemed that booksellers sold fewer German books, German newspapers lost subscribers, and German theaters struggled to fill seats. By the 1840s, Johann Csaplovics was critical of a Hungarian national movement he had once supported. Yet his description of Buda-Pest testifies to its success: "It is remarkable how many Germans here are ashamed of their honorable German origins; and although they know the [German] language quite well, they do not like to speak it with foreigners and would rather be taken for born Magyars."[91]

What do these many details tell us about national life in Buda-Pest? As Lynn Hunt, Iuri Lotman, and other scholars have shown, under certain circumstances, everyday practices (drinking tea, playing cards, and smoking) and language (forms of address and place names) could take on political meanings.[92] In Buda-Pest, men and women inventively used a wide range of symbols and gestures to demonstrate their support for the national cause. Although such displays testify to the real dynamism of the Hungarian national movement, caution is called for when attempting to measure its impact on everyday life in Buda-Pest. Many residents of the twin towns remained immune to the charms of nationalism, and, in their choice of food, dress, amusements, and names, they closely resembled urban dwellers elsewhere in Habsburg Central Europe. The picture that emerges is one in which the impressive advances made by the Hungarian side in literary and public life were not immediately matched by corresponding changes in everyday encounters in the twin towns. There were hints that this might someday happen. For now, however, it was on the dance floor and in cultural life, much more than in houses and neighborhoods, that the Hungarian national movement had its greatest and most lasting impact.

In closing this survey of cultural politics in Buda-Pest, it is tempting to return to the era's fashion magazines, which tirelessly championed the national cause. A good example of this can be seen in an article by Imre Vahot that appeared in *Pesti Divatlap* on October 14, 1844. Describing Buda-Pest as it might appear on October 1, 1950, Vahot presented a thinly veiled catalogue of contemporary complaints in the unimaginative form of describing the distant future.[93] The overall theme is straightforward: by the mid-twentieth century, instead of two nationalities, only one—the Hungarian—will dominate Buda-Pest. The entire population, from countesses to ordinary citizens, will speak Hungarian and only rarely will one hear "foreign" languages in the streets, theaters, schools, or churches: "German sermons will be held in the capital's churches now and again for the sake of a few very old people." Fashions and dances will likewise be exclusively Hungarian. The city's reading public, lukewarm to Hungarian-language publications a century and a half ago, will avidly support thirty Hungarian newspapers, and there will be only one German paper, primarily for foreign visitors. Not all the demands directly addressed national issues: mid-twentieth-century Budapest would also be a cleaner, healthier, and safer city, and one in which poets might buy palaces (wishful thinking!) and people take trains through the Buda Hills. But the national transformation of the towns would be complete, and, by 1950, "one will somehow be able to learn that Budapest was once German only from the German inscriptions on the scarcely legible gravestones in the cemeteries, and our capital can say with proud confidence to the homeland and the nation: 'I am proud that you named me the head and center of Hungary.'"

It would be easy to dismiss this article as yet another piece of journalistic bombast, because national-minded writers in the 1840s frequently scaled rhetorical heights in the hopes of catching their readers' attention.

Not every supporter of the national cause shared Vahot's views. Etelka Schlachta characterized his writings as "arrogant."[94] Nevertheless, it is worth thinking about this article seriously, not for its pedestrian prophesies (many of which would in fact come true), but because it reveals an important facet of "Hungarian Buda-Pest." With Vahot, there is little emphasis on the improvements favored by Széchenyi or the liberalism of the national societies; instead, cultural and linguistic homogeneity are the hallmarks of his urban vision. To Vahot, the Hungarian cause must triumph in every aspect of urban life, no matter what the cost. Vahot was not the first to express such views, but by the 1840s he and other like-minded nationalists had introduced a sharper, more intolerant tone into Buda-Pest's newspapers. In the years that followed, young national activists would carry this xenophobia into the streets as well.

CHAPTER FIVE

Streets and Squares

"Among the debris, ruined houses, ice floes, furniture, beams, and every other obstacle, one could scarcely pass through the narrow streets and only with the most intense effort; . . . everywhere the tottering buildings and collapsing roofs threatened destruction. . . . Only the screams and already hoarse cries for help from those in despair occasionally overwhelmed the thunderous, cracking, rattling noise. One wanted and needed to go in ten directions at once, but could only go in one; one could see hundreds of people in danger and only help one-third and leave the others in the mouth of death; one had to turn back fathers and husbands whose children were already in the boats filled to overflowing and listen to their howls and sobs.

—Baron Miklós Wesselényi, March 14, 1838[1]

Tame today, the Danube River was wild and unpredictable in the nine-teenth century. Floods were a common occurrence, and the one that struck the twin towns in 1838 would be long remembered. Dams protecting Pest from the Danube had given way in the night, and by day large parts of the town were under five to eight feet of water.[2] Warning signs had been appearing for months, as thick blocks of ice downstream had slowly choked the flow of the Danube. Buda, which had no protection against the river, had already flooded several times. Some residents had evacuated Pest, but most remained, wholly unprepared for the terrible destruction in mid-March. It was the worst flood on record—the river rose nearly thirty feet above normal—and it would be weeks before the water retreated. The flood killed 151, and more would have died had it not been for the efforts of people like Wesselényi. At its height, the flooding forced 50,000 from their homes. Fully half of Pest's buildings collapsed, and another quarter were badly damaged; shoddily built houses in the outer districts crumpled by the hundreds, while the more solid structures in Leopold District tended to survive. In monetary terms, the flooding caused nearly 15 million florins of damage in Pest and 2 million more in Buda.

Some observers initially feared that this was a blow from which Pest might not recover. But most were hopeful. "Pest is not lost, Pest will revive with new prosperity, new joy," shouts a character in a novel by Mór Jókai, echoing popular sentiments in the aftermath of the flooding.[3] According to Baron Podmaniczky, the catastrophe captured the attention of millions of people across the Hungarian lands, who subsequently followed developments in Pest with unflagging interest.[4] Donations poured in from far and wide, and Vienna instructed the state bank to loan the towns 3 million florins at low interest. Franz Liszt returned to Hungary for the first time since his childhood to play a benefit concert for the victims of the floods. Under Palatine Joseph's leadership, committees were established to distribute funds and to introduce a new building code for Buda-Pest. This code, the first of its kind in Hungary, set standards for the height of buildings, the thickness of their walls, and procedures for construction. In a nod to public health, it mandated that all houses have at least three rooms and a privy and also banned basement apartments, which were uniformly dank and dark. Predictably, builders often ignored these regulations in the boom that followed. Within four years, well over 1,000 new buildings sprang up in Pest, largely erasing the damage caused by the flood.

Pest rebuilt shed much of its provincial character: the cows and chickens, the low houses, and the winding streets in the center.[5] It was a more "urban" in the sense of having more traffic, fewer empty lots, an emerging factory district, and more monumental buildings. As foreign visitors approvingly noted, Pest was coming to resemble other European cities. But this development did not please all supporters of the Hungarian national cause. Just months after the flood, Bertalan Szemere, who had recently returned from a tour of Western Europe, published a brief but sweeping plan for the reconstruction of Pest.[6] For Szemere, a serious young nobleman from the provinces, the reconstructed city should showcase the Magyars' sophistication and achievements. Szemere wanted more greenery, with grass, trees, and bushes in the squares and with parks ringing the entire city. In the center, arcades would protect pedestrians from rain, and sewers would carry away water and waste. More broadly, a revived Embellishment Commission would develop a plan for streets and neighborhoods and employ architects to design the façades of new buildings (owners would be allowed to dispose of interiors as they saw fit). This top-down urbanism would favor the arts over commerce: "The nation would put everyone in his place; the genius would change places with the 'bungler' [nonguild artisan]." Szemere was confident that the outcome would be something uniquely Hungarian, no matter whether Pest became "an exclusively Hungarian capital, or a world city, which combines the features of all cities."

Szemere's recommendations illustrate perfectly the mix of ambition and ambivalence with which many national leaders regarded Pest. The ambition is easily explained: all agreed that Pest should be a great city, comparable to the capitals of Western Europe. At the same time, however, they also wanted the twin towns to be more manifestly Hungarian, meaning that their public spaces and monumental buildings should somehow reflect the national character. The ensuing attempts to fuse Western mod-els with domestic traditions often produced divisions among activists. It also exposed their ambivalence toward Pest. With few exceptions, the Hungarian leaders were nobles with close links to their home counties. These origins at times showed themselves in the nobility's mistrust or ig-norance of certain aspects of urban life: Szemere's vision of a park-filled city of geniuses leaves suspiciously little room for economic activity and overlooks the towns' pressing social problems. Even among the Hungarian activists who lived full-time in Pest, one often detects an emphasis on style over substance, culture over commerce, and representative architec-ture over required infrastructure.

The same national activists had no qualms about politicizing public space. Fired by the broad vision of a "Hungarian Buda-Pest," they invested street signs, bridges, and buildings with political and national meanings. In this, Hungarian nationalists were hardly unique: a similar impulse had driven the French revolutionaries to rename the Notre Dame Cathedral in Paris the "Temple of Reason" and animated German activists who turned the unfinished Gothic cathedral in Cologne into a symbol of German na-tionhood and unification.[7] In Rome, postunification governments used monuments, road construction, street names, and festivals in their strug-gle to turn Rome into a demonstrably Italian, rather than papal, city.

In Buda-Pest, national activists again found support for their cause in existing political institutions (the National Diet and Pest County), in a civil society built on newspapers and voluntary associations, and in local university students, a new but willful ally. Yet the Hungarian side had to contend with imperial-royal, religious, and local leaders who organized public celebrations, commissioned new buildings, and made key decisions concerning urban development. Until his death in 1847, Palatine Joseph remained an important force in local affairs and continued to support a wide range of cultural and economic initiatives. For example, Joseph en-couraged the construction of a Vienna-Pest railway to spur commerce, sway public opinion, and deflect attention away from more inflammatory issues.[8] The result was a series of skirmishes over the design, use, and meaning of public space. These struggles laid bare the continued tension between the two sides, as well as between the practical and symbolic func-tions of the city.

St. Stephen in Buda

Nineteenth-century writers often described Buda as a town frozen in time. "Ofen [Buda] has remained nearly unchanged for several centuries," re-marked Dr. Anton Jankovich in 1838.[9] Such characterizations ignored Buda's steadily growing population, expanding outer districts, and new buildings. By mid-century, Buda had well over 40,000 residents, which made it one of Hungary's largest towns.[10] The perception of immutability had everything to do with Buda's relationship to Pest, and contemporary writers never tired of describing the towns in binary terms: old/new, unchanging/dynamic, quiet/loud, serene/brash and even male/female (thus Jókai, "beautiful, young, Pest, the teenage bride-to-be of Buda, this old war veteran").[11] But it also stemmed from the varying uses of public space, and both locals and outsiders agreed that Buda—and its Castle District in particular—remained the ceremonial center of the twin towns.

No event illustrated this better than St. Stephen's Day (August 20), today one of the most important national holidays in Hungary. As Hungary's first Christian king, Stephen (r. 997–1038) had done much to spread Roman Christianity among his subjects. Sainthood followed just decades after his death: the canonization of temporal rulers in recently converted lands was a common means of strengthening the church. It was Maria Theresa, however, who helped create St. Stephen's Day in the eighteenth century. Although she is known for dramatically reducing the number of Catholic festivals as part of her effort to make her subjects more hardworking, the pious empress sent the right hand of St. Stephen to Buda and ordered that the holy relic be carried in procession on the saint's feast day. All work was to cease and Catholics had to attend mass. St. Stephen's Day took root slowly, but with Palatine Joseph's active support, it grew into one of the most impressive religious holidays in Hungary, yearly celebrated with devotion and solemnity.[12] In 1818, Emperor-King Francis again decreed that Catholics across the kingdom should observe the feast day.

By the 1820s, the St. Stephen's Day celebration in Buda had become a lavish, theatrical festival rich in royal and religious symbols. The high point of the celebration was the procession bearing the relic. It began at the chapel in the royal palace and ended at the Buda Parish Church (known today as the Matthias Church), where the Archbishop of Esztergom, Hungary's prince-primate, displayed the relic and said mass.[13] First in the procession were the guilds with the banners of their trades; then came elementary, secondary, and university students with their teachers and professors. Monastic and parish priests followed, with town officials on their heels: first the burghers of the outer councils and after them the magistrates of the inner councils. Next came county, judicial, and imperial-royal officials, along with the heads of the university. They were followed by the Archbishop of Esztergom with a large contingent of priests and four deacons bearing the hand of St. Stephen in a silver and crystal box. Behind them came the Palatine and other Habsburgs, accompanied by soldiers and the burgher militias, whose officers marched with drawn swords. The procession was an inspiring sight, as the clerical *Nemzeti Ujság (National Newspaper)* reported: "There is something heart-stirring in a national holiday, and exalted feelings involuntarily fill our breasts, to which the religious rituals send forth a divine ointment."[14] More prosaically, the procession and mass were followed by a day of feasting and games for the population of the towns.

The procession not only showed the ruling house in its full glory, but also revealed the corporate order upon which it rested, as Catholic priests, imperial-royal officials, county nobles, and burghers all played a part in the festivities. It was a cultural performance in which the city "represented itself to itself," meaning that it literally displayed the social and political hierarchy of the city for all to see.[15] The alliance of throne, town, and altar was spatially illustrated in the procession's route from the royal palace to the Buda parish church and in the close proximity of the archbishop and the archduke in the procession. Lest this ideology be lost on anyone, sermons reinforced the imagery with words. In 1839, for example, the priest Aloys Roder described "the Christian burgher" as a person who loves his fatherland, obeys the ruler and his laws, and esteems Christian religion and morality. "Religion," he preached, "is the keystone of the great building of the state and the foundation of all civic order and welfare." The citizens must not only obey the king, but also his subordinates, "and whoever becomes a criminal by disobeying them is a criminal against the Prince himself and bears witness against the divine order."[16]

At the same time, however, the procession concealed as much as it revealed. Although Buda-Pest in the 1840s was still an overwhelmingly Catholic city, its residents included a growing number of non-Catholics. This change was most striking in Pest, which had been almost uniformly Catholic at the turn of the nineteenth century. By the late 1840s, Pest had more than 10,000 Jews and 5,000 Protestants, who, when added to the town's 1,000 Eastern Orthodox, comprised nearly 20 percent of the total population.[17] In physical terms, people walking through Pest in the 1840s would see six Catholic, one Calvinist, one Lutheran, and two Orthodox churches, and if they entered the Orczy House in Theresa District, they would also find two Jewish temples.

Whether the urban population was becoming more secular is harder to quantify. As in other parts of Europe, much of the population was likely to be devout, but among the upper strata of society, both open skepticism and frank displays of religiosity were equally uncommon. Religious language and loyalties nonetheless played a meaningful role in the Hungarian national movement. Contemporaries routinely invoked "the God of the Magyars" (a Magyarok Istene) to bless their endeavors.[18] Religion could be divisive, and Széchenyi warned that the "demon of confessional jealousy" had doomed many associations from the start.[19] But there is evidence that religious differences were slowly losing their salience, at least among the upper classes. Marriages between Catholics and Protestants were increasingly common. The Lutheran Kossuth, for example, had a Catholic wife. Similarly, many voluntary associations brought together Catholics and Protestants (if not Jews) with few apparent tensions.

Hungarian national activists thus felt little connection to the religious festivities in Buda. Journalists often described Easter Monday, Pentecost Monday, and other religious holidays humorously, poking fun at local traditions and behaviors. The authors' condescending tone is a reminder of the social and cultural gap between the commoners who attended these religious festivals and the generally well-born, educated supporters of the Hungarian national movement. By the 1840s, St. Stephen's Day had also come under criticism. Writers carefully avoided references to the Habsburgs or the Catholic Church, and instead disputed the claim that St. Stephen's Day was a national celebration. "Why do we call this a national holiday," asked one newspaper in 1842, "when it is hardly celebrated, except by the Catholics of Buda and Pest?"[20] More pointedly, it continued, how could it be called a Hungarian national celebration when the German element predominated so strongly? Another paper suggested that as part of the festivities, the newly minted Hungarian national anthem should be sung alongside the *Gott erhalte,* the imperial anthem.[21] Although national activists were happy to see the residents of the twin towns showing such enthusiastic devotion to the first king of Hungary, they grumbled, in one paper's words, that "German voices and speech bang the ears, so that the entire feast honoring the first Hungarian king has more the character of an Upper Austrian procession than a national one."[22]

A measure of frustration shaped these words. For decades, the nationalist press and political leaders had called upon churches and temples to introduce the Hungarian language into their services.[23] But the gains in Buda-Pest had been few and far between. Catholic priests continued to say masses in Latin and give their sermons in German, although Hungarian and Slovak homilies could also be heard in Pest. The most famous preacher of the 1820s and 1830s was the Franciscan Stanislaus Albach. Kazinczy called him the "darling of Pest" and noted that his sermons drew peasants and aristocrats alike.[24] Széchenyi had great respect for Albach but disapprovingly added, "He has no Hungarian feeling—entirely German." The critic Bajza glumly wished that the Hungarian side had its own Albach.

The tide slowly began to turn in the 1830s. The National Diet strengthened the Hungarian cause when it passed laws in 1836 and then again in 1840, requiring all religious congregations to keep records of births, deaths, and marriages in Hungarian.[25] The Diet also ordered that within three years clergymen of all faiths know Hungarian, although it did not spell out how this would be measured or enforced. In the 1840s, the Diet opened earnest discussions on how best to introduce the Hungarian language into all Catholic and Protestant elementary schools. Because most Calvinists were Hungarian-speakers, "Protestant" in this case really meant Lutherans, many of whom spoke German or Slovak. But the Lutherans also included several influential Hungarian national activists, such as Count Károly Zay, who in 1840 was appointed inspector-general of the Lutheran church in Upper Hungary. Declaring that his goal was "the Magyarization of our country," Zay immediately ordered that all church correspondence be in Hungarian instead of Latin and proposed that Hungarian be the language of instruction in all Lutheran schools.[26] More ambitiously, Zay wanted to unite Hungary's Calvinist and Lutheran churches, reasoning that a similar union had earlier taken place in Prussia. Zay's proposals were never implemented, in part because they aroused great opposition among Slovak activists, who saw this as a thinly veiled attempt to Magyarize forcibly Hungary's Germans and Slavs. Széchenyi also spoke out against Zay and his program. But his was increasingly a minority view, and many participants in the debates, both Magyars and Slovaks, agreed on one cardinal point, namely, that churches and schools could be used to nationalize the population.

These heated exchanges emboldened a range of nationalists in Buda-Pest. The Lutheran minister Jan Kollár thought in terms of broad Slavic solidarity rather than narrow Slovak nationalism. Yet, in the wake of Zay's actions, he and his followers seceded from the larger, trilingual (German-Hungarian-Slovak) Lutheran community in Pest to form an exclusively Slovak-speaking congregation. By the mid-1840s, the once-united Lutheran church had splintered into three separate congregations: the German with 4,800 members, the Slovak with 1,260, and the Hungarian with 1,025.[27] The Hungarian side had earlier secured a victory of their own. In 1840, Pest's Calvinist congregation decided to stop holding regular services in German, thereby bringing to an end a bilingual tradition that stretched back a quarter century.[28] The Hungarian language also made inroads in Pest's Jewish community in the 1840s. At the same time, a number of Catholic priests began to take part in the Hungarian national societies and to champion the Hungarian language. One of the most visible—and, to Vienna, the most worrisome—was Antal Kronperger, a retired military chaplain and for a time an outspoken supporter of the national cause.[29] As a member of the Industrial Association, he gave free Hungarian lessons to German-speaking apprentices; a police informant later accused him of "contemptible behavior" when he used his contacts in the army to recruit new members for the Protection Association.

But Kronperger was atypical, and most Catholic leaders kept their distance from the Hungarian national movement. Indeed, when liberal members of the National Diet, a group that included many Catholics, broached the question of "mixed" (Catholic-Protestant) marriages, the church hierarchy reacted with alarm. The issue would not be fully settled until the 1890s. For the time being, church leaders began to muster their political forces, urging prelates to participate actively in the National Diets and the lower clergy to take part in county assemblies. They also mobilized Catholics in the realm of civil society, an arena they had formerly neglected. In 1841, the director of the Pest seminary, Ferenc Szaniszló, launched *Religio és Nevelés (Religion and Education)*, the first modern Catholic newspaper.[30] In 1845, Sándor Lipthay, a newspaper editor sympathetic to Catholic interests, founded a new voluntary association, the Assembly for the Common Good, the political conservatives' answer to the predominantly national-liberal social clubs of Pest.[31] The society's 600-plus members included aristocrats, wealthy merchants, imperial-royal officials, and a large number of Catholic priests, a sure sign that it had the endorsement of the church hierarchy. Even Kronperger was brought into line and became the society's director. The church took another decisive step with the Society for the Dissemination of Good and Cheap Books, which it launched in 1848 with more than 1,000 members. This later became the Society of St. Stephen, one of the most influential associations for popular education in the late nineteenth century.

The shift from St. Stephen's Day, a religious festival, to the Society of St. Stephen, a Catholic voluntary association, was a meaningful one. St. Stephen's Day had once brought together the population of Buda-Pest. As late as the 1830s, Dr. Jankovich had suggested that Catholic festivals were properly observed by "the young and old of all estates and of all confessions," adding that he had not witnessed any signs of intolerance between the towns' different religious communities.[32] By the 1840s, however, this sense of unity had been lost, as national activists began to distance themselves from celebrations they thought were too "popular" and said were too "German." If, as Lynn Hunt has suggested, "legitimacy is the general agreement on signs and symbols," the criticisms of St. Stephen's Day can be read as a challenge to the social and political order on display.[33] Their insistence that the towns' religious communities use the Hungarian language likewise challenged the status quo. But the national agitation had some unintended, if foreseeable, consequences. By founding a Slovak-speaking Lutheran congregation, Kollár showed himself to be both an imitator and a competitor to the Magyars. Similarly, although the Catholic leadership rejected the liberal elements of the nationalists' reform program, they showed a remarkable readiness in the 1840s to borrow organizational techniques from the Hungarian activists: associations, newspapers, and even political mobilization in the Diets and assemblies. By the end of the decade, this increasingly contentious public life had overshadowed religious processions in Buda.

Pest, Classical and Imagined

The journalist, poet, librarian, and associational officer, János Garay was a talented portraitist of Buda-Pest. The son of a provincial merchant, Garay was one of thousands of young men who had come to Pest to seek their fortune. In a newspaper article entitled "Street Life," Garay documented a typical day in the center of his adopted city.[34] The streets of Pest were barely watered and swept before people began to pour in from the outer districts: first milkmaids, servants, and peasants laden with produce, flour, chickens, and other products for sale at market. Porters meanwhile opened their houses and café owners made breakfast for the legions of unmarried journeymen and servants. The streets grew louder as they filled with cursing coachmen, bellowing peddlers, and even an Italian selling plaster models who shouted *"figuretti, figuretti."* The poor ate at stalls in the marketplace around 10 a.m., just as the well-to-do made their first appearance. After the shops closed at noon, unmarried lawyers, doctors, journeymen, and students raced to restaurants, and married men went home for lunch. The *beau monde* spent the afternoon strolling, shopping, and visiting, while working people returned to their stalls, workshops, and stores. As dusk approached, the poor tiredly left the center of town, while elegant men gathered on street corners or sauntered to the casino, theaters, or coffeehouses. A final rush came when the Pest theaters let out, but afterward the streetlights illuminated only the occasional straggler. After midnight the streets were empty.

Behind the rich detail, Garay's sketch conveys several generic characteristics of urban life. In the careful dance between rich and poor, moving together but rarely touching, one can discern the spatial and temporal differentiation of social classes. More than in other large cities, Buda-Pest's upper and lower classes still lived in the same neighborhoods and buildings; only the sprawling suburbs (save Leopold District) belonged exclusively to the poor. Similarly, if his use of words like "chaos," "din," and "crowd" reflect common impressions of urban life, Garay's mention of "legions of unmarried men" and "nameless men" are a reminder of its anonymity. Like many writers before him, Garay also compared the city to a theater: "although the players and scenes come on and off the stage every minute, the seats never remain empty for a moment from early morning until late in the evening."[35] Garay's description, in short, gives a sense of what contemporaries called "great-city life" *("nagyvárosi élet").* It is no coincidence that this period also saw the appearance of the first detailed foreign-language guidebooks, which catalogued the twin towns' horse races, fancy shops, hotels, ice-cream parlors, baths, and theaters. All the major Pest newspapers had regular columns with names like "News from the Capital," "Budapest Diary," and "Budapest Observer," which touched on everything from lotteries, gambling, and murders to balls, concerts, and plays.

Pest's growth awakened both pride and concern. By the late 1840s, the town had nearly 100,000 residents, making it twice as large as the next biggest city in Hungary.[36] By some measures, only St. Petersburg and several English and American cities had faster growth rates. Contemporaries spoke of a "second Vienna" and "London on the Danube."[37] Yet rapid urbanization characterized much of Central Europe during this period, as could be seen in Vienna, Berlin, Prague, Breslau, and other urban centers. As in other cities, immigration fueled Pest's growth, especially in the outer districts, where the population more than tripled between 1810 and 1848. The number of houses grew more slowly, and, although many new two- and three-story buildings sprang up, there was also much crowding and, in the eyes of the authorities, social problems on an unprecedented scale.

Traveler J. C. von Thiele called Buda "El Dorado" and said that Pest offered "every attraction of life," but also described hordes of beggars and street children: "Some steal, others are sent by their negligent elders and made to beg, some have a great skill in arousing compassion in passers-by."[38] In the early 1830s, Pest and then Buda banned begging in the streets, and in the 1840s the police forcibly evicted thousands of people from Pest each year, but to little avail.[39] More and more poor people lived in Pest, and their numbers surged when there was an economic downturn in the city or hunger in the countryside.

Along with crowding, rapid movement was another novel aspect of city life. During this period, Pest cemented its position as the commercial, communications, and transportation center of Hungary. Stagecoaches and the mail reached more cities and moved more quickly: the trip from Buda-Pest to Vienna dropped from fifty hours in the 1820s to between eighteen and twenty hours two decades later. Steamships were just as fast and could carry even more passengers and goods. The first steamship made the journey between Vienna and Pest in 1817, and regular traffic developed in the 1830s. The Danube Steamship Society had ten steamships in 1837 and forty-one a decade later. In 1846, steamships carried more than 900,000 passengers.[40] Already in 1836, the Hungarian National Diet passed a law guaranteeing that Pest would be the center of Hungary's future railway network. The first railroad appeared a decade later, with a modest twenty-mile run up the Danube from Pest to Vác; a sixty-mile link to Szolnok opened the following year (and just in time, because it would aid the revolutionary government's flight from the city in late 1848). Within the city itself, hundreds of carriages for hire plied the streets. British travelers compared them favorably to London cabs; locals expressed concern about the reckless driving of carriages belonging to nobles, which fell outside the jurisdiction of the town authorities. Horse-drawn omnibuses were another novelty and famed for their crowding. "They resemble a coop in which the chickens are packed together to the point of bursting," noted one contemporary.[41] That fewer than half the streets in the twin towns were paved did little to ease the flow of traffic.

To many observers, the most obvious measure of the towns' development was the bridge connecting Buda and Pest. Following the expulsion of the Ottomans in 1686, the towns had been connected by a "flying bridge," which was little more than a ferry that swung back and forth across the river on a stout cable fixed to both banks. In 1767, the Royal Treasury built a pontoon bridge by laying long planks over forty boats anchored in the Danube. Over the years, the pontoon bridge became a landmark of old Buda-Pest, and some writers fondly recalled its carved image of St. John Nepomuk, a fourteenth-century Bohemian saint martyred when he was thrown off a Prague bridge.[42] Foreign visitors admired the bridge's ingenuity but worried about crossing it. The pontoon bridge, it was becoming increasingly clear, had serious drawbacks: it had to be dis-

5—The Chain Bridge across the Danube, with Buda's Castle District in the background. This inventive engraving is from 1845, four years before the bridge actually opened to traffic.

mantled during the winter when the Danube froze; it could not easily accommodate the growing traffic between Buda and Pest; it sloped dangerously during the summer, when the water level fell; and it was repeatedly damaged and could break up in strong currents and storms. Detractors also complained about the tolls, which commoners paid but nobles and citizens of the towns did not. In this way, a growing number of people came to see the bridge as an impediment to, rather than as an instrument of, the towns' economic progress.

Serious discussions about a permanent bridge over the Danube started under Joseph II, but the issue caught fire only in the 1820s.[43] Count István Széchenyi was again the spark: on a winter's day in 1821, after ice had prevented him from crossing to the Buda side for his father's funeral, Széchenyi swore to a friend that he would give a year's income for the construction of a bridge over the Danube. He took up the matter again in the late 1820s and by 1832 had formed a voluntary association, the Budapest Bridge Society, to promote the construction of a permanent bridge. Széchenyi then traveled at his own expense to western Europe to gather technical and financial details on bridge construction. At the National Diet of 1832–36, Széchenyi fought for the bridge over the fierce objections of the Buda and

Pest Town Councils, which did not want to give up their substantial toll revenues from the pontoon bridge. Széchenyi's solution that all people crossing the bridge, including nobles, would have to pay a toll caused an uproar in the Diet. The fight for the bridge thus became a struggle to end (at least symbolically) the nobility's exemption from taxes. It is a measure of not only the opposition's growing strength, but also the broad consensus behind Széchenyi's initiative, that, when the Diet finally passed a law in 1836 authorizing the construction of the bridge, it ordered that tolls would be collected from everyone, including nobles. Palatine Joseph soon appointed a joint-stock company to supervise the financing and construction of the bridge, and the cornerstone of the future chain (or suspension) bridge was laid with great ceremony in August 1842.

The permanent bridge linking Buda and Pest was a victory for Széchenyi and his program of liberal economic reform. Széchenyi later turned his attention to the regulation of the lower Danube and Tisza rivers, but the Chain Bridge remained his greatest triumph, and in 1848 he served as minister of public works and transportation. Like the horse races of the 1820s, the bridge would foster economic activity and provide physical proof of what public-spirited aristocrats could accomplish when working together with imperial-royal officials and middle-class professionals. Yet Széchenyi also viewed the bridge through national lenses, predicting that "our country would grow in strength by welding together the sections of Buda and Pest and—by developing everything beautiful, great, and glorious in the heart of the fatherland under the protection of the deity of nationality."[44] In this spirit, the National Diet's law promised that the bridge "will be the property of the nation."[45] Széchenyi's nationalism, however, had a decidedly European cast. As historian George Barany has observed, the bridge brought together Hungarian laborers, Viennese investors, Italian masons, and British experts (its designer was English, and its engineer Scottish).[46] The bridge may have been an offering to the "deity of nationality," but there was nothing distinctly "Hungarian" about it; rather, it was a technological marvel that would have enhanced any European city (fig. 5).

The bridge was only one of many new structures in Pest. Dozens of monumental buildings went up during this period, including the Hungarian National Theater, the Pest Town Hall, the Pest County Hall, and the magnificent National Museum, whose architectural neoclassicism represented the pinnacle of a half century of building in this style. Neoclassical hotels, apartment buildings, and aristocratic palaces also sprang up. This rapid development eclipsed the Baroque and brought the newness of the city into sharp relief. In an 1845 lithograph, for example, the new National Museum is surrounded by an old whitewashed building with a straw roof and a marketplace filled with peasants, wagons, and dogs (fig. 6).[47] But the consistent use of neoclassical architecture helped create the impression of a unified townscape, which visitors and residents alike praised. "It is pleasant

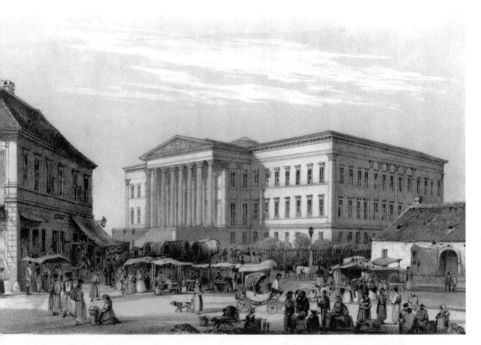

6—Dust, dogs, and Mihály Pollack's splendid National Museum (built 1837–48).

to stride through the streets with an attentive gaze," wrote Thiele, "observing how growing luxury and wealth express themselves in the tasteful construction and decoration of individual buildings."[48]

Concerted building in the neoclassical style made Pest look more like other European cities. A careful observer would have been able to distinguish Pest's neoclassicism from that employed by Karl Friedrich Schinkel in Berlin or Leo von Klenze in Munich, but neoclassical architecture flourished in part because it was international.[49] Mihály Pollack and Josef Hild, the two greatest practitioners of Hungarian neoclassicism, had both received training in German and Italian cities. Moreover, with its functionalism and minimal use of ornament, nineteenth-century classicism also had the advantage of being cheaper than the preceding Baroque and Rococo styles, and it was not uncommon for neoclassical elements to be tacked onto existing buildings. Thus, it proved to be a very adaptable style, used in both sacred and secular architecture, and chosen by aristocrats, burghers, and even well-to-do peasants in the countryside.

Pest did develop its own architectural traditions, and some scholars have characterized Hild's work, with its smooth façades and simple ornamentation, as "Hungarian-flavored classicism."[50] Nonetheless, it was difficult for Hungarian activists to claim neoclassicism as an expressly national style or to argue that the wave of neoclassical construction in itself made

Pest a more "Hungarian" city. This could be seen in the National Museum. Its roots went back to 1802, when Ferenc Széchényi (István's father) donated his collections of rare coins, maps, statues, books, and manuscripts "to the nation." Palatine Joseph was named curator of the collection, which he installed in the Pauline monastery in Pest. In 1807, the National Diet declared the nascent museum a "national institution," and, in the following decades, aristocrats, nobles, and burghers generously added to its collections. The museum was a great source of pride—*Tudományos Gyüjtemény* bragged that it was the first truly "national museum" in Europe—but its quarters were wholly inadequate for its growing collections.[51] The Hungarian National Diet thus voted in 1836 to sponsor a new building for the museum. Designed by Pollack and built between 1837 and 1847, the resulting structure was a handsome marriage of form and function. Although the Hungarian press hailed it as a "national masterpiece" and a "national palace," the museum's Grecian classicism recalled Schinkel's earlier Berlin Museum (1823–30), as well as Robert Smirke's British Museum (1823–46).[52] The "Hungarian" character of the museum derived less from its appearance than from its mission and from the patronage of the National Diet.

The same was true of the new Hungarian-language theater in Pest. Although plans for the theater building dated back to the 1790s, they reached fruition only in the mid-1830s. Pest County played a leading role in this effort, and donations also came from other noble counties, the Pest Town Council, and a host of individuals across the kingdom.[53] The accumulated funds paid for a small plot of land on the outskirts of Pest and a relatively modest building. Its designer, Mátyás Zitterbarth, was from a family of architects and builders who had moved from Austria in the late eighteenth century.[54] Although Zitterbarth would later make a name for himself with the Pest County Hall (1838–40), widely regarded as a high point of Pest neoclassicism, he produced a rather unexceptional design for the Hungarian theater. The theater's interior, which balanced generous gilding and a painting of the nine muses with extensive use of the national colors, partly compensated for the bland exterior. The theater opened to great acclaim in 1837, but its success was guaranteed only in 1840, when the National Diet made it a "national institution" and pledged to support it financially. This allowed the National Theater (as it was now called) to hire better actors and singers, stage more elaborate productions, and in general fulfill its broad goal of cultivating the Hungarian language (productions in other languages were not allowed on its stage). In this respect, the theater was of great importance to the Hungarian national movement, even if was housed in a rather ordinary building.

Against this background, several national activists began to look for alternatives to neoclassical architecture. Their numbers remained small, because most contemporaries welcomed the new buildings in Pest and accepted neoclassicism as a marker of sophistication and progress.[55] But educated Hungarians also knew of the Gothic revival then unfolding in England and the German lands. Széchenyi, who had traveled widely in Europe, argued that Hungary too should possess its own architectural style. In *Buda-Pest's Mud and Dust,* he explained that Hungary must not simply ape its neighbors. "Its buildings must unfailing possess specific features that are not Muscovite, Italian, or German, but must take philosophical measure of Hungary's origins, memories, future, and climate, in short, of every poetic and prosaic circumstance," he wrote.[56] Széchenyi did not indicate what style he had in mind, but he had presented an early argument against neoclassical ("Italian") architecture. Imre Henszlmann, a pioneering archeologist, art historian, and publicist, made an even stronger case in the 1840s. According to Henszlmann, "individuality" and "liveliness" were superior qualities to the universality and serenity of classicism. He therefore urged Magyars not to look abroad for inspiration, but to peer into their own past. According to Henszlmann, Hungarians should "study old masters of national character, and learn from them so that we can create national art from the life surrounding the artist."[57] His argument that art and architecture should reflect local, historical traditions rather than international influences effectively provided the theoretical foundations for Romanticism in the visual arts.

Henszlmann's call for a new, national style found a surprisingly swift response. In 1844, the National Diet opened an international competition for new quarters it hoped to build in Pest. One of the most striking designs came from a young architect named Frigyes Feszl, the son of a Pest stonemason.[58] With its cupola, *Rundbogenstil* arches, and Islamic (Moorish) elements, Feszl's plan for the parliament broke with many of the era's neoclassical conventions. Yet Vienna's resistance and a lack of money doomed the project, and when the Hungarian parliament came to Pest in 1848, it met in the Redoute Hall. Many other nationally minded initiatives likewise failed to get off the ground. What Feszl (and others) did for architecture, for example, István Ferenczy wanted to do for sculpture. After studying in Vienna and Rome, Ferenczy arrived in Pest in the 1820s and was soon making busts and tombs for aristocratic clients. Declaring his intention to create a great national monument, he began work on a bronze equestrian statue of King Matthias, the first of its kind in Hungary. Modeled on the classical statue of Marcus Aurelius in Rome, Ferenczy's King Matthias was to be the Hungarian equivalent to the powerful statue of Joseph II that stood before the Hofburg in Vienna. Ferenczy's plan found only a limited public response, however, and when the 1843–44 National Diet denied his request for support, he abandoned work on the monument and soon gave up sculpture altogether. Széchenyi had no more luck with his proposal for a national pantheon in Buda. Inspired by Westminster Abbey in London and perhaps Santa Croce in Florence, the memorial would have been a cemetery for Hungarian national luminaries past and present.

This architecture of the imagination, as one might call these unbuilt projects, gives an early indication of the historicist, Romantic direction that art and architecture in Hungary would take in the second half of the nineteenth century. Before 1848, however, only a handful of activists were ready to question the dominance of neoclassicism. These challenges are noteworthy because they indicate the degree to which Hungarian nationalists wanted to recreate Buda-Pest in their own image, but it would take time for theorists, artists, and architects to develop widely accepted national motifs. With architecture, then, we can see the remarkable aspirations as well as the practical limits of the Hungarian national movement's impact on the townscape.

Shop and Street Signs

A curious thing happened on August 24, 1842, the day that the cornerstone of the Chain Bridge was laid. The ceremony surrounding this event was especially grand, with Palatine Joseph, Archduke Charles, the archbishop of Esztergom, and other high officials in attendance, along with dozens of aristocrats and political luminaries. Cannons and a band playing the imperial anthem saluted the Habsburgs, and Archduke Charles was the first to use the £200 ivory trowel specially ordered from London. Count Széchenyi, however, was the center of attention, and, when he ceremonially tapped the cornerstone, the cheers turned to "wild shouts of jubilation."[59] Széchenyi's loudest enthusiasts were a group of young men, who reassembled later that evening to celebrate the creator of the Chain Bridge. Their torchlight parade reached his house at 10 p.m., and the youth began to sing and cheer for Széchenyi. Unfortunately, the count was not at home, as his secretary informed the large crowd. The youth persevered and saluted the absent Széchenyi for an hour, albeit with flagging enthusiasm. They next went the house of Lajos Kossuth, who fired them up with a speech generous to Széchenyi and filled with proud references to the Hungarian nation. The count meanwhile waited until after midnight to return to his house, which he entered, unnoticed, through a side gate.

Why had Széchenyi so carefully avoided his young followers? Széchenyi had accepted torchlight serenades before, but by the early 1840s he had grown wary of such noisy tributes. According to police informants, Széchenyi feared that the youth's support would be held against him in Vienna and thereby hinder his reform plans. Neither Széchenyi nor the imperial-royal authorities, however, could fully control what happened in the streets and squares of Buda-Pest. Although fairs, religious celebrations, and observances of the emperor-king's birthday continued as before, they increasingly had to share public space with events organized by supporters of the national cause. Voluntary associations were decisive here: they organized art exhibitions, industrial fairs, awards ceremonies, and public meetings, all of which could draw hundreds and even thousands of guests.

Existing institutions also became much more lively. Meetings of the Pest County assembly had never been dull, but by the 1840s its assemblies had become stormy gatherings that regularly drew scores of noblemen to Pest. It helped that Széchenyi, Kossuth, Nyáry, and other leading liberals regularly took part in the meetings and that the contemporary press described their deliberations and debates. It was said that a nobleman from southern Hungary wanted to buy a small piece of property in Pest County just so that he could participate in its assemblies.

The "Pest Youth" was a key participant in all these events.[60] A mix of university students, lawyers, doctors, writers, poets, and actors, these young men fervently supported Hungarian liberalism and nationalism. They demonstrated their views during sessions of the National Diet in Pressburg, loudly cheering opposition speakers and lustily booing conservatives. They did the same in Pest County Hall. "Those walls," recalled one participant, "have not heard such thunderous cheers since."[61] Some leaders of the Pest Youth joined the national societies, including the National Circle and Protection Association. All who could afford it went to the Hungarian National Theater, where they raucously applauded even second-rate performances. Otherwise they gathered in their rooms or in coffeehouses near the university to drink, debate, and read. Although the students had a deserved reputation for rowdiness, a sympathetic journalist claimed that the coffeehouses had become a "factory of public opinion," where quiet reading, serious discussion, and national agitation had taken the place of wine, cards, carousing, and cursing.[62] The youth, he explained, unanimously supported all forms of national culture (and the Hungarian language above all else), as well as the liberal political leadership, whose portraits adorned the walls of the law students' favorite haunt, the Pilvax Café.

Why did the national idea hold such an attraction for these young men? Scholars sometimes speak of an "intellectual proletariat" as shorthand for the frustrated careerism and woeful employment prospects of a growing number of university graduates in the nineteenth century.[63] In the empires of Central and Eastern Europe, poor but politically aware young men had material reasons to embrace nationalism, with its promise of administrative and teaching positions (once the "foreign" officials and professors had been removed) and the social status that went with them. For Hungary, political scientist Andrew Janos has argued that declining economic prospects in the countryside pushed many young men into the university, where they soon discovered that their prospects as officials, lawyers, scholars, or writers were hardly better.[64] They became Hungary's "marginal men," impecunious intellectuals and underemployed professionals, the foot soldiers of the Hungarian national movement. A strong case can be made for this argument: Hungary already had twice as many lawyers per capita as Austria and too few professional opportunities for the university's 1,000–1,500 students. Moreover, many of these young men had worked as clerks or secretaries at the National Diet in Pressburg, where they had served a political apprenticeship and forged links with the liberal leadership. In Buda-Pest, students directed their frustrations on local targets: university professors, town officials, burghers, and other groups that—at least in the students' eyes—enjoyed power and prosperity but lacked national convictions. In this, they received at least tacit approval from liberal leaders such as Kossuth, who understood them, spoke their language, and encouraged their enthusiasm.

The students thus saw themselves not as "marginal men," but as the vanguard of the national cause in Buda-Pest. If earlier activists had equated national loyalty with language, the Pest Youth accepted this equation as well as its corollary: those who did not publicly support the Hungarian language were disloyal and should be punished. Shopkeepers thereby became an early target of the students' anger. In both Buda and Pest, shop signs were typically written in German, and people went to the *Schuster* for shoes, the *Schneider* for clothes, and the *Tischlermeister* for furniture. The signs themselves were often ornately carved and colorfully painted. In 1832, however, 300 "patriotic-minded youths" signed a petition in protest of German-language shop signs. The petition urged Pest's burghers "to disgrace no longer the streets of our hometown with German signs, but to adorn them with Hungarian ones."[65] The new signs, the youth suggested, would be a natural, outward manifestation of the burghers' loyalty to their homeland. The petitioners expressed their confidence in the burghers, but also issued a not-so-subtle warning: "However, if our gentle remonstrations see no results, we ask for clemency if our breasts, burning for our homeland [and] our language, ignite and burst into a forbidden fire, and perhaps transgress the bounds of civility." Shopkeepers soon learned that these were not idle threats. Teréz Karács recalled that the students discovered a simple "trick," as she put it, to intimidate owners of shops with German-language signs: they threw stones wrapped in a slip of paper into the offending shops, sometimes through the window. On the paper was written, "If there is not a Hungarian sign within 48 hours, not a stone of this building will remain standing."[66] At night, the students—who were never discovered—stole the offending German signs and stacked them in one of the main squares. If the sign, once returned, was not swiftly repainted, then the students stole it again. It is not known how long this campaign lasted, but in the early 1830s many intimidated shopkeepers apparently added Hungarian translations to their shop signs and windows.

The threat of violence and destruction of property that characterize this episode are striking, because neither figures in most accounts of Hungarian nationalism. Yet, if police spies are to be believed, this was not an isolated example. In 1844, in full view of hundreds of people, young men apparently tore down and destroyed a tavern's sign that read *Willkommen;* the report despairingly concluded that "Pest would soon be completely Hungarian, and Germans will be threatened or crushed."[67] Another informant reported that the Pest Youth created an auto-da-fé of *Pester Zeitung*, Eduard Glatz's newspaper. Alajos Degré, a onetime law student and leader of the Pest Youth, boasted in his memoirs that he had entered the Pest German Theater only twice, and both times to disrupt performances.[68] On the second occasion, Degré and other young men whistled down the renowned Belgian violinist Henri Vieuxtemps, who had supposedly broken an earlier promise to perform only in the Hungarian Theater. When Széchenyi condemned the scandal in his newspaper, the Pest youth wanted to give *him* catcalls and were talked out of it only with difficulty.

The local authorities could do little to prevent this unruly behavior. By modern standards, nineteenth-century police forces were woefully understaffed.[69] In the 1830s, as the population of Buda-Pest surpassed 100,000, the total strength of the police was around 265, which included officers, secretaries, night watchmen, and uniformed soldiers (gendarmes in Pest were nicknamed "lobsters" because of their red uniforms).[70] This small force was responsible for the maintenance of public order and security, the apprehension, imprisonment, and punishment of criminals, and the supervision of markets, taverns, beggars, and travelers. It helped that the towns' police captains worked with the imperial-royal authorities, who had a network of paid informants. But reports from these sources could take time to trickle in, and, when they did, administrative gears turned slowly as papers moved from one office to another. Of course, Buda and Pest together garrisoned nearly 10,000 soldiers, many of them from the monarchy's Italian provinces. This was surely a reminder of Vienna's power, but soldiers were of limited use against students who stole shop signs or whistled in the German theater. When the authorities did use the soldiers to restore order—against students and workers in 1831 and against journeymen tailors in 1842—bloodshed was almost always the result.

The nationalist press condemned displays of violence but shared the students' goals, and journalists repeatedly expressed indignation about German-language shop signs in the twin towns. In an article that mixed humor and nationalism, Garay first questioned the logic of the names of individual shops. Was it proper for a cobbler's workshop to be named after the pianist Franz Liszt or for a perfume shop to be named for Minerva, the goddess of wisdom?[71] Although Garay proudly noted the popularity of Hungarian symbols (the crown, flag, and coat of arms) and heroes (Attila, Árpád, and Matthias) on the signs themselves, he conceded that the towns' signs also featured a veritable menagerie of animals. Garay was most critical of shopkeepers whose signs were "still" in German, which he offhandedly referred to as a "guest language." To Garay, shops with signs in both languages were no more acceptable, because they always had German on the top or, if the name appeared on separate doors, on the more heavily trafficked entrance. Garay let his readers draw their own conclusions. Not so another journalist, who angrily asked why the Pest Town

Council had not issued a decree requiring all shop signs to be solely in Hungarian.[72] Denying that this was a meaningless issue, the author also called on the National Diet to address the matter.

National activists soon took aim at street signs as well. Here it was harder for nationalists to argue that town leaders had neglected the Hungarian language, because bilingual street signs had long been common in Buda-Pest. Franz Schams, for example, reported in 1822 that the names of Pest's streets and squares were written in both Hungarian and German.[73] In Buda, bilingual signs already existed in the Castle District, and in 1832, the Buda Town Council ordered that Hungarian and German street signs be placed in all districts.[74] Thus, "Bear Street" in Water District appeared as both *Bärengasse* and *Medve utca*. The street names themselves had varied origins. Longer streets typically bore the names of the towns to which they led. Others took their names from Habsburg rulers and archdukes (Leopold, Joseph, and Alexander) and, much more often, from trades (Miller, Mason, Spurrier, and Brewer) and animals (Three Sheep, Beaver, Raven, and Snake). Looking at a map of early nineteenth-century Pest, it is hard not to credit the town dwellers with a bit of humor, since one could stand at the intersection of Manure and Two Rabbits streets, of Gentlemen and Rag-and-Bone-Man streets, or of Angel and Cemetery streets.

This humor was entirely lost on the nationalist press, which demanded both that the signs should be exclusively in Hungarian and that they should bear more national names. An anonymous 1847 article in the opposition's *Pesti Hirlap* explained the logic of these demands.[75] To the author, Pest's streets were dusty, muddy, and bereft of Hungarian character. National monuments would change this, but the author understood that there was neither money nor support for public statuary, as Ferenczy's ill-fated statue of King Matthias had shown. The author reasoned that historic street names would be a much cheaper solution, particularly because streets in London, Paris, and other European capitals were commonly named for historical figures—for example, Wellington, Nelson, and Marlborough, in London. The author sadly noted that only one in fifty streets in Pest had some historical association; the rest bore the names of trades, animals, and—worst of all—German place names that could not be easily Magyarized, such as Prater, Lerchenfeld, and Florian streets. The only hopeful development was the recent renaming of Magpie Street in Leopold District, which in 1846 became Zrínyi Street in honor of Hungary's famed seventeenth-century poet-warrior. There was no reason why other streets could not be named after medieval kings and recent heroes such as Széchenyi, Kazinczy, and Kölcsey. In conclusion, the author angrily called for "the streets of the capital to receive national and noteworthy names and to be cleansed of the grime of prosaicness and foreignness."

This intolerant conclusion bears closer inspection. Certainly, the author's complaints were not unique. In eighteenth-century America, Benjamin Franklin had grumbled about Philadelphia's bilingual (German-English) street signs and bitterly remarked that German-English translators would soon be required in the Pennsylvania legislature. In Central Europe, nineteenth-century Czech nationalists first demanded bilingual (Czech-German) and then monolingual (Czech only) street signs as part of their campaign to Czechify Prague.[76] After 1989, new regimes in Eastern Europe uniformly purged their cities of communist-era street names. In the early twenty-first century, tensions over the language of street signs continue to simmer in Bilbao, Belfast, Los Angeles, Montreal, Jerusalem, and many other cities and regions. Street names, historian Brian Ladd has concluded, "can be ephemeral, rootless, and inoffensive," yet they can also "contribute to the myths that constitute a collective identity."[77] For political activists, few other features of the cityscape provide such obvious, easy targets.

How did the Hungarian national activists themselves explain their obsession with street names and shop signs? Nationalists attached a semiotic value to street signs, statuary, and other elements of public space. In particular, they believed that everyday symbols could be used to create and strengthen national awareness among the urban population. The 1847 article in the *Pesti Hirlap* shows this plainly, as the writer claimed to have heard several conversations sparked by Zrínyi Street's new name. In one, a Magyar porter explained to his Slovak coworker, with more pride than historical accuracy, what the name meant; in another, the sign prompted a tutor to give his curious student a lesson in Hungarian history. These anecdotes are too good to be true, but they present an idealized picture of how people might acquire national consciousness. The converts in this case include a non-Magyar (the Slovak worker) and the next generation (the student). This model of nationalization held a special appeal for the educated classes, in which their learned culture could painlessly transform willing workers and inquisitive children into proud Magyars. It also sheds new light on the Hungarian side's frequent assertion that Buda-Pest should have a more national appearance. This was not just an end in itself, but, because of the understood power of symbols, the transformation of the townscape would in turn help Magyarize the population as a whole.

Activists also hoped that street signs and markers of the Hungarian national character would influence foreign opinion. Hungarian nationalists had long complained that visitors to Buda-Pest could think that they were in "a town in Germany" rather than in a distinctly Hungarian city.[78] The visitors in these cases were likely fictional—actual travelers rarely had trouble grasping the heterogeneity of Buda-Pest—but the opinions and ideas of other Europeans were of importance to educated Hungarians. The writer for the *Pesti Hirlap*, for instance, argued that, if Pest had historic street names, foreign visitors would see that Magyars were a people with a long history and their own heroes, saints, and luminaries. The concern here is clear: Hungarian nationalists desperately wanted to prove, using every means available to them, that they were a "historical" nation worthy of their own state. Many nineteenth-century Europeans, from Giuseppe Mazzini to Otto von Bismarck, believed that there was a threshold for national states—that is, only nations of a certain size and antiquity (the French, Germans, and Italians) deserved their own states; the small, "unhistorical" nations (ostensibly, the Sicilians, Bretons, and Slovenes) did not.[79] If Buda-Pest more closely resembled London or Paris, it followed that the Magyars deserved their place beside the British and French. With the stakes so high, Hungarian activists found it easy dismiss local traditions and overlook the occasional broken window.

Two events in 1847 gave a clear indication of the changing face of the twin towns. The first was apparently an accident. On February 2, 1847, the Pest theater burned to the ground. The cause of the fire would remain a mystery, but it was a devastating blow to local German-speakers. "The Pest German Theater," explained one contemporary, "was from its founding a mirror to our moral and social interests."[80] Hungarian activists were far less sentimental, and Count Zay spoke for many when he suggested that the large Pest Theater should be rebuilt, but only for Hungarian-language productions; German works would be relegated to the smaller Hungarian National Theater. The now homeless German company performed first in the Castle Theater in Buda and then in a temporary wooden structure in Pest.

On the day this makeshift theater was dedicated, another ceremony took place, this one in Buda. Under the leadership of Gábor Döbrentei, national activists held a large banquet to celebrate their renaming of the Buda Hills. Born in 1785, Döbrentei had been at the center of the national movement for decades. He was connected to the Hungarian Scholarly Society, the National Theater, and, less formally, to the Pest Youth. "Suavity, energy, and patriotism," is how Julia Pardoe described him.[81] On this day, Döbrentei and his followers ceremonially renamed more than fifty hills, valleys, and wells, substituting Hungarian names for their customary German ones. Many of these new names were direct translations, and thus "Eagle Hill" simply changed from *Adlerberg* to *Sashegy*. Others came from Hungarian history: the kings István, Béla, and Matthais all had hills named after them, and several more commemorated the 1686 siege of Buda. As the Buda Town Council later explained, these new names would serve as "public memorials that link the past with the present and speak to the future."[82] The council ordered that the names be used officially from November 1, 1848.

However illuminating, such symbolic acts were only part of the story. Although the twin towns had changed greatly in the 1830s and 1840s, economic, demographic, and in spring 1838, natural forces had dictated much of this development. Its foot soldiers had been enterprising builders, profit-hungry landlords, and aristocrats and bankers armed with capital. Political leaders also played a visible role: they attempted to se. the rules for development—as Palatine Joseph did after the 1838 flood—and sponsored a limited number of representative buildings. Although it did not open until 1849, Széchenyi's Chain Bridge over the Danube had the greatest symbolic importance, and it contributed greatly to the unification of the twin towns. For a small circle of Hungarian national activists, however, this remarkable spurt of building left much to be desired. Urban space, they said, should reflect the national character. Even without the support of leaders like Széchenyi, these insistent journalists and forceful students successfully invested street signs, public buildings, and even religious festivals with national associations.

Most ambitiously, national activists imagined that Buda-Pest could be the undisputed national capital of Hungary.[83] They wanted Buda-Pest to be as grand as London, Paris, and, although they were loath to admit it, Vienna. National activists believed that Buda-Pest's transformation into a genuine capital city depended on the unification and continued improvement of the twin towns. A British traveler echoed this view in the mid-1830s: "In fact, if Hungary is to have a capital, Pesth and Buda united, should be the metropolis. Both have magnificent edifices, chiefly constructed in all the freshness of modern architecture."[84] But the idea of a unified Buda-Pest as a capital city also raised many questions: How would unification take place? What would the relationship be between Vienna and Buda-Pest? What role would the emperor-king play in this capital? Even in the late 1840s, few people could have suspected that these questions would be answered, and in very surprising ways, much sooner than anyone believed possible.

CHAPTER SIX

The Revolutionary Capital

"'Dear brothers!' he began in a whisper. 'I come from Vienna; I have been in the Hungarian capital and experienced great things. Understand that the whirlwind of freedom is at last racing through our old part of the world. Social barriers are falling, the old chains are breaking, and Europe, reborn like a phoenix, wants to be free and the people to embrace one another as brothers.'"

—Ferenc Herczeg, *The Seven Swabians* (1916)[1]

On March 17, 1848, just two days after the outbreak of revolution in Pest, the poet Mihály Vörösmarty sent a letter to Count László Teleki, who was with the National Diet in Pressburg. "A day brings better news than a decade did formerly," he wrote. "With events unfolding as they are, the country cannot be governed from the edge. . . . Only in Pest can you complete what you have been fighting for, and what began here so gloriously."[2] In a few words, Vörösmarty captured the symbolic importance of Buda-Pest to the Hungarian national movement and to the 1848–49 Revolution, just as Ferenc Herczeg (born Franz Herzog) would do nearly sixty years later in his novel *The Seven Swabians*. Much, though certainly not all, of the drama of 1848–49 was played out in Buda-Pest. The script of this drama was in many respects a familiar one, particularly in its opening acts. As in other European capitals, Pest first witnessed revolution in the streets, which surprised and overwhelmed authorities. This was followed by the meeting of a liberal and popularly elected parliament. The old regime—and with it serfdom, censorship, and privilege—seemed to have collapsed overnight, and freedom and solidarity became the watchwords of the day. In Hungary, as elsewhere in Europe, the force of arms would ultimately determine the fate of the revolution, and in 1849 Buda-Pest was occupied by Austrian troops, briefly but dramatically liberated by the Hungarian army, and then taken again by the Austrians. The victors arrested hundreds of revolutionary leaders, shut down clubs and newspapers, banned public demonstrations, and submitted the city to military rule. Similar scenes played themselves out in cities and towns across Europe as monarchical regimes bloodily suppressed liberal, democratic, and nationalist movements.

The 1848–49 Revolution strengthened trends that had been building for decades in Buda-Pest. The revolution offered new possibilities for ordinary men and women to demonstrate their national loyalties and political sympathies. Not all residents joined revolutionary clubs, signed petitions, or marched in the streets, but for many of those who did, the revolution was a political apprenticeship of remarkable duration and intensity.[3] It is tempting to describe the revolutionary experience, with its profusion of symbols, rituals, and martyrs, in almost religious terms, and in her imaginative study of the French Revolution's festivals, historian Mona Ozouf concluded that the revolutionaries had achieved what she calls a "transfer of sacrality." In the place of king and church, they encouraged people's emotional involvement in the secular, liberal, national community.[4] To what extent did a similar process unfold in revolutionary Buda-Pest?

Revolution in the Streets

Starting in Paris, revolution spread like wildfire across Europe in the spring of 1848. In one European capital after another, the "rituals of revolution" unfolded: news from France sparked animated discussions in clubs and coffeehouses and attracted excited crowds into the streets; governments then called out troops to maintain order, and, inevitably, some incident would occur, leading to barricades, street fighting, bloodshed, and the sudden collapse of royal confidence.[5] The panicked authorities either fled, like Louis-Philippe from Paris and Metternich from Vienna, or announced that they were (and always had been) of one mind with the people, as did Friedrich Wilhelm IV of Prussia when he donned the German national colors (black, red, and gold), promised a constitution, and said, with as much sincerity as he could muster, that "from now on Prussia will merge into Germany." The streets became scenes of celebration as "a wave of fraternization swept the continent, uniting the most implausible elements."[6] This euphoria would not last, and, in time, the initiative passed first to popularly elected parliaments, whose leaders looked mistrustfully upon the crowd, and then to soldiers, who brought the revolutionary movements to an end. Until this happened, however, the streets remained a stage upon which the aspirations and conflicts of the revolutions were played out, and festivals, processions, charivari, and protests were a feature of the revolutionary experience across the continent.

Events in Pest closely followed the revolutionary script. The 20,000 people who poured into the streets on March 15 fortified their leaders, cowed the authorities, and helped ensure the swift triumph of the revolution in Hungary. One participant recalled the intoxicating feeling of melting into the crowd: "Now I too belonged to the tribe, without knowing what it planned or where it would go, but I unconditionally trusted my friends and blindly followed them—and would have followed them had they run straight into the jaws of death."[7] Remarkably, no violence accompanied March 15, and the crowds turned celebratory in the exhilarating weeks that followed. By day there were large assemblies in front of the

National Museum, at night torchlight parades, music in the streets, homegrown plays in the theaters, and more cheering. Depending upon one's
perspective, the entire town was either "drunk with joy and happiness" or
"had gone mad"; either way, there was no denying the rapid, total victory
of the crowd over the old regime.[8] Taking their cue from the French, the
Pest revolutionaries swiftly formed the Committee of Public Safety to govern the city and began organizing national guard units to maintain order,
protect property, and defend the new regime.

The March Youth, as the young heroes of the fifteenth were called,
overnight became the tribunes of the revolutionary crowd. These young
students, lawyers, and poets—the Pest Youth of earlier years—readily embraced this role and stoked the fires of fury against Vienna and all that
stood in the way of the sweeping political and social changes they demanded. Their leader was Pál Nyáry, dubbed the Hungarian Revolution's
Danton, who was a spellbinding speaker with radical political views; their
most colorful personality (among many) was the poet Sándor Petőfi,
whose *Nemzeti dal* ("National Song") became the unofficial anthem of the
Hungarian Revolution. Petőfi paraded through the streets with a long cape
and sword (formerly a symbol of nobility, now an indication the old
regime had been overturned), his wife, Júlia Szendrey, cut her hair in imi-
tation of George Sand and proudly wore the Hungarian national colors. To
commemorate their victory, the March Youth rechristened their gathering
place, the Pilvax Café, the "Revolutionary Hall" and founded a newspaper,
appropriately titled *Marczius Tizenötödike (March Fifteenth)*.

Yet the dominance of the March Youth was not complete, even in Pest.
They formed a minority, if a vocal one, on the Committee of Public Safety,
where liberal town officials, guildsmen, merchants, and representatives of
the Hungarian Diet held the majority. More ominously, the National
Guard rapidly became a source of division instead of fostering civic unity
and the revolutionary spirit among the citizenry. National Guard units—
civilian militias—sprang up in cities across Europe in 1848. In Pest, some
master artisans and property owners, formerly the backbone of local militia units and now charged with organizing the National Guard, refused to
admit factory workers, lawyers, students, or Jews. To make matters worse,
the local army commander, who remained loyal to Vienna and hostile to
the Hungarian Revolution, maintained that no weapons were available for
the guardsmen, thus making them a rather toothless force (later inspec-
tions would turn up 14,000 rifles in the army's warehouses).[9]

By late March, negotiations between the National Diet in Pressburg and
the court in Vienna had taken center stage. It was at this juncture that the
Pest masses again inserted themselves into the revolution. On March 29,
when it appeared that the court might refuse to accept the Diet's proposed
reforms, as many as 15,000 people filled the streets to protest the emperor-
king's seeming intransigence.[10] Led by the March Youth, the crowd
marched toward Pest City Hall, angrily roaring, "We don't need a German

government," "They've swindled us in Vienna," and "To arms! To arms!" On the following day, in front of another huge crowd, Petőfi read his openly republican poem, *"A királyokhoz"* ("To the Kings"), which contained the provocative line "No matter what shameless flatterers say, there is no longer a *beloved* king!"[11] He also demanded barricades, although it was unclear against whom they would be directed. Sympathetic newspapers added fuel to the fire, with one reporting that "the entire country is on its feet, the entire nation stands at arms," and another calling on all residents of the country to unite against their common enemy, "the despotic Austrian bureaucracy."[12] In contrast to the euphoric, holiday-like atmosphere of the fifteenth, the mood on the twenty-ninth was darker and more violent. Only the arrival of news that the emperor-king would sign the legislation calmed the crowd and ended the string of mass meetings.

The emperor-king's signature completed the passage of the so-called April Laws, the thirty-one statutes passed in early April that effectively transformed Hungary into a constitutional monarchy. Hungary would be governed by ministers responsible to a parliament that would convene annually in Pest. Suffrage, which was based on property and education qualifications, was extended to approximately one in four adult males, a figure that was far short of the universal suffrage demanded by radicals but high by standards of the nineteenth century (Britain's Great Reform Act of 1832 had given the vote to one in five men). Serfdom was effectively abolished. This "lawful revolution" had its limits: all nobles, no matter how much property or education they possessed, retained the franchise (and they would dominate parliamentary elections in June), Jews were not fully emancipated, the demands of other national leaders (save the Croatians) received no consideration, and the peasants remained burdened with dues and taxes.

Yet for the present, it appeared that "a miracle had happened."[13] What role had the Pest radicals and crowds played in this stunning legislative victory? Historian István Deák has argued that Kossuth shrewdly used these demonstrations to scare Vienna, and, in this sense, the crowds hastened the passage of the April Laws.[14] Yet Kossuth and the political leadership had little taste for barricades or armed civilians, and this set them on a collision course with the March Youth. In a speech delivered in early April, Kossuth said that he considered Buda-Pest to be the "heart of the fatherland" but warned that it could never be its "master."[15] Buda-Pest, in short, was not to be Paris, and for Kossuth and other liberals, the ministers and the parliament, not the streets, should dictate the course of the Hungarian Revolution.

A new Hungarian government under Prime Minister Lajos Batthyány (with Kossuth as minister of finance) established itself in Pest, and its authority was immediately tested in the streets. On April 19, crowds—mobs might be a better word in this context—ran wild through the Jewish quarter of Pest. Spurred on by rather implausible rumors that Jews were throwing stones and pouring hot oil on passers-by on Király (King) Street, the men brushed aside a National Guardsman, beat Jews in the street, and broke the windows of Jewish shops and houses.[16] Journalist Julian Chownitz witnessed the violence: "The crowd advanced in a rage from one place to another, at every moment assaulting solitary pedestrians. . . . If someone had Jewish features, [the crowd] shouted 'Here's one! Smash his head!'"[17] It took hours for the authorities to regain control, and not before several people were wounded. The leading revolutionaries were aghast: Batthyány personally appeared before the crowd to call for calm and later summoned soldiers to back up his words. Albert Pálffy, editor of the radicals' *Marczius Tizenötödike*, thundered that the riots had "defiled" the city; all agreed that the pogrom had cast a shadow over the revolution.[18] Though there would be no repetition of this anti-Semitic violence in Pest, similar pogroms erupted in other Hungarian cities, including Pressburg, where ten Jews were killed and forty were wounded on April 24.

The events of April 19 in Pest were widely condemned, but there was no consensus on their causes or on the best way to prevent further violence. Alleging that a large number of "German petty-bourgeoisie" had dominated these "ragtag mobs," Petőfi and other radicals quickly blamed the rioting on the German-speaking population of Pest, suggesting that it had succumbed to alcohol, religious hatred, and a handful of dangerous orators.[19] Chownitz took this claim a step further, suggesting that "secret emissaries" from Vienna had nursed the Germans' resentments against Jews; the result was "the first evidence of counter-revolutionary agitation in the capital."[20] In newspaper coverage of the rioting, radical writers called on citizens to uphold the principle of fraternity and for the Hungarian government to extend full equality to Jews, but at the same time they also hinted that all German-speakers were traitorous and denied that anti-Semitism existed among Magyars (even as they repeatedly echoed anti-Semitic clichés). Taking no chances, Batthyány's government announced on April 20 that permits would be required for all public demonstrations. Those held without permission or found to have subversive aims would receive three warnings before being broken up with armed force. Further ministerial decrees issued later in the month emphasized that the law was unambiguous in permitting Jews both to join the National Guard and to reside in Pest. In light of "Budapest's present agitated condition," however, the government ordered that Jews be temporarily excused from duty in the National Guard and that all weapons be collected from Jews in Pest.[21] Critics were quick to point out that instead of punishing the rioters, the government seemed to be granting their wishes.

Both the radicals' warnings of counterrevolution and the government's insistence on public order glossed over complex issues at the heart of the anti-Semitic violence. As historian György Spira has shown, the April 19 rioting took place against the background of heightened labor unrest (particularly within the guild system) and growing unemployment. Numerous journeymen drew up petitions, in which they frequently complained about competition from Jewish tailors and craftsmen and submitted them to the town council or the government. The most extreme petitions demanded the exclusion of Jews from the National Guard and the expulsion of all Jews who had settled in Pest since 1838. At the same time, some journeymen took to the streets, where they joined unemployed workers and debtors engaged in a campaign against the payment of rents to landlords, who included a number of Jews. When a large number of National Guardsmen joined in the movement, it decisively weakened local forces charged with maintaining order. This combustible mixture produced the anti-Semitic rioting on April 19. In many respects, the violence in Pest had much in common with the widespread rioting that broke out in eastern France and southwestern Germany in 1848.[22] The leaders in these riots were often guildsmen who felt threatened by Jewish peddlers, shopkeepers, or unlicensed craftsmen.

But the riots had other causes as well. A long tradition of Christian anti-Semitism was undoubtedly an important structural factor. In 1848, moreover, the crowds may also have been responding to the more immediate "threat" of Jewish emancipation. In the nineteenth century, Central European regimes that issued (or prepared to issue) laws granting Jews equal rights as citizens almost always faced a wide range of protests, including hostile pamphlets, petitions, and physical violence against Jews. This was the case in Hungary as well, and the rioting in Pest, Pressburg, and elsewhere effectively took Jewish emancipation off the political agenda for more than a year; only in late July 1849, in the last days of the revolution, would the Hungarian parliament pass a law granting Jews full civil equality. In comparison with economic, religious, and political factors, nationhood played a small role in the riots in Buda-Pest. Although many of the social groups represented in the mobs—journeymen, unemployed workers, and National Guardsmen—had a preponderance of German-speakers, their leaders used the language of economic protest and religious prejudice, rather than that of nationalism. In practice, nationhood became an issue primarily in the interpretation of the rioting. When the radicals claimed that the violence was the work of "German mobs," they were implicitly exonerating all local Hungarian-speakers of guilt. This overlooked the fact that Magyars had been involved in protests against Jews since the beginning of the revolution.[23]

From the perspective of Buda-Pest's Jewish community, the events of April 19 were both threatening and humiliating. Writing a week after the pogrom, one Jewish resident of Pest complained that he had suffered "the crudest insults," and said that he lived in "fear and terrible expectation" of the "most brutal sort" of explosion.[24] In closing his letter, he grimly warned of coming anarchy and added that he was trying to persuade "his people" (*meine Leute*, presumably his relatives or other Jews more generally) to go to Vienna. Many Jews, however, were still willing to stand by the Hungarian Revolution. In late May, for example, "numerous youth" published an appeal to Hungary's Jewish population. Stating that "the Hungarians' homeland is in danger," they called on fellow Jews to volunteer for the Hungarian army *(honvéd)* then being formed. The Magyars, they argued, had long protected the Jews against Germans and Slavs, and, in 1848, had it not been for the anti-Semitic rioting in Pest, Pressburg, and other cities, the Magyar people and their leaders would have "gladly fulfilled the sacred word of equality" and "listened to the commands of fraternity." With its flattering tone and one-sided reading of the recent past, this appeal was likely aimed more at the revolutionary leadership than at the wider Jewish population. Yet it also suggests the eagerness of many Jews to take up arms in defense of the Hungarian lands, just as they had volunteered for national guard units months earlier. This in turn laid the foundation for later arguments explicitly linking military service to citizenship. In a petition sent to parliament on June 24, Hungarian Jewish leaders argued that Jews should be granted full equality with Christians.[25] Invoking the slogan "justice, freedom, and equality," they pointed out that Jewish soldiers were already fighting and dying for Hungary's freedom and stressed their loyalty to Hungary as their homeland: "We want to be equal with all other residents of our homeland—*equal in burdens and sacrifices,* because we are also its sons." If the language was lofty, the message was clear: Hungary's Jews were willing to accept both the rights (legal equality) and duties (military service) of full citizenship.

If this discussion of the streets has moved far from where it started, it is because crowds are inseparable from the wider political struggles of the mid-nineteenth-century revolutions. In many ways, crowds in Pest behaved as they did elsewhere in Europe that year. Two patterns emerge. First, crowds in the streets contributed greatly to the initial successes of the revolutions, but they declined in importance as other forms of criticism and pressure (political clubs, newspapers, petitions, and parliaments) became available. Revolutions everywhere made possible the meteoric rise of soapbox orators, but the political careers of Alphonse de Lamartine in Paris, Adolf Fischhof in Vienna, and Petőfi in Pest were invariably brief. In Hungary, crowds would continue to fill the streets at key points in 1848–49, but never again with the unity or success they had enjoyed in March 1848. Second, crowds posed a difficult test for the revolutionary leadership across Europe. Mass gatherings had the potential to engage the urban lower classes in the revolution—however briefly or indirectly—and the new regimes in part derived their legitimacy from such demonstrations, as was the case in Hungary when 80,000 people celebrated Kossuth's return to Pest in July 1849. Yet even the loudest defenders of "the people" also feared that demagogues could lead the masses astray and turn them into violent mobs. When violence did occur, radicals and liberals were likely to differ on its causes (as they did on most things). Whereas radicals tended to single out "national enemies" and "counterrevolutionaries" as the source of disorder in the streets, liberals looked with suspicion on the radicals themselves, with their ill-considered calls for barricades and re-publics. After April, the Hungarian government faced the problem that revolutionary regimes have always faced: how can revolutions, once they have achieved their initial goals, be stopped?

The Twin Towns in Red, White, and Green

As students of the French Revolution and heirs to the Romantic Era, the participants in 1848 attached great importance to the symbolic di-mension of their struggles. There was a wave of iconoclasm in the first days of each revolution, as people tore down royal coats of arms and cast aside their top hats, frock coats, and wigs, which were seen as symbols of the old order. Outside of France, however, the revolutions stopped at "the foot of the throne," and violent attacks on the royals themselves were un-thinkable. Most revolutionaries were content to rename streets and squares, to insist that national anthems be played, and to plaster every-thing with the national colors. Some symbols were explicitly political: the mania for constitutions, for example, produced constitutional "hats, ties, umbrellas, biscuits, and even a constitutional polka."[26] (Not to be outdone, the Hungarians had their own constitutional *csárdás*.) Other symbols had national resonances. In Prague, the *čamara*, a buttoned jacket, came into vogue in 1848 and remained a symbol of Czech na-tionalism. The prevalence and meaning of such displays often changed over the course of the revolution, yet this explosion of symbolic activity created new possibilities for people to display their political and na-tional allegiances.

There was relatively little destruction or desecration of symbols of imperial-royal authority in Hungary. The Habsburgs themselves remained popular, and newspapers reacted hostilely to Sándor Petőfi's republican poem "To the Kings." Most locals would have supported Kossuth's pro-posal that Emperor-King Ferdinand rule not from Vienna but from Buda. This quixotic but long-popular suggestion had little chance of realization, yet it reflected the Hungarians' belief that theirs was a lawful revolution directed only against Metternich and the evil "Camarilla" surrounding the king and that Buda-Pest, not Vienna, should be the center of the monar-chy. It is also further evidence of how fully Hungary's political leaders un-derstood the importance of symbolic gestures. Kossuth's arrival in Vienna in the first days of the revolution, for example, had been memorable not just because it demonstrated the waning of imperial authority and the waxing of Hungarian influence, but also because the Hungarian delega-tion had been "resplendent in their gala national dress, girt with their richly studded swords, and bearing egret feathers in their caps."[27] When representatives of Vienna later came to Pest, they brought King Matthias's shield as a token of friendship.[28]

From the start, revolutionaries in Buda-Pest insisted on the public display of Hungarian symbols. The response was at first confused, because officials in Buda ordered that imperial colors (black and yellow) and insignia (the double-headed eagle) be removed from public buildings and replaced by the Hungarian tricolor and coat of arms, whereas officials in Vienna conceded only that Hungarian symbols could now appear alongside (and preferably below) the imperial ones.[29] The matter was finally resolved in Act 1848:21 in April, which read:

> § 1. The national colors and coat of arms shall be restored to their ancient rights.
>
> § 2. With the tricolor cockade having been adopted as a civil symbol, it is also established that the national flag and coat of arms shall be used on every public building and public institution, in all public celebrations, and on every Hungarian ship.[30]

If the first paragraph, with its language of restoration rather than of revolution, provides a justification for the law, the second shows clearly the determination of the Hungarian leadership to use symbols to demonstrate the new balance of power. To this end, the revolutionaries in Buda-Pest also ended the state tobacco monopoly and closed the imperial-royal smoke shops—a confident step, to be sure, but one that risked backfiring when the price of cigars immediately rose.[31]

Ordinary people were no less ostentatious. Drawing on a rich repertoire of Hungarian national symbols, most of them created or popularized in the 1830s and 1840s, men and women embraced national dances, songs, poems, and costumes. Consumers could purchase engravings of revolutionary leaders, which began to appear soon after March 15. The engraver Joseph Tyroler, who later printed revolutionary Hungary's banknotes, advertised portraits of Batthyány and Kossuth "in memory of the glorious achievements of our times, as well as of the immortal service of both worthy men in the rebirth of the dear fatherland."[32] Those with deeper pockets could show their support for the revolution through public donations, which became increasingly common after the decision to establish a Hungarian army in late May. The Pest Jewish community loaned the government 50,000 florins without interest, and at the same time offered 100 florins to 100 volunteers who completed three years of service. The well-heeled National Casino likewise placed 20,000 florins and all its silverware "on the altar of the homeland" (a popular phrase in 1848), and a wealthy merchant donated two chests of gold and silver wares, which were displayed in front of the National Museum.[33] Smaller donations, often as little as one florin, also poured in from the countryside, and, in scenes worthy of nineteenth-century opera, women handed over their jewelry to the Hungarian government.

Names also changed to reflect the new conditions. The town of Buda renamed streets in honor of Batthyány and Kossuth, and the Pest Town

Council commemorated the recent events with March 15 Square, Freedom Square, and Free Press Street.[34] In mid-April, the Opposition Circle, long a gathering place for Pest liberals, officially changed its name to the Radical Circle and adopted a new set of bylaws. "The Radical Circle," they read, "is a social club for those who desire to strengthen and give voice to the development of our constitution on the basis of the democratic spirit, liberty, equality, and fraternity."[35] Newspapers hurriedly followed suit: the liberal *Életképek (Sketches of Life)* appended *Népszava (Voice of the People)* to its title, and the conservative *Honderű (Serene Homeland)* was reincarnated first as the radical *Reform (Reform)* and later as the short-lived *Nép-elem (People's Element)*.[36] Other revolutionary titles included *Kossuth Hirlapja (Kossuth's Paper)*, *Munkások Ujsága (Workers' Newspaper)*, *Köztársasági Lapok (Republican Pages)*, and *Die Patriot (The Patriot)*. To emphasize its break with the old regime, the liberal *Pesti Hirlap*, in circulation since 1841, began numbering its issues from one again after March 15, 1848. This was a minor (and inexpensive) alteration, but, like the others described here, it suggested that a new era had dawned.

One of the singular aspects of the Hungarian Revolution was the extent to which it encouraged individuals to adopt new names. There were precedents for this: in the 1790s some Frenchmen had exchanged their Christian names for those of the Roman Republic, and thus Jean had become Gracchus or Brutus.[37] In Hungary in 1848–49, many people with German or Slavic surnames demonstrated their loyalty by voluntarily adopting Hungarian-sounding names. The Pest town councilor Boldizsár Holovits, otherwise a cautious, even conservative, observer of events, took the surname Homonnai. This involved more than a few drinks and a burst of national-minded enthusiasm, because those wishing to change their names had to petition the interior minister and pay a three-florin fee. In this way, the writer and translator Karl Benkert cleverly reversed the syllables of his surname and became Kertbeny. Although some people with German-sounding names translated them directly into Hungarian (hence the draftsman Nikolaus Liebe—in English, Nicholas Love—became Miklós Szerelmey), others were more inventive in their choice of Magyar surnames.[38] The fisherman Jakob Schröder became Jakab Varsai—the rough equivalent in English of going from Jacob Taylor to Jacob Weir or, more loosely, to Jacob the Fish Catcher. Revolution or no, people also had a fondness for aristocratic names: for example, the journalist Karl Lesigan became Károly Andorffy, a name worthy of a count.[39] A number of women, likely widows, also appear in the sources, such as Eleanora Pellett, who changed her surname to Szivesy.[40]

Many of those who adopted new names were Jews. Mihály Táncsics, who organized young Jewish men into their own militia unit, gave each recruit a new, Hungarian-sounding name.[41] Other individuals made the decision on their own. A ministerial announcement from June 1849, for example, approved the request of the medical student Móric Eisler to change his surname to Vasfi, literally, "man of iron."[42] But joining the national community had never been simple for Jews. Non-Jewish writers had long insisted that Jews abandon religious and cultural practices that set them apart from the rest of the population—and these were the writers who viewed Jews with relative tolerance, the ones who did not fantasize about either expelling or converting the Jews en masse. Within the Jewish community, the 1848–49 Revolution gave a strong impetus to religious reformers. In early May, for example, the Magyarization Society circulated a petition calling on "Hungarians of the Mosaic faith" to introduce "changes required by our age" and to abandon all traditions (dress, dietary laws, and the Sabbath) that gave could give rise to charges of separatism.[43] In July 1848, the newly formed Hungarian Central Reform Association began to raise money to purchase church organs for Jewish synagogues and to translate German-language prayer books into Hungarian. In this environment, it is perhaps not surprising that a number of leading Jews converted to Christianity. The converts included several prominent Pest merchants, such as Jónás Kunewalder, who until then had been the head of the Pest Jewish community.[44] Any number of factors—expediency, perceived pressure, revolutionary enthusiasm, and Hungarian national loyalty—may have been at work here, but this was undoubtedly a highly symbolic demonstration of revolutionary solidarity.

Among political radicals, the revolution sparked debates on language and social hierarchy. Invoking the principle of equality, a handful of writers called for people to abandon titles of nobility, a provocative suggestion in Hungary, where nobles made up more than 5 percent of the population and dominated social and political life. To set an example, the young writer Mór Jókay dropped the noble suffix -y from his surname and began writing Jókai. Others called for more egalitarian forms of address, and thus some radicals, inspired by the French Revolution, urged people to address one another simply as *"polgártárs"* (citizen). This practice seems to have taken root in 1848, at least among young people in Pest. "Titles came to an end; the whole world was citizen and citizeness," recalled one revolutionary.[45] Less successful was Mihály Táncsics's suggestion that Hungarian-speakers henceforth address one another as *"kend,"* a term used by peasants. This would be similar to suggesting all Americans call one another "pardner."[46] There were obvious limits to what the wider population would accept—more evidence of the gap between the Pest radicals and most of the political public—yet these efforts suggest the extent to which some enthusiasts hoped to carry the revolutionary struggle into all areas of life.

The emphasis on national symbols also contributed to debates surrounding the role of women in public life. Across Europe, a small number of female activists used the revolutions of 1848 to challenge the traditional exclusion of women from the political community. "When they say the people," wrote Louise Otto, editor of the Saxony-based *Women's News-*

paper, "women do not count."[47] In Hungary, the revolution offered new roles to women, and in its first months women sewed banners, wore the national colors, and took part in street demonstrations. In late April, a new group called the Radical Hungarian Women published a twenty-four-point petition, which asserted that women should "actively take part in public affairs as much as possible," a demand with little precedent in Hungary.[48] The petition was conventional in that it highlighted the role women could play as national-spirited wives and mothers, and it reminded women not to forget "about the woman's realm and responsibilities." But it also encouraged women to take up their pens in service of "freedom, the homeland, and women" and to form a network of associations across the country. Underscoring the significance of symbolic acts, the petition called on women to speak the Hungarian language, purchase domestic goods, wear national costumes, and dance national dances. The experience of women during the Hungarian Revolution was ultimately a mixed one: like men, women held views across the political spectrum and few substantive gains for them came in 1848–49. Yet the revolutionary experience was important in that it mobilized women and laid the groundwork for their seeing themselves as a discrete group of citizens.

But what of those who did not rush to don the national costume, dance the *csárdás,* or address their friends as "citizen"? The forging of national communities often involves attacks on perceived domestic or foreign "enemies," and revolutionaries in Buda-Pest often used symbolic criteria to distinguish friend from foe. The boundaries of the national community, still ill defined in the 1840s, were becoming more distinct. This could be taken to extremes. "Those Hungarian women who avoid the national literature and arts and deem only foreign ones worthy of attention," warned the Radical Hungarian Women, "women who, for example, subscribe to German or French papers and read only foreign books, are forever despised, and we will expel these traitorous, degenerate girls from our circles."[49] The nationalist frenzy affected even Catholic priests, not a group one might expect to embrace revolution. Father János Szerenespataki, for instance, called on his fellow priests to demonstrate their national loyalty by wearing the *atilla*—a braided jacket, part of the national costume—in public and by growing beards since, with few exceptions, the political leadership was bearded.[50] There is an almost comical air to these suggestions, but the priest's concern is obvious: he does not want Catholic leaders to lag in their outward displays of Hungarianness.

What is striking about Buda-Pest in 1848–49 is how rapidly and enthusiastically ordinary men and women adopted the revolution's symbols. In this they were often behaving like their fellows across Europe: the language, colors, and costumes were nationally Hungarian, but the basic symbolic repertoire (flags, slogans, and anthems) was largely the same. Transnational patterns deeply influenced supposedly national symbols. France in particular was the model to be emulated, as was clear from the formation in Buda-Pest of a committee of public safety, the ubiquitous cockades, and the performance of the French anthem at public events.[51] But the Hungarians must also have been watching events elsewhere in the Habsburg Monarchy, where Viennese radicals paraded in black, red, and gold to show their German alignment and Croat activists demanded wider use of their language, colors, clothing, and dances. If the Hungarian case was different, it was only in the breadth and endurance of the political consensus behind the Hungarian language and other national symbols. It was not enough to support the revolutionary cause; one had to do so in the Hungarian language. This was not just the view of radical hotheads. The Hungarian parliament turned away a German-speaking parliamentary deputy who did not know Hungarian, telling him that he had two months to learn the language.[52] Indeed, for some nationalists, language was only the starting point, and they were ready to exclude from the national community anyone who did not look, act, or pray like a "Hungarian."

Club Life During the Revolution

Associational life provides another measure of the impact of the 1848–49 Revolution in Buda-Pest. Social clubs, charitable associations, cultural organizations, and scholarly societies had all been part of the pre-1848 political landscape across Europe, and their numbers, membership, and visibility increased rapidly in 1848. As Jonathan Sperber has written, "Much of the history of the revolution can be understood in terms of the formation of such groups, their affiliation and federation, their mutual interaction, and their role in political mobilization of broad groups of the population."[53] Across the continent, political clubs proliferated with the establishment of freedom of assembly. Over the course of the revolution, associational life became more diverse as club life spread from city to countryside and as democrats, conservatives, Catholics, and others launched their own societies. Paris alone was home to approximately 200 political clubs, and by 1849 the German lands had 1,400 clubs with a total of more than 700,000 members.[54] It is not surprising that one of the first steps later taken by counterrevolutionary regimes was to place strict limits on public meetings and the right to form associations.

Buda-Pest had long been a city of joiners, and voluntary associations had taken on quasi-political roles well before 1848. Although revolutionary Pest was not Paris or Berlin, it still produced a remarkable array of political clubs: the Radical Circle, March Club, Democratic Club, Society for Equality, Pest German Club, and perhaps even a short-lived women's club. Rumors swirled of a secret Czech club in Pest and of covert meetings of Catholic priests in Buda.[55] There were also informal gatherings of ministers, moderates, burghers, and soldiers, and young men gathered in the coffeehouses. The spirit of the revolution infused all these places: "Card playing has entirely ceased in our clubs," bragged one paper, "and without doffing our hats we hold popular assemblies, where speakers announce the free word while standing on chairs."[56] Anything with a scrap of news in it—newspapers, decrees, petitions, and even private letters—might be read aloud in the clubs and coffeehouses.

No association grew more rapidly at the beginning of the revolution than the Radical Circle. The circle played a significant role in the March Revolution in Pest, and, in the following weeks, lawyers, merchants, doctors, and officials, as well as the occasional upholsterer, actor, and clergyman, rushed to join the club.[57] In a clear break with pre-1848 traditions, the Radical Circle openly engaged in politics. In March, for example, it drew up a list of proposed ministers and helped organize a national guard unit.[58] In June, it assembled a list of candidates for elections to the Pest Town Council; according to the newspaperman Chownitz, the authority of the Radical Circle was so great that many districts in the city immediately accepted their candidates. But what sort of politics went on in the Radical Circle? The club included many Pest radicals (one member took subscriptions for a translation of Robespierre's speeches), but no uprisings would be launched from here, and genuine radicals would always constitute a minority.[59] Despite its name, the Radical Circle firmly supported the moderate liberal government, and all but two of the government's ministers were members. It was a place of free discussion, debate, and criticism, as well as a gathering place and a sounding board for supporters of the new government.

A closer look at one of the Radical Circle's assemblies suggests how this might have worked. At the end of April, the Radical Circle held a banquet in honor of a delegation of political leaders from Transylvania. Revolutionaries throughout Europe dreamed of national unification in 1848; for the Hungarians, this meant the return of Transylvania, which had been part of the medieval Hungarian kingdom, but had since been governed by the Ottomans and later by the court in Vienna. The featured speaker was Miklós Wesselényi, a highly respected, nearly blind Transylvanian politician. Describing troubles brewing in southern Hungary, Wesselényi warned that Vienna, with its "infernal cunning," was stirring up Serbs, Croats, and others against the Magyars. He concluded rousingly: "To arms, citizens! . . . Life or death awaits our nation."[60] Members of the Radical Circle greeted Wesselényi's speech with great acclaim, and at a special assembly held the following day, they drafted a petition calling on the government to establish an army, send emissaries to the countryside to rally the population, and declare General Josip Jelačić, recently appointed *Ban* (governor) of Croatia, a traitor and remove him from office.[61] Members of the Hungarian government soon reached the same conclusions: on May 16, the call for ten *honvéd* battalions went out, and on July 11 Kossuth delivered a tremendous speech to parliament in which he asserted that "the homeland is in danger" and won approval to raise a 200,000-strong Hungarian army.[62] As Wesselényi's and Kossuth's language makes clear, even at the height of their success, leading Magyars remained haunted by the specter of being surrounded by enemies. The image of "national death" hovered before the Magyars and filled their speeches; only a strong, unified people, it was believed, could save Hungary from this fate.

Despite such calls for national unity, it was natural for groups that felt insufficiently represented in the Hungarian government (and after the June elections, in parliament) to organize themselves into associations. In early April, an article appeared in a German newspaper calling for the formation of a political club to bring together patriots of all social classes for discussion and the exchange of ideas—in German.[63] With its goal of promoting the common good and strengthening the principles of liberty, equality, and fraternity, the proposed German Club promised to fill a need: "The Magyars have their gathering places; the German-Hungarians are lacking them." The club would promote the cause of the revolution among German-speaking activists of Pest, a group here identified as *Deutschmagyaren*. The Pest German Club, one of the first of its kind in Hungary, began meeting later that month. Although little is known about its operations or its membership, several sources suggest that actors from the German theaters joined in large numbers.[64] The club reportedly hoped to rally support for the German Parliament meeting in Frankfurt and to defend German interests locally, although it did not define what this might mean in practice.

More certain is that the nationalist press savagely attacked the German Club. An early salvo was fired by the newspaper *Reform*, which published an anonymous letter that accused members of the German Club of speaking out against the Hungarian nationality, denouncing those who had Magyarized their names, and barring Magyars from its meetings. The letter concluded bluntly, "One cannot serve two masters. The Germans who dare turn their eyes to Germany should be expelled from the country. Those Germans who live under Hungarian laws and enjoy Hungarian rights are even more culpable if, filled with reactionary tendencies, they throw themselves into foreign arms. They are doubly treasonous. If only the government would step forward against these traitors!"[65] In a more restrained voice, another paper suggested that the Pest German Club was the work of foreigners and asked why the members had set themselves apart from the Hungarian-speaking burghers.[66] In reply, Chownitz defended the club firmly: "Do not look for ghosts where there are none."[67] "Just because we write in German," he added the next day, "it does not change the content of what we say; language is simply a tool." "We see ourselves as patriots," Chownitz asserted, and he invited Hungarian-speakers to take part in the club's meetings. He also defended the club in the Pilvax Café (in spite of loud opposition, he was allowed to speak in German), where he argued that the freedom of assembly applied to the German Club as well.

Chownitz's dream of forging links between the Pest German Club and Hungarian activists quickly dissipated. The club's vice-president condemned Chownitz's activities and denounced him for speaking on behalf of the club. Chownitz responded by declaring that the club's politics were not his own and tendered his resignation.[68] The Hungarian press soon joined in the fray. After describing this incident, one paper warned its readers that the club was dangerous, because it aimed to unite the German population and forge an alliance with German states.[69] The paper also suggested that, if the authorities did not suppress this "separatist enterprise," the Hungarian people should. Noting that the Pest German Club was still holding meetings nearly two months later, a second paper repeated the same refrain and warned that the club represented exclusively German interests. Such accusations should not be taken at face value, because there is little evidence of widespread German national loyalty in Buda-Pest; German-speakers held a wide range of political views. But the diatribes make clear that, at least in the eyes of the Hungarian-language press, the compound *Deutschmagyar* was not an option in 1848: one could be either *Deutsch* (and disloyal) or *magyar* (and loyal), but not both. The edge of Hungarian nationalism was sharpening.

The effects were soon felt in the Buda and Pest Town Halls (see this book's frontispiece). Elections in May and June had returned town governments that solidly supported the revolution, even if many officials had links to the pre-1848 leadership.[70] In Pest, Leopold Rottenbiller, previously vice-mayor, was now elected mayor; in Buda, a master carpenter and property owner named Karl Jakobsohn became mayor. Yet voters also gave council seats to a number of prominent Hungarian activists, including the poet Vörösmarty, the radical Nyáry, the tailor Gáspár Tóth, and the button maker István Szilágyi, all of them outspoken advocates of the national cause. These new councilors immediately made their presence felt in both towns.[71] When Pest's newly elected town council first assembled in early July, it began to use Hungarian in its deliberations. This was a clear break with previous practice, in which records had been kept in Hungarian, but discussions had almost always taken place in German, even after March 15. On paper, councilors still had the right to address the assembly in German, but in practice the more zealous Hungarian-speaking members interrupted or shouted down anyone who tried to speak German. When German-speaking councilors started to stay away from meetings, the nationalist press remarked only that the Magyars were much more hardworking. In Buda, an even smaller number of councilors insisted on speaking Hungarian over the objections of their many colleagues who knew only German. Their intransigence tied up the council for weeks, earning the praise of the newspaper *Kossuth Hirlapja,* which saluted these "fighters of a noble battle for the nationality." Tensions peaked in early August, when a number of German councilors angrily walked out of a meeting. Only weeks later did the Hungarian councilors submit to a compromise, according to which the council would use German in its deliberations and both languages for resolutions and the minutes.[72]

The invective against the German Club and the rousing cheers for the intolerant councilors primarily came from the pens of Pest radicals, who were concurrently trying to found their own political organization. In the radicals' eyes, the revolution was still unfinished, and they continued to call for universal suffrage, full emancipation of Jews, a state-financed school system, and the abolition of church lands. They had their blind spots: radicals thought about "the people" in idealized or abstract terms, yet, when actually confronted with angry journeymen or hungry peasants, they offered little more than sympathy. "I was disappointed," wrote Mihály Táncsics, "because these young people had already sunk into the mire of prejudice in their childhoods," from which "they were not able to extricate themselves."[73] After a number of false starts, radicals founded the Society for Equality, which brought left-wing parliamentary deputies together with the March Youth, creating a coalition of those dissatisfied with the Hungarian government.[74] The club quickly attracted wide support, and by September it had gained more than 1,000 members, including thirty parliamentary deputies. Its meetings were marked by lively debate, and, in what was considered a provocative act, members addressed one another in the familiar form (te), rather than as "gentlemen." As tensions rose between Hungary and Austria in late August and early September, the radicals' rhetoric grew more and more ominous. Attacking Batthyány's government for its moderation, Pál Vasvári said, "The Cabinet should be set aside and those who think themselves capable should take the government into their own hands. They should guillotine the leaders and save the fatherland."[75] Supportive members called for a banquet to rally public opinion and urged the formation of a "vigilante committee" and even a private army to back up their words.

These threats were soon forgotten following the invasion of Hungary by a 40,000-strong imperial army under General Josip Jelačić on September 11, 1848. The members of the Society for Equality immediately threw their support behind the war effort and rallied to the new government formed under the Kossuth's leadership. Hungarian forces stopped Jelačić outside Buda-Pest on September 29, but the war would continue and gain in intensity. In the assessment of István Deák, "The revolutionary phase in the Habsburg lands may well have ended in October 1848; what came later was a war between the Hungarian national government and the other parts of the monarchy."[76] The war also closed a chapter on associational life in Buda-Pest. For much of 1848, political clubs had served an important function in the city. With their assemblies, petitions, speeches, and debates, clubs helped to expand (as in the case of the Radical Circle) and define (as in the German Club) the limits of the political public. Associations continued to operate through the end of the year, but it was increasingly plain that the fate of the revolution would be determined on the battlefield.

"To Fight for the Homeland Is a Beautiful Thing"

The success of the revolutionary Hungarian armies was unique in 1848–49, but in the end they succumbed to overwhelming Austrian and Russian forces. There are many reasons why the collapse did not come earlier: Kossuth's charisma and tireless energy played a major role, as did the unexpected skill of several Hungarian generals. But this resistance would not have been possible without the remarkable support of the wider population, and it is estimated one in two Magyar families contributed to the military struggle in one way or another.[77] In this charged environment, the war effort came to overshadow crowds, symbolic displays, and voluntary associations. In Buda, men and women voluntarily worked to strengthen the fortifications on Castle Hill: the Zichy sisters again led the way, donning simple cotton dresses and pushing wheelbarrows. In Pest, military conflict tamed the radicals, who threw themselves behind the war effort. Petőfi and Vasvári had already enlisted in the army by the end of September, and many other young men followed their example. Those who did not were open to criticism: "To fight for the homeland is a beautiful thing," said one parliamentary deputy, "but to parade around with a red ribbon and cockade is not."[78] Public gatherings in Pest for the remainder of 1848 accordingly had a strong military flavor. Audiences in the National Theater, for example, included large numbers of men in uniform.[79] Similarly, when the Radical Circle held a banquet in honor of visiting Polish revolutionaries in November, the mood, music, and guests were serious, and toasts were somberly drunk to the army and to Kossuth.

The Hungarian armies experienced initial success, but the fighting did not go well in late 1848. At the end of December, with enemy armies rapidly approaching and its own forces nowhere in sight, the Hungarian government, with its banknote press, armaments industry, and parliament in tow, retreated from Buda-Pest to Debrecen in the eastern part of the country. Austrian troops under Field Marshal Windisch-Graetz thus occupied Buda-Pest in early January without firing a shot. A few residents openly welcomed the imperial forces: they included loyal, as well as opportunistic, individuals, such as the engineer and newspaper editor Károly Glembay, who as recently as September had said that it was time for Hungarians "to fight for the welfare and security their beloved homeland with swords rather than pens."[80] But much of the population was more cautious, knowing that occupation meant continued hardships and the quartering of soldiers. For their part, the Austrian authorities rapidly moved to assert control over public life in Buda-Pest: they forbade assemblies and meetings, closed down clubs, casinos, and cultural associations, and banned some newspapers and replaced the editors of others. On February 11, 1849, Windisch-Graetz issued a proclamation warning the Jewish communities of Buda, Pest, and Óbuda that he would hold them collectively responsible and fine them 20,000 florins if any of their members were found spying, spreading rumors, or sending supplies to the Hungarian armies.[81] With great ceremony, the occupying forces disinterred and reburied General Ferenc Lamberg, the imperial-royal commissioner and commander-in-chief murdered by a Pest mob in late September 1848.[82] The authorities also removed Hungarian coats of arms from public buildings and painted the National Museum, the site of so many mass meetings in 1848, Habsburg yellow. In a move that had both symbolic and financial overtones, the occupying authorities declared that all "Kossuth notes" (banknotes issued by the Hungarian government) were now worthless.

If the occupying authorities understood the significance of symbolic gestures, so too did the population of Buda-Pest. Ignoring the ban on associational life, the Radical Circle continued to meet and host loud debates, at least through the end of January.[83] The son of a Pest guild master was arrested for refusing to sit at the table with army officers quartered in his house.[84] The librarian Gábor Mátray, who kept a detailed diary during the occupation, recorded that someone had yelled "Long live Kossuth" in the National Theater and escaped, and that an apprentice had shouted "Jelačić is a scoundrel" to a passing imperial officer and escaped only because the officer thought he had said "Hurrah for Jelačić!"[85] In short, anecdotal evidence suggests that a sizeable part of the population was waiting for the return of the Hungarian army. "We celebrated March 15," wrote one Pest citizen about the first anniversary of the revolution. "True, just secretly. We looked at one another, we clinked glasses, and everyone knew who we were toasting. Our lips were silent, but our hearts were filled with patriotic thoughts."[86] Such displays were not a threat to the occupying forces, but they are again a reminder of the breadth of support for the revolutionary cause in Buda-Pest, as well as an indication of the many ways that it could manifest itself.

The Hungarian leaders repaid this loyalty in full. In spring 1849, the main Hungarian army, which had vanished into the northern mountains in January, suddenly reappeared and won an impressive series of battles under the command of General Artúr Görgey. After months of retreats and evasions, the Hungarians found themselves on the offensive. Instead of carrying the war into Austria, Görgey's forces decided to capture the fortress of Buda, which was guarded by 4,000 determined Austrians. Strategically, the move was a disaster, because it allowed the reeling Austrian forces to regroup and tied up Hungarian forces for weeks. But the siege and capture of Buda had immense political symbolism and at the time were viewed as Hungary's greatest triumph. "Will there be someone," mused Pál Hunfalvy in his diary, "who has seen the siege of Buda, has watched the people of Pest, and has lived there through worries and battles, who will describe these eighteen days as Thucydides would have?"[87] The days following the fall of Buda were filled with a victory parade, a massive celebration in the city park, and a burial procession for fallen Hungarian soldiers (the Austrian commander was thrown in a trench).[88]

In 1848, Kossuth had declared that Buda-Pest would not be the "master" of the revolution. In 1849, however, Hungary's armies fought long and hard to liberate the twin towns—both sides suffered more than 1,000 casualties in the final battle for Buda—and its government and parliament promptly returned when they did. On June 5, 1849, Kossuth reentered Pest in a gilded carriage and was greeted by large, enthusiastic crowds. On June 24, in a highly symbolic act, the minister of the interior officially created "Budapest" from Buda, Pest, and Óbuda. The decree read in part, "The Hungarian state can have only one capital in which Pest chiefly provides the living strength and Buda chiefly provides the ancient historic memory."[89] It continued: "[T]he splendor, strength, power, and greatness of the national capital is dependent on its unity, of which our country, attacked in an unjust war, now stands in most particular need." Revolutionary Hungary now had its capital.

To the dispassionate observer, this newly minted national capital must have looked like an oversized Potemkin village. People were in the streets, Hungarian national symbols were on the walls, and associations had reopened their doors. But the activities of the Radical Circle are again instructive. In June 1849, not long after the recapture of Buda by Hungarian forces, the Radical Circle held two final meetings. The minutes show that, under the Austrians, the circle had successfully prevented a list of its members from falling into the hands of the occupying forces but that its quarters had been devastated, its library dispersed, and its finances ruined.[90] On June 21, the circle's assembly voted unanimously to dissolve the society, resolving that any funds remaining after expenses be used to help the war effort. It was too late. In early July, the Hungarian government was forced to abandon Budapest and move to Szeged in southern Hungary. Austrian and Russian forces occupied the city later that month, making the unification of Budapest a dead letter. The war of independence would end within six weeks; Buda, Pest, and Óbuda would not be united again until 1872–73.

The victorious Austrians attempted to remove all traces of the revolutionary "contagion" from public life in Buda-Pest. They closed political clubs, shut down journals and newspapers, and arrested and imprisoned revolutionary leaders. Dozens of executions followed; the victors sentenced many more people to long prison terms and forcibly inducted *honvéd* soldiers and officers into the imperial army and stationed them throughout the empire. All laws passed during the revolution, starting with the April Laws of 1848, were considered invalid, as were all ministerial decrees. The occupying authorities immediately placed Buda-Pest under a state of siege, which lasted until 1854. They also replaced Hungarian with German as the language of administration, permitted public meetings only with prior approval, and forbade the wearing of the Hungarian national colors or costumes. People who had changed their names were forced to use their old ones, and the famous Café Pilvax was renamed Café Herrengasse. Overlooking no details, the authorities decreed that shop signs could not have red-white-and-green lettering and that, if they had Hungarian wording, it had to appear below the German, which was now required; shopkeepers were given forty-eight hours to repaint their signs.[91] They likewise ordered that entrances to all official buildings be painted black and gold, the imperial colors. Visitors described a changed city. The wife of Rabbi Lipót Löw wrote in her diary, "Pest, which I had seen so happily before, where a warm welcome had always awaited me, now seemed so ugly."[92] Returning to Pest after the collapse of the revolution, Hunfalvy mourned its loss: "Pest is no longer ours, Pest is henceforth our grave."[93]

The revolutionary experience, however, could not be buried so easily. In part, this was because the Habsburgs themselves accepted some of the changes of the revolution, including, most notably, the abolition of serfdom. The principles of constitutional and parliamentary government, full equality for Jews, linguistic rights for all national groups, and expanded civil liberties had also taken firm root in 1848–49 and would form the basis of liberals' political demands in coming decades. Other gains were less tangible but no less significant: the revolution had broken down barriers to participation in public life, allowing a large number of ordinary men and women to demonstrate their political and national convictions in the streets, in associations, and in symbolic displays. Such activities could be divisive, but they underscored the potential of all revolutions to make people feel that they are part of a larger political community.

The Hungarian Revolution thus hastened what Mona Ozouf called a "transfer of sacrality" among the population of Buda-Pest. This process was under way well before 1848, yet the revolutionary experience, as nothing before it, encouraged people to see themselves not as subjects, but as citizens belonging to a national community rather than a particular town, religion, or occupation. In this way, the revolution gave a powerful boost to the process of nationalization. If name changes, voluntary donations, and enlistment in the army are any indication, many town dwellers were eager to show their Hungarian national orientation. Yet they had few other options: German-speakers might adopt a German national orientation, but this was sure to bring down the wrath of Hungarian nationalists and had never had many supporters in Buda-Pest. Hungarian state patriotism—the old *Hungarus* view—remained an influential idea and would reappear throughout the nineteenth century. In Buda-Pest, however, Hungarian nationalists angrily rejected the German Club and its claim to represent German-speaking patriots. For these nationalists, the revolution had raised the bar on how loyalty should be demonstrated: there was no room for hesitation and no tolerance for hyphenation; one was demonstrably "Hungarian" in speech and action, or one was not. This left only dynastic loyalty—a continued attachment to the Habsburg rulers and their supporters in Buda-Pest. But the revolution had undermined the social and political system upon which dynastic loyalty had been built, and the imperial-royal advisors, officials, and soldiers who came to Buda-Pest in 1849 were deeply unpopular. Nor did it help that the Hungarian political leadership refused to recognize Francis Joseph, who had replaced his uncle Ferdinand in December 1848. Nevertheless, the imperial authorities were firmly in control. What this meant for a city that had recently been a revolutionary capital remained to be seen.

CHAPTER SEVEN

The Road to Budapest

"In the history of nationhood in our capital, we have repeatedly been witness to forcible Germanization. There could never be discussion of forcible Magyarization."

—József Kőrösi, head of the Capital Office of Statistics, 1881[1]

The collapse of the 1848–49 Revolution dramatically altered the physical and political landscape of Buda-Pest. The siege of May 1849 had scarred the twin towns, and the Habsburgs' victory later that summer gave them unchallenged authority in Buda-Pest. With its soldiers, administrators, policemen, and handpicked town councilors, the Habsburg side would play an active role in the towns' physical reconstruction, economic development, cultural life, and educational institutions. But did the regime also attempt to Germanize the twin towns, as József Kőrösi and generations of historians would later suggest?[2] And how did the Hungarian side adapt to these new conditions?

Provisional answers to these questions can be found in a census that the Austrian authorities conducted in 1850, just months after the end of the revolution. The aim was to determine the total population, break it down by religion, residency, and other characteristics, and lay the groundwork for military conscription. This would be the first comprehensive count of Hungary's population in decades, and it would include nobles and clergy, who previously had been exempt. But the authorities' decision to gather information about the population's nationality *(Nationalität)*, which they broadly defined in ethnographic rather than in linguistic terms, provoked the most controversy. When published in early 1851, the census reported that the population of Buda-Pest was roughly one-half German and one-third Magyar, with the balance a mix of Jews (who were counted as a separate national group), Slovaks, Serbs, and others.[3] In Buda, Germans (27,939) outnumbered Magyars (7,555) by nearly four to one, and even in Pest, Germans (33,884) held a slight advantage over Magyars (31,965).

Hungarian national activists raised angry objections even before the census was complete. The more empirical pointed out that "nationality" was a fuzzy category and difficult to determine in many cases, particularly because the authorities had not laid out clear criteria. Less-cautious critics alleged that the regime systematically inflated the number of Germans and undercounted Magyars. The mayor of Pest, Szilárd Terczy, voiced these suspicions to the district commissioner in an open letter.[4] To Terczy, the census had produced a "forced majority" of Germans in Pest, in part because census officials had unfairly registered as Germans many residents of Pest, "who in language and thought had already converted entirely to the Hungarian nationality." Terczy's message was obvious: Hungarian-speakers, not German-speakers, formed the largest part of the population of Pest (if not of Buda). Not everyone agreed with Terczy, and the conservative *Pester Zeitung* recalled that, even before the census, the mayor had declared that Magyars comprised a majority in Pest.[5] The paper tartly suggested that the results would have disappointed Terczy even more had the census differentiated between the ethnographic category "Magyar" (*Magyar* in the newspaper) and the geographic-political grouping "Hungarian" *(Ungar)*. Presumably, this would have created a column for people who felt loyal to their Hungarian homeland but were of German, Slovak, or Serb origin. Of course, the paper might also have asked why there were no "divided" or even "Habsburg" options on the census. But the authorities seem not to have fully grasped the political dimensions of the census, which they saw merely as an administrative tool. Yet, by grouping people together into discrete national categories, the census may unintentionally have contributed to the process of nationalization in Buda-Pest.[6] The authorities seemed to have realized this, and when they carried out the next census in 1857, they quietly dropped the category of "nationality."

Despite Terczy's allegations, the Austrian authorities did not pursue policies aimed at the "forcible Germanization" of Buda-Pest in the 1850s. They instead attempted to subdue and then to win over the population.[7] Their heavy-handed use of police and censors weighed equally on all residents, just as their efforts to foster the development of the towns and earn the goodwill of the population had little relation to nationhood. And if the authorities promoted the use of the German language, they also supported Hungarian-language theater, periodicals, and voluntary associations; their aim in the 1850s was simply to denationalize and depoliticize public life. Even in this changed political landscape, however, the idea of a "Hungarian Buda-Pest" continued to motivate national activists, who used a wide range of strategies to demonstrate their opposition to Vienna and promote the Hungarian cause in all corners of the city. The ensuing struggle was often fought in symbolic terms, but political legitimacy lay at its heart: which side possessed the right to not just to govern, but also to put its stamp on Buda-Pest? To this end, both the Habsburgs and their Hungarian opponents attempted to shape public opinion, recognizing that many residents of Buda-Pest remained uncertain in their allegiances and potentially open to recruitment.

Wider political events strongly influenced this contest in Buda-Pest. The collapse of the 1848–49 Revolution opened the door for a decade of neoabsolutist rule from Vienna. The governor-general of Hungary, military men, imperial officials, and reliable locals (the so-called *Gutgesinnte*) firmly held the reins of power in Hungary. Meaningful change would come only in 1859–61, when military defeat in northern Italy, economic crisis, and urban unrest forced Emperor-King Francis Joseph (r. 1848–1916) first to jettison his powerful minister of the interior, Alexander Bach, and then restore parliamentary life throughout the Habsburg lands. In Hungary, this led to elections and the meeting of the Hungarian Diet in Buda. Francis Joseph soon dissolved parliament and Vienna continued to govern Hungary, but the political calculus had changed. In 1865, Vienna and the Hungarian political leadership opened negotiations that resulted in the Compromise of 1867. This agreement made Hungary an equal partner with Austria in the Dual Monarchy and gave its government wide latitude in domestic affairs. The formation of Austria-Hungary not only hastened the unification of Budapest but quickened the tempo of both voluntary and forcible Magyarization as well.[8] The idea of a "Hungarian Budapest," it was clear, would continue to exert a strong influence on political leaders and national activists long after the Austrian officials were gone.

From Rubble to Royal Tours

The newspaper editor Emília Kánya described the devastation of Pest in the aftermath of the 1848–49 Revolution: "Oh, Lord! What has become of our beautiful town? The banks of the Danube have been made nearly unrecognizable. The large Redoute Hall is blasted to ruin, its columns lay scattered on the ground, its windows stare out blackly like the hollows of a giant's blinded eyes."[9] When an American writer came to Pest in 1851, he saw a cannonball that still sat in a woman's parlor and a clergyman's shelled library, leading him to conclude that "it will be long before Pesth recovers from that fearful punishment."[10] Buda, which had been the scene of the fiercest fighting in 1849, was in worse shape, and the royal castle and many surrounding buildings were unusable. In time, the rubble would be cleared and the castle and other structures rebuilt. This would have occurred under any regime, yet, in the tense environment of the 1850s and 1860s, the reconstruction, use, and development of the twin towns took on wider political importance, with the Habsburg authorities and Hungarian nationalists jousting for supremacy in the city.

This competition took place against the background of sustained urban expansion.[11] Local economic growth slowed for much of the 1850s and surged again only in the late 1860s. The total population of the twin towns nonetheless doubled during these decades, and by 1869 the towns had an estimated 269,000 residents, including 202,000 in Pest. Pest's most populous neighborhood, Theresa District, had more residents (70,000) than Hungary's second-largest city (Szeged). Because smallpox, typhus, cholera, and high infant mortality rates continued to check natural increase, immigration remained the engine of growth. The abolition of serfdom increased the flow of peasants from the countryside, and opportunities in construction and industry attracted skilled workers from outside Hungary. On average, Pest added 100 new buildings a year, roughly one-quarter of them two or more stories. (Even in 1872, however, 72 percent of Pest's houses were only one story, compared with 17 percent in Vienna and 5 percent in Berlin.) Rental incomes became a significant source of wealth for property owners, particularly in the more fashionable districts—Leopold District, the Inner City, and parts of Theresa District. New kinds of buildings dotted the cityscape, including factories, railroad stations, department stores, and stock exchanges; the towns now had firehouses, gas lamps, and even a zoo. As historian Károly Vörös has observed, Buda-Pest in 1872 was larger, taller, wealthier, and simply more "urban" than it had been in 1848.

How much credit could Vienna take for this? At first, the imperial authorities seemed interested only in shoring up their rule and intimidating the population.[12] Following the recapture of the city in 1849, the Austrian general Julius von Haynau had overseen a wave of arrests, trials, court-martials, and executions, which culminated in the death by firing squad of Count Lajos Batthyány, the former prime minister, on October 6, 1849. A month later, Haynau ceremonially opened the Chain Bridge across the Danube, and thus the bridge that Széchenyi had deeded to the Hungarian nation now belonged, at least symbolically, to the military authorities. In 1851, the Austrians hanged in effigy more than thirty Hungarian leaders who were in hiding or exile. The Pest Town Council elected as honorary citizens (among others) the Austrian generals Haynau, Jelačić, Radetzky, and Windisch-Graetz; Buda unveiled a sizeable monument to General Hentzi, the Austrian commander who had died in the siege of May 1849. The hastily painted German-language street and shop signs were a further reminder that a new regime was in power, as were the rapidly rebuilt royal palace and fortifications in Buda. After observing the menacing cannons recently mounted on Buda's Palisade Hill (*Blocksberg*, today Gellért Hill), an American visitor dryly remarked that it was "interesting to observe how the Austrians were preparing for future struggles."[13]

A crackdown on public life soon followed. The authorities purged schools of unreliable teachers, placed students and professors under close supervision, and recruited instructors in the Austrian lands. They also closed dozens of newspapers, replaced editors, reintroduced stringent censorship, and supported loyalist newspapers across Hungary. When Imre Vahot, the former editor of *Pesti Divatlap*, wanted to start a new literary magazine, a police official told him that permission would come immediately if he agreed to publish his journal in German; otherwise, it would be impossible.[14] Voluntary associations likewise felt the full weight of repression. At the end of 1851, every society had to reapply for permission to operate, and those that did not were considered dissolved.[15] An imperial patent issued a year later further defined the legal status of voluntary associations: it strictly banned all political societies and reiterated the authorities' right to monitor societies to ensure that they adhered to their stated goals. The number of active associations in Buda-Pest dropped sharply, and those that remained adapted to the changed conditions. The surviving members of the Buda Casino, for example, now kept their minutes in German, subscribed to twice as many German as Hungarian newspapers, and contributed money to help the National Museum acquire portraits of Emperor Francis Joseph and Archduke Albrecht.[16] In a sign of the times, a military band played in the Buda Casino on Friday afternoons.

The German language received a boost across Buda-Pest. The military and civil authorities used German for all internal communications and, more often than not, in their dealings with the wider citizenry.[17] The Buda and Pest Town Councils eventually dropped Hungarian from their minutes and correspondence. In Pest, the town gave 40,000 florins to its German-language theaters but only 16,000 to the Hungarian one. The imperial authorities also promoted the use and study of German in schools, particularly on the secondary level, where German became a compulsory subject. By 1855, professors taught nineteen courses at the university in German, compared with nine in Hungarian and two in Latin; in the same year, Vienna ordered that all secondary school teachers hired in the future be able to teach in German.[18] At the same time, the authorities effectively discouraged people from taking Hungarian-sounding names, and in the 1850s, only a dozen or so people would win official approval to change their surnames. Several people with Hungarian- and Slavic-sounding names in fact took German surnames, but there is no evidence that they did this to show their adherence to the regime or that the authorities had encouraged them.

German did not always come at the expense of Hungarian. As the political situation stabilized, more Hungarian-language newspapers appeared in Buda-Pest, including medical, economic, and legal journals, as well as those aimed specifically at women, Catholics, Protestants, and music enthusiasts. By the end of the 1850s, Pest had forty-four periodicals, thirty-one of them in Hungarian, eleven in German, and two in Slovak.[19] Publishers also provided the expanding reading public with religious publications, almanacs, and novels: by one count, ninety-eight Hungarian-language novels were published in the 1850s, compared with thirty in the preceding three decades.[20] Nor did censorship and police supervision diminish the achievements of the Hungarian National Theater in Pest.[21] In 1850, the authorities required that all theatrical productions receive official approval, threatened directors with jail sentences if there were variations from the script, and ordered the police to attend all performances, including dress rehearsals; references to religious, national, or political issues were strictly forbidden. In this environment, the Hungarian National Theater carefully avoided works that might have antagonized the authorities. Yet the Hungarian Theater flourished, as its troupe performed Shakespeare, French Romantic dramas, and works by local authors (if less commonly, because Buda-Pest's audiences strongly preferred foreign dramas, operas, ballets, and musicals, most anything, it seems, to the Hungarian authors' dramas and tragedies).[22] By the early 1860s, the Hungarian National Theater had surpassed the towns' German theaters in every respect—financially, artistically, and professionally—even if it had also lost some of the pioneering, subversive spirit of its early years.

A number of imperial officials wanted to do more than merely remove politics from cultural life. Some worked actively to foster Hungary's economic development, and this, they hoped, might heal the wounds opened in 1848–49, compensate for the absence of a political life, and weaken the Hungarian national movement.[23] In Buda-Pest, imperial authorities approved useful economic institutions: new grain and stock exchanges, a brewery, and the Pest Lloyd Society, a commercial society founded by the towns' leading merchants in 1853. (Its 600 members included both Christians and Jews, and the society's newspaper, *Pester Lloyd* [Pest Lloyd], soon became the foremost business paper in the country.) They improved the water supply, introduced gas lighting, and backed the construction of a much-needed tunnel on the Buda side of the Chain Bridge. As part of his 1852 and 1857 tours of Hungary, Emperor Francis Joseph visited Buda-Pest, where he took part in military parades, religious ceremonies, and the dedication of statues. He also pardoned imprisoned revolutionaries and allowed some émigrés to return to Hungary. He astutely appropriated Hungarian symbols: in 1857, for example, Francis Joseph wore the uniform of a Hungarian hussar to a performance at the National Theater, where he received a lengthy ovation. In 1858, the town of Pest renamed two squares after the ruler and his popular wife, Elizabeth of Bavaria. Reconciliation between Hungary and the ruling house—if not yet its officials—seemed a possibility.

The Habsburgs' many-sided campaign won some converts. Propelled by their political convictions, loyalty to the dynasty, or material considerations, a number of aristocrats, nobles, burghers, officials, and writers made common cause with the Austrian authorities. The newspaperman Aurél Kecskeméthy wrote in his diary of a tension between his "national and civic senses" but concluded, "I am first of all a citizen of the Austrian Empire, and only as such am I a Hungarian."[24] Kecskeméthy was a correspondent for the semiofficial *Magyar Hirlap (Hungarian Gazette)* and had the ear of the Austrian authorities. Yet the state patriotism he embraced never achieved critical mass in Buda-Pest in the 1850s. Ignoring the regime's economic initiatives and cultural patronage, many Hungarian nationalists instead claimed to see a systematic program of "Germanization." Vienna's educational measures, explained one writer, aimed "to destroy the Magyar nationality and [forcibly] Germanize it along with the other nationalities living in the lands of the Crown of St. Stephen."[25]

Recent historians have been more cautious in their judgments. To C. A. Macartney, the system was nominally Germanizing in that it created a large, German-speaking bureaucracy, but this was not the same thing as creating nationally conscious Germans.[26] As Macartney explains, the regime of the 1850s attempted to depoliticize nationhood entirely, that is, to create a firewall between the cultural realm, in which vernacular languages (Hungarian, Slovak, Romanian, and so on) could be used, and the political sphere, for which German alone was appropriate. Historian Ágnes Deák has also shown that the government in Vienna, itself divided into competing camps, arrived at this cultural policy only gradually and never spelled it out in a single law or decree.[27] Laying to rest a long tradition in Hungarian historiography, she concludes that there was no attempt to de-nationalize or Germanize the population and only halting efforts in Hungary to encourage state patriotism. The result was the regime's heavy-handed but largely neutral cultural policy, to which it added intermittent but largely unsuccessful attempts to win the population's goodwill. Memories of 1848–49 Revolution, still fresh in people's minds, may have frustrated Vienna's efforts, but so too did an increasingly assertive national opposition in Buda-Pest.

The Architects of Resistance

The early 1850s were hard times in Buda-Pest for Hungarian national activists. Some retreated to the countryside, others went to Vienna or more distant cities, and still others eked out a living in the twin towns. Those who remained showed their dissatisfaction when they could: "A joke against Austrian stupidity goes over Pesth with the quickness of thought," noted a foreign visitor.[28] The Hungarian side's prospects improved greatly when the liberal leader Ferenc Deák moved back to Pest in 1854. Under his leadership, large parts of Hungary's political elite continued to insist that the April Laws of 1848 be restored and that the country be reunited before any kind of "normalization" was possible. Deák's measured opposition in turn gave confidence to more confrontational nationalists, who urged the residents of Buda-Pest to show their opposition to the authorities at every turn.

As recent work by Alice Freifeld has shown, national activists succeeded in grafting their agenda onto funerals, festivals, statues, dances, and public holidays.[29] When the authorities smothered social clubs and economic associations, activists rushed to join societies considered to have purely cultural, charitable, or scholarly aims. This allowed associations as diverse as the Natural Science Society, Pest and Buda Women's Associations, and Music Society to take on a new importance in the twin towns. The Pest Arts Society soon had more than 5,500 subscribers, up from 1,000 a decade earlier. People flocked to its exhibits in the Diana baths on the Pest bank of the Danube, where they saw an increasing number of paintings with distinctly Hungarian subjects: peasants, landscapes, and heroic leaders from the distant past. The Society of St. Stephen, a Catholic literary association, had more than 8,000 members, and perhaps because there were few other places to go, its meetings drew political figures such as Deák and Eötvös, as well as university professors, writers, and even a handful of Protestants.

As in the 1840s, the Hungarian cause brought together a wide spectrum of political actors. The case of Count Emil Dessewffy is instructive. A man of action, in the 1840s he had improved his estates, edited a newspaper, and helped found the Conservative Party. No friend of revolution, in 1848 he submitted lists to Vienna of revolutionaries he thought should be punished or pardoned.[30] Dessewffy expected to play a leading role in the 1850s and to act as a mediator between Hungary and the imperial authorities. Unfortunately, Vienna had little interest in negotiation and tended to view these "old conservatives" with suspicion. Nonetheless, the authorities installed Dessewffy as president of the Hungarian Academy of Sciences (the former Scholarly Society), clearly expecting that Dessewffy would keep the membership in line.[31] But if Dessewffy was a reliable political conservative, he could also speak approvingly of the "Magyarization of higher culture" and the "intellectual battles that aim to sustain our nationality."[32] Thus, Dessewffy approved the academy's plans to celebrate the centennial of the birth of Ferenc Kazinczy, the influential early nineteenth-century language reformer.

Unexpectedly, the tumultuous events of 1859 intervened: Austria fought a losing war in Italy, Bach fell from power, and the new government issued the ill-timed, unpopular, and short-lived Protestant Patent, which aimed to make Hungary's Protestant churches more pliable. Against this background, the Kazinczy celebrations of October 1859 turned into a noisy demonstration of Hungarian national pride. Never before had the Academy of Sciences electrified public opinion or filled the streets of Buda-Pest in this manner. Like the Schiller festivals in the Austrian and German lands of the same year, these banquets, parades, and festivals brought people together behind the banner of liberal reforms.[33] But if Schiller was celebrated as the poet of freedom and liberty (rather than as a symbol of German culture), Kazinczy was seen as the "poet of nationality" and hailed for his contribution to Hungarian language reform. Other national celebrations followed in Buda-Pest: on March 15, 1860, students led by the radical Mihály Táncsics attempted to commemorate the outbreak of the 1848–49 Revolution.[34] The local authorities used force against the students, but they could not prevent St. Stephen's Day (August 20) in 1860 from turning into a national demonstration. In Pest, thousands of people, many of them students, journeymen, and young workers, paraded under Hungarian flags, sang Vörösmarty's "Call," and shouted cheers for Garibaldi and the Hungarian leadership.[35] Women appeared in the national costume, and Catholic priests delivered defiant sermons in Hungarian.

The oppositional spirit also took over the dance floor. In the early 1850s, the authorities had discouraged the display of Hungarian national colors, costumes, dances, and music; women who wore black (as a sign of mourning for the 1848–49 revolutionaries) or a combination of red, white, and green could be fined. The police closely monitored balls and social gatherings, where they scrupulously took note of the dances, costumes, and conversations. In 1860, however, the entire carnival season turned into a long nationalist display, as men and women donned Hungarian costumes and refused anything but Hungarian dances.[36] Across Buda-Pest, balls broke down social barriers, bringing together Jews and Christians, as well as aristocrats, nobles, and burghers. As the police vainly attempted to impose order, crowds whistled and booed orchestras that played waltzes and other "German" music. Newspapers rushed to answer their readers' questions about the national costume: should men wear spurs? Did the ancient Magyars wear hats?[37] As one provincial activist later explained, the Hungarian costume "was not just an expression of national feeling, but also had the nature of a demonstration against the existing [political] conditions."[38]

With this sudden, sustained agitation, the Hungarian national movement regained the political initiative, which it would not relinquish even during the ensuing crackdown of the early 1860s. In this context, a number of journalists, architects, and scholars again took up the question of architecture and its relationship to national life. A catalyst was one of the most important architectural commissions of the period, the new Hungarian Academy of Sciences building.[39] The academy began raising funds for its new home in 1858, and donations soon poured in from across the country: aristocrats and wealthy Pest merchants were especially generous, and the town of Pest sold at half price a valuable plot of land at the foot of the Chain Bridge. When the academy solicited designs for the building in 1860 without specifying the architectural style, it sparked a wide-ranging discussion in the press. All sides agreed that the building's façade, its relationship to the Danube, the organization of the interior space, and the total cost were primary considerations. The members of the academy, it soon became clear, favored neoclassical and Gothic models. Even Imre Henszlmann, long a champion of Romantic nationalism in the arts, concluded that "the national elements of architecture do not exist" in Hungary.[40] He inventively explained that this was the result of the Magyars' nomadic roots and their long tradition of using foreign models for their homes, churches, and palaces.

The winning entry, by the Berlin architect Friedrich August Stüler, was for an imposing neo-Renaissance palace, the first major building in this style in Pest (see fig. 7). When completed, its rounded arches, triple façade, and recessed columns placed the building firmly within the classical tradition, just as statues of great thinkers—both European (Galileo, Leibnitz, and Newton) and Hungarian (Miklós Révai, the eighteenth-century linguist)— on the main façade clearly advertised its scholarly mission. The Renaissance style's connotations of civic autonomy and humanist culture had an obvi-

7—Architect Friedrich August Stüler's neo-Renaissance Hungarian Academy of Sciences building (built 1862–65).

ous appeal and made it a favorite of late nineteenth-century builders across urban Europe. In Pest, however, the academy was widely understood to be a bulwark of Hungarian nationhood, and at the building's opening ceremony in December 1865, Dessewffy invoked Hungarian culture as a shield against the alien and often harmful influences of modern scholarship. A handful of critics nevertheless complained that the structure itself was insufficiently "Hungarian." *Vasárnapi Ujság (Sunday Newspaper)* had earlier expressed its regret that the Academy's home would be "foreign," because it would be built in either the German (Gothic) or Italian (Renaissance) style.[41] Some writers held out the hope that a distinctive national architectural idiom would soon emerge: "We do not want to return to the old," wrote two architects, "let us instead look to the future; the style will come from itself and sooner than expected, an independent national architecture will adorn our beautiful homeland."[42]

What shape Hungarian national architecture would take, however, was no clearer now than it had been in the 1840s. Critics and architects could not agree on what was the most suitably national architectural style or whether it was form, function, or ornament (or some combination of the three) that gave a building a distinctly national character.[43] As a result, nearly every architectural tradition could be claimed by the Hungarian

national movement. The leaders of the Academy of Sciences, for example, could defend their choice of the neo-Renaissance style by arguing that it was a deliberate alternative to Vienna's dominant Baroque or simply by pointing out that the cultural and linguistic activities of their institution trumped the building's architectural program. The neo-Gothic style was an obvious alternative, and during this period the Gothic revival found an echo in Hungary. Gothic elements could be seen in Ferenc Wieser's Venetian-inspired Pichler House (built 1855–57) and in Miklós Ybl's eclectic National Riding School (1858). Defenders of the Gothic style trumpeted its associations with craftsmanship and national pride; its detractors saw it as too expensive, too Catholic, and too "German" (despite the fact that Gothic architecture had appeared in many parts of medieval Europe, including Hungary).

The third alternative to classicism and Gothic was architectural "orientalism," which could incorporate everything from Byzantine and Islamic to Indian and Chinese influences. In Buda-Pest, Frigyes Feszl's Vigadó concert hall proclaimed its Hungarian national character through a bold mixture of stylistic elements (see fig. 8). Built between 1859 and 1865, the Vigadó was a Romantic tour de force. Its façade combined Byzantine ornamentation, neoclassical statuary, and Islamic pillars imitating the Moorish architecture of southern Spain. Although experts would have recognized the assembled motifs, Feszl intended the disparate elements to add up to something distinctly Hungarian. It seemed to work, and one critic called Feszl's building a "*csárdás* in stone." This was meant to be sardonic, but it unwittingly acknowledged the connection between the new building and the national movement of the 1830s and 1840s.[44] Later in the nineteenth century, architects such as Ödön Lechner would incorporate folkloric rather than Islamic or Byzantine elements, but the goal of celebrating the uniqueness (and often the Eastern origins) of the Magyars remained the same.

The nationalists' appropriation of three distinct architectural languages in the 1850s and 1860s reflected the general openness of the Hungarian side at this time. This pluralism can also shed light on the place of Jews in this movement. In many respects, the 1850s were difficult times for Hungarian Jewry.[45] The victorious Austrians had invalidated the revolutionary law granting Jewish emancipation and greatly reduced the autonomy of Jewish communities in the Hungarian lands. The authorities also suspended Jewish property rights and required that all Jewish marriages receive official sanction. Gains came only in economic life—the regime's general promotion of industry and trade benefited Jewish and non-Jewish businessmen alike—and in education. In 1849, the Austrians had imposed a huge indemnity on Hungary's Jews for their participation in the revolution, but in 1850 Emperor Francis Joseph halved the fine and ordered that funds be used to establish Jewish schools in Hungary. The civil position of Jews improved only in 1859–61, when imperial decrees allowed them to

8—The "*csárdás* in stone": Frigyes Feszl's Vigadó Hall (built 1859–65).

employ Christian apprentices and servants, opened formerly closed professions and mining towns, and restored their property rights. The short-lived Hungarian Parliament of 1861 established a committee to prepare legislation that would grant Jews full emancipation.

Against this backdrop, the Jewish community in Pest erected a new synagogue, the first sizeable Jewish temple in Hungary. The community had purchased a plot of land on Dohány (Tobacco) Street in 1844, but began to solicit designs only in the mid-1850s after Rabbi Schwab had smoothed over religious divisions within the Pest community, which was increasingly divided between conservatives and moderate reformers—the Neologs, who wanted to introduce new elements into synagogues (organs, choirs, and vernacular sermons) without compromising fundamental religious laws. The Viennese architect Ludwig Förster, who had already built Vienna's main synagogue, was chosen for the project. The resulting structure artfully balanced the needs and traditions of the Jewish community with the expectations and building conventions of a largely Catholic city (see fig. 9).[46] The temple's two towers, for example, referred to the two columns in front of Solomon's temple in Jerusalem and at the same time closely resembled the steeples of a Christian church (Gothic elements on the exterior may have functioned in the same way). Moreover, with its polychromatic bricks, terracotta trim, and striped masonry, the building's façade pointedly recalled the architecture of Moorish Spain, where Jews had peacefully coexisted with Catholics and Muslims for centuries. This style was used for contemporary synagogues in Vienna, Prague, and even New York City, and it reflected the greater self-confidence and visibility of their Jewish communities in the second half of the nineteenth century. As architectural historian Ákos Moravánszky has noted, in most Western cities this orientializing architecture may have set the Jews apart from the rest of the population; in Hungary, however, Jewishness and Hungarianness could overlap in their use of a common "Eastern" architectural language.[47] That Pest architect Frigyes Feszl designed much of the Pest synagogue's interior further strengthened these affinities.

These commonalities perhaps explain why the Dohány Street synagogue was so warmly received. One Jewish writer even claimed that it surpassed Solomon's ancient temple.[48] Its consecration in 1859 drew high-ranking military and civil officials of all faiths: the ceremony struck a balance by closing with a blessing for Francis Joseph and the ruling house, as well as with the choir's performance of the Hungarian anthem, complete with organ accompaniment. But this even-handedness rapidly gave way to full-fledged support for the Hungarian side, as the so-called Festival of Jewish-Magyar Brotherhood (December 19–20, 1860) showed plainly. This event brought together Jews and Christians in the Dohány Street Synagogue, where they prayed, sang Vörösmarty's "Call," and collected money for a statue of the poet Sándor Petőfi. This national-spirited celebration coincided with the refounding of the old Magyarization Society, now called the Israelite Magyar Society, which soon had 918 members.[49] Like its predecessor, the society established a reading room with Hungarian books, held public lectures, and encouraged the use of Hungarian (instead of German or Yiddish) in Jewish schools, shops, and temples. More broadly, it aimed to cement the bond between the Pest Jewish community and Hungarian leaders and, in so doing, to prepare the way for full Jewish emancipation. In 1866, Rabbi Sámuel Kohn would deliver the first Hungarian-language sermon in the Dohány Street synagogue, and, a year later, the Hungarian parliament would pass a law (Act 1867:17) granting Jews equal civil and political rights as individuals.

There were still many doubters. It was not just the Orthodox who rejected the outward symbols of Jewish acculturation in the wider world— the language, clothes, choirs, and organs—and at the so-called Jewish Congress of 1868–69, the Orthodox would formally break with the Neolog majority over the question of language and religious reform.[50] Even some reformers worried about the price of an openly Hungarian alignment. In an address to the Israelite Magyar Society in 1863, Rabbi Sámuel Fischer addressed this issue: "The Israelites have suffered everywhere on the globe, but have only flourished in our homeland [Hungary]; to recognize this is our duty, only in this way will we become Magyar-Israelites [magyar-

9—Echoes of Moorish Spain: Ludwig Förster's Dohány Street Synagogue (built 1854–59).

izraeliták]."[51] But he was quick to add that education must in no way interfere with the Jewish religion, because "the homeland is sacred, but the faith even more so." Rabbi Fischer's hyphenated formulation, "Magyar-Israelites," suggests how one Jewish leader sought to balance his support for the national cause with his religious commitments. Its hyphen likewise echoes earlier alternatives to Hungarian nationalism, with its homogenizing linguistic and cultural pressures.

For now, however, the unreserved supporters of Hungarian nationalism had seized the day. These activists would always remain a small circle within the Jewish community, but they were part of a broad—if fragile—coalition on the Hungarian side. Its leaders' pronounced nationalism may have alienated some supporters of reform in the twin towns, yet it also helped bridge political, social, and religious divisions within the Hungarian camp, which secured its first victories in the early 1860s. Unexpectedly, Francis Joseph's October Diploma (1860) and February Patent (1861) restored Hungarian as the language of administration and education.

Enthusiastic writers claimed that the Hungarian nation was "waking from a dream" or magically born again "like a phoenix"; better yet, it was proof "that the God of the Magyars yet lives . . . and he has not forgotten his chosen people."[52] Already in the summer of 1860, the town councils of Buda and Pest declared that Hungarian would be their official language, which meant that their minutes and communications with other governing bodies would be solely in Hungarian. In a remarkable rerun of the events of 1848, Leopold Rottenbiller again became mayor of Pest in early 1861. At the same time, the newly elected Hungarian Parliament opened in Buda (the exiled Kossuth had received more than 1,000 votes for parliament in Buda-Pest alone).[53] But Francis Joseph was working from his own script, and when the parliament turned intransigent and much of the population refused to pay taxes, the emperor soon dissolved it and installed reliable men at the head of Buda and Pest. Although protesters filled the streets and soldiers had to be used to collect taxes, constitutional government was effectively suspended. Only in 1865 would Rottenbiller return and Deák open negotiations with the crown.

National activists had already made their long-term intentions clear. In 1860, the university in Pest replaced Austrian history and German-language literature with courses in Hungarian history and literature. Over the next year, all professors who did not know Hungarian were simply let go, including an Austrian-born professor of German language and literature who said that, after eight years, he felt at home in Hungary and had wanted to stay; the Austrians' purge after 1849 had been answered in kind. The number of name changes also surged upward: there were no changes in 1859 and only two in 1860, but 213 in 1861 and 332 in the following year.[54] Many of the petitioners had changed their names during the 1848–49 Revolution and were now taking advantage of the new political environment to restore them a dozen years later. One such person was the Pest merchant Ignác Goldstein, who again changed his surname to Arany—a felicitous choice, both meaning "gold" in Hungarian and also the name of the highly regarded poet János Arany.[55] Arany produced some of the finest epic poetry in Hungarian and served as the secretary of the Academy of Sciences and the Kisfaludy Society. But a line he wrote in 1861 is both unsettling and revealing: "In the street dust, stench, German words, filth."[56] Coming from one of the most admired poets of the day, these words did not bode well for Buda-Pest's many German-speakers. This was only one of many indications that national activists would continue their struggle to Magyarize the twin towns, no matter how political conditions changed.

The Unification of Budapest

In 1856, Baron Frigyes Podmaniczky returned to Pest after a trip abroad, his first in ten years. He went to City Park—the only park in Pest—on the outskirts of town. Although it was a Sunday afternoon, the park was nearly deserted. A feeling of despair slowly filled Podmaniczky as he surveyed the neglected park and compared it to the ones he had just seen in Western Europe: "Nowhere was there the smallest trace of progress, comfort, or culture."[57] Like Széchenyi three decades earlier, standing on the banks of the Danube and planning a permanent bridge, Podmaniczky made an emotional vow in City Park. "The tears flowing from my eyes slightly eased the pain in my heart, and as I collected myself, I pledged then to make the advance of our forsaken capital, of which I am so fond, one of the guiding principles of my life." It would be years before Podmaniczky could act on his promise, but this small episode is a reminder of Buda-Pest's continued hold on the national imagination.

Vienna had its own view of the twin towns. In late 1849, the victorious Austrians had nullified the revolutionary government's last-minute creation of Budapest.[58] It was not just that the new regime refused to recognize the validity of decrees and laws issued in 1848–49, but also that Pest had been the seat of the revolution and needed to be punished rather than rewarded with Buda and Óbuda. The authorities instead made Buda their administrative center and at the end of 1849, formally attached Óbuda to it. These moves again made Buda the most important town in Hungary. But Pest could not be entirely ignored, and, in practice, the new regime treated the twin towns as a single administrative unit in several key areas, such as the collection of consumption taxes. With the opening of the Chain Bridge and the tunnel in Buda, the movement of goods and people between the two towns continued to grow. For all their wariness of Pest, then, the Austrians helped pave the way for the eventual unification of the twin towns.

Even in the 1850s, nationalist writers expressed their impatience with these limited gains. Some writers emphasized Buda-Pest's wider importance to the region's economic development. The conservative publicist János Török thus argued that "Buda-Pest must become a commercial link between western and eastern Europe, the importance of which would show itself in the spread of civilization on the Lower Danube."[59] Buda-Pest's boosters also emphasized that the towns should remain the nucleus of national culture. In the words of Baron Zsigmond Kemény, Buda-Pest should be the "center of the revived Hungarian nationality" and "the residential seat [székváros] of a Hungarian homeland united in strength and joined in interests."[60] Buda-Pest, it was hoped, would soon regain the position in economic and cultural life—if not yet in politics—that it had held in the 1830s and 1840s.

These writings set the stage for Mihály Táncsics's remarkable *Our Capital*, which he wrote in prison in 1864.[61] Táncsics's radicalism made him a marginal figure in Hungarian politics, yet *Our Capital* is an unexpectedly mainstream work that fuses strong Hungarian nationalism with an often sophisticated view of urban development. At the outset, Táncsics endorsed the view that Buda-Pest should reflect the Hungarian national character:

"Do not let our capital be like Paris and London: that is, do not let it be a home to maddening luxury, vast wealth, and poverty, the nest of immorality and every vice. Let our capital be the homeland's altar, on which the flame of loyalty to the homeland will ever burn."[62] To Táncsics, everything that differentiated the Magyars from other peoples—their noble nature, honorable character, beautiful dress, and unparalleled language—should distinguish Buda-Pest as well. These aristocratic characteristics are perhaps surprising coming from a defender of the working classes, but by now they had become stock expressions in the national phrasebook. Táncsics also drew on earlier writers in his proposals for urban improvements: with echoes of Palatine Joseph's Embellishment Commission, he called for tree-lined streets, regulation of the flood-prone Danube, larger courtyards in residential buildings, and a ban on basement apartments. His wish list also included more housing for the poor, a second bridge across the Danube, and a promenade in Pest. His proposal that canals be built through Pest to improve cleanliness, transportation, and public health was seconded by Ferenc Reitter, the building director employed by the Vice-Regal Council, who made similar recommendations at the same time.[63]

Our Capital takes a more seditious turn when it comes to Buda. According to Táncsics, the Buda castle and the surrounding neighborhood were too old and damaged to be of use. His solution is to raze the district and start anew. The present regime, he continued, is "the open enemy of our homeland, our nation." The remainder of the book turns into a screed against Austria's colonial exploitation of Hungary and the Habsburgs' preferential treatment of Germans. At one point, Táncsics suggests that workers should be actively recruited from Hungarian-speaking regions in the countryside: "a hale and hearty element must be brought into the population, so that future generations transform into vigorous, full-blooded Magyars."[64] *Our Capital,* in short, pulls together the different models of national-minded urbanism: Széchenyi's emphasis on infrastructural improvements, Szemere's insistence that the city have a pronounced Hungarian character, and Vahot's fantasies of national homogeneity. These visions had grown out of a political movement that was broadly liberal and largely oppositional. But what would happen to the idea of a "Hungarian Buda-Pest" when Vienna largely withdrew from the city?

This occurred in 1867 with the compromise that created Austria-Hungary. With this settlement, Buda-Pest again became a meaningful political center, as was manifestly demonstrated in May 1867, when Francis Joseph came to Buda-Pest for his coronation, the first in the twin towns since 1792. Amid great ceremony, Francis Joseph confirmed the separate status of Hungary within his realm and promised to act as its ruler and protector. Hungary now had a crowned king, an elected parliament, and a ministerial government headed by Count Gyula Andrássy, who earlier had been hanged in effigy for his role in the 1848–49 Revolution. Municipal elections in 1867 returned other '48ers to the leadership of the twin towns. Ferenc Házmán, who had fled to the Ottoman Empire and later lived in America, was elected mayor of Buda, and Móric Szentkirály, a colleague of Kossuth, medical doctor, and reformer, became mayor of Pest. The new town governments quickly turned their attention to needed improvements. In Buda, for example, Házmán called for the demilitarization of the Castle District, the regulation of the Danube, the construction of a second bridge over the Danube, and the development of the town's water supply. Prime Minister Andrássy had his sights on something even bigger: he wanted Buda-Pest to be a representative capital befitting Hungary's place in the Monarchy and Europe. Recognizing that building a capital first required practical reforms, Andrássy actively supported a law (Act 1868:46) that gave the government the right to exercise eminent domain in the interests of commerce, transportation, and embellishment. The prime minister also helped secure necessary credit for large-scale projects from a consortium of Austrian and French bankers.

Andrássy's crowning achievement, and one that enjoyed support across the political spectrum, was Act 1870:10, which established the Metropolitan Board of Public Works, modeled on the London body of the same name.[65] Reflecting the new balance of power in Buda-Pest, the central government appointed half of the board's members, the towns the other half. Charged with development of transportation and infrastructure in Buda-Pest, the board soon assumed authority over most regulatory matters, town planning, the naming of streets, and the opening of major roads through the city. One of its first acts was to open an international competition for a comprehensive plan to direct the long-term development of the city. The winning entry came from a Buda engineer, Lajos Lechner, who made detailed recommendations for the regulation of the Danube, the transformation of the Castle District, and the creation of new industrial zones and residential districts. His plan also called for the construction in Pest of a ring road and radial avenue. With remarkably few alterations, Lechner's plan would serve as the blueprint for the city's development through the end of the nineteenth century. Much of this would be accomplished under Baron Podmaniczky, who served as president of the Board of Public Works from 1873 until 1905. More immediately, the board issued stringent building regulations, which were unpopular with builders and property owners, but resulted in the solid, fireproof, and largely uniform buildings that still dominate central Pest today.

Members of the board also understood the importance of symbolic changes. They renamed numerous streets and squares throughout Buda, Pest, and Óbuda.[66] The ostensible goal was to end duplication and provide streets with more historic and harmonious names. Thus, Pest's Calf Square was renamed Rákóczi Square in honor of the eighteenth-century Transylvanian prince. Nail Street became Eötvös Street, one of many to commemorate the leaders of the 1848–49 Revolution. In total, more than 500 streets received new names, rapidly fulfilling aims first laid out in the nationalist press in the 1840s.

The formation of the Board of Public Works hastened the unification of the towns.[67] Initiative came not from the towns themselves, but from Andrássy and the Hungarian parliament. Already in 1868, parliament had passed laws that unified tax collection and created a common council to oversee schools in Buda and Pest. In 1870, Mór Wahrmann introduced a draft law in parliament calling for formal unification of the two towns. Wahrmann was the grandson of the head rabbi of Pest, a founder of the Israelite Magyar Society, a leader of the Pest Lloyd Society, and a successful merchant. In 1869, just two years after Jewish emancipation, Pest's Leopold District made him the first Jewish member of parliament. The highly visible and politically influential Wahrmann represented a new generation of Jewish leaders in the twin towns. In 1871, the interior minister followed up on Wahrmann's motion and appointed a board of experts to examine the mechanics of unification.

Sharp debates soon erupted in the town halls of Buda and Pest. The Buda Town Council was deeply divided on the question of unification, and some councilors regretted that Buda would lose its separate character and traditions, to say nothing of its claim to be the undisputed capital of Hungary.[68] Szentkirály, the mayor of Pest, likewise expressed his objections to an immediate union of the towns. Buda, he explained, not only had very different interests than Pest, but also was incapable of commercial, industrial, or demographic development and would always be a financial burden on its more dynamic neighbor. Szentkirály held that "the capital of Hungary should be Magyar [*Magyarország fővárosa magyar legyen*]" and for this reason also opposed union with Buda: "I do not say that the town of Buda is not Hungarian-spirited [*magyar érzelmű*], but in its language, in the main and arguably, sole characteristic of nationality, it is only to a limited degree [Magyar]." Szentkirály feared that a unified city council would have many members who would not even be able to read the Hungarian-language minutes. Overlooking Pest's greater population, wealth, and political weight, he darkly warned that "Buda would have an overwhelming influence on Pest."[69]

On the surface, Szentkirály's argument that a unified Budapest should be manifestly "Hungarian" echoed generations of national activists. Yet his suggestion that the national character of the government—and by extension, the city as a whole—was threatened by a comparatively small number of monolingual German-speaking councilors is striking in view of the changes that had taken place since 1867. By this logic, even though advocates of the Hungarian national cause had taken over nearly all positions of power, they remained in constant danger. This warning could support arguments for or against unification; either way, it justified the continued Magyarization of the towns. Not all Hungarian leaders framed the question of unification in strictly national terms: following Andrássy, many simply maintained that Budapest should resemble the other capitals of Europe. When the Hungarian parliament resumed debate on unification in late 1872, the questions of administrative reform, control of the police, and electoral procedures were the most divisive issues. The lower house was united, however, in its conviction that Hungarian alone should be the language of administration in united Budapest, and parliament wrote this into the final draft of Act 1872:36, which spelled out the terms of unification.[70] On December 22, 1872, the law received Francis Joseph's signature and came into force the next day. Buda, Pest, and Óbuda had again become Budapest.

It would be nine months before the new leaders of Budapest took office. A new committee first laid out administrative and electoral districts, defined the number, salaries, and jurisdictions of city officials, and drafted regulations for the entire administration. Meanwhile a terrible cholera epidemic ravaged the city, and the stock market collapse in Vienna also took the shine off unification. Elections were held in September 1873 for the 400-member Metropolitan Council, 200 of whom were to be chosen by the 1,200 highest taxpayers, the other 200 by 15,000 other citizens who possessed the right to vote. Altogether 10,000 voters—just 4 percent of the total population—actually took part in the elections. Finally, on October 25, 1873, the council formally assembled for the first time in the Vigadó Hall. Newspapers enthusiastically described large crowds and councilors in the national dress. Only the German-language *Pester Lloyd* dampened the mood somewhat. Although it agreed that "the capital of Hungary . . . should be Hungarian," it also returned to the language question and warned against ostracizing elected councilors who did not know Hungarian: "Town representatives are not elected to listen uncomprehendingly and remain silent."[71] The Hungarian-language press had little patience for such protests. *Pesti Napló (Pest Diary)* assured its readers that by any measure—population, size, public institutions, or wealth—Budapest occupied "a worthy place among the first-rate metropolises of Europe."[72] At the same time, it expressed its confidence that "the capital of Hungary" would remain the center of cultural, spiritual, and material progress for the Hungarian national movement.

In just a few years, then, the formation of the hyphenated Austria-Hungary had led to the creation of an unhyphenated Budapest. As in earlier periods, support had come from a broad coalition of political actors, including aristocrats (Andrássy, Podmaniczky), burghers (Házmán, Rottenbiller), liberal Jews (Wahrmann), and radicals (Táncsics). Advocates of unification could draw upon a number of well-established economic, administrative, and cultural arguments: they could describe Budapest as a representative capital, an economic engine for the region, or the embodiment of Hungarian national greatness. Their opponents also made historical arguments, if less convincingly. The burghers in Buda, for example, invoked the towns' tradition of self-governance, but this had been a fiction for much of the nineteenth century. Szentkirály's fears that Budapest would somehow be less "Hungarian" also missed the point. With unification in 1872–73, the accretion of power to the Hungarian side was, for all practical purposes, complete. An early twentieth-century British visitor to Budapest rightly observed that "the battle [against the Austrian government] has been won, and it is the chief preoccupation of the Hungarians to prove to the world that they are fitted to take their place in the ranks of modern nations."[73]

As never before, the Hungarian political leadership rallied behind the idea of a monumental city on the Danube. Beginning in 1872, the Board of Public Works laid out a wide ring road (Ringstrasse) and a long, showy avenue (the future Andrássy Avenue) in Pest. Perhaps no building better expressed Hungary's ambitions than the colossal House of Parliament that rose on the Pest side of the Danube in the last decades of the nineteenth century (see fig. 10). Its architect, Imre Steindl, appealed to national pride to defend the building's predominant Gothic style, suggesting that he had attempted to "implant national and individual spirit into the majestic style of the Middle Ages."[74] It helped that Steindl's plan recalled London's Houses of Parliament on the Thames (which in turn brought to mind British constitutional traditions) and that Prime Minister Andrássy was a committed Anglophile. Critics justly pointed out the building's practical needs had been sacrificed in favor of grandiose self-representation (and with some justification, because renovations began just decades after its completion). Predictably, some writers grumbled that a demonstrably "Hungarian" architectural style had not been chosen, even if the interior's national-spirited wall paintings and frescos must have allayed some of their concerns.

The Hungarian parliament building invites comparison with Vienna's, built a decade earlier in the Greek classical style. This was one of many landmarks on Vienna's imposing new Ringstrasse, which was lined with public buildings and private residences. Carl Schorske has shown how the buildings of the Ringstrasse projected the values of Austrian liberalism: progress, education, high culture, municipal self-rule, and parliamentary government.[75] All this was true of monumental architecture in Budapest as well, but with one crucial addition: Hungarian nationalism. Directly and indirectly, the national idea continued to shape urban development in Budapest through the end of the nineteenth century. As a Budapest member of parliament and member of the Board of Public Works wrote in the early 1880s, "Budapest will only have a future, a chance of developing and flourishing, if it becomes entirely Hungarian [ganz ungarisch]."[76] Representational buildings were one matter. How would the new regime put its stamp on the growing population of Budapest?

10—London on the Danube: Imre Steindl's neo-Gothic Parliament building (built 1883–1902).

The Census Revisited

In 1882, József Kőrösi, the highly respected head of the Capital Statistical Office, gave a talk at the Hungarian Academy of Sciences.[77] Kőrösi's subject was the national character of Budapest, both in the past and the present, and he made use of archival sources along with the decennial census he recently had directed. In his speech, Kőrösi claimed that in the medieval era—that is, before the arrival of the Ottomans in 1526—the town of Pest "had been perfectly Magyar" and noted that Magyar, as well as German, mayors had served in Buda. Ottoman occupation had changed these patterns, he showed, with the result that German-speakers gained preponderance in both towns after 1686. This lasted until well into the nineteenth century. How had the situation changed since then? Kőrösi offered a three-part answer. First, he recalculated the results of the 1851 census, this time counting as Hungarian-speakers many of the towns' Jewish residents. Although his estimates confirmed German-speakers dominated Buda, they also showed that in Pest, Hungarian-speakers, rather than being a minority, had actually formed an absolute majority (51.4 percent) of the population. In total, Kőrösi estimated that Hungarian-speakers accounted for 44 percent of the towns' population in 1851, well above the 32 percent originally reported. Second, he showed that by 1881, this figure had risen to 55 percent (compared with 33 percent for German-speakers): for the first time in more than two centuries, Hungarian-speakers represented an absolute majority in Budapest.[78] Last, Kőrösi explained the causes of this transformation. Schools and immigration had been important factors in recent years, but he also proposed more sweeping conclusions. Over the past two centuries, Kőrösi suggested, Budapest had become more and more "Hungarian," no matter what political regime had been in power. Budapest had become a linguistically Hungarian city not through governmental coercion, but through gradual, unalterable, historical processes. To Kőrösi, all signs pointed to the Magyar element growing only stronger in the future.

Kőrösi's findings, which neatly demonstrated the Hungarian character of Budapest in the past, present, and future, had an obvious appeal for national-minded audiences. Subsequent censuses also appeared to bear out his predictions. Budapest grew explosively in last decades of the nineteenth century, as its population, which topped 370,000 in 1880, nearly doubled in the next twenty years. Budapest in 1900 had an estimated 733,000 residents, almost four times as many as it had half a century earlier. According to the 1890 census, 67 percent of the population spoke Hungarian as their mother tongue, and a decade later the figure had risen to 80 percent.[79] The steady influx of hundreds of thousands of Hungarian-speakers from the countryside accounted for much of this change, but the German community was also shrinking. In 1880, 122,454 residents had claimed German as their mother tongue; by 1900 the figure had dropped to 98,515. Bragged a contemporary journalist, "The Germans [in Budapest] are Magyarizing voluntarily and wholeheartedly."[80]

Only in recent years have scholars begun to offer a more complex portrait of language use and nationhood in Budapest.[81] They have highlighted the prevalence of bilingualism (in 1880, 77 percent of the population spoke German and 73 percent Hungarian), the rising number of marriages between speakers of different languages, and the slowness of the resulting generational shifts. Viktor Karády has drawn attention to the varied pace of linguistic change among different religious groups. In the late nineteenth century, the proportion of people who claimed Hungarian as their mother tongue—the key to census figures—was rising among all confessions, and most rapidly among Neolog Jews, thus giving them the highest rates of bilingualism.[82] Because the number of Jews in Budapest increased from roughly 17,000 in 1850 to 71,000 in 1880, this shift had great importance for overall patterns of language use, particularly in the final decades of the century (by 1900, 23 percent of Budapest's population would be Jewish).[83] Karády lists several factors—schools, household service, and improved employment prospects—that pushed all religious groups toward Hungarian but underlines that, for many Jews, the decision to learn Hungarian (or have their children learn it) reflected their national loyalty and desire for social mobility. Péter Hanák has likewise stressed the importance of the Hungarian-speaking elite (the nobility and aristocrats) as a reference group for middle-class social emulation.[84]

What role did coercion play in this process? Was Kőrösi right in asserting that the Magyarization of Budapest in the late nineteenth century was a largely spontaneous process, in which the state and national activists played only secondary roles? Historian Tamás Faragó allows that intolerant voices continued to be heard in the nationalist press and societies, but he also points out that few political leaders had the means or the inclination to push the Hungarian cause into private life and everyday transactions.[85] Although there is much truth to this picture, the same officials had few reservations about intervening in all areas of public life, including streets and squares, cultural institutions, and associational life. In each of these areas, government initiatives overlapped with continued agitation by national activists. The Hungarian side had successfully used this combination throughout the nineteenth century: the only difference in the early 1880s was that the Habsburgs no longer stood in their way. István Deák has succinctly described these nationalist pressures with the term "the chauvinist city."[86]

Theaters are perhaps the best measure of the Hungarians' determination to dominate public space in Budapest.[87] As late as 1867, the city had four German and two Hungarian theaters, and in 1869 the Buda theater director Georg von Gundy established a new German theater on Wollgasse (Wool Street) in Pest's Leopold District. In the following year, however, the Buda Town Council, which itself contained many German-speakers, issued a decree that banned German-language productions in its two theaters: a Hungarian-language company took over one, and the other was soon torn down. The town of Pest also condemned and demolished two of its German theaters, including the "temporary" wooden theater that had stood for eighteen years. Almost overnight, German theater was pushed to the margins of the city. To fill its place, Pest built the Hungarian-language Popular Theater (Népszínház), which opened in 1875 with Francis Joseph and his son Rudolf in attendance. In the same year, the government paid for the expansion and renovation of the National Theater. By the late 1870s, no meaningful competition existed between the Hungarian and German theaters, because the former enjoyed generous subsidies, attracted much larger audiences, and had superior companies. Nonetheless, in 1880, the Pest authorities attempted to revoke the license of the remaining German theater on Wollgasse, a decision backed by the Budapest Metropolitan Council and the nationalist press. "The Germans have lost the battle, which they themselves provoked," crowed a Hungarian newspaper, which added that the city authorities had acted on salutary national principles.[88] Budapest's actions attracted international attention and raised protests in Berlin. Ultimately, only the intervention of the central government allowed the Wollgasse Theater to reopen in late 1880. German theater in Pest would hold on, precariously, for just a decade more.

The city authorities intervened actively in other areas of culture.[89] In 1880, for example, the Budapest council voted to spend 4,000 florins a year to purchase the works of Hungarian-born artists. The city also provided generous support to academies of painting and music; there was also a Hungarian-language drama school, which trained generations of Hungarian actors. In education more generally, both the Budapest and central governments closely supervised the city's schools (and they would later intervene in church-run schools as well). Schools taught students—no matter what their mother tongue—Hungarian history, geography, and civics. In this way, the children of merchants, shopkeepers, artisans, laborers, and peasants could learn what it meant to be "Hungarian."[90] In addition to these nationalist aims, political leaders recognized that the city had too few schools, that teachers' salaries were abysmal, and that 100 to 150 students often crammed into classrooms in the outer districts. In 1868, Budapest initiated a major expansion of its educational system, and, in the same year, the Hungarian Parliament passed a landmark Elementary School Law (Act 1868:38), which made schooling mandatory for all students between the ages of six and twelve, established state-run teacher training schools, and set a standard curriculum. Its provision that all elementary students be educated in their mother tongue, however, had little effect in Budapest, because town and school authorities had already made Hungarian the language of instruction in nearly all of the city's schools. One historian has observed that in 1880—a year in which the census reported 120,000 people whose mother tongue was German—there was not *one* German-language school in Budapest; bilingual (German-Hungarian) instruction was used in only six schools (from a total of more than 100).[91] It is interesting to note that the loudest protests again came from the German School Association in Berlin. In response, 1,200 German-speakers in Budapest signed a petition in which they declared their loyalty to their Hungarian homeland.[92]

The Hungarian side's unrelenting activism in Budapest could be also seen in associational life, an area where the Hungarian leadership seemingly had little to worry about. From the early 1860s onward, associational life in Hungary entered a period of continuous expansion.[93] The Compromise of 1867 and the establishment of liberal governments in both halves of the monarchy had only accelerated this process, with the result that the number of associations in Hungary increased fourfold over the next decade. By 1878, Hungary had 2,701 societies, with more than 593,000 members (by comparison, the Austrian half of the monarchy had more than 8,000 associations). Budapest alone was home to hundreds of societies, which brought together archeologists, meteorologists, Lutheran women, Czech workers, and devotees of Franz Liszt, to name but a few. This rapid growth in associational life was common to many European cities in the late nineteenth century. If the Hungarian case stands out, it may be for the striking reversal that took place after 1867. Societies that just a few years before had struggled for existence now enjoyed official support. The Industrial Association, a hotbed of oppositional activity in the 1840s, had been shut down in the 1850s, but in the late 1860s surviving members refounded it and cooperated closely with the Hungarian government. This was true of many other Hungarian societies, which swiftly became part of the political establishment.

Despite such liberalizaton, not everything had changed. The Hungarian government, it soon became apparent, was just as intolerant of "suspicious" associations as the Austrian regime it had replaced. After 1867 the government introduced no new laws to regulate associations: it simply assumed the right to approve all societies and, when necessary, to supervise or even shut down certain ones (these procedures were spelled out in an 1874 ministerial ordinance). In theory, this power was limited by a provision of the 1868 Nationalities Law (Act 1868:44), which guaranteed all national groups the right to form cultural, educational, and economic associations.[94] In practice, however, the authorities kept a close watch on societies they deemed unreliable and especially those organized by workers and non-Hungarian activists.

Workers' associations in Budapest thus faced an uncertain existence.[95] In the 1850s, the Austrian authorities had quashed workers' burial, self-help, and choral societies; they had tolerated Catholic and later Protestant journeymen's associations, but these failed to attract large memberships. Only the Compromise of 1867 and the subsequent expansion of associational life allowed the formation of a number of broad-based, worker-controlled organizations. The most durable was the Pest-based General Workers Society, which aimed at "the spiritual growth of the working class, as well as the protection and assistance of its material conditions with the goal that henceforth the worker not only be a useful resident of the state, but become a citizen capable of enjoying the liberal constitution."[96] Bucking the trend toward Hungarian in many middle- and upper-class associations, the General Workers Society had three official languages: German, Hungarian, and Slovak. Increased contact with European socialists had an important effect on the society's leadership, whose measured language of citizenship soon gave way to more a combative tone and large demonstrations in support of the Paris Commune in June 1871. The government responded by arresting, imprisoning, and trying the leaders of the General Workers Society. In 1873, the interior minister disbanded the first workers' political party a month after its founding, and the weight of these and other repressive measures crippled the workers' movement in Hungary for decades.

The number of societies that conducted their business in Serb, Slovak, or German likewise dwindled. A handful of Serb and Slovak associations operated in Buda-Pest, but in 1864 the most important of them, the Serb Foundation, moved from Pest to southern Hungary. Another turning point came in 1875, when the Hungarian authorities banned the Slovak Foundation, a cultural association founded in Upper Hungary in 1863, as part of a wider crackdown on Slovak institutions throughout the Hungarian lands.[97] In Buda-Pest, the 1880 census counted more than 20,000

Slovak-speakers, but they had only a few self-help and burial societies; the lively cultural associations of the 1830s and 1840s were by now a distant memory. German-speakers also had a wide range of voluntary associations, but as in earlier decades, few had a pronounced German national character. Perhaps the most visible German-language association was the Pest Lloyd Society. Although its paper at times criticized the Magyars' excesses, the Pest Lloyd Society eventually came to support the Hungarian cause. If its declarations of support at times sounded a bit strained, this perhaps reflected the merchants' uncertainty about their position in an increasingly Hungarian-speaking city. Similar concerns may also have influenced the German-speaking town councilors who allowed—and sometimes even ordered—the closure of Buda-Pest's German-language theaters and schools.

Hints of a German orientation appear farther down the social ladder: in gymnastic societies, sharpshooting clubs, and volunteer fire companies.[98] In the 1860s, a German social club called "Harmony" brought together a small number of engineers and officials for monthly banquets filled with readings, poetry, and songs. As no society before it, the Harmony Club attempted to promote a manifestly German orientation in Buda-Pest. "The German song is a cement," wrote a founding member, "that holds together Germans dispersed across all the lands of the globe."[99] Yet the club also took pains to underline that it was free from all political tendencies and committed to fostering understanding between Germans and Magyars. The Harmony Club was an exception, and most German-language institutions found themselves on the defensive. The sharpshooters still proudly defended their bilingual traditions—"there are no nationalities among us, we are cosmopolitans" declared the Buda Sharpshooters' Club in 1871—but other voluntary associations and trade groups (*ipartestületek*, the successors to the guilds) slowly succumbed to pressure to conduct their business in Hungarian alone.[100] A number of Hungarian national societies encouraged them to do even more. The Central Name-Magyarization Society (1881) encouraged people to undergo what it called a "national baptism" and adopt Hungarian-sounding names. The Hungarian School Society (1886) attempted to introduce Hungarian into kindergartens, burial societies, and churches and also renewed the crusade against Budapest's German-language shop signs.

The significance of these small acts should not be understated. Around 1870, the number of Budapest's residents who claimed as their mother tongue German, Slovak, or some other language besides Hungarian peaked at nearly 150,000.[101] From the 1870s onward, their absolute numbers began to decline, as did their percentage of the total population. High rates of bilingualism and the prominence of German in economic life partially disguised this change, and German, Slovak, Serb, and Yiddish could still be heard in shops, restaurants, businesses, taverns, and houses of worship throughout Budapest.[102] Increasingly, however, these were the everyday languages of an older generation.

The psychic and social tensions caused by this transition are difficult to reconstruct, although two very different early twentieth-century novels provide insightful descriptions of the change. *The Old House* (1914), by the conservative Cécile Tormay, chronicles the rise and fall of the Ulwing family in nineteenth-century Pest. The grandfather, who came from the German lands in the first part of the century, is a confident, successful builder; his beautiful house in the undeveloped Leopold District is a local landmark. By the end of the century, the family business has fallen into ruin, the grandson has committed suicide, and the granddaughter is unhappily married to a Hungarian nobleman. The family house is now a "condemned, quaint old house, uncouthly timid among the powerful new buildings."[103] Its demolition at the end of the novel erases yet another symbol of Budapest's once-proud, German-speaking burghers. The next generation of the family, the granddaughter's sons, will undoubtedly take after their Magyar father.

The second novel, Lajos Hatvany's *Gentlemen and People* (1927), likewise describes several generations of one family—this one, like Hatvany himself, Jewish. It paints a picture of a successful merchant family that speaks German at home. In one scene, the father recognizes that his eldest son must first learn Hungarian if he wants to continue his education in Hungary. The father would prefer to send the boy to Vienna and have him study in German, yet he concedes that "Vienna is far away, the trip is costly, and one must realize that a state is a state and it does what it wants."[104] The new tutor—a university student sporting Magyar dress and a Kossuth beard—fills the son's head with stories of Attila, Saint Stephen, and other national heroes; it is not long before the son, in an early but significant act of rebellion, decides to answer his father's questions not in German, as expected, but in Hungarian. This small act hints at the growing distance between the father and his son's generation.

Larger truths may lurk in these stories. In nineteenth-century Hungary and in Habsburg Central Europe more generally, individuals' national affiliations were not writ in stone. If they wanted, men and women could show their national loyalties by joining a club, adopting a new surname, buying seats at the theater, or choosing a school for their children. For some families, giving preference to the Hungarian language showed at least tacit approval for the nationalist project. Alternately, town dwellers could attempt to ignore the national question altogether, change their minds, or profess loyalty to the Emperor-King, international socialism, or the Catholic Church. In this sense, historians are correct to describe the process by which the population of Budapest became "Hungarian" as spontaneous or unplanned.

But, if it is in the public sphere that people fix their national loyalties, it bears repeating that in late nineteenth-century Budapest people were not choosing between equals. Public life had borne a Hungarian stamp for decades, and, from the 1860s onward, government and town officials, together with national activists, guaranteed that Budapest's theaters, schools, and clubs would be almost exclusively Hungarian in their use of language and national orientation. The city's public life became "Hungarian" long before the population did, and this strongly influenced the choices that people could make. "The existence of a nation," the nineteenth-century French theologian Ernst Renan once said, is a "daily plebiscite."[105] In nineteenth-century Budapest, more and more people appeared ready to vote "Hungarian." But it would have been extremely difficult for them to do otherwise.

The Hungarian Capital

The Present

In June 1892, Emperor-King Francis Joseph came to Budapest to mark the twenty-fifth anniversary of the 1867 Compromise and of his coronation as Hungarian king.[1] He arrived amid escalating controversy over church-state relations, as the Hungarian government prepared to introduce laws, which both Francis Joseph and the Catholic Church opposed, that would introduce state registers, religious equality, acceptance of Judaism as a "received" religion, and, most controversially, obligatory civil marriage. The resulting "culture war" would conclude only in 1895; for a few days in 1892, however, the combatants laid down their weapons to celebrate Francis Joseph's Crown Jubilee. An estimated 300,000 people turned out to see the sixty-one-year-old monarch and his wife as their carriage rolled through the streets of Budapest. To ensure that the day would be memorable, the city leaders had ordered all religious confessions to hold services in the morning, decorated public buildings along the route, and organized a massive torchlight parade and fireworks show in the evening. Francis Joseph repaid his hosts generously, and on June 10, 1892, raised Budapest to the status of "capital city and royal seat" (*fő- és székesváros*).[2] Budapest was now equal in dignity and rank to Vienna. The Dual Monarchy would henceforth have two capitals.

For Hungarian activists, it had long been an article of faith that the twin towns possessed the aura of a national capital. They had promoted this view even in the first half of the century, when the Habsburg monarchs had ruled from Vienna and the National Diet had met in Pressburg. In this respect, Hungary resembles Italy, where enthusiastic nationalists officially declared in 1860 that Rome—and not Turin or Florence—was the national capital, ignoring the fact that Rome was still firmly in the hands of the papacy. Most states, in the process of their development, have had to choose between competing sites for their capital. Both St. Petersburg and Moscow could make a legitimate claim to be the capital of imperial Russia: the former was the seat of the tsar and his government, but the latter was a holy city, the "heart of Russia."[3] In Hungary, the revolutionaries of 1848–49 had unified Budapest and made it their capital, and this remained the goal through the second half of the century. Even after the Compromise of 1867, nationalists continued to insist that the emperor-king should reside in and rule from Budapest: "The Magyar race," read an 1881 newspaper editorial, "will never dissolve into Austria, never recognize another homeland than Hungary, [and] never recognize a ruler other than the Hungarian King, from whom no power could separate us if he lived among us and spoke Hungarian."[4] Francis Joseph would never reside in Budapest, but, by making it a capital and royal seat in 1892, he gave his imprimatur to claims that Hungarian national activists had been making for more than a century.

Budapest had changed greatly during this time. Provincial and small in 1800, Budapest at the end of the century was a brassy metropolis of more than 730,000 residents, which made it the eighth-largest city in Europe, more populous than Rome, Prague, Madrid, or Amsterdam.[5] Visitors compared it to an American city, and there was even a neighborhood called Chicago. Like its American counterparts, Budapest was filled with immigrants: according to the 1890 census, less than 40 percent of the population had been born in the city. These newcomers had helped make Budapest an economic powerhouse—the center of an expanding network of roads and railways and the home to a growing number of department stores, banks, mills, and factories. The era's economic prosperity and cultural flowering also showed in the opulent exteriors of corporate and private residences, as well as in the city's many theaters, cafés, and clubs. One American journalist declared that Budapest had "blossomed out of the primitive and forlorn conditions into the full magnificence of a splendidly appointed modern metropolis."[6] Such observers rarely saw the crowded suburbs, the illegal basement apartments, or the authorities' heartless treatment of the unemployed poor, who were routinely imprisoned or forcibly transported back to their home villages (expellees were given soup and, if the journey took more than twelve hours, two slices of bread).[7]

Late nineteenth-century Budapest was, to all appearances, a manifestly Hungarian city. Visitors remarked upon the new Parliament building, museums, statues, and the political leadership's proud displays on public holidays of the *díszmagyar,* the ceremonial national costume. An Englishwoman marveled at the popularity of national symbols in Budapest, "Could there, for instance, be a people fonder of their flags than the Hungarians? I doubt it. On Sundays and holidays the red, white, and green of the national standard waves and flashes and flaps from every available position."[8] The same visitors would have heard more Hungarian spoken in the streets than earlier in the century. School instruction was almost entirely in Hungarian, which was the leading language of city administration, cultural life, and, increasingly, business as well. In 1896, Budapest had 291 Hungarian-language newspapers (with a total circulation of 52 million), compared with forty-two that appeared in German (13 million).[9] Associational life was even more one-sided: there were scores of Hungarian scholarly, literary, and artistic societies, compared with only a handful of Serb, Czech, Slovak, and German cultural associations. When the last German theater burned to the ground in 1889, the Budapest council simply refused to grant permission for the building of a new one.

Challenges to the regnant Hungarian nationalism nonetheless loomed on the horizon. Across Central Europe, the rise of mass politics in the late nineteenth century transformed the political landscape. Political activists on both the left and the right used expanded suffrage, institutions of civil society, and public demonstrations to mobilize new voters and challenge liberal regimes. In Hungary, the restrictive franchise, the small industrial sector, and governmental repression had long slowed, but could not prevent, the emergence of mass-based political movements. These included political Catholicism, which developed from the church-state struggles of the 1890s. The resulting wave of Catholic activism produced the Catholic People's Party (founded 1895), as well as dozens of Catholic newspapers and hundreds of associations. Political Zionism appeared around the same time. Theodor Herzl, a leader of the Zionist movement, was in fact born in Pest in 1860 but left for good when he was eighteen. Zionism found a limited if influential following in Hungary in the first years of the twentieth century, and in Budapest, Zionists founded a student association and a journal.[10] By far the most consequential new political movement was socialism, which emerged in Budapest against the backdrop of rapid industrialization around the turn of the century. The Hungarian Social Democratic Party was formed in 1890 and stood alongside hundreds of trade associations, workers' clubs, and newspapers. Although the limited franchise on both the parliamentary and city level excluded the Social Democrats from formal political life, their leaders at times used parades, strikes, and mass demonstrations to claim the streets of Budapest.

There were thus many Budapests in the late nineteenth century, not simply the Hungarian national one. In some quarters of the city, the effervescence of national pride would hardly have been felt. In others, it may have been viewed critically. After 1900, a younger generation of political radicals and cultural modernists would turn their backs on their fathers' liberal nationalism. Nevertheless, there is little question that the Hungarian national movement had prevailed in the places that mattered: public spaces, schools, city government, cultural institutions, associational life, and the press. This was the outcome of a century of nationalist agitation—of an unrelenting campaign to nationalize all corners of Budapest. Numerous structural changes and a multitude of smaller developments, some planned, others accidental, had aided the Hungarian cause. The result, however, was plain for all to see: Budapest had become a Hungarian capital.

The Past

In 1882, Ernest Renan famously said that "To forget—and I will venture to say—to get one's history wrong, are essential factors in the making of the nation."[11] This was a lesson that Hungarian nationalists had learned well, and it is a good one to keep in mind when thinking about late nineteenth-century Hungary. One of the most famous paintings of the era was

Gyula Benczúr's monumental *The Recapture of Buda Castle in 1686* (1896) (fig. 11), which is today prominently displayed in the Hungarian National Gallery. The painting was commissioned by the city of Budapest for the grandiose millennium exhibition of 1896, a yearlong celebration of Hungarian national pride and, ostensibly, of the entry of Magyar tribes into the Carpathian Basin 1,000 years earlier. Benczúr had trained in Munich and was from 1883 the director of the Masters School of Painting in Budapest; *The Recapture of Buda Castle* is thus a tour de force of academic historicism. The painting's identifiable subjects are the commanders of the Habsburg-led armies that recaptured Buda in 1686: Prince Charles of Lorraine, the central figure elevated above the fray in three-quarter view on a motionless white horse, and Eugene of Savoy, riding hatless behind on another white horse. To the right, a herald announces the generals and soldiers cheer them; in the foreground, corpses, weapons, and broken cannon testify to the recent fighting. Amid the jumbled mass of Habsburg soldiers and Ottoman prisoners below the mounted figure of Eugene, a turbaned Ottoman prisoner bows his head before a priest brandishing a cross, a further reminder that Christian armies have carried the day.

The dense swirl of figures occupying the left half of the canvas leads the eye to the striking figure in the very center of the painting: a wounded soldier in a rich red uniform brandishing a glinting saber. The outstretched arm and pointing figure of another soldier also draw us to him. The bandages around his head and arm reveal how bravely he has fought, and he alone warily carries his sword in front of him. He turns away from Charles of Lorraine (his sword cuts Charles's boot in two) and the other imperial commanders. His appearance—the richly embroidered coat, the plumed hat, and the full moustache—immediately reveals him to be a Magyar nobleman. How are we to read the relationship between this anonymous but symbolically laden figure and the imperial commanders behind him? In making this painting, Benczúr had apparently wanted to show the deep historical roots of the Austro-Hungarian partnership. In 1686, however, troops from Hungary had comprised no more than 15 percent of the total force: the balance had come from the Habsburg-led Holy Roman Empire and its allies.[12] Benczúr has corrected this imbalance and strongly accented the Hungarian contribution. The Habsburgs' commanders are shown prominently, but also appear distant, motionless, impassive, and untouched by the recent fighting. Almost inevitably, the viewer's eyes—and sympathies—are encouraged to focus on the wary, wounded hero rather than the bewigged imperial leaders.

Once more, the Habsburgs and their supporters have been upstaged by the Hungarians. But why had Vienna repeatedly allowed this to happen, especially before 1867, when it had been, so to speak, in the saddle in Budapest? Admittedly, the imperial-royal authorities never had a free hand in Hungary: the National Diets and noble counties had always been a barrier, and when Vienna did rule without them (under Joseph II in the

11—A national-minded portrayal of the past: Gyula Benczúr, *The Recapture of Buda Castle in 1686* (1896). Erich Lessing / Art Resource, NY

1780s and again in the 1850s), a shortage of resources and manpower limited effective action. Yet, at the beginning of the nineteenth century, Vienna had powerful allies—its officials, large parts of the aristocracy, the burghers, and the Catholic Church. In Buda-Pest, moreover, the Habsburg side had actively contributed to the city's development, as could be seen in the Royal Castle, Buda tunnel, technical college, and the onetime Pest German Theater; under Palatine Joseph, the imperial-royal authorities had laid out Leopold District, the crown jewel of nineteenth-century Pest. There is clearly no one reason why Vienna reaped so few political gains from these many initiatives. It is tempting to follow earlier critics and simply say that Habsburg rule was by definition a policy of "half-deeds and half-ways."[13] Certainly, Vienna mistrusted many of its servants in Buda-Pest and slowly withdrew authority from them (the town councils are a good example of this); it also spurned offers of assistance from other potential supporters, such as Count István Széchenyi. After the death of Palatine Joseph, moreover, the Habsburg side had no natural or charismatic leaders in Buda-Pest.

The Habsburgs had rarely felt the need to court their subjects. The nineteenth-century Habsburg Monarchy was remarkably resilient, surprisingly stable, and largely successful in its social, economic, and cultural modernization.[14] The imperial-royal authorities deserve much credit for these achievements. Decision makers in Vienna, however, were slow to engage in what Oscar Jászi once called "civic education"—namely, to use schools, religious bodies, literature, the press, the army, and other institutions to produce state solidarity and internal cohesion.[15] The Habsburg side made occasional forays in the realm of informal politics—they appeared at public ceremonies, patronized the Hungarian National Museum, and funded sympathetic newspapers—but there was no sustained engagement on the local level and certainly nothing to compare with the Hungarian leadership's many initiatives in the streets, cultural life, and civil society. They failed to realize that, even before the emergence of mass politics at the end of the century, they had to win the "hearts and minds" of their subjects. In this environment, the Habsburg side's natural allies and likely supporters—including aristocrats, Catholic leaders, town officials, merchants, artisans, and Jewish reformers—were open to recruitment from the Hungarian side. Not all would switch allegiances, but enough of them did, with the result that the Habsburgs slowly surrendered their leading role in Budapest. But the Habsburg side left an important legacy. With its control of local administration, education, and the economy, the Vienna had canalized the Hungarian national movement into the streets, clubs, and cultural life, and there it would remain even after the 1867 Compromise. The Hungarian state's relentless Magyarization campaigns of the late nineteenth century owe at least some of their breadth (the attention to surnames, shop signs, and associations) to the oppositional agitation of the 1830s and 1840s.

Why had the Hungarian side succeeded? How had a small circle of national-minded aristocrats, noble landowners, and language enthusiasts gained primacy in the twin towns? Why did their vision of a "Hungarian Budapest" resonate so widely? In their hands, modern nationalism proved to be a remarkably versatile political language. Depending upon who was speaking, the idea of a "Hungarian Budapest" could stand for economic autonomy, urban development, political liberalism, demographic fears, or cultural chauvinism. Over the course of the century, much of the Hungarian side's political dynamism unquestionably came "from above," from the political leadership in the National Diets and Pest County, as well as from a handful of national-minded journalists and club officers. These Hungarian activists liberally borrowed the language and symbols of nationalism from their counterparts across Europe. And like national leaders elsewhere, they used nationalist rhetoric instrumentally—that is, they used it to achieve or consolidate political, economic, and social power. At its best, Hungarian nationalism was connected to cultural innovation and a far-ranging project of liberal reform; at its worst, it entailed linguistic Magyarization and the continued political dominance of the nobility. Both tendencies were present from the beginning, and both shaped the Hungarian national movement in nineteenth-century Budapest.

But why did ordinary people show such enthusiasm for the Hungarian cause in Budapest? What explains the poets who crafted Hungarian verses, the parents who gave their children names from Hungarian history, the women who donned the national costume, and the builders who sought a national architectural style? Although their numbers are difficult to pin down, the supporters of the Hungarian side potentially included the hundreds of readers of nationalist publications in the early 1800s, the thousands of ballroom dancers in the 1840s, and the tens of thousands who cheered Kossuth and other leaders in 1848–49. It would unfair to suggest that these men and women were mindless followers of the national leaders or dupes of nationalist propaganda, just as it would be naïve to suggest that all saw themselves as participants in an egalitarian, oppositional civil society. The Hungarian side's broad liberalism was an obvious draw, but the Hungarian national movement was capacious enough to accommodate people on all points of the political spectrum. Material motives and social anxieties may also have been determining factors in some cases, and it is easy to point to the nobles without land, writers without readers, and students without prospects, all of whom had something tangible to gain from the Hungarian cause. For merchants and masters, the national cause may have held the promise of more customers and higher social status, and if not for themselves, then for their children, whom they made sure learned Hungarian. Some well-to-do women may also have felt it their duty to support their husbands from the gallery of meeting halls; others, like Blanka Teleki and the Zichy sisters, found in nationalism an unprecedented opportunity to play an active role in public life.

All these cases reaffirm the voluntary nature of nineteenth-century nationalism. In a city people could show their national loyalties through everyday actions, by speaking Hungarian, shopping, dancing, subscribing to a newspaper, attending an industrial fair, or joining a club. This gave the Hungarian national movement a genuine openness, and one that allowed thousands of people excluded from formal politics—German-speaking craftsmen, Jewish newspaper editors, and aristocratic women—to demonstrate their political loyalties and Hungarian allegiances. This openness to new recruits was an important legacy of nineteenth-century Hungarian nationalism, although it would be sorely tested from the 1920s onward. National movements nearly always define themselves against an imagined "other" or "enemy." In Buda-Pest, national activists worried aloud about "national death" and spoke ominously of Vienna's policies of Germanization, Pan-Slav movements, and disloyal elements at home. This xenophobic rhetoric lent legitimacy to the newspapers' attacks on Serb dances, the students' violent campaign against German shop owners, and the Protection Association's boycott of Austrian and Bohemian goods. It also cast suspicion on all those people who did not readily demonstrate their national loyalty through language and other symbols. One Central European, Sigmund Freud, once characterized this aggressiveness as the "narcissism of minor differences," an apt reminder that national activists were not so different from their neighbors: they often lived in the same neighborhoods, attended the same dances, went to the same shops, and frequented the same cafes.[16]

Real or imagined, "minor differences" ultimately mattered. Over the course of the century, national activists created a distinctly Hungarian world in Budapest, one complete with its own theaters, balls, newspapers, clubs, and holidays. It later included schools, offices, and businesses. These piecemeal innovations had great consequences, as they allowed an increasing number of residents of Budapest to feel "national" most of the time. Slowly, fitfully, people's loyalties shifted and narrowed, as divided allegiances to king, town, homeland, and religion gave way to national loyalties. In Budapest, the process of nationalization was far from complete. Yet it is nonetheless striking how powerful and tenacious the idea of a "Hungarian Budapest" had proven to be across the nineteenth century. By 1900, the provincial, polyglot world of Ofen-Pest had become little more than a dim memory.

The Future

When the long-serving city councilor Johann/János Haberhauer was elected lord mayor of Budapest in 1897, he immediately Magyarized his name to Halmos.[17] During his mayoralty, thousands of other Budapest residents also adopted more Hungarian-sounding surnames. As before, social status, career considerations, and youthful enthusiasm lay behind these changes; the only difference was the Hungarian government and parliament now promoted the practice much more actively than they had earlier. Hungarian nationalism had always contained elements of coercion and fear, and these grew more pronounced at the turn of the century. For Budapest, this was a period of remarkable technological advance, demographic growth, economic expansion, and cultural ferment, yet, to one astute observer, historian John Lukacs, its writers "had autumn in their hearts."[18] But the tradition of liberal activism also remained strong in Budapest. During the lengthy tenure of Mayor István Bárczy (1908–18), who succeeded Haberhauer/Halmos, the city embarked upon an unprecedented reform program: it took over gas and advertising companies, installed sewers and electrical lines, launched a number of profitable enterprises, and built dozens of new schools and housing for the working poor. This was hardly a solution for Budapest's many social problems, but it was a refreshing alternative to the nationalist wrangling that usually dominated parliamentary politics, Austro-Hungarian relations, and the mainstream press.

To a handful of observers, Budapest no longer deserved to be the center of Hungarian national movement. The city's critics charged that it was alien and disloyal, that the countryside and not the city was the source of the true Hungarianness. There is an obvious irony in this, in light of the continued nationalization of cultural and economic life, the thousands of name changes, and the census returns that showed more and more Hungarian-speakers in Budapest. The accusation that Budapest was somehow "foreign" was an old one. Around 1900, however, it took on new meanings and gained wider resonance. Part of this undoubtedly stemmed from the seemingly universal mistrust with which people in outlying regions seem to view capital cities, from ancient Rome to twenty-first-century Washington. In the countryside, the growth of agrarian and Catholic political movements also fueled hostility. For the tribunes of such movements, Budapest was the source of cultural decadence, capitalist rapacity, and political corruption. Unsurprisingly, a strong current of anti-Semitism often flowed through their attacks. Already in the 1880s, the Pest archdeacon Dr. Pál Kovách wrote that Budapest was "un-Hungarian" (*magyartalan*) and decried the "perverted German dialect" of the Jewish population as well as the "nests of socialism" in the workers' districts.[19] Hungarian writers had once described Budapest as "a holy place, the Mecca of Hungary"; in the early twentieth century, some saw it as "a fever-ridden Sodom."[20] As Lukacs has observed, Budapest had never before been spoken of in these terms.

World War I changed the picture dramatically. Austria-Hungary was destined to lose the war, and, even before its end, Budapest writer Gyula Krúdy mourned the death of his city: "Gradually we must bury the old, loveable Budapest, along with the casualties of war. Budapest has died a hero's death in the World War."[21] The end of the war brought revolution and counterrevolution to Hungary, along with peace treaties that made Budapest the capital of a small, relatively unimportant country.

The story of twentieth-century Budapest goes beyond the scope of this book, but its outlines can be seen, however fleetingly, by considering one last set of name changes. What is today Andrássy Avenue in Pest serves as a good example.[22] Originally, a road called Stonemason Street—*Mauer Gasse* on early maps—ran on its location. In the late nineteenth century, Stonemason Street was replaced by a long, wide, radial avenue of aristocratic residences, museums, tree-lined sidewalks, and later an underground railway. In 1885, Budapest renamed the street in honor of Gyula Andrássy, the former Hungarian prime minister and Austro-Hungarian foreign minister. This name lasted through the interwar period—not so that of two of the squares along the avenue, one of which was named for Benito Mussolini (already in 1936) and the other for Adolf Hitler (1938). These names were abandoned toward the end of World War II, by which time much of the city lay in ruins and more than half its Jewish population had perished. The Soviet Army liberated Budapest, and in 1949 Andrássy Avenue was accordingly renamed in honor of Stalin, and the former Mussolini Square became November 7 Square, to commemorate the Russian Revolution. In the same year, the authorities also annexed the surrounding working-class suburbs, which more than doubled the size of Budapest and increased its population from 1,000,000 to 1,600,000. In 1956, the year of the Hungarian Revolution, Stalin Avenue twice changed names, first to the neutral Avenue of Hungarian Youth and then, in a clear demonstration of fidelity to the Soviets, to the Avenue of the People's Republic. The regime of János Kádár, the first secretary of the Hungarian Socialist Workers Party (1957–88), knew the value of small symbolic gestures, and in 1971 it renamed the onetime Hitler Square after the Hungarian composer Zoltán Kodály. This name remained even after the end of state socialism in 1989. The Avenue of the People's Republic again became Andrássy Avenue, and soon acquired high-end shops, a Burger King, and—with the Goethe Institute and Polish Center—a certain cosmopolitan flair. November 7 Square regained its old name, Octagon. It hardly seems necessary to add that all these street signs are written in Hungarian alone.

Notes

Introduction

1. Mór Jókai, *Kárpáthy Zoltán* (Budapest, [1854] 1956), 139. Unless otherwise noted, all translations in this book are mine.

2. Following Lynn Hunt, political culture is defined as the "values, expectations, and implicit rules that expressed and shaped collective intentions and actions." Hunt, *Politics, Culture, and Class in the French Revolution* (Berkeley, 1984), 10.

3. John Paget, *Hungary and Transylvania*, 2 vols. (Philadelphia, 1850), 1:125.

4. Andersen, cited in Ágnes Ságvári, ed., *Források Budapest múltjából* (hereafter *FBM*), 4 vols. (Budapest, 1971–88), 1:66.

5. R. R. [Johann Christoph Rösler], "Gesellschaftliches Leben in Ofen und Pesth," *Ungarische Miscellen* 1 (1805), 87.

6. Gábor Ágoston, "History of Budapest from Its Beginnings to 1703," in *Budapest: A History from Its Beginnings to 1998*, ed. András Gerő and János Poór, trans. Judit Zinner, Cecil D. Eby, and Nóra Arató (Boulder, 1997), 11–34.

7. György Györffy, *Pest-Buda kialakulása. Budapest története a honfoglalástól az Árpád-kor végi székvárossá alakulásig* (Budapest, 1997), 59–61, 75–76.

8. Karl Malloy, ed., *Das Ofner Stadtrecht. Eine deutschsprachige Rechtssammlung des 15. Jahrhunderts aus Ungarn* (Budapest, 1959); also see Martyn Rady, *Medieval Buda: A Study of Municipal Government and Jurisdiction in the Kingdom of Hungary* (Boulder, 1985).

9. William Hunter, *Travels through France, Turkey, and Hungary, to Vienna, in 1792*, 3rd ed., 2 vols. (London, 1803), 2:167–68. The estates had the right to elect dynasties and not individual kings, who were automatically succeeded by their legitimate heirs.

10. Giorgio Vasari, *Le vite dei più eccellenti pittori, scultori e architetti* (Rome, [1550–68] 1991), 498; also see Thomas DaCosta Kaufmann, *Court, Cloister and City: The Art and Culture of Central Europe, 1450–1800* (Chicago, 1995), 41–46.

11. László Gerevich, ed., *Budapest Története* (hereafter *BPT*), 5 vols. (Budapest, 1973–1980), 2:134.

12. Anonymous poet, cited in László Zolnay, *Mozaikok a magyar újkorból* (Budapest, 1986), 43.

13. Edward Brown, *A Brief Account of Some Travels in Hungaria, Servia . . .* (Munich, [1673] 1975), 166. Emphasis and capitalization in original.

14. Mátyás Bél, *Buda visszavívásáról*, ed. and trans. Balázs Déri (Budapest, [1735–42] 1986), 105; also see *BPT*, 2:417.

15. Robert Townson, *Travels in Hungary with a Short Account of Vienna in the Year 1793* (London, 1797), 88.

16. Imre Palugyay, *Buda-Pest szabad királyi városok leírása* (Pest, 1852), 64.

17. The charters, which took effect in 1711, appear in Palugyay, *Buda-Pest,* 63–68, 303–8. On eighteenth-century town government, see Lajos Schmall, *Adalékok Budapest Székesfőváros történetéhez,* 2 vols. (Budapest, 1899), 1:1–128; Ignác Peisner, *Budapest a XVIII. században* (Budapest, 1900), 63–78; and László Csorba, "Transition from Pest-Buda to Budapest, 1815–1873," in Gerő and Poór, *Budapest,* 73–77.

18. Townson, *Travels in Hungary,* 106.

19. "Pressburgs Trauer!" *Pressburger Zeitung,* October 6, 1784, 1.

20. Joseph's letter is printed in Palugyay, *Buda-Pest,* 73.

21. *BPT,* 3:118, 124; and Vera Bácskai, "Budapest and Its Hinterland: The Development of the Twin Cities 1720–1850," in *Capital Cities and Their Hinterlands in Early Modern Europe,* ed. Peter Clark and Bernard Lepetit (Aldershot, 1996), 183–97.

22. [J. C. Hofmannsegg], *Reise des Grafen von Hofmannsegg in einige Gegenden von Ungarn bis an die türkische Gränze* (Görlitz, 1800), 100.

23. Alfréd Moess, *Pest Megye és Pest-Buda zsidóságának demográfiája 1749–1846* (Budapest, 1968), 21–24; and *BPT,* 3:137–38.

24. Sociologist Rogers Brubaker has recently written about the "wholesale nationalization" of political space in the modern era; this work examines the nationalization of Hungary's largest city in the nineteenth century. See Brubaker, *Nationalism Reframed: Nationhood and the National Question in the New Europe* (Cambridge, 1996), 1–22; as well as Moritz Csáky, "Multicultural Communities: Tensions and Qualities, The Example of Central Europe" in *Shaping the Great City: Modern Architecture in Central Europe, 1890–1937,* ed. Eva Blau and Monika Platzer (Munich, 1999), 43–56; and Jeremy King, "The Nationalization of East Central Europe: Ethnicism, Ethnicity, and Beyond," in *Staging the Past: The Politics of Commemoration in Habsburg Central Europe, 1848 to the Present,* ed. Maria Bucur and Nancy M. Wingfield (West Lafayette, Ind., 2001), 112–52.

25. Spiro Kostof, *A History of Architecture: Settings and Rituals* (New York, 1985), 571–94; Ákos Moravánszky, *Competing Visions: Aesthetic Invention and Social Imagination in Central European Architecture, 1867–1918* (Cambridge, Mass., 1998), 217–83; and Barry Bergdoll, *European Architecture 1750–1890* (Oxford, 2000), 139–70.

26. For English-language works on the Monarchy and the emergence of modern nationalism, see Robert Kann, *The Multinational Empire: Nationalism and National Reform in the Habsburg Monarchy, 1848–1918,* 2 vols. (New York, 1950); C. A. Macartney, *The Habsburg Empire, 1790–1918* (New York, 1969); István Deák, *Beyond Nationalism: A Social and Political History of the Habsburg Officer Corps, 1848–1918* (New York, 1992); and Robin Okey, *The Habsburg Monarchy: From Enlightenment to Eclipse* (New York, 2001). Their bibliographies point to important works in German and other European languages.

27. John Spielman, *The City & the Crown: Vienna and the Imperial Court, 1600–1740* (West Lafayette, Ind., 1993), esp. 185–216.

28. By "national activists," I mean the self-appointed spokesmen and most dedicated supporters of national movements, who are often identifiable as leaders of voluntary associations and regular contributors to newspapers and journals. See Miroslav Hroch, *Social Preconditions of National Revival: A Comparative Analysis of the Social Composition of Patriotic Groups among the Smaller European Nations,* trans. Ben Fowkes (Cambridge, 1985), 14–22.

29. Johann von Csaplovics, *Gemälde von Ungern,* 2 vols. (Pesth, 1829), 1:13.

30. Early nineteenth-century statisticians and geographers frequently counted Jews as a separate national group. See *Buda-Pest, a' magyarok főváros* (Pest, 1845), 7; on the 1851 census, see J. V. Haeufler, *Buda-Pest, Historische-topographische Skizzen von Ofen und Pest und deren Umgebungen*, 3 vols. (Pest, 1854), 3:87.

31. In addition to *BPT*, see János Kósa, *Pest és Buda elmagyarosodása 1848-ig* (Budapest, 1937); László Csorba, "Budapest-gondolat és városegyesítés," *Budapesti Negyed* 1, no. 2 (1993): 14–30; Éva Somogyi, "Budapest als Hauptstadt Ungarns," in *Hauptstädte in Südosteuropa. Geschichte-Function-Nationale Symbolkraft*, ed. Harald Heppner (Vienna, 1994), 29–36; Vilmos Heiszler, "Soknyelvű ország multikulturális központja: Németek és szlovákok a reformkori Pest-Budán," *Budapesti Negyed* 2, no. 4 (1994): 5–22; Gerő and Poór, *Budapest*; Vera Bácskai, Gábor Gyáni, and András Kubinyi, *Budapest története a kezdetektől 1945-ig* (Budapest, 2000); and Alice Freifeld, *Nationalism and the Crowd in Liberal Hungary, 1848–1914* (Baltimore, 2000).

32. On Hungarian nationalism, see Endre Arató, *A nemzetiségi kérdés története Magyarországon, 1790–1848*, 2 vols. (Budapest, 1960); George Barany, "The Awakening of Magyar Nationalism before 1848," *Austrian History Yearbook* 2 (1966): 19–65; Jenő Szűcs, *Nation und Geschichte. Studien* (Budapest, [1974] 1981); Ludwig Gogolák, "Ungarns Nationalitätengesetze und das Problem des Magyarischen National- und Zentralstaates," in *Die Habsburger Monarchie 1848–1918*, vol. 3, *Die Völker des Reiches*, ed. Adam Wandruszka and Peter Urbanitsch (Vienna, 1980), 1207–1303; Laszlo Deme, "Pre-1848 Magyar Nationalism Revisited: Ethnic and Authoritative or Political and Progressive?" *East European Quarterly* 27, no. 2 (1993): 141–69; and Peter F. Sugar, "The More It Changes, the More Hungarian Nationalism Remains the Same," *Austrian History Yearbook* 31 (2000): 127–55.

33. For example, György Kókay, ed. *A magyar sajtó története, 1705–1848* (Budapest, 1979); and Ferenc Kerényi, *Magyar színháztörténet, 1790–1873* (Budapest, 1990).

34. On "sinking islands," see Oszkár Jászi, *A nemzeti államok kialakulása és a nemzetiségi kérdés* (Budapest, [1912] 1986), 98; A. J. P. Taylor, *The Habsburg Monarchy, 1809–1918* (New York, [1948] 1965), 25; and Dennison Rusinow, "Ethnic Politics in the Habsburg Monarchy and Successor States: Three 'Answers' to the National Question," in *Nationalism and Empire: The Habsburg Monarchy and the Soviet Union*, ed. Richard L. Rudolph and David F. Good (New York, 1992), 245–49.

35. For example, Macartney, *Habsburg Empire*, 725; and Péter Hanák and Ferenc Mucsi, eds., *Magyarország története 1890–1918*, 2 vols. (Budapest, 1988), 1:417–18. For a more careful examination, see *BPT*, 4:452–54.

36. The following have been especially useful: Gary Cohen, *Politics of Ethnic Survival: Germans in Prague, 1861–1918* (Princeton, N.J., 1981); Max Engman, in collaboration with Francis W. Carter, A. C. Hepburn, and Colin A. Pooley, eds., *Ethnic Identity in Urban Europe* (New York, 1992); Michael Hamm, *Kiev: A Portrait, 1800–1917* (Princeton, N.J., 1993); Jeremy King, *Budweisers into Czechs and Germans: A Local History of Bohemian Politics, 1848–1948* (Princeton, N.J., 2002); and Norman Davies and Roger Moorhouse, *Microcosm: Portrait of a Central European City* (London, 2002)

37. See especially Benedict Anderson, *Imagined Communities: Reflections on the Origin and Spread of Nationalism*, rev. ed. (London, 1991); Craig Calhoun, "Nationalism and Ethnicity," *Annual Review of Sociology* 19 (1993): 211–39; Peter Alter, *Nationalism*, 2nd ed. (London, 1994), 1–15; Virginia Tilley, "The Terms of the Debate: Untangling Language about Ethnicity and Ethnic Movements," *Ethnic and Racial Studies* 20, no. 3 (1997): 506–11; and David A. Bell, *The Cult of the Nation in France: Inventing Nationalism, 1680–1800* (Cambridge, Mass., 2001), 1–21.

38. See Hunt, *Politics, Culture and Class;* Geoff Eley, "Nations, Publics, and Political Cultures: Placing Habermas in the Nineteenth Century," in *Habermas and the Public Sphere,* ed. Craig Calhoun (Cambridge, Mass., 1993), 289–339; Pieter Judson, *Exclusive Revolutionaries: Liberal Politics, Social Experience, and National Identity in the Austrian Empire, 1848–1914* (Ann Arbor, Mich., 1996); and Nancy Bermeo and Philip Nord, eds. *Civil Society Before Democracy: Lessons from Nineteenth-Century Europe* (Lanham, Md., 2000).

39. Civil society is a zone of communication and association rooted in institutions independent of the state. For civil society in pre-1848 Hungary, see András Gergely and János Veliky, "A politikai közvélemény fogalma Magyarországon a XIX. század közepén," *Magyar Történelmi Tanulmányok* 7 (1974): 5–42; and Gábor Pajkossy, *Polgári átalakulás és nyilvánosság a magyar reformkorban* (Budapest, 1991).

40. For example, George L. Mosse, *The Nationalization of the Masses: Political Symbolism and Mass Movements in Germany from the Napoleonic Wars through the Third Reich* (Ithaca, N.Y., 1975); Charles Tilly, *Coercion, Capital and European States AD 900–1900* (Oxford, 1990); Isaiah Berlin, "The Bent Twig: On the Rise of Nationalism," in *The Crooked Timber of Humanity: Chapters in the History of Ideas,* ed. Henry Hardy (New York, 1991), 238–61; and Liah Greenfeld, *Nationalism: Five Roads to Modernity* (Cambridge, Mass., 1992).

41. My approach to these issues draws upon Judson, *Exclusive Revolutionaries;* and Roger Chickering, *We Men Who Feel Most German: A Cultural Study of the Pan-German League, 1886–1914* (Boston, 1984).

42. Mihály Táncsics, *Fővárosunk* (Pest, 1867), 27–28.

1: Buda-Pest, Ofen-Pest

1. Townson, *Travels in Hungary,* 76–77.

2. Ibid., 76–90.

3. Ibid., 82.

4. Ibid., 100.

5. As Rusinow notes, Galicia, Dalmatia, and Habsburg Italy were exceptions to this rule. See Rusinow, "Ethnic Politics," 246; for similar views, see Taylor, *Habsburg Monarchy,* 24; Macartney, *Habsburg Empire,* 88; and Okey, *Habsburg Monarchy,* 9.

6. For example, István Széchenyi to Palatine Joseph, August 12, 1838, in *Gróf Széchenyi István levelei,* ed. Béla Majláth, 3 vols. (Budapest, 1889–91), 2:558–59; on the prevalence of German in the town halls, see István Baraczka, "A magyar nyelv ügye Pest, Buda és Óbuda közigazgatásában," *Tanulmányok Budapest Múltjából* (hereafter *TBM*) 8 (1940): 51–52; Peisner, *Budapest a XVIII. században,* 200; and *BPT,* 3:152–53. On cultural life, see *BPT,* 3:193–205; and Wolfgang Binal, *Deutschsprachiges Theater in Budapest. Von den Anfängen bis zum Brand des Theaters in der Wollgasse (1889)* (Vienna, 1972), 27–37.

7. *BPT,* 3:132.

8. Marton Schwartner, *Statistik des Königreichs Ungern,* 2 vols. (Ofen, 1809–11), 1:118–56.

9. Schwartner, *Statistik,* 1:121.

10. W. A. C. de Jonge, *Pesth en Presburg in 1843. Aanteekeningen uit het Reis Journaal* (n.p., 1843), 11. For a later version of the same, see Francis E. Clark, *Old Homes of New Americans: The Country and the People of the Austro-Hungarian Monarchy and Their Contribution to the New World* (Boston, 1913), 175–77.

11. Péter Hanák, *The Garden and the Workshop* (Princeton, N.J., 1998), 60.

12. András Vályi, *Magyar Országnak leírása*, 3 vols. (Buda, 1796–99), 3:77.

13. Schmall, *Adalékok*, 1:322–24.

14. Townson, *Travels*, 422.

15. Franz Schams, *Vollständige Beschreibung der königlichen Freystadt Pest* (Pest, 1821), 109; for a similar description, see J. G. Kohl, *Reise in Ungarn*, 2 vols. (Dresden, 1842), 1:358–59.

16. In addition to the works cited in the introduction, see especially E. J. Hobsbawm, *Nations and Nationalism Since 1780: Programme, Myth, Reality*, 2nd ed. (Cambridge, 1992), 14–45; and Geoff Eley and Ronald Grigor Suny, "Introduction: From the Moment of Social History to the Work of Cultural Representation," in *Becoming National: A Reader*, ed. Eley and Suny (New York, 1996), 3–37.

17. Charles S. Maier, "City, Empire, and Imperial Aftermath: Contending Contexts for the Urban Vision," in Blau and Platzer, *Shaping the Great City*, 25–41 (quotation 30).

18. Elek Fényes, *Magyarország leirása*, 2 vols. (Pest, 1847), 2:212.

19. Townson, *Travels*, 77.

20. *BPT,* 3:49, 66–67, 257.

21. Csaplovics, *Gemälde von Ungern*, 1:172.

22. Éva H. Balázs, *Hungary and the Habsburgs 1765–1800: An Experiment in Enlightened Absolutism*, trans. Tim Wilkinson (Budapest, 1997), 307–11.

23. Hofmannsegg, *Reise*, 107.

24. József Zoltán, *A barokk Pest-Buda élete. Ünnepségek, szórakozások, szokások* (Budapest, 1963), 226; Macartney, *Habsburg Empire*, 106; and *BPT,* 3:192, 397–98.

25. Vályi, *Magyar Országnak leírása*, 3:74.

26. Joseph, cited in *BPT,* 3:185; also see Schmall, *Adalékok*, 1:49–54.

27. Hunter, *Travels through France*, 2:164–65. The building would gain notoriety after the 1848–49 Revolution, when it was used as a prison and execution site for the defeated revolutionaries.

28. Schmall, *Adalékok*, 1:325–30 (quotation 326).

29. Moritz Csáky, "Die Hungarus Konzeption. Eine 'realpolitische' Alternative zur magyarischen Nationalstaatsidee," in *Ungarn und Österreich unter Maria Theresia und Joseph II*, ed. Anna M. Drabek, Richard G. Plaschka, and Adam Wandruszka (Vienna, 1982), 71–89. For the parallel form of "Bohemianism," see Jiří Kořalka, *Tschechen in Habsburgerreich und in Europa 1815–1914* (Munich, 1991), 27–37, 51–64.

30. Macartney, *Habsburg Empire*, 88; also see Okey, *Habsburg Monarchy*, 11–25.

31. Henry Marczali, *Hungary in the Eighteenth Century* (Cambridge, 1910), 142.

32. Gusztáv Thirring, *Magyarország népessége II. József korában* (Budapest, 1938), 126, 132–33.

33. Thirring, *Magyarország népessége*, 132.

34. Johann Springer, *Statistik des österreichischen Kaiserstaates*, 2 vols. (Vienna, 1840), 1:200.

35. Townson, *Travels in Hungary*, 101–102. Emphasis in original.

36. See Sugar, "The Rise of Nationalism in the Habsburg Empire," *Austrian History Yearbook* 3, no. 1 (1967): 111–16; and Macartney, *Habsburg Empire*, 90.

37. Domokos Kosáry, *Művelődés a XVIII. századi Magyarországon* (Budapest, 1980), 323–39.

38. Ferenc Kazinczy, cited in Kosáry, *Művelődés*, 325; on the lodges in Buda and Pest, see Lajos Abafi, *A szabadkőművesség története Magyarországon* (Budapest,

[1900] 1993), 157–59, 181–83; and Gábor Vermes, "Ideál és valóság: Szabadkőművesek Magyarországon a 18. században," in *Emlékkönyv L. Nagy Zsuzsa 70. születésnapjára*, ed. János Angi and János Barta (Debrecen, 2000), 93–104.

39. *Magyar Hírmondó*, April 14, 1784, 235–36, in *Magyar Hírmondó. Az első magyar nyelvű újság*, ed. György Kókay (Budapest, 1981), 163–64.

40. Joseph, cited in Balázs, *Hungary and the Habsburgs*, 211.

41. The decree appeared in Hungarian translation in *Magyar Hírmondó*, June 5, 1784, 345–49, in Kókay, *Magyar Hírmondó*, 164–67; also see Kosáry, *Művelődés*, 432–41.

42. On Pest County, see Gyula Szekfű, *Iratok a magyar államnyelv kérdésének történetéhez 1790–1848* (Budapest, 1926), 32–33; and Pest County to Joseph II, January 21, 1790, Országos Széchényi Könyvtár, Kézirattár *Fol. Hung.* 164, ff. 419–23.

43. Townson, *Travels in Hungary*, 141.

44. L. A. Hoffmann, *Babel. Fragmente über die jetzigen politischen Angelegenheiten in Ungarn* (Gedrückt im römischen Reiche, 1790), 89–91.

45. Gyula Mérei and Károly Vörös, eds. *Magyarország története 1790–1848*, 2 vols. (Budapest, 1980), 1:58–59.

46. Decsy, *The Pannonian Phoenix, or the Hungarian Language Risen From the Ashes* (1790), cited in Margaret C. Ives, *Enlightenment and National Revival: Patterns of Interplay and Paradox in Late 18th Century Hungary* (Ann Arbor, Mich., 1979), 179–85.

47. For the wider impact of the French Revolution, see Alter, *Nationalism*, 39–41; Hobsbawm, *Nations and Nationalism*, 18–21; Stuart Woolf, introduction to *Nationalism in Europe, 1815 to the Present*, ed. Woolf (London, 1996), 2–15; and Bell, *The Cult of the Nation*.

48. Dugonics, *Etelka* (1788), cited in Ives, *Enlightenment and National Revival*, 54–57, 161–67 (quotation 161). *Etelka* was in fact a thinly disguised political satire. See Kosáry, *Művelődés*, 320, 662–63.

49. Cited in Ives, *Enlightenment and National Revival*, 163.

50. János Váczy, "A nemzeti felbuzdulás (1790)," *Századok* 48, nos. 4–5 (1914): 260.

51. Kosáry, *Művelődés*, 301–22; and Ferenc Bíró, *A felvilágosodás korának magyar irodalma* (Budapest, 1994), 119–42.

52. János Mazsu, *The Social History of the Hungarian Intelligentsia, 1825–1944* (Boulder, 1997), 35–36.

53. Péczeli, cited in Bíró, *A felvilágosodás*, 127.

54. See Emil Niederhauser, *The Rise of Nationality in Eastern Europe* (Budapest, 1981), 195–208; Endre Arató, *A magyarországi nemzetiségek nemzeti ideológiája* (Budapest, 1983); and Laszlo Deme, "Pre-1848 Magyar Nationalism."

55. George Barany, "Hoping against Hope: The Enlightened Age in Hungary," *American Historical Review* 76, no. 2 (1971): 319–57 (quotation 348); also see Sugar, "The More It Changes."

56. See Anderson, *Imagined Communities*, 37–42; Hobsbawm, *Nations and Nationalism*, 51–63; Niederhauser, *Rise of Nationality*, 45–55; and, for two insightful case studies, see Wolfgang Kessler, *Politik, Kultur und Gesellschaft in Kroatien und Slawonien in der ersten Hälfte des 19. Jahrhunderts* (Munich, 1981); and Hugh LeCaine Agnew, *Origins of the Czech National Renascence* (Pittsburgh, 1993).

57. Eley and Suny, "Introduction," 7; also see Hroch, *Social Preconditions;* Anderson, *Imagined Communities*, esp. 37–82; and Agnew, *Czech National Renascence*, 51–92.

58. György Bessenyei, *Magyardom* (1778), cited in Ives, *Enlightenment and National Revival*, 99–105 (quotation 100).

NOTES TO PAGES 28-33

59. [Anon.], *Hazafiak tüköre* (1790), cited in Ives, *Enlightenment and National Revival*, 190–94 (quotation 192).

60. Herder made this statement in *Ideen zur Philosophie der Geschichte der Menschheit* (1791); see Holm Sundhaußen, *Der Einfluß der Herderschen Ideen auf die Nationsbildung bei den Völkern der Habsburger Monarchie* (Munich, 1972), 64–97.

61. Révai, cited in Bíró, *A felvilágosodás*, 127.

62. Kazinczy to István Pronay, May 22, 1790, in ed., *Kazinczy Ferenc levelezése*, ed. János Váczy, 22 vols. (Budapest, 1890–1927), 2:82–85.

63. Hroch, *Social Preconditions*, 160–65.

64. József Gvadányi, *Egy falusi nótáriusnak budai utazása . . .* (Budapest, 1978), 18.

65. The translation is from Ives, *Enlightenment and National Revival*, 176.

66. Townson praised the university library in Pest, but reported that it was "not much frequented." Townson, *Travels in Hungary*, 79, as well as G. F. Cushing, "Books and Readers in 18th-Century Hungary," *Slavonic and East European Review* 47, no. 108 (1969): 57–77; *BPT*, 3:200–205; and Kosáry, *Művelődés*, 529–33.

67. *BPT*, 3:209–10, 482.

68. Éva H. Balázs, *Berzeviczy Gergely, a reformpolitikus 1765–1795* (Budapest, 1967), 192–98.

69. Anna Fábri, *Az irodalom magánélete. Irodalmi szalonok és társaskörök Pesten, 1779–1848* (Budapest, 1987), 72–79.

70. Macartney, *Habsburg Empire*, 140–42; and Szekfű, *Iratok*, 55–56.

71. *FBM*, 1:117; on the Jacobin movement, see Mérei and Vörös, *Magyarország története 1790–1848*, 1:159–212.

72. Hofmannsegg, *Reise*, 120–21.

73. "Buda," *Hadi- és Más Nevezetes Történetek*, July 27, 1790, 109. R. J. W. Evans has pointed out that in Hungarian (though not in German or English), one can differentiate between voluntary *magyarosodás* and enforced *magyarosítás*. In this study, I have translated both words as "Magyarization" but, when needed, added adjectives to capture the original meaning. See Evans's compelling article: "Language and State Building: The Case of the Habsburg Monarchy," *Austrian History Yearbook* 35 (2004): 1–24.

74. Members of the National Playing Company *(Nemzeti Játszó Társáság)* to Pest County, August 22, 1795, in *A vándorszínészettől a Nemzeti Színházig*, ed. Ferenc Kerényi, (Budapest, 1987), 42–44.

75. Csokonai, cited in G. F. Cushing, "The Birth of National Literature in Hungary," *Slavonic and East European Review* 38, no. 91 (1959–60): 464.

76. The quotation is from András Vályi, who used these words to describe Buda. See Vályi, *Magyar Országnak leírása*, 323. On the importance of place for national movements, see George White, *Nationalism and Territory: Constructing Group Identity in Southeastern Europe* (Lanham, Md., 2000), esp. 1–44.

2: Mud, Dust, and Horses

1. Riehl, cited in David Blackbourn, *The Long Nineteenth Century: A History of Germany, 1780–1918* (New York, 1998), 128.

2. Antal Lábán, "Kortörténeti titkos jelentések Bécsből a száz év előtti magyarságról," *Századok* 56, nos. 1–5 (1922): 306–29 (quotations 318); also see Cushing, "Birth of National Literature," 471; and Loránt Czigány, *The Oxford History of Hungarian Literature: From the Earliest Times to the Present* (Oxford, 1984), 120–22.

NOTES TO PAGES 33-40

3. László Waltherr to Julianna Kamocsay, May 7, 1819, in Kerényi, *A vándorszínészettől,* 111; for the newspaper: "Magyar Ország," *Magyar Kurir,* May 11, 1819, 296–97.

4. Macartney, *Habsburg Empire,* 147–98.

5. Raymond Erickson, "Vienna in Its European Context," in *Schubert's Vienna,* ed. Erickson (New Haven, Conn., 1997), 11–16.

6. Francis, cited in Oscar Jászi, *The Dissolution of the Habsburg Monarchy* (Chicago, [1929] 1961), 83. Emphasis in original

7. Jászi, *Dissolution,* esp. 135–40; also see Okey, *Habsburg Monarchy,* 68, 79, 97.

8. Linda Colley, *Britons: Forging the Nation, 1707–1837* (New Haven, Conn., 1992).

9. *BPT,* 3:309.

10. [Anon.], "Némelly hazafiúi emlékeztető szavak a' Magyarok Nemzeti Lelke, és Charactere felől," *Tudományos Gyüjtemény* 6, no. 6 (1822): 30–56 (quotations 42, 43); and István Vedres, "A Magyar Nemzeti Lélekről egy két szó," *Tudományos Gyüjtemény* 6, no. 11 (1822): 55–75 (quotation 58).

11. *BPT,* 3:428, 432–33, 450–51.

12. Vera Bácskai, *A vállalkozók előfutárai. Nagykereskedők a reformkori Pesten* (Budapest, 1989), 33–34.

13. Schams, *Freystadt Pest,* 71; also see Paget, *Hungary and Transylvania,* 1:145.

14. Kohl, *Reise in Ungarn,* 1:189.

15. J. C. v. Thiele, *Das Königreich Ungarn,* 6 vols. (Kaschau, 1833), 6:13.

16. On the population and houses, see *BPT,* 3:257–58, 373–74; and Paget, *Hungary and Transylvania,* 1:145.

17. *BPT,* 3:374, 425.

18. Johann Csaplovics ("Slavic fortress") cited in *BPT,* 3:267–68.

19. *BPT,* 3:108.

20. Ibid., 99, 300.

21. There were an estimated seventy-three Jewish artisans in 1820. *BPT,* 3:332.

22. Jakab Pólya, *A Pesti Polg. Kereskedelmi Testület és a Budapesti Nagy Kereskedők és Nagyiparosok Társulata története* (Budapest, 1896), 32–70.

23. *BPT,* 3:307.

24. Bácskai, *A vállalkozók előfutárai,* 16–19.

25. Townson, *Travels in Hungary,* 76. Hunter used nearly identical language to describe a poorer neighborhood of Buda: "The streets are narrow, straggling, and dirty, and the houses, which have a miserable appearance, are tenanted chiefly by Jews." Hunter, *Travels through France,* 2:156.

26. Sándor Büchler, *A zsidók története Budapesten a legrégibb időktől 1867-ig* (Budapest, 1901), 351–61; and *BPT,* 3:386.

27. Moess, *Pest Megye,* 15–25.

28. Franz Schams, *Vollstandig Beschreibung der köngl. freyen Haupt Stadt Ofen* (Ofen, 1822), 635–47 (quotations 646–47); also see Carol Herselle Krinsky, *Synagogues of Europe: Architecture, History, Meaning* (Cambridge, Mass., 1985), 155–57.

29. Moess, *Pest Megye,* 60–70; Michael K. Silber, "A Jewish Minority in a Backward Economy: An Introduction," in *Jews in the Hungarian Economy 1760–1945,* ed. Silber (Jerusalem, 1992), 3–25; Vera Bácskai, "A pesti zsidóság a 19. század első felében," *Budapesti Negyed* 8, no. 2 (1995), 5–21; and, more generally, Géza Komoróczy, ed., *A zsidó Budapest. Emlékek, szertartások, történelem,* 2 vols. (Budapest, 1995), 1:97–147.

198

30. Thiele, *Königreich Ungarn,* 6:82.

31. Paget, *Hungary and Transylvania,* 1:144.

32. Macartney, *Habsburg Empire,* 173–74.

33. Sándor Domanovszky, *József nádor élete és iratai,* 4 vols. (Budapest, 1925–44), 1:437–39 (quotation 437).

34. On the Embellishment Commission, see *BPT,* 3:259–64, 313; Csorba, "Transition," 78–79; Mihály Pásztor, *A százötven éves Lipótváros* (Budapest, 1940), 134–36; and Gábor Preisach, *Budapest városépítésének története. Buda visszavételétől a kiegyezésig* (Budapest, 1960), 41–52.

35. G. L. Feldmann, *Pesth und Ofen. Neuester und vollständiger Wegweiser durch beide Städte und ihre Umgebungen* (Leipzig, 1844), 24.

36. On the theater, see Binal, *Deutschsprachiges Theater,* 85–99; and Alice Freifeld, "The De-Germanization of the Budapest Stage," in *Germany and Eastern Europe: Cultural Identities and Cultural Differences,* ed. Keith Bullivant, Geoffrey Giles, and Walter Pape (Amsterdam, 1999), 154–55.

37. Paget, *Hungary and Transylvania,* 1:276.

38. Frigyes Podmaniczky, *Egy régi gavallér emlékei* (Budapest, 1984), 35.

39. Gábor Döbrentei to Ferenc Kazinczy, November 16, 1811, in Kerényi, *A vándorszínészettől,* 94.

40. [Róza Széppataki] Déry, *Emlékezései,* 2 vols. (Budapest, 1955), 1:216.

41. Kazinczy, cited in *BPT,* 3:506–7.

42. Fredrik Barth, introduction to *Ethnic Groups and Boundaries,* ed. Barth, (Boston, 1969), 9–38; Chickering, *We Men Who Feel Most German;* and Woolf, introduction, 7.

43. Schams, *Freystadt Pest,* 72–73.

44. Joseph, cited in János Poór, "'Emléke törvénybe iktattatik.' József nádor (1776–1847)," *Budapesti Negyed* 2, no. 1 (1994): 19–34 (quotation 26).

45. Marie Tanner, *The Last Descendant of Aeneas: The Habsburgs and the Mythic Image of the Emperor* (New Haven, Conn., 1993).

46. Heinz Dollinger, "Das Leitbild des Bürgerkönigtums in der europäischen Monarchie des 19. Jahrhunderts," in *Hof, Kultur und Politik im 19. Jahrhundert,* ed. Karl Ferdinand Werner (Bonn, 1985), 325–64.

47. Grillparzer, cited in Jászi, *Dissolution,* 78.

48. Macartney, *Habsburg Empire,* 159–62 (quotation 159). On newspapers in Hungary, see Kósa, *Pest és Buda elmagyarosodása,* 176–88; and Domokos Kosáry, *Society and Culture in Eighteenth-Century Hungary,* trans. Zsuzsa Béres and rev. Christopher Sullivan (Budapest, 1987), 138.

49. For recent treatments, see Moritz Csáky, "Die Hungarus-Konzeption"; Fábri, *Az irodalom magánélete,* 95–370; László Sziklay, *Pest-Buda szellemi élete a 18–19. század fordulóján* (Budapest, 1991); László Tarnói, ed., *Deutschsprachige Lyrik im Königreich Ungarn um 1800* (Budapest, 1996); and Tarnói, ed., *Literatur und Kultur im Königreich Ungarn um 1800. Im Spiegel Deutschsprachiger Prosatext* (Budapest, 2000).

50. Tarnói, *Literatur und Kultur,* 143–51, 153–57.

51. Bredeczky, cited in Csáky, "Die Hungarus-Konzeption," 84; also see István Fried, "Über die Kultur des deutschen Bürgertums von Pesth-Ofen am Anfang des 19. Jahrhunderts," *Német Filológiai Tanulmányok* 9 (1975): 95–111; and Tarnói, *Deutschsprachiger Lyrik,* 253–54, 330.

52. The quotation comes from Gregor Berzeviczy, who in fact wanted to retain Latin as the official language. As cited in Julius Kornis, *Ungarische Kulturideale*

1777–1848 (Leipzig, 1930), 176. Also see Szekfű, *Iratok,* 62–104, 270–318; and Macartney, *Habsburg Empire,* 176–77, 183–85.

53. Szekfű, *Iratok,* 276–77.

54. Ibid., 285–88.

55. *Az irodalom magánélete,* 178–86; also see Gábor Vermes, "Retreat and Preparation: The Prelude to Hungary's Age of Reform," *Hungarian Studies* 16, no. 2 (2002): 263–76.

56. *BPT,* 3:489–92.

57. Révai, cited in Fábri, *Az irodalom magánélete,* 187.

58. Fábri, *Az irodalom magánélete,* 219–27.

59. István Horvát, *Nagy Lajos és Hunyadi Mátyás hires magyar királyoknak védelmeztetések a' nemzeti nyelv ügyében* (Pest, 1815), 17, 50.

60. István Horvát, *Mindennapi (1805–1809)* (Budapest, 1967), 131, 133.

61. József Gööž, *Budapest története* (Budapest, 1896), 166; and Antal Lábán, "Kortörténeti titkos jelentések," 321.

62. *BPT,* 3:492–98; and László Deme, "Writers and Essayists and the Rise of Magyar Nationalism in the 1820s and 1830s," *Slavic Review* 43, no. 4 (1984): 624–40.

63. See János Zvornik, "Gondolatok a' Magyar tudós társaság legelső munkájáról," *Tudományos Gyüjtemény* 15, no. 2 (1831): 42–57 (quotation 45); Gábor Sebestyén, "A Magyar Nyelvnek, a' mértékes Versekre, minden más Nyelvek felett való alkalmatos volta," *Tudományos Gyüjtemény* 6, no. 5 (1822): 50–58 (quotations 53–54); and Endre Kunoss, "A Nyelvünkbeni idegen szavakról," *Tudományos Gyüjtemény* 15, no. 11 (1831): 88–105 (quotation 104).

64. Alajos Mednyánszky, "Hazafiúi gondolatok a' Magyar nyelv kiterjesztése dolgában," *Tudományos Gyüjtemény* 6, no. 1 (1822): 3–37 (quotation 30); also see Deme, "Pre-1848 Magyar Nationalism," 634. Mednyánszky later became a member of the Hungarian Scholarly Society and a high-ranking imperial-royal official.

65. Alajos Mednyánszky, "Hazafiúi gondolatok," 3.

66. Isidór Guzmics, "A' nyelvnek hármas befolyása az ember' emberisítésébe, nemzetisítésébe és hazafiúsításába," *Tudományos Gyüjtemény* 6, no. 8 (1822): 3–36 (quotation 18).

67. Franz Schams, *Freystadt Pest,* 110–11.

68. Karács, cited in Györgyi Sáfrán, ed., *Teleki Blanka és köre* (Budapest, 1963), 144–45.

69. János Csaplovics, "Ethnographiai értekezés Magyar Országról," *Tudományos Gyüjtemény* 6, no. 3 (1822): 37–65 (quotations 60–62).

70. See the perceptive remarks in Evans, "Language and State Building," esp. 8–13.

71. Sarolta Vay, *Régi magyar társasélet* (Budapest, 1986), 368–79.

72. Gyula Viszota, ed., *Gróf Széchenyi István naplói,* 6 vols. (Budapest, 1925–39), 1:166 (December 13, 1815). Emphasis in original.

73. Gyula Viszota, "Gróf Széchenyi István és a magyarországi lóversenyek megalapitása," *Magyar Gazdaságtörténelmi Szemle* 11, nos. 1–2 (1904): 5–18; and George Barany, *Stephen Széchenyi and the Awakening of Hungarian Nationalism, 1791–1841* (Princeton, N.J., 1968), 180–83.

74. Széchenyi to Count István Fáy, April 4, 1830, in Majláth, *Gróf Széchenyi István levelei,* 1:159–61.

75. Bermeo and Nord, *Civil Society,* xx–xxii; also see Joseph Bradley, "Subjects into Citizens: Societies, Civil Society, and Autocracy in Tsarist Russia," *American Historical Review* 107, no. 4 (2002): 1094–123.

76. Cohen, *Politics of Ethnic Survival,* 52–63; David Blackbourn and Geoff Eley, *The Peculiarities of German History: Bourgeois Society and Politics in Nineteenth-Century Germany* (Oxford, 1984), 196; Hans-Peter Hye, "Vereinswesen und bürgerliche Gesellschaft in Österreich," *Beiträge zur historischen Sozialkunde* 18, no. 3 (1988): 86–97; and Judson, *Exclusive Revolutionaries,* 18–28.

77. Haus-, Hof- und Staatsarchiv (hereafter HHStA) *Minister Kolowrat Akten,* 1847/62, but cf. Gábor Pajkossy, "Egyesületek Magyarországon és Erdélyben 1848 előtt," *Korunk* 4, no. 4 (1993): 107.

78. Vay, *Régi magyar társasélet,* 179–81; and *BPT,* 420–21.

79. On the casino and associational movement, see Mihály Ilk, *A Nemzeti Casino százéves története 1827–1926* (Budapest, 1927); Barany, *Stephen Széchenyi,* 167–73; Bettina Gneiße, *István Széchenyis Kasinobewegung im ungarischen Reformzeitalter (1825–1848)* (Frankfurt am Main, 1990); Pajkossy, "Egyesületek"; and András Gerő, *Modern Hungarian Society in the Making: The Unfinished Experience,* trans. James Patterson and Enikő Koncz (Budapest, 1995), 19–21.

80. Széchenyi, cited in Barany, *Stephen Széchenyi,* 112, 218.

81. Ibid., 134.

82. István Széchenyi, *Hitel* (Pest, 1830), 174–75; also see *A' Pesti Casino tagjainak A.B.C. szerint való feljegyzése és annak alapjai 1828* (Pest, 1828).

83. For "schools of public life," see Pajkossy, *Polgári átalakulás;* and James Sheehan, *German Liberalism in the Nineteenth Century* (Chicago, 1978), 13–17; for "enlightened sociability," see Margaret Jacob, *Living the Enlightenment: Freemasonry and Politics in Eighteenth-Century Europe* (New York, 1991), 1–21.

84. Széchenyi to Count Károly Eszterházy, October 26, 1828, in Majláth, *Gróf Széchenyi István levelei,* 1:102–4.

85. Géza Fülöp, *A magyar olvasóközönség a felvilágosodás idején és a reformkorban* (Budapest, 1978), 87–137.

86. Horváth, cited in Gneiße, *Kasinobewegung,* 125.

87. Széchenyi, *Hitel,* 162–65; and Barany, *Stephen Széchenyi,* 144, 211.

88. István Széchenyi, *Világ vagy is felvilágosító töredékek némi hiba 's előitélet eligazitására* (Pest, 1831), 90–92, 509, 516.

89. Széchenyi to Miklós Wesselényi, June 15, 1832, in Majláth, *Gróf Széchenyi István levelei,* 1:226–27.

90. Robert J. W. Evans, "Hungary and the Habsburg Monarchy 1840–1867: A Study in Perceptions," *Etudes Danubiennes* 4, no. 2 (1988): 24.

3: Club Life

1. Leopold Hevánszky, *Dank-Rede gehalten als die Cholera-Seuche in der Stadt Pesth nachgelassen hatten . . .* (Pesth, [1831]), 4–5.

2. Police informant, cited in *BPT,* 3:463.

3. Palugyay, *Buda-Pest,* 308–16; István Barta, "Az 1831. évi pesti koleramozgalom," *TBM* 14 (1961): 445–70; and Mérei and Vörös, *Magyarország története 1790–1848,* 2:674–78.

4. Ferenc Pulszky, *Életem és korom,* 2 vols. (Budapest, 1958), 1:65–68.

5. Julia Pardoe, *The City of the Magyar,* 3 vols. (London, 1840), 1:217.

6. "Wanderung durch Pesth," *Die Grenzboten* 3, no. 36 (1847): 411–20 (quotation 412).

7. Judson, *Exclusive Revolutionaries,* 20; also see Cohen, *Politics of Ethnic Survival,* esp. 52–63.

8. Pajkossy, "Egyesületek"; Keith Hitchins, "Hilfsvereine auf Gegenseitigkeit in Ungarn, 1830–1941," *Internationale Revue für Soziale Sicherheit* 46, no. 3 (1993): 93–116; Gerő, *Modern Hungarian Society,* 19–43; and Robert Nemes, "Associations and Civil Society in Reform-Era Hungary," *Austrian History Yearbook* 32 (2001): 25–45.

9. "Lokal-Zeitung," *Der Spiegel,* May 18, 1844, 320.

10. *Regélő Pesti Divatlap,* November 19, 1843, 1301; and Magyar Országos Levéltár (hereafter MOL) P 1073 11 cs. 19. t., 1–31.

11. On Batthyány, see András Molnár, "Az egyesületek szerepe Batthyány Lajos politikai pályafutásában (1840–1847)," *Századok* 130, no. 1 (1996): 3–28.

12. *Regélő Pesti Divatlap,* January 14, 1844, 58–59.

13. Károly Kecskeméti, *La Hongrie et le réformisme libéral. Problèmes politiques et sociaux (1790–1848)* (Rome, 1989), 303–9.

14. For a critical discussion of civil society, see Harold Mah, "Phantasies of the Public Sphere: Rethinking the Habermas of Historians," *Journal of Modern History* 72, no. 1 (March 2000): 153–82.

15. MOL P 1073 1.-4. k. and Országos Széchényi Könyvtár, Kézirattár *Fol. Hung.* 2182; more generally, see Mór Gelléri, *Ötven év a magyar ipar történetéből 1842–1892* (Budapest, 1892).

16. MOL P 1073 6. cs. 6 t., 163–64, 195–96.

17. Imre Vahot, "Fényes Elek," *Pesti Divatlap,* March 12, 1846, 201–5; and Attila Paládi-Kovács, *Fényes Elek* (Budapest, 1976).

18. Péter Hanák, "Polgárosodás és urbanizáció (Polgári lakáskultúra Budapesten a 19. században)," *Történelmi Szemle* 27 (1984): 124–27.

19. "Wanderung durch Pesth," *Die Grenzboten* 3, no. 36 (1847): 411–20 (quotation 419).

20. MOL A 105 *Informations-Protokolle,* November 21 and 29, 1845; and Miklós Füzés, *Batthyány Kázmér* (Budapest, 1990), 54–59.

21. Peter Evan Turnbull, *Austria,* 2 vols. (London, 1840), 2:259–73.

22. HHStA *Minister Kolowrat Akten,* 1846/2335; and Judson, *Exclusive Revolutionaries,* 22–23.

23. The circulation figures are from Kósa, *Pest és Buda,* 188.

24. Pajkossy, *Polgári átalakulása,* 10–16.

25. Theresa Pulszky, *Memoirs of a Hungarian Lady,* 2 vols. (London, 1850), 4.

26. HHStA *Minister Kolowrat Akten,* 1845/221 and 1845/679; for Sedlnitzky: MOL A 105 *Informations-Protokolle,* February 25, 1845; also see Julius Marx, *Die wirtschaftlichen Ursachen der Revolution von 1848 in Österreich* (Graz, 1965), 62–72.

27. HHStA *Konf. Akten,* 1845/70; and MOL A 45 *Acta Praesidialia,* 1845/78.

28. MOL N 22 *Praesidialia,* 1845/9.

29. MOL R 104.II.K.56 "Igazgató választmányi jelentés a Védegyleti Közgyűlésre," November 17, 1845.

30. Gelléri, *Ötven év,* 112; and Elza Horváth, *A Védegylet története* (Budapest, 1911), 35.

31. HHStA *Konf. Akten A* 1845/666; and MOL A 45 *Acta Praesidialia* 1845/289 and 1845/477.

32. [Karl Zay], *Der ungarische Schutzverein* (Leipzig, 1845). Other pamphlets included Ferenc Pulszky, *Actenstücke zur Geschichte des ungarische Schutzvereins* (Leipzig, 1847); Auguste de Gerando, *Ueber den öffentlichen Geist in Ungarn* (Leipzig, 1848); and *Magyar szózatok* (Hamburg, 1847), which contains important speeches by Kázmér Batthyány and Kossuth.

33. MOL N 22 *Ep. Off.* 1845/14; and MOL A 105 *Informations-Protokolle,* April 23, 1845.

34. Cited in Ilk, *A Nemzeti Casino,* 34.

35. Béla Dezsényi, "A Nemzeti Kör a negyvenes évek irodalmi és hírlapi mozgalmaiban," *Irodalomtörténeti közlemények* 57 (1953): 172–84.

36. MOL A 105 *Informations-Protokolle,* December 5, 1846; also see Pajkossy, *Polgári átalakulás;* and Iván Zoltán Denés, "The Value System of Liberals and Conservatives in Hungary, 1830–1848," *Historical Journal* 36, no. 4 (1993): 825–50.

37. *Az Ellenzéki Kör pénztári számadása 1847ik év April 1től 1848ik év Martius 31ig* (Pest, 1848); Viszota, *Gróf Széchenyi István naplói,* 6:733 (February 25, 1848) for Széchenyi's attack; and Dezsényi, "A Nemzeti Kör," 184–95.

38. *Pesti Hirlap,* February 5, 1846, 81; also see Kohl, *Reise in Ungarn,* 1:304.

39. MOL P 1073 21.cs. 47. t., 174–75; MOL P 1073 18. cs. 40. t., 23; Mór Gelléri, *Az magyar ipar úttőrői. Élet- és jellemrajzok* (Budapest, 1887), 117–22; Gyula Mérei, *Magyar iparfejlődés 1790–1848* (Budapest, 1951), 304–6; and Gábor Nyárády, *Az első magyar iparműkiállítás* (Budapest, 1962), 143.

40. Béla Pukánszky, *Német polgárság magyar földön* (Budapest, [1940]); Arató, *A nemzetiségi kérdés;* and Heiszler, "Soknyelvű ország," 8–16.

41. See especially Cohen, *Politics of Ethnic Survival,* as well as Rusinow, "Ethnic Politics"; Karl F. Bahm, "Beyond the Bourgeoisie: Rethinking Nation, Culture, and Modernity in Nineteenth-Century Central Europe," *Austrian History Yearbook* 29 (1998): 19–35; and King, "Nationalization of East Central Europe."

42. Palugyay, *Buda-Pest,* 239, 510–29; and *BPT,* 3:335–36.

43. Bácskai, *A vállalkozók előfutárai,* 77–90, 174–96.

44. András Poros, "A pesti iparos- és kiskeredőpolgárság részvétele az ellenzéki irányitásu szervezetekben az 1840-es években," in *Nyolc tanulmány a XIX. századi magyar történet köréből,* ed. Csilla Csorba and András Gerő (Budapest, 1978), 92.

45. MOL P 1073 6. cs. 6. t., 156–57, 189–90.

46. Csanády, cited in Gelléri, *Ötven év,* 123.

47. Kósa, *Pest és Buda,* 249–55; and Baraczka, "A magyar nyelv ügye."

48. "Kivonat egy pesti napkönyvből," *Társalkodó,* March 17, 1832, 85–86; András Koleda, "Buda sz. k. Főváros határozati a magyarnyelve terjesztés ügyében," *Társalkodó,* August 1, 1832, 239–40; and "Magyarország és Erdély," *Sürgöny,* September 3, 1840, 73–74.

49. Schmall, *Adalékok,* 176–77.

50. Árpád Tóth, "Hivatali szakszerűsödés és a rendi minták követése," *TBM* 25 (1996): 40–41.

51. On Rottenbiller and Holovits, see Zsigmond Barna, *Emlék-beszéd. . .* (Pest, 1871); and MOL A 105, *Informations-Protokolle,* May 2, 1845, February 13, 1847, and March 20, 1847.

52. Fried, "Über die Kultur," 100–101; and Czigány, *Hungarian Literature,* 124–26.

53. Cited in István Fried, "Haza, állam, nemzet a magyarországi német sajtóban a XIX. század első felében," *Magyar Könyvszemle* 105, no. 3 (1989): 247–61 (quotation 250).

54. *Der Schmetterling,* cited in Fried, "Haza, állam, nemzet," 252.
55. Carl Maria Benkert, "Vorwart," in *Jahrbuch des deutschen Elementes in Ungarn,* ed. Benkert (Budapest, 1846), 1–10 (quotation 7).
56. On Glatz, see Arató, *A nemzetiségi kérdés,* 2:288–89; and Ruprecht Steinacker, *Eduard Glatz. Der Sprecher des deutschen Bürgertums in Ungarn vor 1848* (Munich, 1964).
57. Eduard Glatz, "Reversales," reprinted in Benno Imendörffer, ed., "Eduard Glatz: *Deutsche Xenien von und für Ungarn,*" *Südostdeutsche Forschungen* 4, no. 1 (1939): 70–126 (quotation 86). The title refers sardonically to mixed (Catholic-Protestant) marriages of the era, which the Catholic Church permitted only if the couple gave a pledge (*Reversales*) to raise all their children as Catholics.
58. *Pesti Első Temetkezési Egyesület alapszabály könyvecskéje/Erster Pesther Leichen-Verein Statuten Büchlein* (Pest, 1842).
59. *A' Pesti Polgári Czél-Lövész Egylet Névkönyve 1846dik évre/Album der Pesther bürgerlichen Scheiben-Schützen Gesellschaft für das Jahr 1846* (Pest, [1846]); and Schmall, *Adalékok,* 2:251–56.
60. MOL A 105 *Informations-Protokolle,* February 13, 1847; MOL R 151 *Az Ellenzéki Kör jegyzőkönyve,* minutes of February 7, 1848 meeting; and Dezsényi, "A Nemzeti Kör" 187.
61. MOL A 105, *Informations-Protokolle,* July 21, 1845; on Vienna's actions, see MOL A 105 *Informations-Protokolle,* January 15, 1839; and Piroska Szemző, *A "Pesther Zeitung": Egy XIX-ik századbeli kormánylap története* (Budapest, 1941).
62. Fényes, *Magyarország leírása,* 1:32.
63. Büchler, *A zsidók története;* Lajos Venetianer, *A magyar zsidóság története* (Budapest, [1922] 1986); William O. McCagg, *A History of Habsburg Jews, 1670–1918* (Bloomington, 1989); and Catherine Horel, *Juifs de Hongrie 1825–1849. Problèmes d'assimilation et d'émancipation* (Strasbourg, 1995).
64. Jacob Katz, "The Identity of Post-Emancipatory Hungary Jewry," in *A Social and Economic History of Central European Jewry,* ed. Yehuda Don and Victor Karády (New Brunswick, N.J., 1990), 13–31; Karády, *Zsidóság, Polgárosodás, Asszimiláció. Tanulmányok* (Budapest, 1997); and Kati Vörös, "How Jewish is Jewish Budapest?" *Jewish Social Studies* 8, no. 1 (2001): 88–125.
65. Moess, *Pest Megye,* 60–70; also see *BPT,* 3:397.
66. Henrik Pollák, "Adatok a magyar izraeliták statisztikájához," in *Első magyar zsidó naptár és évkönyv 1848-ik szökőévre* (Pest, 1848), 137–42.
67. Dezső Márkus, ed., *Magyar Törvénytár. 1836–1868 évi törvényczikkek* (Budapest, 1896), 175–76.
68. For example, Budapest Fővárosi Levéltár IV. 1202/a. *Pest város Tanácsülési jegyzőkönyve,* December 2, 1846.
69. "Fővárosi hirnök," *Hetilap,* January 5, and February 23, 1847, 27, 248.
70. Ferdinand Nagy, "Pest jelenleg anyagi és szellemi szempontbul," *Hasznos Mulatság,* November 21, 1840, 165–66.
71. Jacob Katz, *A House Divided: Orthodoxy and Schism in Nineteenth-Century Central European Jewry,* trans. Ziporah Brody (Hanover, N.H., 1998), 43–45.
72. Mihály Halprin, "Zsidó szózat," *Pesti Hirlap,* April 11, 1845, 240; also see Kohl, *Reise in Ungarn,* 1:384–85.
73. For its bylaws, see *Társalkodó,* April 16, 1846, 117–18; as well as Venetianer, *A magyar zsidóság,* 135–47; and Horel, *Juifs de Hongrie,* 151–52.
74. Márton Diósy, "A Honi Izraeliták Között Magyar Nyelvet Terjesztő Egylet . . . ," in *Zsidó naptár,* 83–93 (quotations 83–86).

75. For its bylaws and their approval, see MOL N 22 *Misc. off.* 1842/68; and HHStA *Konf. Akten A* 1846/597.

76. Ignácz Schlesinger, "Közlemények a nehéz kézmüveket . . . ," in *Zsidó naptár,* 207–10.

77. Venetianer, *A magyar zsidóság,* 140–42.

78. Michael K. Silber, "The Entrance of Jews into Hungarian Society in Vormärz: The Case of the 'Casinos,'" in *Assimilation and Community: The Jews in Nineteenth-Century Europe,* ed. Jonathan Frankel and Steven Zipperstein (Cambridge, 1992), 291–93, 303.

79. Police informant, cited in Barany, *Stephen Széchenyi,* 171.

80. Silber, "A Jewish Minority," 6–8.

81. MOL N 22 73. cs. *Polit. et Int.* 1844/28/1; also see Silber "The Entrance of Jews into Hungarian Society," 304–6.

82. Piroska Szemző, *Német írók és pesti kiadóik a XIX. században (1812–1878)* (Budapest, 1931), 39–50, 67–74.

83. On the Kunewalders, see MOL P 1073 8. cs. 7. t.; *Regélő Pesti Divatlap,* March 28, 1844, 395; and Károly Vörös, *Budapest legnagyobb adófizetői 1873-ban* (Budapest, 1979), 62.

84. MOL N 22 *Misc. Off.* 1845/1, minutes of January 9, 1845, meeting of the Protection Association's Pest chapter.

85. MOL P 1073 10. cs. 17. t. Köveskál chapter to the National Executive Committee, July 19, 1846.

86. MOL P 1073 14 cs. 26 t. Merchants Corporation of Neusohl to the Industrial Association, December 27, 1845.

87. De Gerando, *Ueber den öffentlich Geist,* 426.

4: Women and Cultural Politics

1. Kossuth, cited in Gabriella D. Szvoboda, *Barabás Miklós 1810–1898* (Budapest, 1983), 42.

2. *BPT,* 3:540–42; and Szvoboda, *Barabás Miklós,* 39–55.

3. See Colley, *Britons,* 237–82; Partha Chatterjee, *The Nation and Its Fragments: Colonial and Postcolonial Histories* (Princeton, N.J., 1993), 116–57; and for Hungary, Martha Lampland, "Family Portraits: Gendered Images of the Nation in Nineteenth-Century Hungary," *East European Politics and Society* 8, no. 2 (1994): 287–316.

4. Szekfű, *Iratok,* 175–76. There were two nonstandard systems for naming months, one based on the liturgical calendar and another on the seasons. In Hungarian, January could therefore be *január, boldogasszony hava* ("month of the Blessed Virgin"), or *télhó* ("winter month"). A number of newspapers, national societies, and noble counties regularly used the non-standard forms in the early nineteenth century.

5. Szekfű, *Iratok,* 399, 482, 510–11, 612–13; Gábor Pajkossy, "Problems of the Language of State in a Multinational Country: Debates at the Hungarian Diets of the 1840s," in *Etudes historiques hongroises 1990,* 6 vols. (Budapest, 1990), 2:97–110; and János Varga, *A Hungarian Quo Vadis: Political Trends and Theories of the Early 1840s,* trans. Éva D. Pálmai (Budapest, 1993), 51–59.

6. Fényes, *Magyarország leirása,* 1:30, succinctly lays out these arguments.

7. Arató, *A nemzetiségi kérdés,* 1:106–36; Barany, "Awakening," 41–45; and Anderson, *Imagined Communities,* 78–82.

8. Stanley B. Kimball, "The Matica Česká, 1831–61: The First Thirty Years of a Literary Foundation," in *Czech Renascence of the Nineteenth Century*, ed. Peter Brock and H. Gordon Skilling (Toronto, 1970), 53–73.

9. *A Kisfaludy-Társaság szabályai és személyzete 1838* (Buda, 1838); and Lajos Kéky, *A százéves Kisfaludy-Társaság (1836–1936)* (Budapest, 1936), 22–102 (quotation 75).

10. Paget, *Hungary and Transylvania*, 1:146. Emphasis in original.

11. MOL A 105 *Informations-Protokolle*, March 8 and April 12, 1839.

12. Széchenyi, cited in *BPT*, 3:499.

13. Eric Hobsbawm, *The Age of Revolution, 1789–1848* (New York, [1962] 1996), 269; also see Barany, "Awakening," 32.

14. The Serb Foundation (*Matica Srbska*) and its activities are described in János Török, "A Tököly-intézet és a Matica Srbska," *Hazánk* 1 (1858): 648–52; Arató, *A nemzetiségi kérdés*, 1:89–94; and Vasileje Krestić, "Egyesületek, pártok és érdekképviseleti szervek a magyarországi szerbeknél," in *Híd a századok felett*, ed. Péter Hanák and Marianna Nagy (Pécs, 1997), 179–97.

15. Jozef Karpat, "The Transition of the Slovaks from a Non-Dominant Ethnic Group to a Dominant Nation," in *Ethnic Groups and Language Rights*, ed. Sergij Vilfan (New York, 1993), 135–54.

16. On the Society for the Friends of Slovak Literature (*Spolok Milovňikov Teči a Literatúri Slowenskéj*) and Kollár, see Sziklay, *Pest-Buda szellemi élete*, 118–20; Heiszler, "Soknyelvű ország," 16–22; and Stanley J. Kirschbaum, *A History of Slovakia: The Struggle for Survival* (New York, 1995), 94–101.

17. King, "Nationalization of East Central Europe," 122.

18. Bajza uses the terms "magyarodás" and "magyarosítás" interchangeably. *FBM*, 1:152–53.

19. Jean-Jacques Rousseau, *The Government of Poland*, trans. Willmore Kendall (Indianapolis, [1772] 1985), 19.

20. Isser Woloch, *The New Regime: Transformations of the French Civic Order, 1789–1820s* (New York, 1994), 172–207 (quotation 177).

21. *BPT*, 3:474.

22. On Eichholz/Tölgyessy, see "Magyarország és Erdély," *Hirnök*, August 26, 1839, n.p.; also see Szekfű, *Iratok*, 399, which contains the text of Act 1844:2; and Pajkossy, "Problems."

23. For example, Vienna's cautious deliberations over the proposed *Nevelési Társulat* (1842), in HHStA *Minister Kolowrat Akten*, 1844/1801.

24. Gelléri, *Ötven év*, 78–95.

25. "II. Iparegylet," *Életképek*, November 6, 1844, 622–24.

26. László Buky, "A nők nemzetiség' nemtőiként tekintve," *Regelő Pesti Divatlap*, July 30, 1843, 304–6.

27. Katalin Szegvári Nagy, *A nők művelődési jogaiért folytatott harc hazánkban (1777–1918)* (Budapest, 1969), 23–49; and Katalin Fehér, "Reformkori sajtóviták a nők művelődésének kérdéseiről," *Magyar Könyvszemle* 111, no. 3 (1995): 247–63.

28. Kultsár, cited in Fehér, "Reformkori sajtótviták," 248.

29. Éva Takáts, "Némelly észrevételek Tekéntetes Kultsár István Úrnak, azon értekezésére, mellyet 1822-ik esztendő második felében közöl a' leánykák házi neveléséről," *Tudományos Gyüjtemény* 6, no. 12 (1822): 36–42.

30. Fáy, cited in Fehér, "Reformkori sajtótviták," 255; also see Nagy, *A nők művelődési jogaiért*, 30–32.

NOTES TO PAGES 92-98

31. Fáy, cited in Fehér, "Reformkori sajtótviták," 255.

32. See "Frauen Emancipation," *Der Ungar,* August 26, 1845, 797–98.

33. Teleki, "Szózat a magyar főrendű nők nevelése ügyében," *Pesti Hirlap,* December 9, 1845, 377; also see Antonia de Gerando, *Gróf Teleki Blanka élete* (Budapest, 1892).

34. MOL A 105 *Informations-Protokolle,* March 4, March 23, and July 14, 1846.

35. Blanka Teleki to Franciska Gyulay Wass, August 15, 1846, in Sáfrán, *Teleki Blanka,* 365.

36. HHStA *Konf. Akten,* 1846/1811.

37. Both students cited in Emőd Farkas, *Az 1848–49-iki szabadságharcz hősnői,* 2 vols. (Budapest, 1910), 1:94–5.

38. László Siklossy, *A régi budapesti erkölcse* (Budapest, 1972), 166–74; Katalin F. Dózsa, "Budapest—Divatváros," *TBM* 26 (1997): 89–110; and Dózsa, "A társasági élet szerepe a XIX. században Budapest világvárossá válásában," *TBM* 28 (1999): 303–18.

39. Anton Jankovich, *Pesth und Ofen mit ihren Einwohnern, besonders in medicinischer und anthropologischer Hinsicht* (Ofen, 1838), 154–65 (quotation 155).

40. Imre Vahot, "Budapesti Szemle," *Pesti Divatlap,* February 12, 1846, 137–38.

41. See "Nemzeti bál köntös," *Tudományos Gyüjtemény* 16, no. 1 (1832): 131; and Szekrényessy, "Magyar nyelv-daliák," *Társalkodó,* March 20, 1833, 92.

42. Szekrényessy, "Táncmulatság a' Pesti Nemzeti Casinóban," *Társalkodó,* February 20, 1833, 57.

43. See the tailor Pál Kersztessy's "Figyelmeztetés a' divat ruhák készítés tárgyában" in MOL P 1073 17. cs. 39. t.; and the actress Déryné's *Emlékezései,* 2:225.

44. "'Szalmatűz' magyar közmondás," *Társalkodó,* April 4, 1835, 107–8.

45. MOL A 105 *Informations-Protokolle,* February 10, 1843.

46. MOL A 105 *Informations-Protokolle,* February 3, 1843.

47. Petőfi, "Batthyányi és Károlyi grófnék," in *Petőfi Sándor összes költeményei,* 2 vols. (Budapest, 1956), 1:224–25.

48. Adolf Frankenburg, *Emlékiratok,* 3 vols. (Pest, 1868), 3:31–32.

49. "A télhó 15-iki tánczvigalom a fővárosban," *Pesti Divatlap,* January 19, 1845, 89–90; "Budapesti Ujdonságok," *Nemzeti Ujság,* January 19, 1845, 43; and *Jelenkor,* January 23, 1845, 40.

50. MOL A 105 *Informations-Protokolle,* January 27, 1845.

51. "Tánczvigalom Pesten," *Életképek,* January 18, 1845, 97–98.

52. "A Védegylet mint Pártarabló," *Honderű,* June 16, 1846, 469–73.

53. *Pesti Divatlap,* January 26, 1845, 138.

54. Domokos Kosáry, "Kossuth és a Védegylet," *Magyar Történettudományi Intézet Évkönyve* (1942): 477.

55. Paget, *Hungary and Transylvania,* 2:265; and Katalin Dózsa, "How the Hungarian National Costume Evolved," in *The Imperial Style: Fashions of the Habsburg Era* (New York, 1980), 74–87.

56. Imre Vahot, "Üdv és hála hölgyeinknek a nemzetiség szent nevében!" *Pesti Divatlap,* March 6, 1845, 297–98.

57. A dance card from the Pest Circle's ball lists two Polish, three French, and thirteen Hungarian dances. MOL R 150 "Tánczrend a Pesti Kör tánczvigalmában. Télútóhó 18-án 1846."

58. "Néhány szó a nemzeti tánczról," *Pesti Divatlap,* February 25, 1845, 249–51.

59. Podmaniczky, *Emlékei*, 115–25.

60. *Pesti Divatlap*, December 1, 1844, 145.

61. "Nemzeti Szinház," *Életképek*, July 10, 1844, 52–54.

62. Anderson, *Imagined Communities*, 102; Calhoun, "Nationalism and Ethnicity," 222; and Eley and Suny, "Introduction," 7–9.

63. *Honderű*, February 17, 1846, 136.

64. Kálmán Isoz. "A Pest-budai Hangászegyesület és nyilvános hangversenyei (1836–1851)," *TBM* 3 (1934): 170–72; also see "Heti Szemle," *Honderű*, April 19, 1844, 259.

65. Andrew Janos, *The Politics of Backwardness in Hungary, 1825–1945* (Princeton, N.J., 1982), 35–83.

66. On Sparta, see Lajos Pongrácz, "Fényűzés és egyszerűség. Adalékul a védegyleti eszmékhez," *Életképek*, January 18, 1845, 69–71; and MOL A 105 *Informations-Protokolle*, April 5, 1845.

67. "Carneval naplója," *Honderű*, February 10, 1846, 114.

68. Quotations from *Pesti Divatlap*, March 2, 1845, 290; and *Életképek*, March 8, 1845, 324; also see *Der Ungar*, March 1, 1845, 196.

69. Mirjam Moravcová, "Die Tschechischen Frauen im Revolutionären Prag 1848/49," in *1848/49 Revolutionen in Ostmitteleuropa*, ed. Rudolf Jaworski and Robert Luft (Munich, 1996), 75–96.

70. Hunt, *Politics, Culture, and Class*, 81.

71. On "national symbolization," see Chickering, *We Men Who Feel Most German*; and Katherine Verdery, "Whither 'Nation' and 'Nationalism,'" *Daedalus* 122 (1993): 37–46.

72. Cohen, *Politics of Ethnic Survival*, 123–49.

73. Rogers Brubaker and Frederick Cooper, "Beyond 'Identity,'" *Theory and Society* 29, no. 1 (2000): 27–28.

74. Podmaniczky, *Emlékei*, 76, 209. The foremost statistician of the era, Elek Fényes, estimated in 1837 (on the basis of surnames in death registers) that only one-fifth of Pest's population was Magyar, although he was quick to mention that almost everyone understood both German and Hungarian. See Fényes, *Magyar Országnak, 's a' hozzá kapcsolt tartományok mostani állapotja statistickai és geographiai tekintetben*, 2 vols. (Pest, 1837–43), 2:385.

75. Jankovich, *Pesth und Ofen*, 132–36 .

76. Feldmann, *Pesth und Ofen*, 6.

77. Pukánszky, *Német polgárság*, 136–66.

78. Károly Vörös, ed., *Pest-Budai hétköznapok* (Budapest, 1966), 41–53.

79. Baron Andrian-Werburg's oppositional pamphlet, *Oesterreich und dessen Zukunft*, was published anonymously and without permission, yet it circulated widely in the Habsburg lands. Vörös, *Pest-Budai hétköznapok*, 50.

80. Kohl, *Reise in Ungarn*, 1:316.

81. Kósa, *Pest és Buda*, 270–71; and Arató, *A nemzetiségi kérdés*, 2:282–86.

82. Glatz, "Die modernen Wiedertäufer," in *Deutsche Xenien*, 102.

83. The figures are for all of Hungary. See Simon Telkes, *Hogy magyarositsuk a vezetékneveket?* 4th ed. (Budapest, 1906), 55–57; and Viktor Karády and István Kozma, *Név és nemzet. Családnév-változtatás, névpolitika és nemzetiségi erőviszonyok Magyarországon a feudalizmustól a kommunizmusig* (Budapest, 2002), 33–47.

84. [J. Palgrave Simpson], *Letters from the Danube*, 2 vols. (London, 1847), 1:254.

85. Kohl, *Reise in Ungarn*, 1:314–15.

86. *Hetilap*, May 6, 1845, 186.

87. On Fáy, see Ferencz Badics, *Fáy András életrajza* (Budapest, 1890), 609. *A magyar bor-ismertető egyesület* (The Society for the Popularization of Hungarian Wine) is described in Fényes, *Magyar Országnak*, 2:405.

88. Kohl, *Reise in Ungarn*, 1:190–202, 282–83 (quotation 191); on Hungarian cuisine, see John Lukacs, *Budapest 1900: A Historical Portrait of a City and Its Culture* (New York, 1988), 76–80; and Michael Jacobs, *Budapest: A Cultural Guide* (Oxford, 1998), 42–46.

89. [Simpson], *Letters from the Danube*, 1:253–54.

90. The police report is printed in László Révész, "Das Junge Ungarn 1825–1848," *Südost-Forschungen* 25 (1966): 100–102.

91. Johann v. Csaplovics, *England und Ungern, Eine Parallele* (Halle, 1842), 127.

92. Hunt, *Politics, Culture, and Class;* Iurii M. Lotman, "The Decembrist in Daily Life (Everyday Behavior as a Historical-Psychological Category)," in *The Semiotics of Russian Cultural History*, ed. Lotman, Lidiia Ia. Ginsburg, and Boris A. Uspenskii (Ithaca, N.Y., 1985), 95–149; and T. H. Breen, "'Baubles of Britain': The American and Consumer Revolutions of the Eighteenth Century," *Past & Present* 119 (1988): 73–104.

93. [Imre Vahot], "Fővárosi hirek a jövő század közepén," *Pesti Divatlap*, October 14, 1844, 9–10.

94. Vörös, *Pest-Budai hétköznapok*, 46.

5: Streets and Squares

1. *FBM*, 1:56–60 (quotation 58).

2. Palugyay, *Buda-Pest*, 316–20; Pásztor, *Lipótváros*, 138–42; and *BPT*, 3:293–96.

3. Jókai, *Kárpáthy Zoltán*, 222.

4. Podmaniczky, *Emlékei*, 97.

5. Pásztor, *Lipótváros*, 139.

6. Bertalan Szemere, "Pest jövendőjérül szépitési tekintetben," *Tarsalkodó*, May 12, 1838, 145–47; also see *BPT*, 3:297.

7. Hunt, *Politics, Culture, and Class*, 52–57; Mona Ozouf, *Festivals and the French Revolution*, trans. Alan Sheridan (Cambridge, Mass., 1988), 126–57; and Bruno Tobia, "Urban Space and Monuments in the 'Nationalization of the Masses,'" in Woolf, *Nationalism*, 171–91.

8. Varga, *Hungarian Quo Vadis*, 5–18.

9. Jankovich, *Pesth und Ofen*, 3.

10. Palugyay, *Buda-Pest*, 172–73.

11. Jókai, *Kárpáthy Zoltán*, 139.

12. "Szent István, első magyar apostoli király ünnepe," *Hazánk* 1 (1858): 557–60; Kósa, *Pest és Buda*, 84–86; and *BPT*, 3:412–13.

13. Schams, *Haupt Stadt Ofen*, 279–94.

14. *Nemzeti Ujság*, August 23, 1843, 540.

15. The quotation is from Robert Darnton, *The Great Cat Massacre and Other Episodes in French Cultural History* (New York, 1984), 107–43 (quotation 124).

16. Aloys Roder, *Der Christliche Bürger in einer Kanzelrede am Festtage des heiligen Stephan ersten König von Ungarn, geschildert in der Festung Ofen 1839* (Buda, 1839), 11.

17. *BPT,* 3:397–98.

18. See Lajos Kossuth's letter to Hugo Hoffmann, MOL R 104.II.K.27, January 11, 1845.

19. Széchenyi, *Világ,* 69.

20. "Pesti Posta," *Regélő Pesti Divatlap,* August 25, 1842, 664–66.

21. *Honderű,* August 24, 1844, 127–28.

22. *Pesti Divatlap,* August 28, 1845, 701–2.

23. For example, "Jelességek," *Tudományos Gyüjtemény* 7, no. 5 (1823): 112; and Pál Kún, "Egyesüljünk," *Társalkodó,* August 17, 1843, 259–61; more generally, see Fényes, *Magyar Országnak,* 2:385–86; Kósa, *Pest és Buda,* 81–93; and *BPT,* 3:400–404.

24. Kazinczy and Széchenyi, cited in Kósa, *Pest és Buda,* 82–83.

25. Szekfű, *Iratok,* 482, 510–11.

26. On Zay, see [R. W. Seton-Watson], *Racial Problems in Hungary* (London, 1908), 65–70; Arató, *A nemzetiségi kérdés,* 2:115–18; and Varga, *Hungarian Quo Vadis,* 61–67.

27. József Székács, *A magyarhoni Ágost. Hitv. Evang. Egyház egyetemes névtára* (Pest, 1848), 19.

28. The Calvinist community was largely Hungarian-speaking, but had offered German-language services since 1816, when Palatine Joseph had married a northern German princess who was a Calvinist. On the end of this tradition, see *Jelenkor,* January 22, 1840, 25.

29. For Vienna's reports on Kronperger, see MOL A 45 *Acta Praesidialia* 1845/80; and MOL A 105 *Informations-Protokolle,* February 11 and May 2, 1845.

30. János Kiss and János Sziklay, ed., *A Katholikus Magyarország,* 2 vols. (Budapest, 1902), 1:495–500, 534–36; and Csaba Fazekas, "The Dawn of Political Catholicism in Hungary, 1844–1848," *Hungarian Studies* 13, no. 1 (1998/99): 13–26.

31. MOL A 39 *Acta Generalia,* 1846/4295; *A Közhasznu Gyülde tiszteleti helybeli és vidéki rendes tagjainak névsora betűrenddel, s alapszabályai* (Pest, 1846–47); and Dezsényi, "A Nemzeti Kör," 177–82.

32. Jankovich, *Pesth und Ofen,* 139–40.

33. Hunt, *Politics, Culture, and Class,* 54.

34. János Garay, "Az utca élete," in *Buda-Pest, a' magyarok fővárosa,* ed. József Waldapfel (Budapest, n.d.), 141–43.

35. Garay, "Az utca élete," 142.

36. *BPT,* 3:374–75. By one count, Pest was the 42nd largest city in Europe in 1846, and 23rd when combined with Buda and Óbuda. In the Habsburg lands, only Vienna and Milan had more residents than Buda-Pest.

37. Kohl, *Reise in Ungarn,* 209.

38. Thiele, *Königreich Ungarn,* 6:82–83.

39. *BPT,* 3:423–25.

40. *BPT,* 3:323–26.

41. Gyula Antalffy, *Reformkori magyar városrajzok* (Budapest, 1982), 206.

42. Cécile Tormay, *The Old House,* trans. E. Torday (New York, 1922), 27.

43. *BPT,* 3:290–92; and Barany, *Stephen Széchenyi,* 97n, 273–76.

44. Széchenyi, cited in Barany, *Stephen Széchenyi,* 276.

45. Márkus, *1836–1868 évi törvényczikkek,* 65–66.

46. Barany, *Stephen Széchenyi,* 276

47. Rudolf Alt, *Buda-Pest* (Pest, 1845), 33.

48. Thiele, *Königreich Ungarn,* 6:52–53.

49. Kostof, *History of Architecture*, 563–83; and Bergdoll, *European Architecture*, 121–35.

50. Anna Zádor and Jenő Rados, *A klasszicizmus építészete Magyarországon* (Budapest, 1943), 11–38.

51. [Anon.], "Europában alkotott Nemzeti Muzeumok között első volt a' Magyar Országi," *Tudományos Gyüjtemény* 16, no. 4 (1832): 97–113; also see Palugyay, *Buda-Pest*, 372–77.

52. The Industrial Union used these phrases in *Hetilap*, February 27, 1846, n.p.

53. Kerény, *Magyar színháztörténet*, 224–30.

54. *BPT*, 3:526–27.

55. See *Pesti Hirlap*, December 29, 1841, 870.

56. István Széchenyi, *Buda-Pesti por és sár*, ed. Ervin Fenyő (Budapest, 1995), 118.

57. Henszlmann, cited in *BPT*, 3:530; also see Kósa, *Pest és Buda*, 198.

58. *BPT*, 3:530, 534–36; and Dénes Komárik, "Az 1844-es pesti országháza-tervpályázat," *TBM* 19 (1972): 251–83.

59. MOL A 105 *Informations-Protokolle*, September 2, 1842; also see Nyárády, *Az első magyar iparműkiállítás*, 86–89.

60. Révész, "Das Junge Ungarn," 92–104; and *BPT*, 3:502–503.

61. Alajos Degré, *Visszaemlékezéseim* (Budapest, [1884] 1983), 88.

62. Imre Vahot, "Kávéházak," in Waldapfel, *Buda-Pest*, 127–30.

63. For discussions of youth and nationalism, see Cohen, *Politics of Ethnic Survival*, 209–15; Hroch, *Social Preconditions*, 148–49; and Greenfeld, *Nationalism*, 295–309.

64. Janos, *Politics of Backwardness*, 42–43.

65. Országos Széchényi Könyvtár, Kézirattár *Quart. Hung.* 625, December 1832.

66. Kárács, cited in Sáfrán, *Teleki Blanka*, 146.

67. Révész, "Das Junge Ungarn," 101-2; on the newspaper, see MOL A 105 *Informations-Protokolle*, April 14, 1845.

68. Degré, *Visszaemlékezéseim*, 89–99.

69. Jonathan Sperber, *Rhineland Radicals: The Democratic Movement and the Revolution of 1848–1849* (Princeton, N.J., 1991), 88–91.

70. Fényes, *Magyar Országnak*, 2:378, 398; and *BPT*, 3:394–95.

71. Garay, "Boltcimerek," in Waldapfel, *Buda-Pest*, 31–33; also see "Pesti magyarosodás," *Hasznos Mulatság*, January 12, 1833, 29–30.

72. "Heti Szemle," *Honderű*, April 29, 1843, 577.

73. Schams, *Freystadt Pest*, 74; also see Jankovich, *Pesth und Ofen*, 12; Kósa, *Pest és Buda*, 255–58; and Pásztor, *Lipótváros*, 171–83.

74. "Utczák' nevei Budán és Pozsonyban már magyarúl is," *Társalkodó*, December 8, 1832, 392.

75. "Fővárosunk' prózaisága," *Pesti Hirlap*, January 12, 1847, 811–12.

76. Cohen, *Politics of Ethnic Survival*, 3, 148–49.

77. Brian Ladd, *Ghosts of Berlin: Confronting German History in the Urban Landscape* (Chicago, 1997), 208–15 (quotation 214).

78. For example, Franz Schams, *Freystadt Pest*, 110–11; "Kivonat egy pesti napkönyvből," *Társalkodó*, March 17, 1832, 85–86; Antal Kiss, "A buda-pesti magyarosodás ügyében," *Hasznos Mulatságok*, April 3, 1841, 108; and "Julia," *Nemzeti Ujság*, December 13, 1844, 391–93.

79. Hobsbawm, *Nations and Nationalism*, 31–45; and Alter, *Nationalism*, 61.

80. Binal, *Deutschsprachiges Theater*, 211–15 (quotation 213).

81. Pardoe, *City of the Magyar,* 2:141.

82. Kósa, *Pest és Buda,* 257–61 (quotation 258).

83. See "Budapesti Szemle," *Pesti Divatlap,* December 9, 1847, 1592–93, which observed that Hungary had two capitals and complained that a pronounced "Teutonic element" was present in both. It called on the National Diet to meet in Pest, not Pressburg.

84. [Anon.], *Austria and the Austrians,* 2 vols. (London, 1837), 291; also Kohl, *Reise in Ungarn,* 1:158.

6: The Revolutionary Capital

1. Ferenc Herczeg, *A hét sváb,* 3rd ed. (Budapest, [1916] 1920), 8.

2. Vörösmarty to Teleki, March 17, 1848, in *Teleki László 1810–1861,* ed. Zoltán Horváth, 2 vols. (Budapest, 1964), 2:141.

3. Jonathan Sperber, *The European Revolutions, 1848–1851* (Cambridge, 1984), 148–78; also see Jaworski and Luft, *1848/49 Revolutionen in Ostmitteleuropa;* Alex Körner, ed., *1848—A European Revolution? International Ideas and National Memories of 1848* (New York, 2000); R. J. W. Evans and Harmut Pogge von Strandmann, eds., *The Revolutions in Europe 1848–1849* (Oxford, 2000); and Dieter Dowe et al., eds., *Europe in 1848: Revolution and Reform,* trans. David Higgins (New York, 2001).

4. Ozouf, *Festivals and the French Revolution,* 262–82.

5. See Manfred Gailus, "The Revolution of 1848 as 'Politics of the Streets,'" in Dowe, *Europe in 1848,* 779–98; and Jonathan Sperber, "Festivals of National Unity in the German Revolution of 1848–1849," *Past & Present* 136 (1992): 114–38.

6. Sperber, *European Revolutions,* 116.

7. Degré, *Visszaemlékezéseim,* 178.

8. For descriptions of the town, see Degré, *Visszaemlékezéseim,* 191 ("drunk with joy") and Ferenc Pulszky, *Életem és korom,* 2 vols. (Budapest, [1880] 1958), 1:332 ("gone mad").

9. György Spira, *A Pestiek Petőfi és Haynau között* (Budapest, 1998), 40–52.

10. László Deme, *The Radical Left in the Hungarian Revolution of 1848* (Boulder, 1976), 40–43; and Spira, *Petőfi és Haynau között,* 74–76.

11. Petőfi, cited in Deme, *Radical Left,* 47. Emphasis in original.

12. "Az ingerültség folyton növekszik," *Életképek,* April 2, 1848, in *1848 napi-sajtója,* ed. Ferenc Bay (Budapest, 1948), 42–44; and *Pesti Hirlap,* April 2, 1848, in Bay, *1848 napi-sajtója,* 45–46.

13. István Deák, *The Lawful Revolution: Louis Kossuth and the Hungarians, 1848–1849* (New York, 1979), 99.

14. Deák, *Lawful Revolution,* 94–96.

15. Kossuth, cited in Deme, *Radical Left,* 31.

16. Deák, *Lawful Revolution,* 113–15; and Spira, *Petőfi és Haynau között,* 125–33.

17. Julian Chownitz, *Geschichte der ungarischen Revolution . . . ,* 2 vols. (Stuttgart, 1849), 1:78.

18. Pálffy, cited in Deme, *Radical Left,* 48.

19. Spira, *Petőfi és Haynau között,* 132–33

20. Chownitz, *Geschichte,* 1:75.

21. Jenő Zsoldos, ed., *1848–1849 a magyar zsidóság életében* (Budapest, 1998), 112–13.

22. Sperber, *European Revolutions*, 123; and Christhard Hoffmann, Werner Bergmann, and Helmut Walser Smith, eds., *Exclusionary Violence: Antisemitic Riots in Modern Germany* (Ann Arbor, Mich., 2002), esp. 1–21, 43–65.

23. Already on March 17, the cloth merchant István Nádosy (at least by name, a Magyar) was the first to object to Jews serving in the National Guard. On April 18, a lawyer by the name of Pazár (again, likely a Magyar name) was the first to read anti-Semitic demands to crowds gathered in front of the National Museum.

24. Zsoldos, *1848–1849*, 120–21.

25. Ibid., 178–80. Emphasis in original.

26. Jiří Kořalka, "Revolutions in the Habsburg Monarchy," in Dowe, *Europe in 1848*, 153, 162.

27. Deák, *Lawful Revolution*, 74.

28. Podmaniczky, *Emlékei*, 259.

29. Erzsébet F. Kiss, *Az 1848–1849-es magyar minisztériumok* (Budapest, 1987), 51–52.

30. Márkus, *1836–1868 évi törvényczikkek*, 244.

31. Pulszky, *Életem és korom*, 1:334.

32. *Der Ungar*, April 11, 1848, 688, in Zsoldos, *1848–1849*, 96.

33. "Nemzeti áldozatkészség," *Pesti Hirlap*, May 25, 1848, in Bay, *1848 napi-sajtója*, 60–61.

34. Mór Jókai, "Forradalom vér nélkül," *Életképek Népszava*, March 19, 1848, 377–82.

35. MOL R 151 *Az Ellenzéki Kör jegyzőkönyve*, minutes of April 16, 1848 assembly.

36. Domokos Kosáry, *The Press During the Hungarian Revolution of 1848–1849* (Boulder, 1986). Kosáry notes (p. 45) that the number of periodicals in Hungary rose from 65 in 1847 to 152 during the revolution.

37. R. R. Palmer, *Twelve Who Ruled* (Princeton, N.J., 1969), 147.

38. On name changes, see [Márton Szentivány], *Századunk névváltoztatásai* (Budapest, 1895), 15–22; and György Spira, *Vad tűzzel* (Budapest, 2000), 83–84. "Tailor" is a common translation of "Schroeder," if not the only possible one. Naturally, it had always been both easier and more common for people to switch between different first names—for "John" to call himself either Johann or János.

39. Hungarian orthography does not use double consonants, so the second "f" in Andorffy was a superfluous but aristocratic flourish, since a number of old noble families in Hungary had similar names (e.g., the Counts Dessewffy).

40. Changing one's name was nothing new to women, who did so when they married. On Pellett/Szivesy, see Budapest Fő~városi Levéltár IV. 1106/a. *Buda város 1848–1849.évi iratai*, 1848/99.

41. Mihály Táncsics, *Életpályám* (Budapest, 1949), 245. Non-Jewish members of the March Youth also joined Táncsics's unit.

42. *Közlöny*, June 26, 1849, 526, in Zsoldos, *1848–1849*, 230–31.

43. "A pesti és aradi zsidók reformtervei," *Pesti Hirlap*, May 3, 1848, 393, in Zsoldos, *1848–1849*, 115–16; "A Magyar Középponti Reformegylet felhívása," *Kossuth Hirlapja*, August 10, 1848, 159, in Zsoldos, *1848–1849*, 192–94.

44. *Hetilap*, April 11, 1848, 459.

45. [Mária Csapó] Mrs. Sándor Vachott, *Emlékiratok (Szemelvények)* (Budapest, 1935), 72.

46. Táncsics, *Életpályám*, 242. Táncsics himself had changed his name from the more Slavic-sounding Stancsics.

47. Otto, cited in Gabriella Hauch, "Did Women Have a Revolution? Gender Battles in the European Revolution of 1848/49," in Körner, *A European Revolution*, 65.

48. "A Radikál Magyar Hölgyek Kivánatai," *Életképek Népszava*, April 30, 1848, 521-23; also see Susan Zimmermann, *Die bessere Hälfte*. *Frauenbewegungen und Frauenbestrebungen im Ungarn der Habsburgermonarchie, 1848 bis 1918* (Vienna, 1999); and Robert Nemes, "Women in the 1848-1849 Hungarian Revolution," *Journal of Women's History* 13, no. 3 (2001): 193-207.

49. "A Radikál Magyar Hölgyek Kivánatai," 523.

50. János Szerenespataki, "Fölszólitás a magyar papsághoz," *Nemzeti Ujság*, April 6, 1848, 1089.

51. Deme, *Radical Left*, 9-13.

52. Kořalka, "Revolutions in the Habsburg Monarchy," 153.

53. Sperber, *European Revolutions*, 157-63; also see Michael Wettengel, "Party Formation in Germany: Political Associations in the Revolution of 1848," in Dowe, *Europe in 1848*, 529-57.

54. Rüdiger Hachtmann, "The European Capital Cities in the Revolution of 1848," in Dowe, *Europe in 1848*, 356-59.

55. For rumors of Czechs, see *Életképek Népszava*, May 18, 1848, 665; of priests, *Pesti Divatlap*, May 13, 1848, 613.

56. *Pesti Divatlap*, March 21, 1848, 375.

57. Of 139 new members admitted on April 16, 46 were lawyers (33 percent of the total), 27 merchants (19 percent), 24 other "professionals" (17 percent), 15 officials (11 percent), 5 manufacturers and craftsmen (4 percent), 5 clerks (4 percent), 5 newspaper editors and writers (4 percent), 4 students and tutors (3 percent), 3 clergymen (2 percent), 2 men connected to the theater (1 percent), 2 army officers (1 percent) and 1 landowner (1 percent). No occupational information was listed for 31 other new members. MOL R 151 *Az Ellenzéki Kör jegyzőkönyve*, minutes of April 16, 1848 assembly.

58. Chownitz, *Geschichte*, 1:168; and Spira, *Petőfi és Haynau között*, 43, 273.

59. MOL R 151 *Az Ellenzéki Kör jegyzőkönyve*, minutes of May 29, 1848 meeting; and Gyula Kéry, ed., *A magyar szabadságharcz története napi-krónikákban* (Budapest, 1899), 518.

60. "Wesselényi a magyar szabadságért," *Pesti Hirlap*, May 1, 1848, in Bay, *1848 napi-sajtója*, 56-58.

61. "Politikai lakoma" and "Körgyülés," *Pesti Divatlap*, May 6, 1848, 580-81.

62. Deák, *Lawful Revolution*, 144-45; for a text of Kossuth's speech, see Gábor Pajkossy, *Kossuth Lajos* (Budapest, 1998), 86-89.

63. Ignaz August [Beyse], "Ein Pester deutscher Clubb," *Pesther Zeitung*, April 7-8, 1848, 3434, 3438-39.

64. Marta S. Lengyel, *Egy tévelygő Habsburg-alattvaló a 19. század derekán* (Budapest, 1985), 71-72; and Spira, *Petőfi és Haynau között*, 150-54.

65. *Reform*, April 30, 1848, 63.

66. *Marczius Tizenötödike*, May 8, 1848, 184, cited in Lengyel, *Egy tévelygő Habsburg-alattvaló*, 72.

67. Chownitz, cited in Lengyel, *Egy tévelygő Habsburg-alattvaló*, 72-73.

68. *Reform*, May 14, 1848, 97; and Lengyel, *Egy tévelygő Habsburg-alattvaló*, 74.

69. *Pesti Divatlap*, May 13, 1848, 613; and *Kossuth Hirlapja*, July 20, 1848, 74.

70. Spira, *Petőfi és Haynau között*, 288–92.

71. "Fővárosi ujdonságok," *Kossuth Hirlapja*, July 5 and August 5, 1848, 15, 139–40.

72. "Fővárosi ujdonságok," *Kossuth Hirlapja*, August 9, 1848, 154.

73. Táncsics, *Életpályám*, 255.

74. László Deme, "The Society for Equality in the Hungarian Revolution of 1848," *Slavic Review* 31, no. 1 (1972): 71–88. The club's name pointedly recalled the French Revolution's radical "Society of Equals."

75. Vasvári, cited in Deme, "Society for Equality," 80.

76. István Deák, "Revolutions and the Many Meanings of Freedom in the Habsburg Monarchy," in *Revolutions and the Meaning of Freedom in the Nineteenth Century*, ed. Isser Woloch (Stanford, Calif., 1996), 260.

77. R. J. W. Evans, "1848–1849 in the Habsburg Monarchy," in Evans and von Strandmann, *Revolutions in Europe*, 203.

78. Wearing red alone (instead of the tricolor) had been a mark of political radicalism since the beginning of the revolution. Pál Hunfalvy, *Napló 1848–1849* (Budapest, 1986), 159.

79. On the theater, see Kerényi, *Magyar színháztörtenet*, 355; on the Radical Circle, see Kéry, *A magyar szabadságharcz története*, 650–51.

80. Spira, *Petőfi és Haynau között*, 453.

81. Zsoldos, *1848–1849*, 227–28.

82. Gábor Mátray, *Töredék jegyzemények Magyarország történetéből 1848/49-ben* (Budapest, 1989), 59, 86–87.

83. Spira, *Petőfi és Haynau között*, 470.

84. Spira, *Vad tűzzel*, 92.

85. Mátray, *Töredék jegyzemények*, 72, 99.

86. György Gracza, cited in Freifeld, *Nationalism and the Crowd*, 84.

87. Hunfalvy, *Napló*, 272.

88. Freifeld, *Nationalism and the Crowd*, 85.

89. The decree is translated in Ágnes Ságvári, *Budapest: The History of a Capital* (Budapest, 1973), 89–90; also see Spira, *Petőfi és Haynau között*, 600–602.

90. MOL R 151 *Az Ellenzéki Kör jegyzőkönyve*, minutes of June 11 and 24, 1849, meetings.

91. Imre Waldherr, "Geringer és Haynau a Lánchídon," in *Küzdelem, bukás, megtorlás*, ed. Gyula Tóth (Budapest, 1978), 495–96.

92. Zsoldos, *1848–1849*, 270–73.

93. Hunfalvy, *Napló*, 350.

7: The Road to Budapest

1. József Kőrösi, *Budapest nemzetiségi állapota és magyarosodása az 1881-diki népszámlálás eredményei szerint* (Budapest, 1882), 39.

2. On Germanization, see, Kőrösi, *Budapest nemzetiségi állapota*; Jászi, *Dissolution*, 100; and Endre Kovács and László Katus, eds., *Magyarország története 1848–1890*, 2 vols. (Budapest, 1979), 1:466–69.

3. The figures appear in Haeufler, *Buda-Pest, historische-topographische Skizzen*, 3:87; also see Dezső Dányi, *Az 1850. és 1857. évi népszámlálás* (Budapest, 1993); and Ágnes Deák, '*Nemzeti egyenjogúsítás.' Kormányzati nemzetiségpolitika Magyarországon 1849–1860* (Budapest, 2000), 59–79.

4. For Terczy's letter, see *Pesti Napló,* April 29, 1851, 2.

5. "Pest, am 1. Mai," *Pester Zeitung,* May 2, 1851, 507–8.

6. On censuses in general, see Anderson, *Imagined Communities,* 166; Deák, *Nemzeti egyenjogúsítás,* 77; and King, "Nationalization of East Central Europe," 128–29.

7. The material in this chapter draws upon Albert Berzeviczy, *Az absolutismus kora Magyarországon 1849–1865,* 3 vols. (Budapest, 1922); György Szabad, *Hungarian Political Trends Between the Revolution and the Compromise (1849–1867),* trans. Éva Pálmai (Budapest, 1977); *BPT,* 4:117–320; Deák, *Nemzeti egyenjogúsítás;* and Freifeld, *Nationalism and the Crowd,* 89–188.

8. Useful discussions of Magyarization can be found in Anderson, *Imagined Communities,* 102–11; Rusinow, "Ethnic Politics"; and Jeremy King, "Austria versus Hungary: Nationhood, Statehood, and Violence since 1867," in *Nationalitätenkonflikte im 20. Jahrhundert,* ed. Philipp Ther and Holm Sundhaussen (Wiesbaden, 2001), 163–79.

9. Emília Kánya, *Réges-régi időkről (Egy 19. századi írónő emlékiratai),* ed. Anna Fábri and Bori Kiss (Budapest, 1998), 110.

10. Charles Loring Brace, *Hungary in 1851: With an Experience of the Austrian Police* (London, 1852), 33.

11. This paragraph draws upon *BPT,* 4:185–89, 195–99.

12. An extensive list of the regime's transgressions can be found in Ödön Wildner, *Buda és Pest közigazgatásának története az 1849–1865. évi abszolutizmus és provizórium alatt* (Budapest, 1937).

13. Brace, *Hungary in 1851,* 31.

14. Imre Vahot, *Emlékiratai,* 2nd ed. (Budapest, 1890), 203–8.

15. For associational life in the 1850s, see Moriz Stubenrauch, *Statistische Darstellung des Vereinswesens im Kaiserthume Österreich* (Vienna, 1857), 1–6; *BPT,* 4:266; and Deák, *Nemzeti egyenjogúsítás,* 301–5.

16. *A Budavári Casino-Egylet,* 23–32.

17. Technically, German was simply the language of inner communication in Hungary, that is, the language used within the imperial administration. Officials were required to respond to citizens in their own languages, and thus there were at least ten languages of outer communication in the Monarchy, of which Hungarian was one. In practice, many officials in Buda-Pest did not know Hungarian. See Deák, *Nemzeti egyenjogúsítás,* 191–224, 309.

18. Berzeviczy, *Az absolutismus kora,* 1:235–36; *BPT,* 4:290–98; Kovács and Katus, *Magyarország története 1848–1890,* 1:466–477; and Deák, *Nemzeti egyenjogúsítás,* 248–87.

19. *BPT,* 4:280. According to Loránt Czigány, many of these publications were the mediocre products of low quality writers. See Czigány, *Hungarian Literature,* 198.

20. Deák, *Nemzeti egyenjogúsítás,* 300.

21. On theatrical life in the 1850s, see Berzeviczy, *Az absolutismus kora,* 1:235, 2:488–510; Edit Császár Mályusz, "A főváros színházi életének megmagyarosodása (1843–1878)," *TBM* 15 (1963): 451–66; Freifeld, "The De-Germanization of the Budapest Stage," 163–67; and Deák, *Nemzeti egyenjogúsítás,* 307–12.

22. "Újévi szózat a nemzeti szinház ügyében," *Napkelet,* January 3, 1858, 15; and *Vasárnapi Ujság,* August 31, 1862, 417.

23. Deák, *Nemzeti egyenjogúsítás,* 333–38; and Freifeld, *Nationalism and the Crowd,* 127–38, 144–55.

24. Kecskeméthy, cited in Géza Buzinkay, "A Challenge for Intellectuals: Austro-Hungarians with Two Languages," in *Hungary and European Civilization*, ed. György Ránki (Budapest, 1989), 323.

25. Gyula Schvarcz, cited in Deák, *Nemzeti egyenjogúsítás*, 251.

26. Macartney, *Habsburg Empire*, 441–42.

27. Deák, *Nemzeti egyenjogúsítás*, 333–38.

28. Brace, *Hungary in 1851*, 24. For more on small acts of resistance in the early 1850s, see Ágnes Deák, "Társadalmi ellenállási stratégiák Magyarországon az abszolutista kormányzat ellen 1851–1852-ben," *Aetas* 4 (1995): 27–59.

29. Freifeld, *Nationalism and the Crowd*, 138–87; also see Berzeviczy, *Az abszolutizmus kora*, 2:482–87, 511–31.

30. Deák, *Lawful Revolution*, 244–45.

31. For its revised bylaws, see "A Magyar Tudományos Akadémia új alapszabályai," *Hazánk* 2 (1859): 99–104; also see Kovács and Katus, *Magyarország története 1848–1890*, 1:610–12.

32. "Gróf Dessewffy Emil akadémiai megnyitó beszéd," *Vasárnapi Ujság*, January 5, 1862, 1–3.

33. Judson, *Exclusive Revolutionaries*, 85–86; and Freifeld, *Nationalism and the Crowd*, 166–72.

34. Táncsics, *Életpályam*, 314–21; also see Gerő, *Modern Hungarian Society*, 240–41.

35. "Sz. István ünnepe Budapesten," *Napkelet*, August 26, 1860, 554–55; also see *FBM*, 1:231–32.

36. See *Pester Lloyd*, January 28, 1860, 3, for a ball organized by Pest's Jewish community; "Pesti napló," *Pesti Napló*, January 12, 1860, on the refusal to waltz; and *Pesti Napló*, January 26, 1860, 3, for the official regulations on dances.

37. János Oroszhegyi, "Egy szó a magyar öltözet körül," *Napkelet*, April 1, 1860, 219–20.

38. Albert Berzeviczy, *Régi emlékek, 1853–1870* (Budapest, 1907), 121.

39. Zsigmond Pál Pach, ed., *A Magyar Tudományos Akadémia másfél évszázada 1825–1975* (Budapest, 1975), 103–5; also see István Gorove, "A magyar Akadémia házáról," in *Gattajai Gorove István emlékezete. Gyűjtemény irodalmi s szónoklati hagyatékaiból* (Budapest, 1860), 200–205.

40. Imre Henszlmann, "Das Gebäude der ungarischen Akademie," *Pester Lloyd*, January 31 and February 1, 1861, n.p.

41. "A magyar akadémiai palota tervek," *Vasárnapi Ujság*, March 2, 1862, 100–101.

42. Hencz and Bergh, "Hazai épitészetünk ügyében," *Vasárnapi Ujság*, February 24, 1861, 91; also see László Gerő, *Pest-Buda épitészete az egyesítéskor* (Budapest, 1973), 157; and Morávanszky, *Competing Visions*, 66–74, 217–21.

43. On nationalism and architecture, see Moravánszky, *Competing Visions*, 217–83; and Barry Bergdoll, *European Architecture*, 139–70.

44. "Csárdás in stone" is a loose but workable translation of Edvard Hansen's phrase, "auskristallirter Tschardasch." Hansen, cited in István Gábor, *A Vigadó története* (Budapest, 1978), 37.

45. János Gyurgyák, *A zsidókérdés Magyarországon. Politikai eszmetörténet* (Budapest, 2001), 56–61.

46. Krinsky, *Synagogues of Europe*, 157–59; Rudolf Klein, "Keresztények számára már érthető, zsidók számára még emészthető," *Budapesti Negyed* 2, no. 2 (1994): 28–41; and Komoróczy, *A zsidó Budapest*, 1:150–58.

47. Moravánszky, *Competing Visions*, 234.

48. Franz Xaver Kempf, *Geschichte und Bau des neuen Israelitischen Kultus-Tempels in Pest* (Pest, 1859), 7; for a more modest description, see "Az izraelita templom fölszentelése," *Budapesti Hirlap*, September 7, 1859, 2.

49. "Magyarító Egylet," *Allgemeine Illustrirte Judenzeitung*, November 23, 1860, 131–32; and "Die erste Jahresversammlung des 'Izraelita Magyar Egylet,'" *Allgemeine Illustrirte Judenzeitung*, June 27, 1862, 201–6.

50. Gyurgyák, *A zsidókérdés*, 215–21; and Katz, *A House Divided*.

51. Sámuel Fischer, *Egy komoly szó hazánk izraelitáinak magyarosodása érdekében* (Pest, 1863), 30–31.

52. László Rákosi, "Jelen átalakulásunk házi szellemei," *Napkelet*, November 18, 1860, 737–40.

53. *BPT*, 4:251–55.

54. Telkes, *Hogy magyarositsuk a vezetékneveket?* 59–65; and Karády and Kozma, *Név és nemzet*, 34–47.

55. MOL D 189 *Magyar Kancellária*, 1862/208 and 1862/291.

56. The oft-quoted line reads, "Az utcán por, bűz, német szó, piszok." See Arany, "Vojtina ars poétikája," in *Verses Budapest*, ed. Aladár Komlós (Budapest, 1968), 45–46.

57. Podmaniczky, *Emlékei*, 339–40.

58. *BPT*, 4:299–316; and Csorba, "Budapest-gondolat."

59. Török's article appeared on the fourth anniversary of the 1849 unification of Buda-Pest. János Török, "Buda-Pest," *Pesti Napló*, June 24, 1853, in *Török János publicisztikai és nemzetgazdasági nemély dolgozatai* (Pest, 1858), 57–59.

60. Kemény, cited in Csorba, "Budapest-gondolat," 22.

61. Táncsics was allowed to publish *Fővárosunk* only in 1867. Also see *BPT*, 4:299–300.

62. Táncsics, *Fővárosunk*, 11–12.

63. Ferencz Reitter, *Duna-Szabályozás Buda és Pest között* (Pest, 1865).

64. Táncsics, *Fővárosunk*, 27–28.

65. Dezső Márkus, ed., *Az 1869–1871. évi törvényczikkek* (Budapest, 1896), 123–27; also see László Siklóssy, *Hogyan épült Budapest? (1870–1930)* (Budapest, 1931).

66. Lajos Schmall, *Buda-Pest utczái és térei* (Budapest, 1906).

67. Albert Gardonyi, *A főváros egyesítésére vonatkozó okmányok gyűjteménye* (Budapest, 1913); *BPT*, 4:11–16; and Csorba, "Budapest gondolat," 27–30.

68. "Pest und Ofen oder Pest-Ofen," *Pester Lloyd*, August 11, 1871, 3; and Viktória Czaga, "A főváros egyesítése a budaiak szemszögéből," *TBM* 28 (1999): 13–22.

69. *FBM*, 1:290–92.

70. Act 1872:36.89.§. mandated that the city's "official administrative language *(hivatalos ügykezelési nyelve)* is exclusively the official state language, that is, Hungarian." *FBM*, 1:295–302 (quotation 301).

71. "Pest, 24 Oktober," *Pester Lloyd*, October 25, 1873, 2.

72. "Budapest, Oct. 25," *Pesti Napló*, October 26, 1873, 1.

73. Francis H. E. Palmer, *Austro-Hungarian Life in Town and Country* (New York, 1903), 61.

74. Steindl, cited in Moravánszky, *Competing Visions*, 68; also see *Az Ország Háza: Buda-Pesti Országháza-tervek 1784–1884/The House of the Nation: Parliament Plans for Buda-Pest, 1784–1884* (Budapest, 2000), esp. 356–71.

75. Carl E. Schorske, *Fin-de-Siècle Vienna: Politics and Culture* (New York, 1981), 24–115

76. Alexander Országh, *Budapest's oeffentliche Bauten in den Jahren 1868–1882* (Budapest, 1884), 224.

77. The talk was published as Kőrösi, *Budapest nemzetiségi állapota*, 1–45; also see Josef Kőrösi, *Die Hauptstadt Budapest im Jahre 1881. Resulte der Volksbeschreibung und Volksbezählung* (Berlin, 1881).

78. The 1881 census in fact asked people about their "mother tongue" (*anyanyelv, Muttersprache*) and not their nationality. Kőrösi conceded that language and nationality were not always identical, and he provided a careful analysis of bilingualism in Budapest. At the same time, he also stated that "the entire world" equated language with nationality and therefore freely used the census results to characterize the national character of the city and its population.

79. *BPT*, 4:452–54; also see Éva Windisch, "A magyarországi német nemzetiségi mozgalom előtörténete (1867–1900)," *Századok* 98, nos. 4 and 6 (1964): 635–60, 1104–29; and Horst Haselsteiner, "Budapest als Hauptstadt des ungarischen Reichsteiles der Habsburgermonarchie," in *Hauptstädte in europäischen Nationalstaaten*, ed. Theodor Schieder and Gerhard Brunn (Munich, 1983), 121–33.

80. Adolf Ágai, *Utazás Pestről Budapestre 1843–1907* (Budapest, [1908] 1998), 313.

81. Zoltán Tóth, "Was wird im Schmeltztiegel geschmolzen? Assimilationswesen in Pest in der zweiten Hälfte des 19. Jahrhunderts," in *Wien-Prag-Budapest. Blütezeit der Habsburgmetropolen*, ed. Gerhard Melinz and Susan Zimmermann (Budapest, 1996), 210–18; and Tamás Faragó, "A főváros népe: sokszínűség és beolvadás," in *Az egyesített főváros. Pest, Buda, Óbuda*, ed. Gábor Gyányi (Budapest, 1998), 75–110.

82. Viktor Karády, "Egyenlőtlen elmagyarosodás, avagy hogyan vált Magyarország magyar nyelvű országgá," in *Magyarország társadalomtörténete*, ed. György Kövér, 2 vols. (Budapest, 1995), 2:302–36.

83. Komoróczy, *A zsidó Budapest*, 2:362.

84. Péter Hanák, "Urbanizáció és asszimiláció Budapesten a dualizmus korában," in Hanák and Nagy, *Híd a századok fellet*, 227–35.

85. Faragó, "A főváros népe," 98–99. Also see Rusinow, "Ethnic Politics," 253, which observes that state pressures towards nationalization were "contributory and facilitative" rather than primary.

86. István Deák, *Assimilation and Nationalism in East Central Europe During the Last Century of Habsburg Rule* (Pittsburgh, 1983), 13.

87. Binal, *Deutschsprachiges Theater*, 212–14, 382–85; Mária Bódis, "Színi élet a Duna két partján, 1867–1885," *TBM* 27 (1998): 117–22; and Freifeld, "The De-Germanization of the Budapest Stage," 167–71.

88. Kosmopolita, "A magyar ügy diadala a főváros közgyűlésén," *Pesti Napló*, 2–3.

89. *BPT*, 4:277–98, 487–513; also see Kovács and Katus, *Magyarország története 1848–1890*, 2:844–50, 1399–1405.

90. Eugen Weber describes a similar process in provincial France in *Peasants into Frenchmen: The Modernization of Rural France, 1870–1914* (Stanford, Calif., 1976), 303–38.

91. Béla Bellér, *A magyarországi németek rövid története* (Budapest, 1981), 111.

92. "Budapest német ajkú polgárainak tüntetése," *Pesti Hirlap*, May 1, 1882, 3–4; also see Freifeld, *Nationalism and the Crowd*, 245–46.

93. See Pajkossy, "Egyesületek," 108; and Gyula Vargha, *Magyarország egyletei és társulatai 1878-ban* (Budapest, 1881), 362–94.

94. The law appears in English translation in Seton-Watson, *Racial Problems,* 429–33.

95. Oszkár Sashegyi, ed., *Munkások és parasztok mozgalmai Magyarországon 1849–1867* (Budapest, 1959), esp. 469–74; and *BPT,* 4:265–75.

96. For its bylaws, see *FBM,* 1:247–50.

97. Seton-Watson, *Racial Problems,* 274–92; and Loránt Tilkovszky, "Budapesti szlovák és cseh egyesületek történetéhez," *Századok* 132, no. 6 (1998): 1305–21.

98. See *A Pesti Torna-Egylet Alapszabályai/Statuten des Pester Turn-Vereines* (Pest, 1866); and Károly Demény and István Tatár, *A Budapesti (Budai) Torna Egylet 60 éves története 1869–1929* (Budapest, 1929), 8–19.

99. August Imendörfer, *Der deutsche gesellige Verein "Eintracht" 1863–1888. Ein Erinnerungsblatt zur Feier des 25-jährigen Bestandes* (Budapest, 1888), 1–45 (quotation 17); also see Pukánszky, *Német polgárság,* 149.

100. Károly Kimnach, ed., *Jelentés a Budai Polgári Lövész-egylet által 1871-ben tartott százados ünnepélyről* (Buda, 1872), 46.

101. *BPT,* 4:452.

102. R. J. W. Evans usefully observes that "functional polyglossia" continued to grow in the Monarchy through 1914, but that it "lacked more and more the support of any ideological commitment in official, establishment, or intellectual circles." See Evans, "Language and State Building," 22.

103. Tormay, *The Old House,* 282.

104. Lajos Hatvany, *Urak és Emberek,* 2 vols. (Budapest, [1927] 1963), 1:76–84 (quotation 77). I would like to thank Howard Lupovitch for directing me to this novel.

105. Ernest Renan, "What Is a Nation?" in *The Nationalism Reader,* ed. Omar Dahbour and Micheline R. Ishay (Amherst, N.Y., 1999), 143–55 (quotation 154).

Conclusion

1. *FBM,* 2:267–69; and Freifeld, *Nationalism and the Crowd,* 263–65.

2. *FBM,* 2:44–45.

3. Richard Wortman, "Moscow and Petersburg: The Problem of Political Center in Tsarist Russia, 1881–1914," in *Rites of Power: Symbolism, Ritual, and Politics Since the Middle Ages,* ed. Sean Wilentz (Philadelphia, 1985), 244–71 (quotation 266).

4. "Székesváros vagy főváros?" *Pesti Hirlap,* January 7, 1881, 1–2.

5. Tamás Faragó, "Die Budapester Bevölkerungsentwicklung und die Zuwanderung 1840 bis 1941," in Zimmermann and Melinz, *Wien-Prag-Budapest,* 61, 68.

6. Albert Shaw, "Budapest: The Rise of a New Metropolis," *Century Magazine* 44, no. 2 (1892): 163–79 (quotation 163).

7. Susan Zimmermann, *Prächtige Armut: Fürsorge, Kinderschutz und Sozialreform in Budapest* (Sigmaringen, Germany, 1997), 78.

8. H. Ellen Browning, *A Girl's Wanderings in Hungary,* 2nd ed. (London, 1897), 248.

9. On the press, associations, and theater, see *BPT,* 4:454, 494, 497.

10. Gyurgyák, *Zsidókérdés,* 243–54.

11. Renan, "What Is a Nation?" 145.

12. *BPT,* 2:426.

13. The quotation comes from Grillparzer, cited in Jászi, *Dissolution*, 44. Kann, *Multinational Empire*, 1:28, likewise describes "the history of the application of expedients instead of solution."

14. See István Deák, "Cause for Despair? (Some Remarks on the Mood of Pessimism in the Late Habsburg Monarchy)," in *Polgárosodás Közép-Európában / Verbürgerlichung in Mitteleuropa*, ed. Éva Somogyi (Budapest, 1991), 87–96; Gary B. Cohen, *Education and Middle-Class Society in Imperial Austria, 1848–1918* (West Lafayette, Ind., 1996); and Okey, *Habsburg Monarchy*, 396–401.

15. Jászi, *Dissolution*, 24–27.

16. Sigmund Freud, *Civilization and Its Discontents*, ed. and trans. James Strachey (New York, [1930] 1961), 72.

17. Pukánszky, *Német polgárság*, 101; also see Karády and Kozma, *Név és nemzet*, 64–76.

18. Lukacs, *Budapest 1900*, 12.

19. Pál Kovách, *Budapest és környéke, a magyar nemzetiség és nyelv szempontjából tekintve* (Budapest, 1880), 4, 52–53.

20. For Budapest as Mecca, see "Pest és a Magyarok," *Pesti Divatlap*, January 22, 1846, 73–76; for Sodom, see Lukacs, *Budapest 1900*, 187.

21. Gyula Krúdy, "The Golden Age of Budapest," in *Krúdy's Chronicles*, ed. and trans. John Bátki (Budapest, 2000), 197–201.

22. The various names are listed in Violetta Hidvégi, "Kezdetben Radiálstrassénak hívták," *Budapesti Negyed* 1, no. 1 (1993): 197–201.

Bibliography

Primary Sources

Archival and Library Collections

Budapest Fővárosi Levéltára
Buda város 1848–1849. évi iratai (IV. 1106/a)
Pest város Tanácsülési jegyzőkönyvek (IV. 1202/a)

Haus-, Hof- und Staatsarchiv
Konf. Akten
Konf. Akten A
Minister Kolowrat Akten

Magyar Országos Levéltár
Magyar Kancellária (A 39, A 45, A 105, D 189)
Archivum Palatinale Secretum Archiducis Josephi (N 22)
Kisebb testületi, egyesületi és intézményi fondok (P 1073)
1526 utáni gyűjtemény—R szekció (R 104, R 150, R 151)

Országos Széchényi Könyvtár, Kézirattár
Fol. Hung.
Quart. Hung.

Newspapers and Periodicals

Allgemeine Illustrirte Judenzeitung
Budapesti Hirlap
Életképek
Die Grenzboten
Hadi- és Más Nevezetes Történetek
Hasznos Mulatságok
Hazánk
Hetilap
Hirnök
Honderű
Jelenkor
Kossuth Hirlapja
Magyar Kurir
Marczius Tizenötödike

Napkelet
Nemzeti Ujság
Pester Lloyd
Pester Zeitung
Pesti Divatlap
Pesti Hirlap
Pesti Napló
Pressburger Zeitung
Reform
Der Spiegel
Társalkodó
Tudományos Gyüjtemény
Der Ungar
Ungarische Miscellen
Vasárnapi Ujság

Other Primary Materials

Alt, Rudolf. *Buda-Pest/Pesth und Ofen*. Pest: Hartleben 1845.
Bay, Ferenc, ed. *1848 napi-sajtója*. Budapest: Officina, 1948.
Bél, Mátyás. *Buda visszavívásáról*. Edited and translated by Balázs Déri. Budapest: Zrínyi, [1735–42] 1986.
Brace, Charles Loring. *Hungary in 1851: With an Experience of the Austrian Police*. London: Richard Bentley, 1852.
Brown, Edward. *A Brief Account of Some Travels in Hungaria, Servia* . . . Munich: Finnisch-Ugrischen Seminar an der Universität, [1673] 1975.
Browning, H. Ellen. *A Girl's Wanderings in Hungary*. 2nd ed. London: Longmans, Green, 1897.
A Budavári Casino-Egylet félszázados története 1841–1891. Budapest: Athenaeum, 1891.
Chownitz, Julian. *Geschichte der ungarischen Revolution*. . . 2 vols. Stuttgart: Rieger, 1849.
Csaplovics, Johann von. *England und Ungern. Eine Parallele*. Halle: Renger, 1842.
———. *Gemälde von Ungern*. Pesth: C. A. Hartleben, 1829.
Csapó, Mária [Mrs. Sándor Vachott]. *Rajzok a multból. Emlékiratok (Szemelvények)*. Budapest: 1935.
Degré, Alajos. *Visszaemlékezéseim*. 2 vols. Budapest: Szépirodalmi Könyvkiadó, 1983.
Déry, [Róza Széppataki]. *Emlékezései*. Edited by Pál Réz. 2 vols. Budapest: Szépirodalmi Könyvkiadó, 1955.
Az Ellenzéki Kör pénztári számadása 1847ik év April 1-től 1848ik év Martius 31-ig. Pest: Beimel, 1848.
Az első magyar zsidó naptár és évkönyv 1848-ik szökőévre. Pest: Landerer és Heckenast, 1848.
Eötvös, Joseph. *The Village Notary: A Romance of Hungarian Life*. Translated by Otto Wenckstern. New York: D. Appleton, 1850.
Feldmann, G. L. *Pesth und Ofen. Neuester und vollständiger Wegweiser durch beide Städte und ihre Umgebungen*. Leipzig: Verlags-Magazin, 1844.
Fényes, Elek. *Magyar Országnak,'s a' hozzá kapcsolt tartományoknak mostani állapotja statistikai és geographiai tekintetben*. 6 vols. Pest: Trattner-Károlyi, 1837–43.

————. *Magyarország leirása.* 2 vols. Pest: Beimel, 1847.

Fischer, Sámuel. *Egy komoly szó hazánk izraelitáinak magyarosodása érdekében.* Pest: Emich Gusztáv, 1863.

Források Budapest múltjából. Edited by Ágnes Ságvári. 5 vols. Budapest: Budapest Főváros Levéltára, 1971–88.

Frankenburg, Adolf. *Emlékiratok.* 3 vols. Pest: Emich Gusztáv, 1868.

Gardonyi, Albert. *A főváros egyesítésére vonatkozó okmányok gyűjteménye.* Budapest: Székesfővárosi Házinyomda, 1913.

Gerando, Auguste de. *Ueber den öffentlichen Geist in Ungarn.* Leipzig: J. J. Weber, 1848.

Gvadányi, József. *Egy falusi nótáriusnak budai utazása.* . . Budapest: Magvető Kiadó, 1978.

Haeufler, J. V. *Buda-Pest, Historische-topographische Skizzen von Ofen und Pest und deren Umgebungen.* 3 vols. Pest: Gustav Emich, 1854.

Hatvany, Lajos. *Urak és Emberek.* 2 vols. Budapest: Szépirodalmi Könyvkiadó, 1963.

Herczeg, Ferenc. *A hét sváb.* 3rd ed. Budapest: Singer és Wolfner, [1916] 1920.

Hevánszky, Leopold. *Dank-Rede gehalten als die Cholera-Seuche in der Stadt Pesth nachgelassen hatten.* . . Pesth: [1831].

Hoffmann, L. A. *Babel. Fragmente über die jetzigen politischen Angelegenheiten in Ungarn.* Gedrückt im römischen Reiche: 1790.

Hofmannsegg, J. C. *Reise des Grafen von Hofmannsegg in einige Gegenden von Ungarn bis an die türkische Gränze.* Görlitz: C. G. Anton, 1800.

Horvát, István. *Nagy Lajos és Hunyadi Mátyás hires magyar királyoknak védelmeztetések a' nemzeti nyelv ügyében.* Pest: Trattner János Tamás, 1815.

Hunfalvy, Pál. *Napló 1848–1849.* Edited by Aladár Urbán. Budapest: Szépirodalmi Könyvkiadó, 1986.

Hunter, William. *Travels through France, Turkey, and Hungary, to Vienna, in 1792.* 3rd ed. 2 vols. London: J. White, 1803.

Imendörfer, August. *Der deutsche gesellige Verein "Eintracht" 1863–1888. Ein Erinnerungsblatt zur Feier des 25-jährigen Bestandes.* Budapest: Franklin-Verein, 1888.

Imendörffer, Benno, ed. "Eduard Glatz: *Deutsche Xenien von und für Ungarn.*" *Südostdeutsche Forschungen* 4, no. 1 (1939): 70–126.

Jahrbuch des deutschen Elementes in Ungarn. Edited by Karl Benkert. Budapest, 1846.

Jankovich, Anton. *Pesth und Ofen mit ihren Einwohnern, besonders in medicinischer und anthropologischer Hinsicht.* Ofen: Universitäts-Schriften, 1838.

Jókai, Mór. *Kárpáthy Zoltán.* Budapest: Szépirodalmi Könyvkiadó, [1854] 1956 .

Jonge, W. A. C. de. *Pesth en Presburg in 1843. Aanteekeningen uit het Reis Journaal.* 1843.

Kempf, Franz Xaver. *Geschichte und Bau des neuen Israelitischen Kultus-Tempels in Pest.* Pest: Gustav Emich, 1859.

Kerényi, Ferenc, ed. *A vándorszínészettől a Nemzeti Színházig.* Budapest: Szépirodalmi Könyvkiadó, 1987.

Kéry, Gyula, ed. *A magyar szabadságharcz története napi-krónikákban.* 2 vols. Budapest: Franklin-Társulat, 1899.

Kimnach, Károly, ed. *Jelentés a Budai Polgári Lövész-egylet által 1871-ben tartott százados ünnepélyről.* Buda: M. Királyi Egyetemi Könyvnyoma, 1872.

Kohl, J. G. *Reise in Ungarn.* 2 vols. Dresden: Arnold, 1842.

Kőrösi, József. *Budapest nemzetiségi állapota és magyarosodása az 1881-diki népszámlálás eredményei szerint.* Budapest: M. T. Akadémia Könyvkiadó-hivatala, 1882.

Kovách, Pál. *Budapest és környéke, a magyar nemzetiség és nyelv szempontjából tekintve.* Budapest: "Hunyadi Mátyás" Intézet, 1880.

A Közhasznu Gyűlde tiszteleti helybeli és vidéki rendes tagjainak névsora betűrenddel, s alapszabályai. Pest: 1846–47.

Krúdy, Gyula. "The Golden Age of Budapest." In *Krúdy's Chronicles,* edited and translated by John Bátki, 197–201. Budapest: Central European University Press, 2000.

Magyar Hírmondó. Az első magyar nyelvű újság. Edited by György Kókay. Budapest: Gondolat Kiadó, 1981.

Márkus, Dezső, ed. *Az 1869–1871. évi törvényczikkek.* Budapest: Franklin-Társulat, 1896.

———. *Magyar Törvénytár. 1836–1868 évi törvényczikkek.* Budapest: Franklin-Társulat, 1896.

Mátray, Gábor. *Töredék jegyzemények Magyarország történetéből 1848/49-ben.* Edited by Katalin Fülep. Budapest: Szépirodalmi Könyvkiadó, 1989.

Mitglieder des Mercantil-Casino in Pesth. Pest: 1848.

Országh, Alexander. *Budapest's oeffentliche Bauten in den Jahren 1868–1882.* Budapest: Pester Buchdruckerei, 1884.

Az Országos Védegylet alapszabályai. n.p., n.d.

Paget, John. *Hungary and Transylvania; With Remarks on their Condition, Social Political and Economical.* Philadelphia: Lea & Blanchard, 1850.

Palmer, Francis H. E. *Austro-Hungarian Life in Town and Country.* New York: G. P. Putnam's Sons, 1903.

Palugyay, Imre. *Buda-Pest szabad királyi városok leirása.* Pest: Landerer és Heckenast, 1852.

Pardoe, Julia. *The City of the Magyar.* 3 vols. London: George Virtue, 1840.

A' Pesti Casino tagjainak A.B.C. szerint való feljegyzése és annak alapjai 1828. Pest: 1828.

Pesti első temetkezési egyesület alapszabály könyvecskéje/Erster Pesther Leichen-Verein Statuten Büchlein. Pest: 1842.

A' Pesti Polgári Czél-Lövész Egylet Névkönyve 1846dik évre/Album der Pesther bürgerlichen Scheiben-Schützen Gesellschaft für das Jahr 1846. Pest: [1846].

A Pesti Torna-Egylet Alapszabályai/Statuten des Pester Turn-Vereines. Pest: Erste ungarische Vereins-Buchdruckerei, 1866.

Podmaniczky, Frigyes. *Egy régi gavallér emlékei.* Edited by Ágota Steinert. Budapest: Helikon Kiadó, 1984.

Pulszky, Ferenc. *Actenstücke zur Geschichte des ungarische Schutzvereins.* Leipzig: 1847.

———. *Életem és korom.* 2 vols. Budapest: Szépirodalmi Könyvkiadó, 1958.

Pulszky, Theresa. *Memoirs of a Hungarian Lady.* 2 vols. London: H. Colburn, 1850.

Renan, Ernest. "What Is a Nation?" In *The Nationalism Reader,* edited by Omar Dahbour and Micheline R. Ishay, 143–55. Amherst, N.Y.: Humanity Books, 1999.

Roder, Aloys. *Der Christliche Bürger in einer Kanzelrede am Festtage des heiligen Stephan ersten König von Ungarn, geschildert in der Festung Ofen 1839.* Ofen: 1839.

Rousseau, Jean-Jacques. *The Government of Poland.* Translated by Willmore Kendall. Indianapolis: Hackett, 1985.

Schams, Franz. *Vollständige Beschreibung der königl. freyen Haupt Stadt Ofen in Ungern.* Ofen: Königl. Universitäts Buchdruckerey Schriften, 1822.

———. *Vollständige Beschreibung der königlichen Freystadt Pest in Ungern.* Pest: Hartleben, 1821.

Schwartner, Marton. *Statistik des Königreichs Ungern.* 2 vols. Ofen: Königl. Universitäts-Schriften, 1809–11.

Shaw, Albert. "Budapest: The Rise of a New Metropolis." *Century Magazine* 44, no. 2 (1892): 163–79.

Simpson, J. Palgrave. *Letters from the Danube.* London: R. Bentley, 1847.

Springer, Johann. *Statistik des österreichischen Kaiserstaates.* 2 vols. Vienna: F. Beck, 1840.

Stubenrauch, Moriz. *Statistische Darstellung des Vereinswesens im Kaiserthume Österreich.* Vienna: Kaiserlich-königlichen Hof- und Staatsdruckerei, 1857.

Széchenyi, István. *Buda-Pesti por és sár.* Edited by Ervin Fenyő. Budapest: Balassi Kiadó, 1995.

———. *Gróf Széchenyi István levelei.* Edited by Béla Majláth. 3 vols. Budapest: Athenaeum, 1889–91.

———. *Gróf Széchenyi István naplói.* Edited by Gyula Viszota. 6 vols. Budapest: Magyar Történelmi Társulat, 1925–39.

———. *Hitel.* Pest: Petrózai Trattner J. M. és Károlyi István, 1830.

———. *Világ vagy is felvilágosító töredékek némi hiba 's előitélet eligazitására.* Pest: Landerer, 1831.

Székács, József. *A magyarhoni Ágost. Hitv. Evang. Egyház egyetemes névtára.* Pest: Landerer és Heckenast, 1848.

Szekfű, Gyula. *Iratok a magyar államnyelv kérdésének történetéhez 1790–1848.* Budapest: Magyar Történelmi Társulat, 1926.

Táncsics, Mihály. *Életpályám.* Budapest: Révai, 1949.

———. *Fővárosunk.* Pest: Bartalits Imre, 1867.

Thiele, J. C. von. *Das Königreich Ungarn.* 6 vols. Kaschau: Theile'schen Erben, 1833.

Tormay, Cécile. *The Old House.* Translated by E. Torday. New York: Robert M. McBride, 1922.

Tóth, Gyula. *Küzdelem, bukás, megtorlás.* Budapest: Szépirodalmi Könyvkiadó, 1978.

Townson, Robert. *Travels in Hungary with a Short Account of Vienna in the Year 1793.* London: G. G. and J. Robinson, 1797.

Turnbull, Peter Evan. *Austria.* 2 vols. London: J. Murray, 1840.

Vahot, Imre. *Emlékiratai.* 2nd ed. Budapest: Kocsi Sándor, 1890.

Vályi, András. *Magyar Országnak leírása.* 3 vols. Buda: A' Királyi Universitásnak Betűivel, 1796–99.

Vay, Sarolta. *Régi magyar társasélet.* Edited by Ágota Steinert. Budapest: Magvető Könyvkiadó, 1986.

Vörös, Károly, ed. *Pest-Budai hétköznapok.* Budapest: Történeti Múzeum, 1966.

Waldapfel, József, ed. *Buda-Pest, a' magyarok fővárosa.* Budapest: Franklin-Társulat, n.d.

Zay, Karl. *Der ungarische Schutzverein.* Leipzig: Otto Wigand, 1845.

Zsoldos, Jenő, ed. *1848–1849 a magyar zsidóság életében.* Budapest: Múlt és Jövő Kiadó, 1998.

Selected Secondary Sources

Agnew, Hugh LeCaine. *Origins of the Czech National Renascence.* Pittsburgh: University of Pittsburgh Press, 1993.

Ágoston, Gábor. "History of Budapest from Its Beginnings to 1703." In *Budapest: A History from Its Beginnings to 1998,* edited by András Gerő and János Poór, 11–34. Boulder, Colo.: Social Sciences Monographs, 1997.

Alter, Peter. *Nationalism.* 2nd ed. London: Edward Arnold, 1994.

Anderson, Benedict. *Imagined Communities: Reflections on Origins and Spread of Nationalism.* Rev. ed. London: Verso, 1991.

Antalffy, Gyula. *Reformkori magyar városrajzok.* Budapest: Panorama, 1982.

Arató, Endre. *A magyarországi nemzetiségek nemzeti ideológiája.* Budapest: Akadémiai Kiadó, 1983.

———. *A nemzetiségi kérdés története Magyarországon, 1790–1840.* 2 vols. Budapest: Akadémiai Kiadó, 1960.

Bácskai, Vera. "Budapest and Its Hinterland: The Development of Twin Cities 1720–1850." In *Capital Cities and Their Hinterlands in Early Modern Europe,* edited by Peter Clark and Bernard Lepetit, 183–97. Addershot: Scholar Press, 1996.

———. "A pesti zsidóság a 19. század első felében." *Budapesti Negyed* 8, no. 2 (1995): 5–21.

———. *A vállalkozók előfutárai. Nagykereskedők a reformkori Pesten.* Budapest: Magvető Könyvkiadó, 1989.

Bácskai, Vera, Gábor Gyáni, and András Kubinyi. *Budapest története a kezdetektől 1945-ig.* Budapest: Budapest Főváros Levéltára, 2000.

Bahm, Karl F. "Beyond the Bourgeoisie: Rethinking Nation, Culture, and Modernity in Nineteenth-Century Central Europe." *Austrian History Yearbook* 29 (1998): 19–35.

Balázs, Éva H. *Hungary and the Habsburgs 1765–1800: An Experiment in Enlightened Absolutism.* Translated by Tim Wilkinson. Budapest: Central European University Press, 1997.

Baraczka, István. "A magyar nyelv ügye Pest, Buda és Óbuda közigazgatásában." *Tanulmányok Budapest Múltjából* 8 (1940): 51–59.

Barany, George. "The Awakening of Magyar Nationalism before 1848." *Austrian History Yearbook* 2 (1966): 19–54.

———. "Hoping against Hope: The Enlightened Age in Hungary." *American Historical Review* 76, no. 2 (1971): 319–57.

———. *Stephen Széchenyi and the Awakening of Hungarian Nationalism, 1791–1841.* Princeton, N.J.: Princeton University Press, 1968.

Barta, István. "Az 1831. évi pesti koleramozgalom." *Tanulmányok Budapest Múltjából* 14 (1961): 445–70.

Barth, Fredrik, ed. *Ethnic Groups and Boundaries.* Boston: Little, Brown, 1969.

Bell, David A. *The Cult of the Nation in France: Inventing Nationalism, 1680–1800.* Cambridge, Mass.: Harvard University Press, 2001.

Bellér, Béla. *A magyarországi németek rövid története.* Budapest: Magvető Kiadó, 1981.

Bergdoll, Barry. *European Architecture, 1750–1890.* Oxford: Oxford University Press, 2000.

Bermeo, Nancy, and Philip Nord, eds. *Civil Society Before Democracy: Lessons from Nineteenth-Century Europe.* Lanham, Md.: Rowman & Littlefield, 2000.

Berzeviczy, Albert. *Az absolutismus kora Magyarországon 1849–1865.* 3 vols. Budapest: Franklin Társulat, 1922.

Binal, Wolfgang. *Deutschsprachiges Theater in Budapest. Von den Anfängen bis zum Brand des Theaters in der Wollgasse (1889).* Vienna: Böhlau, 1972.

Bíró, Ferenc. *A felvilágosodás korának magyar irodalma.* Budapest: Balassi Kiadó, 1994.

Blackbourn, David. *The Long Nineteenth Century: A History of Germany, 1780–1918.* New York: Oxford University Press, 1998.

Blackbourn, David, and Geoff Eley. *The Peculiarities of German History: Bourgeois Society and Politics in Nineteenth-Century Germany.* Oxford: Oxford University Press, 1984.

Bradley, Joseph. "Subjects into Citizens: Societies, Civil Society, and Autocracy in Tsarist Russia." *American Historical Review* 107, no. 4 (2002): 1094–123.

Breen, T. H. "'Baubles of Britain': The American and Consumer Revolutions of the Eighteenth Century." *Past & Present* 119 (1988): 73–104.

Brubaker, Rogers. *Nationalism Reframed: Nationhood and the National Question in the New Europe.* Cambridge: Cambridge University Press, 1996.

Brubaker, Rogers, and Frederick Cooper. "Beyond 'Identity.'" *Theory and Society* 29, no. 1 (2000): 1–47.

Büchler, Sándor. *A zsidók története Budapesten a legrégibb időktől 1867-ig.* Budapest: Franklin-Társulat, 1901.

Buzinkay, Géza. "A Challenge for Intellectuals: Austro-Hungarians with Two Languages." In *Hungary and European Civilization,* edited by György Ránki, 321–29. Budapest: Akadémiai Kiadó, 1989.

Calhoun, Craig. "Nationalism and Ethnicity." *Annual Review of Sociology* 19 (1993): 211–39.

Chatterjee, Partha. *The Nation and Its Fragments: Colonial and Postcolonial Histories.* Princeton, N.J.: Princeton University Press, 1993.

Chickering, Roger. *We Men Who Feel Most German: A Cultural Study of the Pan-German League, 1886–1914.* Boston: Allen & Unwin, 1984.

Cohen, Gary. *The Politics of Ethnic Survival: Germans in Prague, 1861–1914.* Princeton, N.J.: Princeton University Press, 1981.

Colley, Linda. *Britons: Forging the Nation, 1707–1837.* New Haven, Conn.: Yale University Press, 1992.

Csáky, Moritz. "Die Hungarus Konzeption. Eine 'realpolitische' Alternative zur magyarischen Nationalstaatsidee." In *Ungarn und Österreich unter Maria Theresia und Joseph II,* edited by Anna M. Drabek, Richard G. Plaschka, and Adam Wandruszka, 71–89. Vienna: Verlag der Österreichischen Akademie der Wissenschaft, 1982.

———. "Multicultural Communities: Tensions and Qualities, The Example of Central Europe." In *Shaping the Great City: Modern Architecture in Central Europe, 1890–1937,* edited by Eva Blau and Monika Platzer, 43–56. Munich: Prestel, 1999.

Csorba, László. "Budapest-gondolat és városegyesítés." *Budapesti Negyed* 1, no. 2 (1993): 14–30.

———. "Transition from Pest-Buda to Budapest, 1815–1878." In *Budapest: A History from Its Beginnings to 1998,* edited by András Gerő and János Poór, 69–102. Boulder, Colo.: Social Sciences Monographs, 1997.

Cushing, G. F. "The Birth of National Literature in Hungary." *Slavonic and East European Review* 38, no. 91 (1959–60): 459–75.

———. "Books and Readers in 18th-Century Hungary." *Slavonic and East European Review* 47, no. 108 (1969): 57–77.

Czigány, Lóránt. *The Oxford History of Hungarian Literature: From the Earliest Times to the Present.* Oxford: Oxford University Press, 1984.

Darnton, Robert. *The Great Cat Massacre and Other Episodes in French Cultural History.* New York: Basic Books, 1984.

Davies, Norman, and Roger Moorhouse. *Microcosm: Portrait of a Central European City.* London: Jonathan Cape, 2002.

"*Nemzeti egyenjogúsítás.*" *Kormányzati nemzetiségpolitika Magyarországon 1849–1860.* Budapest: Osiris Kiadó, 2000.

———. Deák, Ágnes. "Társadalmi ellenállási stratégiák Magyarországon az abszolutista kormányzat ellen 1851–1852-ben." *Aetas* 4 (1995): 27–59.

Deák, István. *Assimilation and Nationalism in East Central Europe During the Last Century of Habsburg Rule.* Pittsburgh: University of Pittsburgh Press, 1983.

———. *Beyond Nationalism: A Social and Political History of the Habsburg Officer Corps, 1848–1918.* New York: Oxford University Press, 1990.

———. "Cause for Despair? (Some Remarks on the Mood of Pessimism in the Late Habsburg Monarchy)." In *Polgárosodás Közép-Európában/Verbürgerlichung in Mitteleuropa*, edited by Éva Somogyi, 87–96. Budapest: MTA Történettudományi Intézet, 1991.

———. *The Lawful Revolution: Louis Kossuth and the Hungarians, 1848–1849.* New York: Columbia University Press, 1979.

———. "Lawful Revolutions and the Many Meanings of Freedom in the Habsburg Monarchy." In *Revolution and the Meanings of Freedom in the Nineteenth Century*, edited by Isser Woloch, 280–314. Stanford, Calif.: Stanford University Press, 1996.

Deme, László. "Pre-1848 Magyar Nationalism Revisited: Ethnic and Authoritative or Political and Progressive?" *East European Quarterly* 27, no. 2 (1993): 141–69.

———. *The Radical Left in the Hungarian Revolution of 1848.* Boulder, Colo.: East European Quarterly, 1976.

———. "The Society for Equality in the Hungarian Revolution of 1848." *Slavic Review* 31, no. 1 (1972): 71–88.

———. "Writers and Essayists and the Rise of Magyar Nationalism in the 1820s and 1830s." *Slavic Review* 43 (1984): 624–40.

Denés, Iván Zoltán. "The Value System of Liberals and Conservatives in Hungary, 1830–1848." *Historical Journal* 36, no. 4 (1993): 825–50.

Dezsényi, Béla. "A Nemzeti Kör a negyvenes évek irodalmi és hirlapi mozgalmaiban." *Irodalomtörténeti közlemények* 57 (1953): 163–204.

Dollinger, Heinz. "Das Leitbild des Bürgerkönigtums in der europäischen Monarchie des 19. Jahrhunderts." In *Hof, Kultur und Politik im 19. Jahrhundert*, edited by Karl Ferdinand Werner, 325–64. Bonn: L. Röhrscheid, 1985.

Domanovszky, Sándor. *József nádor élete és iratai.* 4 vols. Budapest: Magyar Történelmi Társulat, 1925–1944.

Dowe, Dieter et al., eds. *Europe in 1848: Revolution and Reform.* Translated by David Higgins. New York: Berghahn Books, 2001.

Dózsa, Katalin. "How the Hungarian National Costume Evolved." In *The Imperial Style: Fashions of the Habsburg Era*, edited by Polly Cone, 74–87. New York: Metropolitan Museum of Art, 1980.

Eley, Geoff. "Nations, Publics, and Political Cultures: Placing Habermas in the Nineteenth Century." In *Habermas and the Public Sphere*, edited by Craig Calhoun, 289–339. Cambridge, Mass.: MIT Press, 1992.

Eley, Geoff, and Ronald Grigor Suny, eds. *Becoming National: A Reader.* New York: Oxford University Press, 1996.

Engman, Max, in collaboration with Francis W. Carter, A. C. Hepburn, and Colin G. Pooley, eds. *Ethnic Identity in Urban Europe.* New York: New York University Press, 1992.

Erickson, Raymond. *Schubert's Vienna.* New Haven, Conn.: Yale University Press, 1997.

Evans, R. J. W. "1848–1849 in the Habsburg Monarchy." In *The Revolutions in Europe 1848–1849*, edited by Evans and Harmut Pogge von Strandmann, 181–206. Oxford: Oxford University Press, 2000.

———. "Hungary and the Habsburg Monarchy 1840–1867: A Study in Perceptions." *Etudes Danubiennes* 4, no. 2 (1988): 18–39.

———. "Language and State Building: The Case of the Habsburg Monarchy." *Austrian History Yearbook* 35 (2004): 1–24.

Fábri, Anna. *Az irodalom magánélete. Irodalmi szalonok és társaskörök Pesten 1779–1848.* Budapest: Magvető Könyvkiadó, 1987.

Faragó, Tamás. "Die Budapester Bevölkerungsentwicklung und die Zuwanderung 1848 bis 1941." In *Wien-Prag-Budapest. Blütezeit der Habsburgmetropolen*, edited by Gerhard Melinz and Susan Zimmermann, 58–72. Vienna: Promedia, 1996.

———. "A főváros népe: sokszínűség és beolvadás." In *Az egyesített főváros. Pest, Buda, Óbuda*, edited by Gábor Gyányi, 75–110. Budapest: Városháza, 1998.

Farkas, Emőd. *Az 1848–49-iki szabadságharcz hősnői.* 2 vols. Budapest: Rózsa Kálmán, 1910.

Fazekas, Csaba. "The Dawn of Political Catholicism in Hungary, 1844–1848." *Hungarian Studies* 13, no. 1 (1998/99): 13–26.

Fehér, Katalin. "Reformkori sajtóviták a nők művelődésének kérdéseiről." *Magyar Könyvszemle* 111, no. 3 (1995): 247–63.

Freifeld, Alice. "The De-Germanization of the Budapest Stage." In *Germany and Eastern Europe: Cultural Identities and Cultural Differences*, edited by Keith Bullivant, Geoffrey Giles, and Walter Pape, 148–73. Amsterdam: Rodopi, 1999.

———. *Nationalism and the Crowd in Liberal Hungary, 1848–1914.* Baltimore, Md.: Johns Hopkins University Press, 2000.

Fried, István. "Haza, állam, nemzet a magyarországi német sajtóban a XIX. század első felében." *Magyar Könyvszemle* 105 (1989): 247–61.

———. "Über die Kultur des deutschen Bürgertums von Pesth-Ofen am Anfang des 19. Jahrhunderts." *Arbeiten zur Deutschen Philologie* 9 (1975): 95–110.

Fülöp, Géza. *A magyar olvasóközönség a felvilágosodás idején és a reformkorban.* Budapest: Akadémiai Kiadó, 1978.

Gábor, István. *A Vigadó története.* Budapest: Zeneműkiadó, 1978.

Gelléri, Mór. *Az magyar ipar úttörői. Élet és jellemrajzok.* Budapest: Dobrowsky és Franke, 1887.

———. *Ötven év a magyar ipar történetéből 1842–1892.* Budapest: Pesti Könyvnyomda, 1892.

Gerevich, László, ed. *Budapest Története.* 5 vols. Budapest: Akadémiai Kiadó, 1973–1980.

Gergely, András and János Veliky. "A politikai közvelemény fogalma Magyarországon a XIX. század közepén." *Magyar Történelmi Tanulmányok* 7 (1974): 5–42.

Gerő, András. *Modern Hungarian Society in the Making: The Unfinished Experience.* Translated by James Patterson and Enikő Koncz. Budapest: Central European University Press, 1995.

Gerő, András, and János Poór, eds. *Budapest: A History from Its Beginnings to 1998.* Translated by Judit Zinner, Cecil D. Eby, and Nóra Arató. Boulder, Colo.: Social Science Monographs, 1997.

Gerő, László. *Pest-Buda építészete az egyesítéskor.* Budapest: Műszaki Könyvkiadó, 1973.

Gneiße, Bettina. *István Széchenyis Kasinobewegung im ungarischen Reformzeitalter (1825–1848). Ein Beitrag zur Erforschung der Anfänge der nationalliberalen Organisation im vormärzlichen Ungarn.* Frankfurt am Main: Peter Lang, 1990.

Gogolák, Ludwig. "Ungarns Nationalitätengesetze und das Problem des Magyarischen National- und Zentralstaates." In *Die Habsburger Monarchie 1848–1918.* Vol. 3, *Die Völker des Reiches,* edited by Adam Wandruszka and Peter Urbanitsch, 1207–1303. Vienna: Verlag der österreichischen Akademie der Wissenschaften, 1980.

Greenfeld, Liah. *Nationalism: Five Roads to Modernity.* Cambridge, Mass.: Harvard University Press, 1992.

Györffy, György. *Pest-Buda kialakulása. Budapest története a honfoglalástól az Árpádkor végi székvárossá alakulásig.* Budapest: Akadémiai Kiadó, 1997.

Gyurgyák, János. *A zsidókérdés Magyarországon. Politikai eszmetörténet.* Budapest: Osiris Kiadó, 2001.

Hamm, Michael. *Kiev: A Portrait, 1800–1917.* Princeton, N.J.: Princeton University Press, 1993.

Hanák, Péter. *The Garden and the Workshop: Essays on the Cultural History of Vienna and Budapest.* Princeton, N.J.: Princeton University Press, 1998.

———. "Polgárosodás és urbanizáció (Polgári lakáskultúra Budapesten a 19. században)." *Történelmi Szemle* 27 (1984): 123–44.

Hanák, Péter, and Ferenc Mucsi, eds. *Magyarország története 1890–1918,* 2 vols. Budapest: Akadémiai Kiadó, 1988.

Hanák, Péter, and Marianna Nagy. *Híd a századok felett.* Pécs: University Press, 1997.

Haselsteiner, Horst. "Budapest als Hauptstadt des ungarischen Reichsteiles der Habsburgermonarchie." In *Hauptstädte in europäischen Nationalstaaten,* edited by Theodor Schieder and Gerhard Brunn, 121–33. Munich: R. Oldenbourg, 1983.

Heiszler, Vilmos. "Soknyelvű ország multikulturális központja. Németek és szlovákok a reformkori Pest-Budán." *Budapesti Negyed* 2, no. 4 (1994): 5–22.

Hitchins, Keith. "Hilfsvereine auf Gegenseitigkeit in Ungarn, 1830–1941." *Internationale Revue für Soziale Sicherheit* 46, no. 3 (1993): 93–116.

Hobsbawm, Eric J. *The Age of Revolution, 1789–1848.* New York: Vintage Books, 1996.

———. *Nations and Nationalism Since 1780: Programme, Myth, Reality.* Cambridge: Cambridge University Press, 1992.

Horel, Catherine. *Juifs de Hongrie 1825–1849. Problèmes d'assimilation et d'émancipation.* Strasbourg: Revue d'Europe Centrale, 1995.

Horváth, Zoltán. ed. *Teleki László 1810–1861.* 2 vols. Budapest: Akadémiai Kiadó, 1964.

Hroch, Miroslav. *Social Preconditions of National Revival in Europe: A Comparative Analysis of the Social Composition of Patriotic Groups among the Smaller European Nations.* Translated by Ben Fowkes. Cambridge: Cambridge University Press, 1985.

Hunt, Lynn. *Politics, Culture, and Class in the French Revolution.* Berkeley: University of California Press, 1984.

Hye, Hans-Peter. "Vereinswesen und bürgerliche Gesellschaft in Österreich." *Beiträge zur historischen Sozialkunde* 18 (1988): 86–96.

Ilk, Mihály. *A Nemzeti Casino százéves története 1827–1926.* Budapest: Franklin-Társulat, 1927.

Isoz, Kálmán. "A Pest-budai Hangászegyesület és nyilvános hangversenyei (1836–1851)." *Tanulmányok Budapest Múltjából* 3 (1934): 165–79.

Ives, Margaret C. *Enlightenment and National Revival: Patterns of Interplay and Paradox in Late 18th Century Hungary.* Ann Arbor, Mich.: University Microfilms International, 1979.

Jacob, Margaret. *Living the Enlightenment: Freemasonry and Politics in Eighteenth-Century Europe.* New York: Oxford University Press, 1991.

Jacobs, Michael. *Budapest: A Cultural Guide.* Oxford: Oxford University Press, 1998.

Janos, Andrew. *The Politics of Backwardness in Hungary, 1825–1945.* Princeton, N.J.: Princeton University Press, 1982.

Jászi, Oscar. *The Dissolution of the Habsburg Monarchy.* Chicago: University of Chicago Press, 1961.

———. *A nemzeti államok kialakulása és a nemzetiségi kérdés.* Budapest, Gondolat, 1986.

Judson, Pieter M. *Exclusive Revolutionaries: Liberal Politics, Social Experience, and National Identity in the Austrian Empire, 1848–1914.* Ann Arbor: University of Michigan Press, 1996.

Kann, Robert. *The Multinational Empire: Nationalism and National Reform in the Habsburg Monarchy, 1848–1918.* 2 vols. New York: Columbia University Press, 1950.

Karády, Viktor. "Egyenlőtlen elmagyarosodás, avagy hogyan vált Magyarország magyar nyelvű országgá." In *Magyarország társadalomtörténete,* edited by György Kövér and Gábor Gyáni, 2:302–36. 2 vols. Budapest: Nemzeti Tankönyvkiadó, 1995.

———. *Zsidóság, Polgárosodás, Asszimiláció. Tanulmányok.* Budapest: Cserépfalvi Kiadása, 1997.

Karády, Viktor, and István Kozma. *Név és nemzet. Családnév-váltotatzás, névpolitika és nemzetiségi erőviszonyok Magyarországon a feudalizmustól a kommunizmusig.* Budapest: Osiris Kiadó, 2002.

Karpat, Jozef. "The Transition of the Slovaks from a Non-Dominant Ethnic Group to a Dominant Nation." In *Ethnic Groups and Language Rights,* edited by Sergij Vilfan, 135–54. New York: New York University Press, 1993.

Katz, Jacob. *A House Divided: Orthodoxy and Schism in Nineteenth-Century Central European Jewry.* Translated by Ziporah Brody. Hanover, N.H.: University Press of New England, 1998.

Kecskeméti, Károly. *La Hongrie et le réformisme libéral. Problèmes politiques et sociaux (1790–1848).* Rome: Il Centro Di Ricerca, 1989.

Kéky, Lajos. *A százéves Kisfaludy-Társaság (1836–1936).* Budapest: Franklin Társulat, 1936.

Kerényi, Ferenc, ed. *Magyar Színháztörténet 1790–1873.* Budapest: Akadémiai Kiadó, 1990.

Kessler, Wolfgang. *Politik, Kultur und Gesellschaft in Kroatien und Slawonien in der ersten Hälfte des 19. Jahrhunderts.* Munich: Oldenbourg, 1981.

Kimball, Stanley B. "The Matica Česká, 1831–61: The First Thirty Years of a Literary Foundation." In *Czech Renascence of the Nineteenth Century,* edited by Peter Brock and H. Gordon Skilling, 53–73. Toronto: University of Toronto Press, 1970.

King, Jeremy. "Austria versus Hungary: Nationhood, Statehood, and Violence since 1867." In *Nationalitätenkonflikte im 20. Jahrhundert,* edited by Philipp Ther and Holm Sundhaussen, 163–79. Wiesbaden: Harrassowitz Verlag, 2001.

———. *Budweisers into Czechs and Germans: A Local History of Bohemian Politics, 1848–1948.* Princeton, N.J.: Princeton University Press, 2002.

———. "The Nationalization of East Central Europe: Ethnicism, Ethnicity, and Beyond." In *Staging the Past: The Politics of Commemoration in Habsburg Central Europe, 1848 to the Present,* edited by Maria Bucur and Nancy M. Wingfield, 112–52. West Lafayette, Ind.: Purdue University Press, 2001.

Kirschbaum, Stanley J. *A History of Slovakia: The Struggle for Survival.* New York: St. Martin's Press, 1995.

Kókay, György, ed. *A magyar sajtó története 1705–1848.* Budapest: Akadémiai Kiadó, 1979.

Komoróczy, Géza, ed. *A zsidó Budapest. Emlékek, szertartások, történelem.* 2 vols. Budapest: MTA Judaisztikai Kutatócsoport, 1995.

Kořalka, Jiří. "Revolutions in the Habsburg Monarchy." In *Europe in 1848: Revolution and Reform,* edited by Dieter Dowe et al., 145–69. Translated by David Higgins. New York: Berghahn Books, 2001.

———. *Tschechen in Habsburgerreich und in Europa 1815–1914.* Munich: R. Oldenbourg, 1991.

Körner, Axel, ed. *1848—A European Revolution? International Ideas and National Memories of 1848.* New York: Palgrave Macmillan, 2000.

Kósa, János. *Pest és Buda elmagyarosodása 1848-ig.* Budapest: n.p., 1937.

Kosáry, Domokos. "Kossuth és a Védegylet." *Magyar Történettudományi Intézet Évkönyve* (1942): 421–536.

———. *Művelődés a XVIII. századi Magyarországon.* Budapest: Akadémiai Kiadó, 1980.

———. *The Press During the Hungarian Revolution of 1848–1849.* Boulder, Colo.: Social Science Monographs, 1986.

Kostof, Spiro. *A History of Architecture: Settings and Rituals.* New York: Oxford University Press, 1985.

Kovács, Endre, and László Katus, eds. *Magyarország története 1848–1890.* 2 vols. Budapest: Akadémiai Kiadó, 1979.

Krestić, Vasileje. "Egyesületek, pártok és érdekképviseleti szervek a magyarországi szerbeknél." In *Híd a századok felett,* edited by Péter Hanák and Marianna Nagy, 179–97. Pécs: University Press, 1997.

Krinsky, Carol Herselle. *Synagogues of Europe: Architecture, History, Meaning.* Cambridge, Mass.: MIT Press, 1985.

Ladd, Brian. *Ghosts of Berlin: Confronting German History in the Urban Landscape.* Chicago: University of Chicago Press, 1997.

Lampland, Martha. "Family Portraits: Gendered Images of the Nation in Nineteenth-Century Hungary." *East European Politics and Society* 8, no. 2 (1994): 287–316.

Lengyel, Marta S. *Egy tévelygő Habsburg-alattvaló a 19. század derekán.* Budapest: Akadémiai Kiadó, 1985.

Lotman, Iurii M. "The Decembrist in Daily Life (Everyday Behavior as a Historical-Psychological Category)." In *The Semiotics of Russian Cultural History,* edited by Iurri M. Lotman, Lidiia Ia. Ginsburg, and Boris A. Uspenskii, 95–149. Ithaca, N.Y.: Cornell University Press, 1985.

Lukacs, John. *Budapest 1900: A Historical Portrait of a City and Its Culture.* New York: Grove Weidenfeld, 1988.

Macartney, C. A. *The Habsburg Empire 1790–1918.* London: Weidenfeld & Nicolson, 1968.

Mah, Harold. "Phantasies of the Public Sphere: Rethinking the Habermas of Historians." *Journal of Modern History* 72, no. 1 (March 2000): 153–82.

Maier, Charles S. "City, Empire, and Imperial Aftermath: Contending Contexts for the Urban Vision." In *Shaping the Great City: Modern Architecture in Central Europe, 1890–1937*, edited by Eva Blau and Monika Platzer, 25–41. Munich: Prestel, 1999.

Marczali, Henry. *Hungary in the Eighteenth Century*. Cambridge: Cambridge University Press, 1910.

Marx, Julius. *Die wirtschaftlichen Ursachen der Revolution von 1848 in Österreich*. Graz: Böhlau, 1965.

Mazsu, János. *The Social History of the Hungarian Intelligentsia, 1825–1944*. Boulder, Colo.: Social Science Monographs, 1997.

McCagg, William O. *A History of Habsburg Jews, 1670–1918*. Bloomington: Indiana University Press, 1989.

Mérei, Gyula. *Magyar iparfejlődés 1790–1848*. Budapest: Közoktatásügyi Kiadóvállalat, 1951.

Mérei, Gyula, and Károly Vörös, eds. *Magyarország története 1790–1848*. 2 vols. Budapest: Akadémiai Kiadó, 1980.

Moess, Alfréd. *Pest Megye és Pest-Buda zsidóságának demográfiája 1749–1846*. Budapest: Magyar Izraeliták Országos Képviseletének kiadása, 1968.

Molnár, András. "Az egyesületek szerepe Batthyány Lajos politikai pályafutásában (1840–1847)." *Századok* 130, no. 1 (1996): 3–28.

Moravánszky, Ákos. *Competing Visions: Aesthetic Invention and Social Imagination in Central European Architecture, 1867–1918*. Cambridge, Mass.: MIT Press, 1998.

Nagy, Katalin Szegvári. *A nők művelődési jogaiért folytatott harc hazánkban (1777–1918)*. Budapest: Közgazdasági és Jogi Könyvkiadó, 1969.

Nemes, Robert. "Associations and Civil Society in Reform-Era Hungary." *Austrian History Yearbook* 32 (2001): 25–45.

———. "The Politics of the Dance Floor: Civil Society and Culture in Nineteenth-Century Hungary." *Slavic Review* 60, no. 4 (2001): 802–23.

———. "Women in the 1848–1849 Hungarian Revolution." *Journal of Women's History* 13, no. 3 (2001): 193–207.

Niederhauser, Emil. *The Rise of Nationality in Eastern Europe*. Translated by Károly Ravasz and revised by Bertha Gaster. Budapest: Corvina, 1981.

Nyárády, Gábor. *Az első magyar iparműkiállítás*. Budapest: Közgazdasági és Jogi Könyvkiadó, 1962.

Okey, Robin. *The Habsburg Monarchy: From Enlightenment to Eclipse*. New York: St. Martin's Press, 2001.

Ozouf, Mona. *Festivals and the French Revolution*. Translated by Alan Sheridan. Cambridge, Mass.: Harvard University Press, 1988.

Pajkossy, Gábor. "Egyesületek Magyarországon és Erdélyben 1848 előtt." *Korunk* 4 (1993): 103–9.

———. *Kossuth Lajos*. Budapest: Új Mandátum, 1998.

———. *Polgári átalakulás és nyilvánosság a magyar reformkorban*. Budapest: MTA Történettudományi Intézet, 1991.

———. "Problems of the Language of State in a Multinational Country: Debates at the Hungarian Diets of the 1840s." In *Études historiques hongroises 1990*. Vol. 2, *Ethnicity and Society in Hungary*, edited by Ferenc Glatz, 97–110. Budapest: Institute of History of the Hungarian Academy of Sciences, 1990.

Pásztor, Mihály. *A százötven éves Lipótváros.* Budapest: Budapest Székesfőváros Hazinyomdája, 1940.

Peisner, Ignác. *Budapest a XVIII. században.* Budapest: Singer és Wolfner, 1900.

Poór, János. "'Emléke törvénybe iktattatik.' József nádor (1776–1847)." *Budapesti Negyed* 2, no. 1 (1994): 19–34.

Poros, András. "A pesti iparos- és kiskeredőpolgárság részvétele az ellenzéki irányitásu szervezetekben az 1840-es években." In *Nyolc tanulmány a XIX. századi magyar történet köréből,* edited by Csilla Csorba and András Gerő, 89–111. Budapest: Eötvös Loránd Egyetem, 1978.

Preisach, Gábor. *Budapest városépítésének története: Buda visszavételétől a kiegyezésig.* Budapest: Műszáki Könyvkiadó, 1960.

Pukánszky, Béla. *Német polgárság magyar földön.* Budapest: Franklin Társulat, [1940].

Rady, Martyn. *Medieval Buda: A Study of Municipal Government and Jurisdiction in the Kingdom of Hungary.* Boulder, Colo.: Social Science Monographs, 1985.

Révész, László. "Das Junge Ungarn 1825–1848." *Südost-Forschungen* 25 (1966): 72–119.

Rusinow, Dennison. "Ethnic Politics in the Habsburg Monarchy and Successor States: Three 'Answers' to the National Question." In *Nationalism and Empire: The Habsburg Empire and the Soviet Union,* edited by Richard L. Rudolph and David F. Good, 243–67. New York: St. Martin's, 1992.

Sáfrán, Györgyi, ed. *Teleki Blanka és köre.* Budapest: Szépirodalmi Könyvkiadó, 1963.

Ságvári, Ágnes, ed. *Budapest: The History of a Capital.* 4 vols. Translated by Kornél Balás and Károly Rávász. Budapest: Corvina, 1973.

Schmall, Lajos. *Adalékok Budapest Székesfőváros történetéhez.* 2 vols. Budapest: Székesfőváros Kiadása, 1899.

———. *Buda-Pest utczái és térei.* Budapest: Székesfőváros Házinyomdája, 1906.

Schorske, Carl E. *Fin-de-Siècle Vienna: Politics and Culture.* New York: Vintage Books, 1981.

Seton-Watson, R. W. *Racial Problems in Hungary.* London: A. Constable, 1908.

Sheehan, James. *German Liberalism in the Nineteenth Century.* Chicago: University of Chicago Press, 1978.

Siklóssy, László. *Hogyan épült Budapest? (1870–1930).* Budapest: Fővárosi Közmunkák Tanácsa, 1931

———. *A régi Budapest erkölcse.* Budapest: Corvina, 1972.

Silber, Michael. "The Entrance of Jews into Hungarian Society in Vormärz: The Case of the 'Casinos.'" In *Assimilation and Community: The Jews in Nineteenth-Century Europe,* edited by Jonathan Frankel and Steven J. Zipperstein, 284–323. Cambridge: Cambridge University Press, 1992.

———, ed. *Jews in the Hungarian Economy 1760–1945.* Jerusalem: Magnes Press, 1992.

Somogyi, Éva. "Budapest als Hauptstadt Ungarns." In *Hauptstädte in Südosteuropa. Geschichte, Function, Nationale Symbolkraft,* edited by Harald Heppner, 29–36. Vienna: Böhlau, 1994.

Sperber, Jonathan. *The European Revolutions, 1848–1851.* Cambridge: Cambridge University Press, 1984.

———. *Rhineland Radicals: The Democratic Movement and the Revolution of 1848–1849.* Princeton, N.J.: Princeton University Press, 1991.

Spielman, John P. *The City & the Crown: Vienna and the Imperial Court, 1600–1740.* West Lafayette, Ind.: Purdue University Press, 1993.

Spira, György. *A Pestiek Petőfi és Haynau között.* Budapest: Enciklopédia Kiadó, 1998.

———. *Vad tűzzel.* Budapest: Osiris, 2000.

Sugar, Peter. "The More It Changes, the More Hungarian Nationalism Remains the Same." *Austrian History Yearbook* 31 (2000): 127–55.

———. "The Rise of Nationalism in the Habsburg Empire." *Austrian History Yearbook* 3, no. 1 (1967): 91–120.

Szabad, György. *Hungarian Political Trends Between the Revolution and the Compromise (1849–1867).* Translated by Éva Pálmai. Budapest: Akadémiai Kiadó, 1977.

Szemző, Piroska. *Német írók és pesti kiadóik a XIX. században (1812–1878).* Budapest: Pfeifer F., 1931.

Szentivány, Márton. *Századunk névváltoztatásai.* Budapest: Hornyánszky Viktor, 1895.

Sziklay, László. *Pest-Buda szellemi élete a 18–19. század fordulóján.* Budapest: Argumentum Könyvkiadó, 1991.

Szűcs Jenő. *Nation und Geschichte. Studien.* Budapest: Corvina, 1981.

Szvoboda, Gabriella D. *Barabás Miklós 1810–1898.* Budapest: Képzőművészeti Kiadó, 1983.

Tarnói, László, ed. *Deutschsprachige Lyrik im Königreich Ungarn um 1800.* Budapest: Germanistisches Institut, 1996.

———, ed. *Literatur und Kultur im Königreich Ungarn um 1800. Im Spiegel Deutschsprachiger Prosatext.* Budapest: Argumentum Kiadó, 2000.

Taylor, A. J. P. *The Habsburg Monarchy, 1809–1918.* New York: Harper & Row, 1965.

Telkes, Simon. *Hogy magyarositsuk a vezetékneveket?* 4th ed. Budapest: M. Kir. Állami Nyomda, 1906.

Thirring, Gusztáv. *Magyarország népessége II. József korában.* Budapest: Magyar Tudományos Akadémia, 1938.

Tilley, Virginia. "The Terms of the Debate: Untangling Language about Ethnicity and Ethnic Movements." *Ethnic and Racial Studies* 20, no. 3 (1997): 497–522.

Tóth, Árpád. "Hivatali szakszerűsödés és a rendi minták követése." *Tanulmányok Budapest Múltjából* 25 (1996): 27–60.

Tóth, Zoltán. "Was wird im Schmeltztiegel geschmolzen? Assimilationsweisen in Pest in der zweiten Hälfte des 19. Jahrhunderts." In *Wien-Prag-Budapest. Blütezeit der Habsburgmetropolen,* edited by Gerhard Melinz and Susan Zimmermann, 210–18. Vienna: Promedia, 1996.

Varga, János. *A Hungarian Quo Vadis: Political Trends and Theories of the Early 1840s.* Translated by Éva D. Pálmai. Budapest: Akadémiai Kiadó, 1993.

Venetianer, Lajos. *A magyar zsidóság története.* Budapest: Könyvértékesítő Vállalat, 1986.

Verdery, Katherine. "Whither 'Nation' and 'Nationalism.'" *Dædalus* 122 (1993): 37–46.

Vermes, Gábor. "Retreat and Preparation: The Prelude to Hungary's Age of Reform." *Hungarian Studies* 16, no. 2 (2002): 263–76.

Vörös, Károly. *Budapest legnagyobb adófizetői 1873-ban.* Budapest, Akadémiai Kiadó, 1979.

Weber, Eugen. *Peasants into Frenchmen: The Modernization of Rural France, 1870–1914.* Stanford, Calif.: Stanford University Press, 1976.

White, George. *Nationalism and Territory: Constructing Group Identity in Southeastern Europe.* Lanham: Rowman & Littlefield, 2000.

Windisch, Éva. "A magyarországi német nemzetiségi mozgalom előtörténete (1867–1900)." *Századok* 98, nos. 4 and 6 (1964): 635–60, 1104–29.

Woloch, Isser. *The New Regime: Transformations of the French Civic Order, 1789–1820s.* New York: W. W. Norton, 1994.

———, ed. *Revolution and the Meanings of Freedom in the Nineteenth Century.* Stanford, Calif.: Stanford University Press, 1996.

Woolf, Stuart. *Nationalism in Europe, 1815 to the Present.* London: Routledge, 1996.

Wortman, Richard. "Moscow and Petersburg: The Problem of Political Center in Tsarist Russia." In *Rites of Power: Symbolism, Ritual and Politics Since the Middle Ages,* edited by Sean Wilentz, 244–71. Philadelphia: University of Pennsylvania Press, 1985.

Zádor, Anna, and Jenő Rados, *A klasszicizmus építészete Magyarországon.* Budapest: Magyar Tudományos Akademia, 1943.

Zimmermann, Susan. *Die bessere Hälfte? Frauenbewegungen und Frauenbestrebungen im Ungarn der Habsburgermonarchie, 1848 bis 1918.* Vienna: Promedia, 1999.

———. *Prächtige Armut: Fürsorge, Kinderschutz und Sozialreform in Budapest.* Sigmaringen: Jan Thorbecke, 1997.

Zoltán, József. *A barokk Pest-Buda élete. Ünnepségek, szórakozások, szokások.* Budapest: Budapest Fővárosi Szabó Ervin Könyvtár, 1963.

Index

Hungarianness, 76, 104, 141, 164, 188
Hungarus loyalty, 21, 150. *See also* Habsburg loyalists; Hungarian patriotism
Huns, 4, 26
Hunt, Lynn, 101, 104, 114, 191n2
Hunter, William, 5, 198n25

Industrial Association, 62, 63, 69–72, 79–82, 91, 113, 176
industrialization, 15, 57, 64, 108, 169, 183
Israelite Magyar Society. *See* Magyarization Society
Italians, 17–18, 27, 115, 128
Italy, 5, 9, 11, 83, 87, 98–99, 119, 121, 125, 154, 159, 181, 194n5

Janos, Andrew, 123
Jászi, Oscar, 35, 185
Jelačić, General Josip, 143, 146, 148, 155
Jews: associations of, 78–79, 140, 157, 164, 183; discrimination against, 34, 39–40, 52, 79–80, 133–36, 198n25; emancipation of, 19, 30, 60, 77, 80–81, 135, 146, 150, 162, 164, 170; Habsburgs and, 77, 162–63, 170–71; Hungarian national movement and, 10, 13, 34, 76–81, 162–65, 179; Hungarian Parliament and, 136, 163–64, 170; merchants, 39, 77–81, 157; name changes of, 103, 139; National Diet and, 77; and pogrom in Pest (1848), 133–36, 213n23; population of, 6, 8–9, 17, 40–41, 76–77, 111, 152, 174, 193n30; in public life, 12, 72, 79–81, 160, 162–65; religious reform and, 140, 163; in Revolution of 1848–49, 132–37, 139–40; students, 78, 91; and synagogues, 40, 111, 163–65, *165*
Jókai, Mór, 3, 108, 110, 140
Joseph, Palatine (Archduke), 41–46, 47, 49, 57–58, 59–60, 66, 82, 83, 108–110, 118, 120, 122, 129, 168, 185
Joseph II (Emperor), 7, 18–29, 35, 40, 42, 46, 48, 90, 117, 121, 184
journeymen, 70, 77, 91, 114, 115, 125, 135, 146, 159, 177
Judson, Pieter, 61

Kádár, János, 190
Karács, Teréz, 52, 91
Karadžić, Vuk, 88–89
Karády, Viktor, 174
Karlsbad Decrees, 46
Katz, Jacob, 77
Kazinczy, Ferenc, 28, 45, 48, 49, 51, 112, 126, 159
Kecskeméthy, Aurél, 157
Kecskeméti, Károly, 62
Kisfaludy, Károly, 33, 44, 50, 87, 89, 166; *The Tatars in Hungary*, 33, 44, 49
Kisfaludy Society, 87, 89, 166
Kodály, Zoltán, 190
Kohl, J. G., 37, 103–4
Kölber carriage-making firm, 69–70
Kollár, Jan, 88, 113–14
Kőrösi, József, 152, 173–75, 219n78
Kossuth, Lajos, 10, 83–84, 86, 87, 93, 98, 122, 166, 169, 179; associations and, 60–67; as journalist, 60, 65; as National Diet leader, 60, 68, 86, 104, 124; in Pest County, 123; and *Pesti Hirlap*, 65; and Revolution of 1848–49, 69, 111, 133–38, 143, 146–49, 187
Kronperger, Antal, 113–14
Kultsár, István, 48–49
Kunewalder, Jónás, 80–81, 140

Landerer, Lajos, 70
Latin language, 21, 22, 46, 102, 112; official status of, 7, 10, 17, 24, 30, 47–50, 71, 84, 86, 199n52; publications in, 5, 25, 30, 49–50. *See also* schools
Lechner, Lajos, 169
Lechner, Ödön, 162
Leopold I (Emperor-King), 6
Leopold II (Emperor-King), 25, 30
liberalism, 3, 9, 46, 73, 77, 92, 130–31, 150, 177, 186–87; associations and, 54–58, 64–69, 71, 81–82, 106, 114, 139; economic, 55–58, 118; and Hungarian national movement, 101, 114, 123, 172, 133; of political leadership, 10, 60, 68, 85–86, 113, 123–24, 133, 136–37, 158–59, 171, 176–77, 183, 188